TEACHER DEVE...

Series Editor: A... Hargreaves

CHANGING TEACHERS, CHANGING TIMES

Centr...

Please ...tem ... befor...

TITLES IN THE TEACHER DEVELOPMENT SERIES:

Margaret Buchmann and Robert E. Floden:
Detachment and Concern: Conversations in the Philosophy of Teaching and Teacher Education

Andy Hargreaves and Michael G. Fullan (eds):
Understanding Teacher Development

Andy Hargreaves:
Changing Teachers, Changing Times: Teachers' Work and Culture in the Postmodern Age

Michael Huberman (trans. Jonathan Neufeld):
The Lives of Teachers

William Louden:
Understanding Teaching: Continuity and Change in Teachers' Knowledge

Les Tickle:
Reflective Professional Practice: The Induction of New Teachers

CHANGING TEACHERS, CHANGING TIMES

Teachers' Work and Culture in the Postmodern Age

Andy Hargreaves

CONTINUUM
London and New York

CONTINUUM
The Tower Building,
11 York Road
London SE1 7NX

370 Lexington Avenue
New York
NY 10017-6550

First published 1994
Reprinted 1995, 1996, 1998, 2000

British Library Cataloguing-in Publication Data
A catalogue record for this book is available from the British Library.

ISBN 0–304–32257–1 (hardback)
       0–8264–5443–7 (paperback)

Typeset by Colset Pte Ltd, Singapore
Printed and bound in Great Britain by
Redwood Books, Trowbridge, Wiltshire

This book is dedicated to my mother and late father. Although denied the benefits of the education they merited and deserved, they always appreciated its value. After my father's death, my mother unhesitatingly supported my own education through and beyond the compulsory years, sometimes at considerable personal sacrifice. Sacrifice is one of the most unfashionable yet underrated human virtues. For my mother, and those of her sex, her class and her time, it was the supreme way to care. Especially for those who give it, sacrifice needs no repayment; only acceptance and redemption. It is to those who have sacrificed themselves for their children's future, and to my mother in particular, that this book is dedicated.

Contents

Series Editor's Introduction   ix

Preface and Acknowledgements   xiii

PART ONE   CHANGE

1   Devices and Desires
     The Process of Change   3
2   The Malaise of Modernity
     The Pretext for Change   22
3   Postmodernity or Postmodernism?
     The Discourse of Change   38
4   Postmodern Paradoxes
     The Context of Change   47

PART TWO   TIME AND WORK

5   Time
     Quality or Quantity? The Faustian Bargain   95
6   Intensification
     Teachers' Work – Better or Worse?   117
7   Guilt
     Exploring the Emotions of Teaching   141

PART THREE   CULTURE

8   Individualism and Individuality
     Understanding the Teacher Culture   163
9   Collaboration and Contrived Collegiality
     Cup of Comfort or Poisoned Chalice?   186
10   The Balkanization of Teaching
     Collaboration That Divides   212

P.T.O

Contents

11 Restructuring
Beyond Collaboration   241

Name Index   265

Subject Index   269

Series Editor's Introduction

In Britain and Australia, they call it teaching. In the United States and Canada, they call it instruction. Whatever terms we use, we have come to realize in recent years that the teacher is the ultimate key to educational change and school improvement. The restructuring of schools, the composition of national and provincial curricula, the development of benchmark assessments – all these things are of little value if they do not take the teacher into account. Teachers don't merely deliver the curriculum. They develop, define it and reinterpret it too. It is what teachers think, what teachers believe and what teachers do at the level of the classroom that ultimately shapes the kind of learning that young people get. Growing appreciation of this fact is placing working with teachers and understanding teaching at the top of our research and improvement agendas.

For some reformers, improving teaching is mainly a matter of developing better teaching methods, of improving instruction. Training teachers in new classroom management skills, in active learning, cooperative learning, one-to-one counselling and the like is the main priority. These things are important, but we are also increasingly coming to understand that developing teachers and improving their teaching involves more than giving them new tricks. We are beginning to recognize that, for teachers, what goes on inside the classroom is closely related to what goes on outside it. The quality, range and flexibility of teachers' classroom work are closely tied up with their professional growth – with the way that they develop as people and as professionals.

Teachers teach in the way they do not just because of the skills they have or have not learned. The ways they teach are also grounded in their backgrounds, their biographies, in the kinds of teachers they have become. Their careers – their hopes and dreams, their opportunities and aspirations, or the frustration of these things – are also important for teachers' commitment, enthusiasm and morale. So too are relationships with their colleagues – either as supportive communities who work together in pursuit of common goals and continuous improvement, or as individuals working in isolation, with the insecurities that sometimes brings.

As we are coming to understand these wider aspects of teaching and teacher development, we are also beginning to recognize that much more than pedagogy, instruction or teaching method is at stake. Teacher development, teachers' careers, teachers' relations with their colleagues, the conditions of status, reward and leadership under which they work — all these affect the quality of what they do in the classroom.

This international series, Teacher Development, brings together some of the very best current research and writing on these aspects of teachers' lives and work. The books in the series seek to understand the wider dimensions of teachers' work, the depth of teachers' knowledge and the resources of biography and experience on which it draws, the ways that teachers' work roles and responsibilities are changing as we restructure our schools, and so forth. In this sense, the books in the series are written for those who are involved in research on teaching, those who work in initial and in-service teacher education, those who lead and administer teachers, those who work with teachers and, not least, teachers themselves.

This book is my personal contribution to the series. The purpose of a series editor's introduction is normally not just to describe a book, but also to show its profile and prominence. When the book in question is one's own, this is obviously difficult. Instead of evaluating the text, therefore, I shall endeavor to summarize it, and to outline some of my purposes in writing it.

"The rules of the world are changing. It is time for the rules of teaching to change with them." These are the closing sentences of *Changing Teachers, Changing Times*, a discussion of the changing nature of teachers' work and culture in a rapidly changing postmodern world. The analysis presented is broad in its scope, provocative in style and continually grounded in richly described examples of what teachers think, say and do.

My argument is that our basic structures of schooling and teaching were established for other purposes at other times. Many of our schools and teachers are still geared to the age of heavy mechanical industry with isolated teachers processing batches of children in classes or standards, in age-based cohorts. While society moves into a postindustrial, postmodern age, our schools and teachers continue to cling to crumbling edifices of bureaucracy and modernity; to rigid hierarchies, isolated classrooms, segregated departments and outdated career structures. The book describes seven fundamental dimensions of the postmodern social condition, and the challenges they pose for teachers and their work. I hope readers will find that my analysis of this postmodern context of teaching has theoretical originality, but also clarity. The subject of postmodernity is too important to be left to academic intellectuals, to be written about in esoteric, inaccessible ways. I have therefore tried to set out the postmodern agendas for teachers' work for a broader audience, without compromising their intellectual richness.

Drawing on intensive interviews with teachers at all levels, this book portrays what happens when society changes but the basic structures of teaching and schooling do not. Teachers become overloaded, they experience intolerable guilt, their work intensifies, and they are remorselessly pressed for time. More and more is added on to existing structures and responsibilities, little is taken away, and still less is completely restructured to fit the new expectations of and demands upon teaching. My book sets out to give a practical and realistic sense of these working realities of teaching, as teachers experience them now.

It also addresses some of the attempts to restructure teaching; their benefits and their drawbacks. Teacher collaboration can provide a positive platform for improvement. It can also degenerate into stilted and unproductive forms of contrived collegiality. Administrators can challenge the restrictive culture of teacher isolation and individualism, but inadvertently eradicate all semblances of creativity and individuality with it. Teachers can sometimes get extra time away from their classes to plan and prepare with one another, but may have less control over how they use it. Secondary schools might weaken the traditional boundaries between the balkan states we have come to know as subject departments, only to see other boundaries, and self-interested sub-groups emerge in their place. In this sense, my book sets out to take a hard-edged look at actual efforts to restructure teachers' work. It is an analysis that is neither cynical nor sentimental, but realistically grounded in the words and work of teachers' currently experiencing changes of this kind.

Changing Teachers, Changing Times is a book that respects and represents teachers and teaching, but not sentimentally or self-indulgently. It is a book written for teachers and those who work with teachers, and a book for researchers who want to understand teaching better.

Andy Hargreaves

Preface and Acknowledgements

This book is about how teaching is changing and about the choices and challenges facing teachers as we move into the postmodern age. It sets out to provide an accessible yet rigorous account of postmodern society – the kind of society we are now entering – and the distinctive changes it is creating and will create in teachers' work. It does this by giving a careful and respectful hearing to how teachers themselves are already experiencing change in their work. Teachers' words and teachers' work are at the heart of this book – a book that seeks to build bridges between the daily lives of teachers and the profound social changes taking place all around them. It calls for an understanding of these complex social, indeed global changes; and of teachers themselves.

The way most of us have experienced and understood teachers is in terms of what, for good or ill, they have done for us or indeed to us as children. As adults, however, only a few of us have had much opportunity to understand and appreciate what it is that teachers have done to them by other people.

For many years now, in classrooms and in staffrooms, I have studied the working lives of teachers. With children I have been a teacher, and with adults, I continue to be so. I have taught teachers and worked with teachers. My next-door neighbors are teachers, my wife is a teacher, a number of her relatives are teachers, and some of my best friends are teachers. In one way or another, formally and less so, I spend a lot of my time listening to teachers talk about their work and their world.

Notwithstanding the adverse comments people sometimes make about teachers talking "shop" whenever they meet, even at parties, engaging with teachers about their working lives is not an uninteresting task. On the contrary, beneath the stories and the gossip, and often right there within them, teachers' lives are packed with complexity and surprise. Learning about teachers' working lives is a continuous process of unending discovery. At one level, there is so much diversity. The concerns of older teachers are often different from those of younger ones. Secondary teachers see their work differently from elementary or primary teachers, and teachers of some subjects differently from teachers of others. Men teachers tend to view what they do differently from women teachers, teachers in one country or system differently from teachers in another, and teachers in the present differently from their counterparts in the past.

Just as fascinating is the fact that behind all the variations and vicissitudes among teachers' working lives are a number of profound and persistent regularities of teaching that define what most teachers do in most educational settings, most of the time. That teachers work largely with age-segregated classes; that they teach mainly alone, in isolation; that they ask questions to which they already know the answer; that they assess and care for their students without having their students assess and care for them: these are some of the most fundamental and indeed sacred regularities of teachers' work. In a world experiencing and encountering rapid change, however, these regularities are now coming to be questioned. If they are to be questioned effectively, one of the most central regularities of all that must be addressed is that of how teachers are treated; for in the main, teachers have not been treated very well.

In England and Wales, policymakers tend to treat teachers rather like naughty children; in need of firm guidelines, strict requirements and a few short, sharp evaluative shocks to keep them up to the mark. In the United States, the tendency is to treat and train teachers more like recovering alcoholics: subjecting them to step-by-step programs of effective instruction or conflict management or professional growth in ways which make them overly dependent on pseudo-scientific expertise developed and imposed by others.

Measures like these are disrespectful. They fail to show regard for teachers' professionalism in terms of their ability and duty to exercise their discretionary judgments in the circumstances and with the children they know best. They are also impractical. By dealing only with issues of knowledge, skill and compliance in trying to make teachers more effective, they fail to deal with other vital influences on the nature and quality of teachers' work. These are the teacher's *purpose*, which drives what the teacher does; the kind of *person* the teacher is, in their life as well as their work, and how this affects their teaching; the *context* in which teachers work, which limits or liberates them in terms of what they can achieve; and the *culture* of the teaching community and how teachers' relationships (or lack of them) with their colleagues can support or subvert them in their efforts to improve the quality of what they offer to their students.

This book is about these influential but often elusive aspects of teachers' work — about the personal, moral, cultural and political dimensions of teaching. It examines these aspects and their implications for teaching in the context of times of rapid and far-reaching change within teachers' work, as well as in the world beyond it; postindustrial, postmodern times when the fundamental regularities of teaching and teachers' work are being questioned.

The argument I develop here is built upon an understanding of teachers themselves, and of how they experience their work and the ways it is changing. It rests on many hours of listening to teachers who have generously given their time to talk about their working lives. Here, I owe particular gratitude to the Ontario teachers in 12 elementary schools who participated in a study of teachers' work and uses of preparation or planning time, from which much of the evidence in this book is derived. Chapter 10 draws on data collected in a number of secondary schools whose teachers were either anticipating or already experiencing immense changes in their work in the context of a government mandate to restructure Grade 9. My thanks go out to these teachers also, for sharing their perceptions so honestly and openly at a time of unsettling change for them. Rouleen Wignall worked in half the schools in the elementary teacher study, contributed to the analysis, and co-authored the final report. Bob Macmillan worked with me in one of the secondary schools reported in Chapter 10 and contributed substantially to the analysis of how teachers were experiencing change in that school. I am grateful to both Rouleen and Bob for their continuing colleagueship and support, and to Bob for permission to present some of our joint work here as part of Chapter 10. My former graduate student, Betty Tucker, has also kindly allowed me to draw on some of her data about teacher Employee Assistance Programs in Chapter 7, and I would like to thank her for this too.

Many people have given me intellectual support and stimulation in developing the ideas and analyses that comprise this book. David Hargreaves first drew my (and many of my colleagues') attention to the importance of teacher cultures as long ago as the late 1970s. Judith Warren Little, Milbrey McLaughlin, Ann Lieberman, Leslie Siskin, Sandra Acker, Bill Louden, Peter Grimmett, Jennifer Nias and Peter Woods have deepened and extended my understanding of that field. Jonathan Neufeld has intrigued me with his quirky conceptions of time, and John Smyth has given me a timely exposure to his alternative conceptions of teachers' work. Michael Fullan first brought to my attention the importance and complexity of educational change, and worked with me as an inspiring and unselfish collaborator in understanding and interpreting it. My friend (also artist and art teacher) Frank Lotta is responsible for introducing me to the intellectual wonders of postmodernism, Ted Gordon added to that understanding, and with another friend and close colleague, Ivor Goodson, I have enjoyed the most stimulating ongoing conversations about its significance and its meaning. Gunnar Handal, Sveinung Vaage, Karen Jensen and the students of the Faculty of Education graduate seminar at the University of Oslo supportively helped me work through my ideas on postmodernity and teachers' work when they were in their embryonic stages. Linda Grant, David Lennox and the Ontario Public School Teachers' Federation encouraged me to connect my work and ideas with ordinary teachers in Ontario and across Canada – they never give up on respecting and recognizing teachers' professional rights and opportunities to connect intelligently and interactively with research that impacts on their work and their world, nor do they allow researchers like myself to neglect their responsibilities to contribute openly and effectively to that interaction.

Leo Santos has miraculously unscrambled my hieroglyphics in preparing the typescript and his cheerful and energetic support, which is helpful beyond measure, is highly valued. Lastly, my wife and teenage children, Stuart and Lucy, have, as always, managed to tolerate the eccentricity and endure the distractedness that usually accompanies my efforts at book-writing, especially in the later stages. To them, I promise to fix the doorbell, get the ironing completed on time again, and atone for my guilt in any other ways deemed appropriate now all this is over. As well as their tolerance, of course, I also appreciate the warmth, good humor and cheerful skepticism about some of my more "creative" ideas that characterize our household and that make my work and life more pleasurable and rewarding. Home is where the heart is – and also humility!

Chapters 5–9 in this book build on material that has already been published elsewhere in one form or another, and I am grateful to the permission given by various journals and publishers to reprint it here. These include:

Taylor & Francis publications and *Qualitative Studies in Education* for material in Chapter 5 (first published as Hargreaves, A. (1990), "Teachers' work and the politics of time and space", *Qualitative Studies in Education*, 3(4), 303–20).

Taylor & Francis publications and the *Journal of Education Policy* for material in Chapter 11 (published as "Restructuring restructuring", *Journal of Education Policy*, forthcoming).

Teachers College Press and *Teachers College Record* for material in Chapter 6 (first published as Hargreaves, A. (1992), "Time and teachers' work: An analysis of the intensification thesis", *Teachers College Record*, 94(1), 87–108).

Teachers College Press for material in Chapter 10 (published as "Balkanized secondary schools and the malaise of modernity", in Siskin, L. and Little, J. W. (eds), *Perspectives on Departments*, forthcoming).

Pergamon Press and *Teaching and Teacher Education* for material in Chapter 7 (first published as Hargreaves, A. and Tucker, E. (1991), "Teaching and guilt: Exploring the emotions of teaching", *Teaching and Teacher Education*, 7(5/6), 491–505).

Pergamon Press and the *International Journal of Educational Research* for material in Chapter 8 (first published as Hargreaves, A. (Fall 1992), "Individualism and individuality: Reinterpreting the teacher culture", *International Journal of Educational Research*).

Corwin Press and Sage Publications for material in Chapter 9 (first published as Hargreaves, A. (1991), "Contrived collegiality: The micropolitics of teacher collaboration", in Blase, J. (ed.), *The Politics of Life in Schools*. New York: Sage).

PART ONE

CHANGE

Chapter 1

Devices and Desires
The Process of Change

INTRODUCTION

This book is about changing teachers. It looks at how teachers and teaching have changed in recent years and assesses the changes teachers will face in the future. It examines how politicians and administrators want to change teachers along with the reforms they propose and the measures they take to do that. Last of all, the book is about how and why teachers actually *do* change, about what it is that impels or inspires them to change (or indeed, not to change) in the first place.

The process by which teaching is changing and teachers are changed, I shall show, is systemically ironic. Good intentions are persistently and infuriatingly turned on their heads. Even the most well intentioned change devices which try to respect teachers' discretionary judgments, promote their professional growth and support their efforts to build professional community are often self-defeating because they are squeezed into mechanistic models or suffocated through stifling supervision. Extra time awarded away from classroom duties can be taken back through closer monitoring and regulation of how it should be used. Professional development can be turned into bureaucratic control, mentor *opportunities* into mentor *systems*, collaborative cultures into contrived collegiality. In these ways, many administrative devices of change do not just undermine teachers' own desires in teaching. They threaten the very desire to teach itself. They take the heart out of teaching.

The reasons for these ironies of change are to be found in the wider social context in which schools operate and of which they are a part. The fundamental problem here, I will argue, is to be found in a confrontation between two powerful forces. On the one hand is an increasingly postindustrial, postmodern world, characterized by accelerating change, intense compression of time and space, cultural diversity, technological complexity, national insecurity and scientific uncertainty. Against this stands a modernistic, monolithic school system that continues to pursue deeply anachronistic purposes within opaque and inflexible structures. Sometimes school systems actively try to resist the social pressures and changes of postmodernity. More often they try to respond with seriousness and sincerity, but they do so with an administrative apparatus that is

3

cumbersome and unwieldy. Educationally, this central struggle presents itself in a number of ways.

First, as the pressures of postmodernity are felt, the teacher's role expands to take on new problems and mandates – though little of the old role is cast aside to make room for these changes. Second, innovations multiply as change accelerates, creating senses of overload among teachers and principals or head-teachers responsible for implementing them. More and more changes are imposed and the timelines for their implementation are truncated. Third, with the collapse of moral certainties, old missions and purposes begin to crumble, but there are few obvious substitutes to take their place. Fourth, the methods and strategies teachers use, along with the knowledge base which justifies them, are constantly criticized – even among educators themselves – as scientific certainties lose their credibility. If the knowledge base of teaching has no scientific foundation, educators ask, "on what can our justifications for practice be based?" What teachers do seems to be patently and dangerously without foundation.

It is not simply that modernistic school systems are the problem, and postmodern organizations the solution. Postmodern societies themselves, we shall see, are loaded with contradictory possibilities, many of which have yet to be worked out. But it is in the struggles between and within modernity and postmodernity that the challenge of change for teachers and their leaders is to be found. It is through these conflicts that the realization of educational restructuring as an opportunity for positive change or a mechanism of retraction and restraint will be realized. It is here that the battle for teacher professionalism, as the exercise of wise, discretionary judgment in situations that teachers understand best, will be won or lost.[1]

The book is an argument about teaching and change, and it draws on a wide range of experience, evidence, and argument to achieve that purpose. Much of the book, particularly Chapters 5–9, draws specifically and extensively on a study I conducted with Rouleen Wignall, in the late 1980s, of elementary teachers, their perceptions of their work and their relationships with colleagues.[2] The argument of the book is, in this sense, not only illuminated by the words of teachers themselves, but also springs directly from those words and the sense I have tried to make of them. I do, of course, draw on and actively try to develop theories about teaching and teachers' work, but always in active dialogue with the data. In much of the writing on teaching and teachers' work, teachers' voices have either been curiously absent, or been used as mere echoes for preferred and presumed theories of educational researchers. Teachers' voices, though, have their own validity and assertiveness which can and should lead to questioning, modification and abandonment of those theories wherever it is warranted. In this book, we will see that teachers' words do not merely provide vivid examples of theories at work. They also pose problems and surprises for those theories.

There are four key themes running through the text. As the title suggests, *change* is the overriding one. But there are also three vital domains through which change exerts its impact on the nature and organization of teaching. These are *work*, *time* and *culture*. To orientate the reader to these key themes, I want to signpost each of them in this introduction before developing them in greater depth within the main text.

The Substance of Change

People are always wanting teachers to change. Rarely has this been more true than in recent years. These times of global competitiveness, like all moments of economic crisis, are producing immense moral panics about how we are preparing the generations of the future in our respective nations. At moments like these, education generally and schools in particular become what A. H. Halsey once called "the wastebasket of society"; policy receptacles into which society's unsolved and insoluble problems are unceremoniously deposited.[3] Few people want to do much about the economy, but everyone — politicians, the media and the public alike — wants to do something about education.

With so many traditional Western economic strongholds looking increasingly precarious in the context of an expanding global marketplace, school systems and their teachers are being charged with onerous tasks of economic regeneration. They are being pushed to place more emphasis on mathematics, science and technology, to improve performance in basic skills, and to restore traditional academic standards on a par with or superior to those of competing economies.

In addition to economic regeneration, teachers in many lands are also being expected to help rebuild national cultures and identities. Global economic integration, as expressed in growing economic union within Europe and the Free Trade Agreement in North America, is sowing fears of national disintegration among countries like Britain and Canada — fears that they will lose their cultural and political identities and distinctiveness. In response to economic globalization and multicultural migration, schools in many parts of the world are therefore being expected to carry much of the burden of national reconstruction. In an effort to resurrect traditional values and senses of moral certainty, school curricula, for instance, are being packed with new content which stresses historical, geographical and cultural unity and identity — content which teachers must master and cover.

Last and by no means least, schools and their teachers are being expected to meet these heightened demands in contexts of severe fiscal restraint. Hard-pressed states facing economic retrenchment and the welfare burdens of an aging population are divesting themselves of much of their financial commitment to schooling and expecting schools and their teachers, through market competition and frugal self-management, to stand more on their own feet.

Ideological compliance and financial self-reliance have therefore become the twin realities of change for many of today's schools and their teachers. Across many parts of the planet, the effects of these realities are clearly visible in a multiplicity of reforms and innovations with which teachers are now having to deal. These are what make up the *substance* of change, the actual changes which teachers must address. Two examples – England and Wales, and the United States – illustrate the range and character of these reforms.

In England and Wales, rampant and remorseless change imposed from above has become a pressing and immediate feature of teachers' working lives. The introduction of a subject-by-subject, stage-by-stage National Curriculum; the establishment of detailed, age-related attainment targets; the inauguration of a nationwide system of standardized testing; the creation of a new public examination system; and, most recently, a threatened reversion to traditional teaching methods in primary schools – these are just some of the numerous, simultaneously imposed changes with which teachers are having to cope.[4]

These important and pressing changes are what David Hargreaves and David Hopkins call *branch changes*: significant, yet specific changes of practice, which teachers can adopt, adapt, resist or circumvent, as they arise.[5] Beneath them are even deeper transformations at the very roots of teachers' work which address and affect how teaching itself is defined and socially organized. Such *root changes* include the introduction of compulsory performance appraisal to regulate teachers' methods and standards; the shift to local management of schools as a way of making teachers and their leaders (as a matter of sheer survival) more dependent on and responsive to the market force of parental choice between schools; and draconian measures to make teacher education more utilitarian and less reflective and questioning, by allocating huge proportions of trainee teachers' time to practical training in schools, at the expense of purportedly irrelevant or harmful theory in university education faculties. Alongside all these root changes, there is also the sheer cumulative impact of multiple, complex, non-negotiable innovations on teachers' time, energy, motivation, opportunities to reflect, and their very capacity to cope.

The British case of multiple, mandated change is perhaps an extreme one. It is extreme in its frantic pace, in the immense scope of its influence, and in the wide sweep of its legislative power. More than anything, however, it is extreme in the disrespect and disregard that reformers have shown for teachers themselves. In the political rush to bring about reform, teachers' voices have been largely neglected, their opinions overridden, and their concerns dismissed. Change has been developed and imposed in a context where teachers have been given little credit or recognition for changing themselves, and for possessing their own wisdom to distinguish between what reasonably *can* be changed and what cannot.

England and Wales may be an exaggerated case of rapid and fundamental educational change, but it is not an isolated one. In the United States, while educational policy at the federal level has little legislative force and is mostly expressed through public documents and debates, the pervasive doubts that such documents have fuelled about the ability of anachronistic school systems to develop the sophisticated skills and competences needed to meet the economic challenges of the twenty-first century have provoked numerous attempts to undertake a complete restructuring of the organization of teaching and learning in schools.

The change represented in many US restructuring efforts has shown rather more respect for teachers' abilities and been more inclusive of their efforts than the change represented by top-down UK reform. Even so, patterns of change by compliance that characterized earlier waves of US educational reform have by no means been eliminated, and their persistence often undermines other change efforts and indeed can be passed off as restructuring itself. For instance, many US teacher leadership programs select, reward and evaluate their teachers, not according to multiple criteria of excellence and professional growth, but according to teachers' adherence to approved models of teaching, often ones that place a premium on basic skills.[6] Similarly, evaluations of the implementation of manipulative, problem-solving approaches to mathematics teaching in California show that teachers commonly fail to implement them because of the persistence of parallel programs that emphasize direct instruction in basic skills – programs which are also tied to student testing and teacher appraisal.[7] Restructuring efforts notwithstanding, the *substance* of change for US teachers is therefore not only complex, but also often contradictory. Old waves and new waves of reforms create confusing cross-currents of change that can be difficult to negotiate and that can even drag teachers under.

The changes that are prevalent in Britain and the United States are also to be found in different ways in Canada, Australia, New Zealand, in other countries of the OECD, and in many more nations besides. Accelerating educational change is a global phenomenon! Why are teachers encountering so much change? Where does it come from? What does it mean?

Satisfactory answers to questions about the substance and context of educational change cannot be found in enigmatic clichés which assert that change is all around us, or that the only certain thing about the future is the inevitability of change. Aphorisms such as these are best left to pop psychology books on personal change, human potential or corporate improvement.

Nor can satisfactory answers be found by sticking to the specifics of each particular change in each particular country. In principle, school-based management, for instance, can be a good thing or a bad thing. Where extensive decision-making powers are indeed handed over to individual schools, it can lead to diversity, innovation and teacher empowerment. But when school-based management is implemented in a system where public funding is scarce and bureaucratic control over curriculum and assessment has been retained or reinforced, this can lead to self-seeking competitiveness around narrowly defined goals of basic skills or academic success. Here, school-based management can lead not to devolution of decision-making but displacement of blame.[8] The benefits and drawbacks of school-based management for teachers cannot therefore be evaluated properly in the abstract, but only in relation to parallel evaluations of school financing, and of curriculum and assessment control.

Contemporary patterns of educational reform are systemic and interconnected. As Sarason advises, the different components of educational reform
should be addressed as a whole, in their interrelationships, as a complex system.[9] In education, as in other walks of life, things go together. It is the inter-
relationship of changes that lends them a particular coherence; that gives them
one particular thrust rather than another. Meaningful and realistic analysis of
educational change therefore requires us to do more than balance out the advantages and disadvantages of particular reforms like school-based management. It
requires us to relate part to whole — the individual reform to the purpose and
context of its development. And it requires us to look at the interrelationships
between the different parts in the context of that whole. There are *big pictures*
of educational change, and it is important to look at them.

THE CONTEXT OF CHANGE

Chapters 2–4 will analyze the broad *substance* of educational change as it is
affecting teachers, and the *context* from which it springs. Essentially, I shall
argue, what is at work in the construction of current patterns of educational
change is a powerful and dynamic struggle between two immense social forces:
those of modernity and postmodernity.

Modernity is a social condition that is both driven and sustained by Enlightenment beliefs in rational scientific progress, in the triumph of technology over
nature, and in the capacity to control and improve the human condition by
applying this wealth of scientific and technological understanding and expertise to social reform.[10] *Economically*, modernity begins with the separation of
family and work through the rational concentration of production in the factory
system, and culminates in systems of mass production, monopoly capitalism
or state socialism as ways of increasing productivity and profitability. In
modernistic economies, expansion is essential to survival. *Politically*, modernity
typically concentrates control at the center with regard to decision-making,
social welfare and education, and, ultimately, economic intervention and regulation as well. *Organizationally*, this is reflected in large, complex and often
cumbersome bureaucracies arranged into hierarchies, and segmented into
specializations of expertise. In the bureaucracies of modernity, functions are
differentiated rationally and careers ordered in logical progressions of rank and
seniority. The *personal* dimensions of modernity have been widely commented
upon. In modernity, there is system and order, and often some sense of collective
identity and belonging too. But the price of rationality is also a loss of spirit or
magic; what Max Weber described literally as *disenchantment* in comparison
with premodern existence.[11] The scale of organizational life and its rational
impersonality can also lead to estrangement, alienation and lack of meaning in
individual lives.

Secondary schools are the prime symbols and symptoms of modernity.

Their immense scale, their patterns of specialization, their bureaucratic complexity, their persistent failure to engage the emotions and motivations of many of their students and considerable numbers of their staff – these are just some of the ways in which the principles of modernity are expressed in the practice of secondary education. In many respects, state secondary education has become a major component of the malaise of modernity.

Most writers locate the origins of the *postmodern* condition somewhere around the 1960s.[12] Postmodernity is a social condition in which economic, political, organizational and even personal life come to be organized around very different principles than those of modernity. *Philosophically* and *ideologically*, advances in telecommunications along with broader and faster dissemination of information are placing old ideological certainties in disrepute as people realize there are other ways to live. Even scientific certainty is losing its credibility, as supposedly *hard* findings on such things as decaffeinated coffee, global warming, breast cancer screening or even effective teaching are superseded and contradicted by new ones at an ever increasing pace. *Economically*, postmodern societies witness the decline of the factory system. Postmodern economies are built around the production of smaller goods rather than larger ones, services more than manufacturing, software more than hardware, information and images more than products and things. The changing nature of what is produced along with the technological capacity to monitor shifts in market requirements almost instantaneously, reduce the need for stock and inventory. Units of enterprise shrink drastically in scale as a result. Flexible accumulation is now the driving economic principle as profitability becomes dependent on anticipation of and rapid responsiveness to local and changing market demands.

Politically and *organizationally* the need for flexibility and responsiveness is reflected in decentralized decision-making, along with flatter decision-making structures, reduced specialization and blurring of roles and boundaries. If the organizational metaphor of modernity is the compartmentalized egg-crate, then that of postmodernity is the moving mosaic. Roles and functions now shift constantly in dynamic networks of collaborative responsiveness to successive and unpredictable problems and opportunities. *Personally*, this restructured postmodern world can create increased personal empowerment, but its lack of permanence and stability can also create crises in interpersonal relationships, as these relationships have no anchors outside themselves, of tradition or obligation, to guarantee their security and continuance.

The postmodern world is fast, compressed, complex and uncertain. Already, it is presenting immense problems and challenges for our modernistic school systems and the teachers who work within them. The compression of time and space is creating accelerated change, innovation overload and intensification in teachers' work. Ideological uncertainty is challenging the Judaeo-Christian tradition on which many school systems have been based, and raising crises of identity and purpose in relation to what their new missions might be. Scientific uncertainty is undermining the claims of a sure knowledge base for teaching and

9

making each successive innovation look increasingly dogmatic, arbitrary and superficial. And the search for more collaborative modes of decision-making is posing problems for the norms of teacher isolation on which teachers' work has been based, as well as problems for many school leaders who fear for their power as they worry about how far collaboration might go.

Much of the future of teaching will depend on how these distinctive challenges of postmodernity are realized and resolved within our modernistic schools and school systems.

THE PROCESS OF CHANGE

How will teachers actually respond to these changes? How *do* teachers change — at this moment or any other? What makes teachers change in the face of change, and what makes them dig in their heels and resist? Questions such as these concern what is commonly referred to as the *change process*: the practices and procedures, the rules and relationships, the sociological and psychological mechanisms which shape the destiny of any change, whatever its content, and which lead it to prosper or falter. If we are to understand the specific impact upon teachers of educational change in the postmodern world, we must also understand the place of teachers in the change process more generally. While concerns about the change process run through the book as a whole, I want to give it particular emphasis in this opening chapter.

Compared to the rather meager body of research on the context and substance of educational change, there is now a rich store of literature, research and practical understanding on the change *process*. In the field of school improvement, many maxims have been gleaned from this research and applied as a result of it. These include the observations that change is a process not an event;[13] that practice changes before beliefs;[14] that it is better to think big, but start small;[15] that evolutionary planning works better than linear planning;[16] that policy cannot mandate what matters;[17] that implementation strategies which integrate *bottom-up* strategies with *top down* ones are more effective than *top-down* or *bottom-up* ones alone;[18] and that conflict is a necessary part of change.[19] Of course, close inspection of these principles reveals that some are less self-evident and more contestable than they first appear. It took legislative force at the level of the European courts to mandate the abolition of corporal punishment in British schools, for instance. It is hard to say that this mandate did not matter! Similarly, Wideman has found that practice changes before beliefs only under the particular conditions of imposed change.[20] Elsewhere, practice and beliefs tend to change interactively and together. However, while there is certainly a tendency to overstate these principles and to oversell them as manipulable *rules* of change, most of them rest on the fundamentally sound understanding that teachers, more than any others, are the key to educational change.

Changes can be proclaimed in official policy, or written authoritatively on paper. Change can look impressive when represented in the boxes and arrows of administrators' overheads, or enumerated as stages in evolutionary profiles of school growth. But changes of this kind are, as my Northern English grandmother used to say, just *all top show*! They are superficial. They do not strike at the heart of how children learn and how teachers teach. They achieve little more than trivial changes in practice. Neither do changes of buildings (like open-plan ones), textbooks, materials, technology (like computers), nor even student groupings (as in mixed-ability groups) unless profound attention is paid to processes of teacher development that accompany these innovations. The involvement of teachers in educational change is vital to its success, especially if the change is complex and is to affect many settings over long periods of time. And if this involvement is to be meaningful and productive, it means more than teachers acquiring new knowledge of curriculum content or new techniques of teaching. Teachers are not just technical learners. They are social learners too.[21]

Recognizing that teachers are social learners draws our attention not just to their *capacity* to change but also to their *desires* for change (and indeed for stability). This book looks at the desires teachers themselves have to change their practice, or to conserve the practice they already value (and we shall see that these things are by no means mutually exclusive). If we can understand teachers' own desires for change *and* for conservation, along with the conditions that strengthen or weaken such desires, we will get valuable insights from the grassroots of the profession, from those who work in the frontlines of our classrooms, about *how* change can be made most effectively, as well as *what* we should change and *what* we should preserve. Getting up close to teachers in this way does not mean endorsing and celebrating everything that teachers think, say and do. But it does mean taking teachers' perceptions and perspectives very seriously.

Political and administrative *devices* for bringing about educational change usually ignore, misunderstand or override teachers' own *desires* for change. Such devices commonly rely on principles of compulsion, constraint and contrivance to get teachers to change. They presume that educational standards are low and young people are failing or dropping out because the practice of many teachers is deficient or misdirected. The reason why teachers are like this, it is argued, is that they are either unskilled, unknowledgeable, unprincipled or a combination of all three. The remedy for these defects and deficiencies, politicians and administrators believe, needs to be a drastic one, calling for decisive devices of intervention and control to make teachers more skilled, more knowledgeable and more accountable.[22] Underpinning many of these devices for changing teachers is the presumption that teachers have somehow fallen short, and that intervention by others is needed to get them up to scratch.

Many devices of change, predicated on these assumptions, have become familiar fare in strategies for educational reform. They include mandated and purportedly teacher-proof curriculum guidelines, imposition of standardized testing to control what teachers teach, saturation in new teaching methods of supposedly proven effectiveness, career bribery through programs of teacher leadership linked to pay and incentives, and market competitiveness between schools to secure change through teachers' instinct for survival as they struggle to protect their schools and preserve their jobs. These policy devices for changing teachers are poorly synchronized with teachers' own desires for change. Such desires spring from dispositions, motivations and commitments of a very different nature than those which opportunistic politicians, impatient administrators and anxious parents often imagine and presume.

At the heart of change for most teachers is the issue of whether it is *practical*. Judging changes by their practicality seems, on the surface, to amount to measuring abstract theories against the tough test of harsh reality. There is more to it than this, though. In the ethic of practicality among teachers is a powerful sense of what works and what doesn't; of which changes will go and which will not – not in the abstract, or even as a general rule, but for *this* teacher in *this* context.[23] In this simple yet deeply influential sense of practicality among teachers is the distillation of complex and potent combinations of purpose, person, politics and workplace constraints. It is through these ingredients and the sense of practicality which they sustain, that teachers' own desires for change are either constructed or constrained. To ask whether a new method is practical is therefore to ask much more than whether it works. It is also to ask whether it fits the context, whether it suits the person, whether it is in tune with their purposes, and whether it helps or harms their interests.[24] It is in these things that teachers' desires concerning change are located; and it is these desires that change strategies must address.

In recent years, there have been serious and widespread attempts to establish closer congruence between the devices and desires of change. There have been efforts to involve teachers more in the change process, to create more *ownership* of change among the teaching force, to give teachers more opportunities for leadership and professional learning, and to establish professional cultures of collaboration and continuous improvement. Much of this book analyzes the fate of this new wave of strategies which seek to secure change through professional development. While these moves are to be applauded in many respects, I will show that they also contain some important and disturbing ironies. Paramount among these is that the more reformers systematically try to bring the *devices* of change in line with teachers' own *desires* to change, the more they may stifle the basic *desire* to teach itself.

Desire is imbued with "creative unpredictability"[25] and "flows of energy".[26] The basis of creativity, change, commitment and engagement is to be found in desire, but from the organization's standpoint, so too is danger. In *desire* is to be found the creativity and spontaneity that connects teachers emotionally and sensually (in the literal sense of feeling) to their children, their colleagues and their work. Desire is at the heart of good teaching. According to the *Shorter Oxford English Dictionary*, desire is "that emotion which is directed to the attainment or possession of some object from which pleasure or satisfaction is expected; longing, craving, a wish". In teaching, such desires among exceptional and particularly creative teachers are for fulfilment, intense achievement, senses of breakthrough, closeness to fellow humans, even love for them.[27]

For instance, there is growing evidence that many teachers and students already have a rich experience of informal and spontaneous cooperation and collaboration in their school lives.[28] While innovations in teaching methods and professional development usefully concentrate on cooperation and collaboration as a focus for improvement, they often do so in ways that are contrived and controlled — making *safe simulations* of cooperation and collaboration from which the dangers of spontaneity, sensuality and creativity have been removed. Cooperative learning strategies among students, and mentor systems or peer coaching systems among teachers exemplify how desire can be denuded or deadened when feelings and emotions are subject to administrative control.

In Chapter 4 we will see that innovation as safe simulation is becoming one of the dominant strategies of educational change: increasingly so as change strategies move from the clinical worlds of knowledge and technique into the volatile and unpredictable domains of human feeling and emotion. In the remainder of the book, we will see how this change process works itself out in three important domains of teaching: work, time and culture.

WORK

Teachers and their associations frequently describe and dignify what they do as a profession, skilled craft or career. Teaching, however, is also fundamentally a kind of work. This is not to suggest that teaching is unduly laborious in the way that much low-grade manual work is. I simply want to point out in line with Connell's pioneering analysis of teachers' work that teaching is also a job: a set of tasks and human relationships that are structured in particular ways.[29] Similarly, the school — that place where most paid teachers teach — is more than an empty shell of walls and windows; more even than a learning environment for its students. The school is also a workplace for its teachers — just like the hospital is for a surgeon, the office for a clerk, and the shop floor for a factory worker. This workplace is structured through resources and relationships which can make the job easier or harder, fruitful or futile, rewarding or dispiriting.

The popular image of teachers' work is of work performed in classrooms with children — asking questions, issuing directions, giving advice, keeping order, presenting material, marking children's work, or correcting their mistakes. These activities and the preparation needed to organize them are the stuff of teaching for most people. Despite all the investment in staff development and inservice training, classroom teaching, even for teachers, remains central to the definition of what teaching is.

There are many other aspects to teachers' work, though — ones which have taken on increasing importance in recent years. To some extent, in parents' nights, staff meetings or marking books at home, these other parts of the job have always been there. But their invisibility has meant that they have not been part of the public face of teaching. When members of the public judge teachers, and do so on the basis of the many teachers they themselves have known over the years, they judge them through children's eyes – eyes that have seen the teacher teaching, but not preparing, marking or meeting. This is why, to the public, teachers' work often seems less difficult and demanding than it really is.

In recent years, these parts of the teacher's work that extend beyond the classroom have become more complex, numerous and significant. For many teachers, work with colleagues now means much more than structured staff meetings or casual conversations. It may also involve collaborative planning, being a peer coach for a partner, being a mentor for a new teacher, participating in shared staff development or sitting on review committees to discuss the individual cases of children with special needs. Meetings with parents now frequently extend beyond perfunctory parents' nights to more regular consultations, telephone calls and extended report cards. The growing threats of litigation and the escalating demands of accountability have also created a proliferation of notes of permission and explanation along with other form-filling and paperwork.

Many of these tasks are onerous. Some are trivial and unnecessary. But not all are a dreary distraction from the essential tasks of classroom teaching. Indeed, there is growing evidence that proper and positive attention to matters outside the classroom can significantly improve the quality of what goes on within it. Involvement in decision-making, constructive work with colleagues, shared commitment to continuous improvement – these things have been recorded as having a demonstrable impact on student achievement.[30]

By no means are all of these extra demands and commitments educationally positive, though. Work outside the classroom has many different implications for teachers and their effectiveness, depending on what it is and how it is organized. Here again is the central problem. Individually, we know what many of the recent changes in teachers' work *are*. Collectively, we are much less certain about what they *mean*!

Two of the main explanations are those of *professionalization* and *intensification*. *Professionalization* emphasizes changes in and extensions to the teacher's role that signify greater professionalism. In this position, teaching is seen as becoming more complex and more skilled with teachers being involved more in leadership roles, partnership with colleagues, shared decision-making and providing consultancy to others in their own areas of expertise.[31]

A second position points to deterioration and deprofessionalization in teachers' work. These accounts portray teachers' work as more routinized and deskilled, with teachers having less discretion to exercise their professional judgments that seem most suited to their own children in their own classes. Teachers are depicted as being treated almost like recovering alcoholics: needing to adopt step-by-step methods of instruction, or to comply with imposed tests and curricula in order to be effective. Overall, teachers' work is described as becoming increasingly *intensified*, as pressures accumulate and innovations multiply under conditions of work that fail to keep pace with these changes and even fall behind. Under this view, the rhetoric of professionalism simply seduces teachers into consorting with their own exploitation.

The theoretical debates between professionalization on the one hand, and intensification and deskilling on the other are not just matters of academic curiosity. They pose absolutely fundamental questions about the nature of teachers' work and how it is changing. Is it getting better or worse, more skilled or less skilled, more professionalized or less so? And how do teachers *feel* about the nature of their work and the changes in it? How does the way that teachers' work is now structured relate to teachers' purposes, to the kinds of people teachers are, and to the workplaces in which teachers operate? How does change affect teachers, so that they are able or unable to effect change themselves?

TIME

Chapters 5–7 address these vital questions about teachers and their work. One of the most basic, constitutive features of teachers' work is that of time. This is the subject of Chapters 5 and 6. Shortage of time is one of the perennial complaints of teachers and teaching. In studies of educational change, school improvement, curriculum implementation and staff development, shortage of time repeatedly appears as one of the chief implementation problems. Scarcity of time makes it difficult to plan more thoroughly, to commit oneself to the effort of innovation, to get together with colleagues, or to sit back and reflect on one's purposes and progress. How much time teachers get away from classroom duties, to work with colleagues or just to reflect on their own, is a vital issue for matters of change, improvement and professional development.

Time, though, is much more than a quantity that can be given or taken away, inflated or reduced (although it is certainly also that). Time is a perception as well as a property. Different people perceive time differently. We will see that teachers and administrators often have very different perceptions of time in teaching and its relationship to educational change. This is partly a gender issue, for the relationship between administrators and teachers is most often a relationship between men and women respectively. But it is also a question of how teachers and administrators each experience the teaching context and the place of change within it. Teachers and administrators, I will argue, perceive time in teaching and change very differently. These differences are rooted in how teachers and administrators respectively are located in relation to the structure of teachers' work. And they are differences that can lead to profound misunderstandings and struggles about teaching, change and time itself, as administrators typically compress the timelines of change that their teachers try to hold back! Understanding the complexity and interrelatedness of this problem, I shall show, requires synthesis of different but compatible theoretical approaches which enable us to appreciate that time in teaching is at once a technically manageable resource, a subjectively varying perception and an object of political struggle.

Chapter 6 then examines some commonly held claims in the study of teachers' work, that the experience and organization of time has itself changed with time. This argument is known as the intensification thesis: the thesis that time in teaching is becoming more compressed, with worrying consequences. Because this thesis is so widely stated but so weakly demonstrated, I will explore how it stands up against the experiences and perceptions of teachers themselves. The intensification thesis will therefore be interrogated with teachers' own voices; with what they themselves have to say about time and work. We shall see that these voices offer some support for the intensification thesis, but also some surprises. The teachers' voices in Chapter 6 articulate many unexpected statements that cast serious doubts upon parts of the thesis.

In Chapter 7, I turn to the emotional dynamics of teaching; to how teachers feel about their work. Looking at the specific case of teaching and guilt, I examine how these dynamics emerge from the ways in which the work of teaching is structured. In moderation, guilt can be the inner voice of conscientiousness. But in excess, I will argue, guilt can produce burnout, cynicism and exit from the profession. There is much about the way in which teachers' work is presently structured that produces such guilt gluts and all their side effects. In particular, I will show that teachers can be especially guilt prone, when they feel they may be hurting those for whom they care, because of excessive and conflicting demands, unending expectations, and uncertain criteria of professional achievement within the workplace.

CULTURE

Chapter 7 shows that uncertainty in teaching can contribute to the guilt that many teachers feel. In teaching, the work is never over, more can always be done, things can always be improved. In these conditions, teachers by definition can never do enough. Other research also indicates that uncertainty can lead to reduction of risk, safety in teaching methods and as a result, lowering of student expectations and achievement.[32] If uncertainty has always been a pervasive quality of teaching, the collapse of scientific certainty and with it, a supposedly sure knowledge base for teaching (in methods of *proven* success, for instance) promises to exaggerate its influence still further.

If there is a wish to reduce some of the unhelpful uncertainties of teaching, then means other than technical, scientific ones must therefore be found. One commonly advanced solution is to build professional cultures of teaching among small communities of teachers in each workplace, who can work together, provide mutual support, offer constructive feedback, develop common goals, and establish challenging but realistic limits regarding what can reasonably be achieved. It is upon this argument about reducing teacher uncertainty that much of the case for developing cultures of collaboration among teachers has come to rest.

Chapters 8–10 deal closely and controversially with the issue of teacher collaboration, and with the role played by teacher cultures in educational change, more widely. I will not spend much time going over the relatively well trodden ground that makes the case for collaboration in terms of its contribution to school improvement, professional growth and student achievement. Enough eulogies have been written already on this subject. Collaboration is now widely proposed as an organizational solution to the problems of contemporary schooling, just as it is proposed as a flexible solution to rapid change and the need for greater responsiveness and productivity in business corporations and other organizations more widely. Collaborative decision-making and problem solving is a cornerstone of postmodern organizations.

My purpose in this book is neither to praise collaboration nor to bury it. My concern, rather, is with its meanings, realizations and consequences. Again, the words of teachers will serve as our guide here in unravelling the conceptual woolliness of collaboration. Many controversies are to be found in those words and in the understandings they generate. In Chapter 8, we will find that well-intentioned drives to create collaborative cultures and to expunge the culture of teacher isolation and individualism from our schools are in serious danger of eliminating individuality among teachers, and with it the disagreeable creativity that can challenge administrative assumptions and be a powerful force for change.

Chapter 9 takes up the theme of collaboration in earnest, and draws a distinction between *collaborative cultures* and *contrived collegiality*. Collaboration can be a device to help teachers work together to pursue and review their own purposes as a professional community, or it can be a way of reinscribing administrative control within persuasive and pervasive discourses of collaboration and partnership. Collaboration, in this sense, can be a burden as well as a blessing, especially once administrators take it over and convert it into models, mandates, and measurable profiles of growth and implementation. For the spontaneous, unpredictable and dangerous processes of teacher-led collaboration, administrators too often prefer to substitute the safe simulation of contrived collegiality: more perfect, more harmonious (and more controlled) than the reality of collaboration itself.

Like time, collaboration is a central point of struggle between administrators and teachers, and even among administrators themselves. Though current patterns of collaboration have been precipitated by postmodern conditions, hierarchical bureaucracies persistently try to regulate such collaboration and reintegrate it into modernistic systems as new strategies of regulation and control. In the debates and struggles surrounding the meaning of collaboration can be seen some of the central conflicts between modernity and postmodernity with which our schools and teachers are now wrestling.

Chapter 10 turns to forms of collaboration which divide as much as they unite. Drawing on data collected among secondary school teachers, it shows how the modernistic secondary school system has *balkanized* its teachers into departmental *cubbyholes*. While this has created a measure of collaboration within departments, collaboration across subject boundaries has become severely restricted, creating pedagogical inconsistency, competitive territoriality and lack of opportunities for teachers to learn from and support each other.

Data from innovative secondary schools, however, suggest that many attempts to eradicate traditional forms of *balkanization* simply reconstruct it in other ways. Many such schools try to secure shared visions and common values organized around innovative curricula, alternative pedagogies, widened systems of assessment and reporting and so on. Despite their radical content, these programs of reform, I shall argue, often just substitute one modernistic mission for another. This time, though, the balkanization occurs not between departments, but between the avant garde and the rearguard, between insiders and outsiders, or between the old and the young. Secondary schools, I shall argue, if they are to avoid balkanization and all its problems must search for more postmodern patterns of organization and collaboration that are pluralistic and flexible in nature, instead of ones that seek to contrive or impose whole-school consensus across their entire staffs.

FUTURES

Moving on from the empirical data, the final chapter looks at possible futures for change among teachers. It sketches out different possible scenarios for educational restructuring. In itself, we shall find, restructuring is not a self-evident solution to the crises affecting teachers and their schools. Nor are school culture, professional development or educational leadership. In ethical and practical terms, rather, what matters in all these domains is how the conflicts will be worked out between bureaucratic control and teacher empowerment most immediately, and between modernity and postmodernity more widely. It is through these struggles that the future cultures, capacities and commitments of teachers will be constructed.

Every change involves a choice: between a path to be taken and others to be passed by. Understanding the context, process and consequences of change helps us clarify and question these choices. Which choices we make will ultimately depend on the depth of that understanding but also on the creativity of our strategies, the courage of our convictions, and the direction of our values. Accordingly, the book closes not with definitive rules for improvement, lists of successful practice, or any other spurious certainties. Rather, it sets out some of the choices we face, along with their moral and practical implications when we encounter educational change or are making such change ourselves in this postmodern world. For if we can come to understand the possible futures of change, we may be more able to take charge of such change in the future.

NOTES

1. This notion of professional action as the exercise of discretionary judgment within conditions of unavoidable and perpetual uncertainty is outlined most clearly by Donald Schön in *The Reflective Practitioner*, San Francisco, Jossey-Bass, 1983. It is a notion of professionalism that is very different from the more conventional one, which is grounded in notions of esoteric knowledge, specialist expertise and public status.

2. The initial project report is Hargreaves, A. and Wignall, R., *Time for the Teacher: A Study of Collegial Relations and Preparation Time Use among Elementary School Teachers*, Transfer Grant Project 51/1070, Toronto, Ontario Institute for Studies in Education.

3. Halsey, A. H., Heath, A. and Ridge, J., *Origins and Destinations*, Oxford, Oxford University Press, 1980.

4. I have discussed the impact of these interconnected reforms more extensively in my book on *Curriculum and Assessment Reform*, Milton Keynes, Open University Press and Toronto, OISE Press, 1989. The refusal in 1993 of teachers to administer National Curriculum tests, and the establishment of a committee under Sir Ron Dearing to look into the impact of testing demands on teachers' work, points to the limited effectiveness of reform by compliance.

5. See Hargreaves, D. and Hopkins, D., *The Empowered School*, London, Cassell, 1991.

6. Such practices are documented in Popkewitz, T. and Lind, K., "Teacher incentives as reforms: Teachers' work and the changing control mechanisms in education", *Teachers College Record*, 90, 1989, 575–94; Smyth, J. and Garman, N., "Supervision as school reform: A critical perspective", *Journal of Education Policy*, 4(4), 1989, 343–61; and Hargreaves, A. and Dawe, R., "Paths of professional development: Contrived collegiality, collaborative culture and the case of peer coaching", *Teaching and Teacher Education*, 6(3), 1990, 227–41.

7. This is revealed in a collection of related studies published in *Educational Evaluation and Policy Analysis*, 12(3), Fall 1990.

8. For extensive discussions of the possibilities and problems of school-based management, see Caldwell, B. and Spinks, J. M., *The Self-Managing School*, Lewes, Falmer Press, 1988, and Caldwell, B. and Spinks, J. M., *Leading the Self-Managing School*, London and Washington, DC, Falmer Press, 1992. For more trenchant critiques of the principles and practices of educational self-management, see the collection of papers in Smyth, J. (ed.), *The Socially Critical Self-Managing School*, London and Washington, DC, Falmer Press, Forthcoming.

9. Sarason, S., *The Predictable Failure of Educational Reform*, San Francisco, Jossey-Bass, 1990.

10. The literature on modernity is reviewed and discussed in Chapter 2.

11. Weber, M., *General Economic History*, New Brunswick, NJ, and London, Transaction Books, 1981. Weber, M., *Economy and Society: An Outline of Interpretive Sociology*, New York, Bedminster Press, 1968.

12. The literature on postmodernity and its major characteristics is reviewed and discussed in Chapter 4.

13. Fullan, M., with Stiegelbauer, S., *The New Meaning of Educational Change*, New York, Teachers College Press; Toronto, OISE Press and London, Cassell, 1991.

14. Huberman, M. and Miles, M., *Innovation Up Close*, New York: Plenum, 1984.

15. Fullan, M., *What's Worth Fighting For in the Principalship*, Toronto, Ontario Public School Teachers' Federation, 1988.

16. Louis, K. S. and Miles, M., *Improving the Urban High School*, New York, Teachers College Press, 1990.

17. McLaughlin, M., "Learning from experience: Lessons from policy implementation", *Educational Evaluation and Policy Analysis*, 9, 171–8; and McLaughlin, M., "The Rand change agent study revisited: Macro perspectives and micro realities", *Educational Researcher*, December 1990, 11–16.

18. Hopkins, D., "School improvement in an era of change", in Ribbins, P. and Whale, E. (eds), *Improving Education: The Issue Is Quality*, London, Cassell, 1992.

19. Lieberman, A., Darling-Hammond, L. and Zuckerman, D., *Early Lessons in Restructuring Schools*, New York, National Center for Restructuring Education, Schools, and Teaching (NCREST), 1991.

20. Wideman, R., "How secondary school teachers change their classroom practices", Ed.D. thesis, Toronto, University of Toronto, 1991.

21. One of the ironies of contemporary educational reform is that advocates of a socially grounded experiential approach to children's learning often hold teachers responsible for respecting the social character of children's learning, but do not see that teachers are social learners themselves. Children have been the victims and teachers the villains – the ones who interpose themselves and their requirements between young people and the experiential possibilities of learning.

22. I have developed this argument more extensively in "Teaching quality: A sociological analysis", *Journal of Curriculum Studies*, 20(3), 1988, 211–32; See also Darling-Hammond, L. and Berry, B., *The Evolution of Teacher Policy*, Santa Monica, CA, Rand Corporation.

23. Doyle, W. and Ponder, G., "The practicality ethic in teacher decision-making", *Interchange*, 8(3), 1977–78, 1–12.

24. These questions of context, purpose and person in teaching are addressed more extensively in Fullan, M. and Hargreaves, A., *What's Worth Fighting For? Working Together for Your School*, Toronto, Ontario Public School Teachers' Federation; Andover, MA, The Network; Milton Keynes, Open University Press; and Melbourne, Australian Council for Educational Administration, 1991.

25. Lash, S., *Sociology of Postmodernism*, London and New York, Routledge, 1990, 66. My

alliterative distinction here owes much aesthetically, but little theoretically, to a similarly worded but substantively different distinction drawn by P. D. James in her novel, *Devices and Desires*, London, Faber & Faber, 1990. (The phrase originally comes from the Anglican *Book of Common Prayer*.)

26. Deleuze, G. and Guattari, F., *Anti-Oedipus, Capitalism and Schizophrenia*, New York, Viking Press, 1977, p. 26.

27. Woods, P., "Teaching and creativity", in *Teacher Skills and Strategies*, London and Washington, DC, Falmer Press, 1990.

28. This evidence is reviewed and described in Chapter 9.

29. Connell, R., *Teachers' Work*, Sydney and New York, George Allen & Unwin, 1985. Connell's analysis stands out against many other theoretical analyses of teachers' work by the way it is grounded in richly described empirical data, as well as in theoretical application.

30. As, for example, in Rosenholtz, S., *Teachers' Workplace*, New York, Longmans, 1989.

31. The discussion of intensification and professionalization is developed fully in Chapter 6.

32. This is shown most strikingly in Rosenholtz's study of teacher development, workplace culture and student outcomes in Tennessee elementary schools. See Rosenholtz, *op. cit.*, note 30.

Chapter 2

The Malaise of Modernity
The Pretext for Change

UNDERSTANDING CHANGE

In any talk about schooling, corporate analogies are common. Yet they are also contested. Schools are not businesses. Children are not products. Educators aren't usually out to make a profit. Schools and corporations, however, are not absolutely unalike. Larger secondary schools in particular share with many business corporations a number of important characteristics. These include large numbers of staff, delineated hierarchies of command, divisions of specialized responsibility, demarcation of tasks and roles, and challenges to achieve consistency and coordination. When the corporate world encounters major crises and undergoes profound transitions, human service organizations like hospitals and schools should pay close attention, for similar crises may soon affect them.

Few observers of the social world around them can be unaware of the monumental changes now taking place in the corporate world. Restructuring, downsizing, relocation and even extinction are the realities of organizational change which many corporations and their employees are having to face. Businesses are being broken up. Organizational hierarchies are being flattened as layers of bureaucracy are swept away. Leadership and the way it is exercised is undergoing extraordinary transformations. As traditional structures wither and new ones emerge, these patterns of change are sometimes celebrated in eulogies of personal empowerment or of organizational learning and development. At other times, the celebrations are but thinly veiled euphemisms for corporate collapse, managerial ruthlessness or calculated bankruptcy. Depending on one's value standpoint, and sometimes on the situation as well, these transformations in corporate life can be either heroic or horrendous. Either way, their impact in the corporate world and beyond is formidable.

The social tranformations we are witnessing on the cusp of the millennium extend far beyond the corporate world alone. Extensive changes in economic and organizational life are being accompanied by and also interrelated with equally profound changes in the organization and impact of knowledge and information, in the global spread of ecological danger along with growing public awareness of that danger, in the geopolitical reconstruction of the global map, in the restitution and reconstitution of national and cultural identities, and even in the redefinition and restructuring of human selves. While in one sense, change is ubiquitous, the social pendulum is always swinging, and there is nothing new under the sun, the juxtaposition of these extensive changes at one historical moment amounts to more than one more shift of social fashion. Indeed, it is not too dramatic to claim that these combined and connected changes mark the decline of one key sociohistorical period and the advent of another. With the former Czechoslovakian President and intellectual, Vaclav Havel, I want to argue that these combined changes mark "the end of the modern era" – or at least the beginning of that end.[1] This significant sociohistorical shift poses extremely important challenges for us all around the turn of the century. Given their role in preparing the generations of the future, the implications of these changes for teachers are particularly important. Yet, while the reverberations of change are now beginning to be felt in the educational world, they are often only vaguely understood. Indeed, the generic literature on educational change has dealt with them rather poorly.

The educational change literature is replete with theories and understandings of what has come to be known as *the change process*. Addressing the more generic aspects of educational change, this literature has helped us appreciate how change gets implemented, how people make changes themselves and how change persists and becomes institutionalized over time.[2] However, intensive and cumulative attention to the change process has also often led to what Robert Merton called *goal displacement*.[3] Goal displacement happens when we become so fascinated with the means by which we pursue our goals that these means ultimately take the place of the goals themselves. The original goals then become neglected or forgotten. Preoccupation with the change process is often like this. As efforts are channelled into implementation, the reasons for making the change in the first place fade quickly into the background. As a result, people who are affected by change often wonder what the change is for. They are unclear about its origins or purpose, and its relevance to them. While we now have an impressive professional discourse of change *process*, our attention to the *purpose* and *context* of change, and to discourses through which it might be interpreted and expressed, is relatively impoverished. In this chapter and the two that follow it, I want to develop just such a discourse of change context; one that is appropriate to the momentous sociohistorical transformations with which we are now being confronted.

This discourse is grounded in the central proposition that the challenges and changes facing teachers and schools are not parochially confined to education but are rooted in a major sociohistorical transition from a period of *modernity* to one of *postmodernity*. Schools and teachers are being affected more and more by the demands and contingencies of an increasingly complex and fast-paced, postmodern world. Yet their response is often inappropriate or ineffective – leaving intact the systems and structures of the present, or retreating to comforting myths of the past. Schools and teachers either cling to bureaucratic solutions of a modernistic kind: more systems, more hierarchies, more laid on change, more of the same. Or they retreat nostalgically to premodern myths of community, consensus and collaboration, where small is beautiful and friendships and allegiance tie teachers and others together in tight, protected webs of common purpose and belonging. In many respects, schools remain modernistic and in some cases even premodern institutions that are having to operate in a complex postmodern world. As time goes by, this gap between the world of school and the world beyond it is becoming more and more obvious. The anachronistic nature of schooling is increasingly transparent. It is this disparity that defines much of the contemporary crisis of schooling and teaching.

This chapter briefly summarizes the major characteristics of the era of modernity, an era which is generally on the wane but one which has set remarkably resilient assumptions and conditions within which schools and teachers now operate, and to which they continue to cling as the vortex of change swirls all around them. The next two chapters then turn to a detailed analysis of the emerging postmodern condition itself, and the challenges it is presenting to teachers and their work as they face a new century. In this first section of the book, the discussion will sometimes take us away from the immediate world of the school to the society surrounding it. But without an understanding of context, of where all the pressures and changes are coming from, there can be no clarity or coherence about the changes as we experience them. And without clarity or coherence, we can exert little control or direction over the future of education and the role that teachers will play there. Without a theory of context, educational change is a mystical or meaningless process that cannot be adequately conceptualized or controlled by those who experience it. So it is with a theory of context that we must begin.

THE MALAISE OF MODERNITY

Although schooling is an ancient invention, its contemporary forms and mass availability were constructed and established within quite specific social conditions. These have been labelled by various social theorists as conditions of *modernity*.[4] Exactly how modernity should be periodized is a matter of dispute among such theorists, but most seem to locate its onset around the time of the Enlightenment, the age of Reason. Beyond that, some writers also separate out a further, more advanced stage of modernity which they call late or high modernity.[5] The beginning of this latter period is commonly located around the mid- to late nineteenth century, with its widespread acceptance being achieved in the aftermath of World War II. Turner summarizes the origins and evolution of modernity like this:

> Modernity arises with the spread of western imperialism in the
> sixteenth century; the dominance of capitalism in northern

Europe . . . in the early seventeenth century; the acceptance of
scientific procedures with the publication of the works of Francis
Bacon, Newton and Harvey; and preeminently with the
institutionalization of Calvinistic practices and beliefs in the
dominant classes of northern Europe. We can follow this process
further through the separation of the household and the
economy, and the creation of the institution of motherhood in
the nineteenth century. Although the idea of the citizen can be
traced back to Greek times via the independent cities of the
Italian state . . ., the citizen as the abstract carrier of universal
rights is a distinctively modern idea . . .[6]

If the nomenclature and periodization of modernity are somewhat contested, its dominant characteristics are more widely acknowledged and agreed.
At root, modernity rests upon Enlightenment beliefs that nature can be transformed and social progress achieved by the systematic development of scientific
and technological understanding, and by its rational application to social and
economic life. Compared to premodern societies, the condition of modernity is
one in which the spheres of economic production and human reproduction
become segregated from one another. Family and workplace are no longer contiguous. Industrialization brings with it the factory system, culminating in
systems of mass production and consumption within high modernity. In the
words of Max Weber, economic life and organizational life more generally
undergo *rationalization*.[7] The modern factory system gathers large numbers of
workers together in single locations where time and motion can be finely
calibrated and carefully regulated through bureaucratic hierarchies of supervision and control. For Alvin Toffler, high modernity is the era of the *smoke-
stack*.[8] It is built on economies of *scale*.[9] Monopoly capitalism in the first
world or state socialism in the second are its culminating patterns of economic
organization.

As Jürgen Habermas and, more recently, David Harvey have argued, the
social and historical project of *modernity* was pursued chiefly in the name
of social emancipation as a way of lifting humanity out of the particularism,
paternalism and superstition of premodern times.[10] The project of modernity

amounted to an extraordinary intellectual effort on the part of
Enlightenment thinkers to develop objective science, universal
morality and law and autonomous art according to their inner
logic. The idea was to use the accumulation of knowledge
generated by many individuals working freely and creatively for
the pursuit of human emancipation and the enrichment of daily
life. The scientific domination of nature promised freedom from
scarcity, want and the arbitrariness of natural calamity. The
development of rational forms of social organization and rational
modes of thought promised liberation from the irrationalities of

myth, religion, superstition, release from the arbitrary use of power as well as from the dark side of our own human natures. Only through such a project could the universal, eternal and the immutable qualities of all humanity be revealed.[11]

Harvey goes on to note that the twentieth-century experience of war and military catastrophe dramatically shattered this optimism.[12] The meaning of modernity has in this sense become laden with ambiguity, enshrining positive and negative connotations alike. Drawing on the classical writings of Max Weber on modernization, and particularly on bureaucracy and the rationalization of social life, Bryan Turner analyzes these ambiguities in some depth. For Weber, he says:

> Modernity is . . . the consequence of a process of modernization by which the social world comes under the domination of ascetism, secularization, the universalistic claims of instrumental rationality, the differentiation of the various spheres of the lifeworld, the bureaucratization of economic, political and military practices, and the growing monetarization of values. . . .
>
> The essential feature of Weber's view of modernity is, however, its ambiguity. Modernization brings with it the erosion of meaning, the endless conflict of polytheistic values, and the threat of the iron cage of bureaucracy. Rationalization makes the world orderly and reliable, but it cannot make the world meaningful.[13]

Modernity has always been a double-edged phenomenon. It has possessed the potential to enhance the human condition but also to impoverish it. This can be seen in a number of arenas.

1. *Economically*, modernity has promised efficiency, productivity and prosperity but, especially in its later stages, it has also created workplaces and labor processes which separate management from workers, planning from execution and head from hand. These labor processes, it has been argued, break down workers' tasks into smaller and smaller measurable components, deskilling people's work and subjecting it to ever increasing degrees of technical control.[14]

Teachers too, it has been suggested, have been subjected to and subjugated by this deskilled labor process. Their work, it is argued, has been defined and their powers of discretion delimited by the technical controls of standardized tests, "teacher-proof" curriculum packages and guidelines, and step-by-step models of teaching imposed from above. In teachers' workplaces, as in others, the measures designed to increase technical control have often ironically undermined it, by creating problems of meaning, motivation and morale among teachers struggling to work more intuitively, more emotionally and more morally than these technical controls permit.[15]

2. *Politically*, modernity has seen the consolidation of the nation state as a military force, and the creation of the welfare state as a supposedly civilizing and elevating one.[16] The rise of the state and the role of the state within high modernity have been exceptionally important.[17] State structures have become increasingly strong, centralized and interventionist. Through the application of Keynesian economics, they have taken increasing responsibility for supporting, coordinating and intervening in the conditions of economic production and for securing social progress through welfare reforms. Sweden's social democratic state, Britain's postwar welfare state, and Lyndon Johnson's US War on Poverty are some of the most significant exemplars of the politics of high modernity. Communist societies extended these processes of state coordination, intervention and control even further.

The modern state is the planned state. Its segregation of business zones from residential ones concentrates social life into different compartments, function by function. Its expressways and motorways have been designed to increase speed of communication, its skyscrapers to conserve scarce urban space, its welfare apartment blocks and housing estates to remove urban squalor. In the name of social and technological efficiency on the one hand and planned human improvement on the other, the modern state both protects and patrols the populace in ever-widening nets of regulation, control and intervention. This applies to education too.[18]

Across the world, one of the most important and pervasive state reforms has been mass education. On the one hand, mass education was won as a right by an increasingly franchised and politically organized populace. It entitled and enfranchised young people to have access to educational and social opportunities. On the other hand, mass education also trained the future labor force and sustained social order and control. In the words of one critic, it was nothing less than an *ideological state apparatus*.[19] The relationship between education and the modern state, therefore, has not been consistently benign.

Modern school systems, as educational historians like Hamilton and Goodson have noted, emerged as factory-like systems of mass education designed to meet the needs of manufacturing and heavy industry. They processed pupils in batches, segregated them into age-graded cohorts called *classes* or *standards*, taught them a standardized course or curriculum, and did this through teacher-centered methods of lecturing, recitation, question-and-answer and seatwork.[20] These systems of mass elementary education, for an increasingly massified society, with large laboring classes, were supplemented by more selective systems of state and private secondary education for commercial and social elites. With the expansion of equal opportunities alongside mounting concerns about unskilled labor forces, uncompetitive economies and shortfalls of human capital, secondary education was increasingly made available to all. It too became part of mass schooling.

The conditions of modernity have set the parameters and assumptions within which our secondary schools in particular, along with their teachers, developed and now operate. Punctuated lesson periods, age-segregated classes, the subject-based academic curriculum, and paper and pencil testing – all those things that now make up "*real*" secondary school teaching, the seemingly natural, normal and reasonable ways to organize a curriculum and to teach – are therefore highly specific sociohistorical products. A key argument of this book is that these extant practices and structures of secondary school teaching may now have outlived their usefulness, being no longer appropriate for a society in which the conditions and assumptions of modernity upon which state secondary schooling was founded are losing their force and relevance.

3. *Organizationally*, the politics and economics of modernity have had significant and systematic effects on institutional life, including schooling. Most of today's secondary schools are quintessentially modernistic institutions. Characteristically immense in size, balkanized into a maze of bureaucratic *cubbyholes* known as subject departments, and precariously articulated by that geometric labyrinth known as the school schedule or timetable, secondary schools have struggled hard to improve opportunity and choice for swelling numbers of young people, but at significant cost. This has been a cost of impersonality and alienation for their students, and bureaucratic inflexibility and unresponsiveness to change among their staffs. American secondary schools have been likened to shopping malls; British comprehensive schools to over-crowded airports.[21] The metaphors are not flattering. As large and often cumbersome organizations, many secondary schools seem to mesh poorly with the academic, personal and social needs of their students and with the needs for fruitful professional development, continuous learning, and flexible decision making among their staff.

The current crisis of secondary education is not just a problem of size, impersonality or inflexibility, though. It is not even a problem of failing to meet the economic challenges of global competitiveness. It is a problem, rather, of a balkanized, specialized, modernistic school system confronting new and complex conditions of postmodernity. As I argued in the previous chapter, secondary schools are both symbols and symptoms of the malaise of modernity. Their large, complex, bureaucratic structures are ill suited to the dynamic and varying needs of the postmodern world: needs for more relevant and engaging student learning, for more continuous and connected professional development, and for more flexible and inclusive decision-making.[22]

4. *Personally*, the effects of modernistic bureaucracies extend right through to the formation and fulfilment of individual selves and identities. This is not to imply that bureaucracies are all bad. At their best, they replace patronage and nepotism with impartial judgments that recognize qualifications and expertise. Corporate bureaucracies can also offer certain kinds of personal reward and satisfaction. As Leinberger and Tucker found when they revisited the corporate "organization men" whom William H. Whyte had first studied in the 1950s, organizations offered long-term security in exchange for company loyalty, and

a clear sense of place in the wider structure.[23] Corporate bureaucracies offered both security of prospects and prospects of security. For this, however, there was a price.

One thing that many corporate bureaucracies valued in their employees was "the well rounded personality". But as Leinberger and Tucker note:

> the well rounded personality, so beloved by the corporate
> personnel officers Whyte interviewed, could be counted on to
> eschew eccentricity of any kind . . . and to have no rough edges
> that would prevent smooth integration into the social machinery.[24]

Corporations appeared to value the construction of pleasing personalities more than the expression of inner selves. Personalities had to be marketable and malleable in the context of company needs. And so the achievement of security, advancement and sense of place also involved some sacrifice of the self, to a greater or lesser degree. Whyte himself put it like this. In terms of "company loyalty", he said:

> all the new emphases [in the 1950s] call for a closer spiritual
> union between the individual and the Organization. As the
> prophets of belongingness have maintained, greater fealty to the
> Organization can be viewed as a psychological necessity for the
> individual. In a world changing so fast, in a world in which he
> must forever be on the move, the individual desperately needs
> roots, and the Organization is a logical place to develop them.
> There are some highly practical forces at work to compel
> more loyalty. With the great increase in fringe benefits, the
> development of pension and annuity plans, the individual's
> self-interest is bound up more tightly than before in continued
> service in one organization. Why, then, should a man leave a
> company?[25]

Why indeed? Except, perhaps, when company needs and individual needs are not identical. As Whyte himself continued:

> One of the hazards of the life we lead, says a man now poised at
> the top threshold of the top management of one of our largest
> corporations, is the loss of well-defined objectives. What is the
> purpose? What is the end? I was deeply a part of my job in the
> chemical division. My wife and I were deeply a part of the
> community; I was contributing and was effective. Then they
> asked me to come to New York – the VP in charge told me that
> by coming here, I'd have a box seat in the "Big Time." If his
> guess has been bad, it's a terrible waste. I hope the company
> isn't playing checkers with me. I feel a lack. I don't know what
> I'm being groomed for . . .[26]

29

Not surprisingly, when corporate credibility began to be questioned from the 1960s and 1970s onwards, the literature of social psychology took up the organizational suppression of the self as one of its overriding themes. Ervin Goffman used metaphors of human drama to describe social interaction as the art of impression management.[27] Eric Berne popularized interpersonal relations as a set of games people play.[28] There was renewed interest in George Herbert Mead's classical distinction between the unconstrained and innovating "I", and the other-directed, socially regulated "Me".[29] R. D. Laing distinguished between inner "true" selves and socially conditioned "false" ones.[30] And in studies of teaching, Jennifer Nias, along with other sociologists of teaching, pointed to differences between what she called the substantial self which strove to realize its own purposes and the situational self of the teacher which was compromised by the constraints of circumstance.[31] In their different ways, all these writings expounded a humanistic critique of modernity and the organizations which had come to dominate it. Modernistic bureaucracies alienated the human spirit. They emptied work of its meaning. They separated workers from their inner selves.

These problems applied to teaching just as much as they did to other occupations. Unreasonable demands and constraints could reduce much teaching to survival, or, even worse, permit strategies of survival to pass for teaching itself. Throughout the 1970s and 1980s writers like Westbury, Woods and myself showed how a lot of teaching consisted of *coping strategies* that teachers had evolved over the years to deal with situational constraints, accountability demands, testing requirements, shortages of resources and conflicting expectations.[32] Studies of teaching showed how teachers had to struggle hard to define and defend worthwhile selves in the face of all these demands – to preserve and express the people that they were, and to protect and promote the moral purposes which gave meaning to their work.[33]

Some teachers succeeded in sustaining the self and even found exceptional environments where it could flourish.[34] Many had to revise their goals for self-realization downwards to fit the realistically limited opportunities their schools provided.[35] And by mid to late career, many other teachers gave up on self-realization altogether in the workplace, and became cynical or disenchanted, resisting change in their staffrooms, and lowering levels of commitment and performance in the classroom.[36] Reforms in teacher education and teacher development in the United States have sought to remedy these problems by trying to improve the quality of teachers' working lives. I will return to these efforts throughout this book. For now, it simply needs to be stressed that in modernistic school systems, sustaining and realizing the self has been a constant struggle for teachers, whose purposes, commitments and very desires to teach have been persistently obstructed and undermined by the bureaucratic structures in which they work.

THE CRISIS OF MODERNITY

By the 1970s, there were growing signs that the age of modernity may have been approaching its end. Continuing ambiguities have always pervaded the modern condition. But towards the end of the 1960s and the beginning of the 1970s, the magnitude of the difficulties created by modern economies, modern states and modern patterns of organization were becoming immense. Through the 1970s and beyond, these difficulties reached such crisis proportions that they began to generate a set of powerful pretexts for change in economic, political and organizational life: the change that we have come to call postmodernity.

1. *Economically*, high modernity was becoming exhausted.[37] Mass consumption and mass production had been its foundations of wealth creation and capital accumulation. Increased consumption was stimulated by increased production. Economic expansion was the order of the day. In the 1970s, however, the West was plunged into dramatic economic collapse. Most immediately, this was precipitated by the world oil crisis of 1973. However, difficulties faced by modern economies had been intensifying long before this. One way modern economies had continued to expand was by opening up international markets and spreading their opportunities for profit-making across geographical space. But by the 1970s, these markets were becoming saturated and exhausted. Expansion and profitability had also been sustained by incurring increasing debts and deferring costs and losses over time. But by the 1970s, these too were becoming overwhelming. With the rise of new industrializing nations outside the West that were unencumbered by the legacies of old infrastructures or by powerful traditions of trade unionism, many Western economies found it increasingly hard to compete with the cheaper labor costs and greater technological initiative of their overseas competitors. Not just the efficiency, but the very viability of modern Western economies was seriously in doubt.

2. *Politically*, the crisis of Western economies quickly led to what O'Connor called a fiscal crisis of the state.[38] Modern Western economies had been run along the lines of Keynesian economics which fostered and legitimated direct state intervention in industrial production and economic life more generally. The Keynesian state regulated consumer supply and demand by intervening in the business cycle, regulating interest rates, imposing wage restraints, etc. It took communications, basic utilities and raw materials into public ownership in order to create cheap and stable infrastructures for profitable production. Sometimes it even took out major shareholdings in or secured overall control of particular companies where it deemed this to be in the general economic and public interest. More than this, the state expanded its investment in education, medicine and social welfare as ways of responding to rising social aspirations, "buying off" potential dissent, creating and sustaining a technically educated and physically healthy labor force, and generally trying to construct conditions of sufficient social harmony for economic productivity to prosper.[39]

31

The modern state has been the inalienable partner of the modern economy. Functionally, structurally, and at the highest levels even personally (in terms of intermarriage, social networks, shared school backgrounds, and the like), state and economy have been firmly wedded together. In the context of a collapsing economy, however, the state's once shrewd investments in education, social welfare and public ownership quickly came to be viewed as expensive luxuries that taxpayers could no longer afford. More than this, with profits in decline and people out of work, the state (and schooling with it) no longer appeared to be doing its job. As well as being expensive, the state also seemed to be manifestly inefficient. The benevolent, interventionist state rapidly came to be regarded as the bungling and intrusive state. It was fast losing its legitimacy.[40] Such crises of legitimacy in Western states became very much the norm from the late 1970s onwards. These crises of finance and legitimacy in the state created powerful pretexts for "rolling back the state" and reforming the educational and social welfare systems of Western societies. These reforms, we shall see, impact considerably on the work of teachers.

3. *Organizationally*, bureaucracies in corporations and bureaucracies in the state have increasingly been blamed for precipitating and perpetuating economic and social inefficiency and injustice. For Charles Taylor, a fundamental part of what he calls *the malaise of modernity* has been the overwhelming dominance within organizations and social life more generally of instrumental reason (or what Habermas calls technical rationality) as the basis for judgment and planning.[41] Narrowness of vision, inflexible decision-making, unwieldy structures, linear planning, unresponsiveness to changing client needs, the sacrifice of human emotion for clinical efficiency and the loss of meaningful senses of community have all become increasingly apparent and worrying features of the later stages of modernity. For these reasons, the organizations of modernity with their bureaucratic structures and hierarchical forms of leadership have come under powerful pressures to change.

CONCLUSION

Modernity has survived for centuries; its more recent forms for decades. It is not yet clear whether our generation will be witness to its complete demise, to the end of an epoch. Many facets of modernity clearly are in retreat or under review — standardization, centralization, mass production and mass consumption among them. Deeper continuing structures of power and control in society may not be eliminated quite so easily. They may, however, be changing their form: renovated and refurbished with postmodern façades of accessibility and diversity.

Whether these changes are judged to be deep or superficial, it is evident that the processes and practices of modernity in the economy, the state and the daily lives of organizations are being significantly revised and restructured;

sometimes by design, more often by sheer financial necessity. Schools and educational systems are latecomers to these changes, though. As Shedd and Bacharach put it:

> Private organizations are working to rid themselves of the inflexible and noncompetitive features of the mass production, assembly-line industrial model of management. At the same time, states, schools and even some teacher unions are standardizing textbooks, exams, and procedures and dividing responsibility for the learning process into smaller and smaller segments. Teachers are isolated in their individual classrooms, structurally discouraged from exchanging knowledge either of the students they share or the teaching techniques they have discovered, and encouraged to leave all decisions affecting more than their own specific classrooms to "management".[42]

In the face of postmodern pressures for greater flexibility, improved responsiveness, speed of change and dispersal of control, two educational responses have been evident. One, most visible within secondary schooling, but also often pervading the imposed testing and curriculum requirements of entire systems, has been to restore and reinforce the crumbling edifice of modernity, by defending departmentalism, reasserting traditional school subjects, standardizing teaching strategies and imposing system-wide testing. In the face of the postmodern challenge of a complex, diverse and rapidly changing world, the very rigidity of these methods makes them fated to fail.

A second response has been more apparent in smaller primary or elementary schools which often have a little more flexibility to innovate. This has been to retreat behind the ramparts of romantic progressivism, and build close-knit, collaborative communities of a premodern kind among their teachers (and sometimes their parents) in pursuit of common visions of educational improvement. As we shall see in later chapters, despite its capacity to harness human energies and commitment, and to be responsive to local needs, this response can also be politically rather naive; ill-equipped to operate in a complex world of vested interests and conflicting values. Given these conditions of conflict and complexity, this response seems more able to establish enclaves of experimentation (especially in more protected middle class communities) than to generate and sustain larger waves of system-wide change.[43] Moreover, the nostalgic search for smaller communities of collaboration and consensus tends to overlook the presence of those less virtuous and less readily acknowledged premodern qualities of paternalism and parochialism through which many (often male) principals and headteachers manage and motivate their (mainly female) teaching staff.[44] It was, of course, this very paternalism which modernistic bureaucracies were meant to eliminate. In this sense, the fact that many elementary school principals and primary school headteachers refer to their schools as "families" is not without irony.

Neither reasserting the bureaucratic practices of modernity, nor retreating to protected communities more reminiscent of the premodern age, seem to be appropriate or effective responses to the complex challenges of the postmodern world. The search for other solutions is not easy. But an essential first step is to begin to understand; to look more closely at the nature of the complexity, at the scale of the challenge, and at the distinctive problems and possibilities that postmodernity creates for teachers and schools.

Chapter 4 looks in detail at seven major dimensions of postmodernity and the challenges they pose for teachers and their work. It connects the changing work of teachers to the changing world in which they live. Before undertaking that analysis, however, it is important to recognize that the word *postmodern* is widely used among social theorists, aesthetic critics and the general public as well. Fashionable though they have become, however, terms like postmodernism and postmodernity have been given many different meanings. This can give rise and has given rise to considerable confusion. The next brief chapter, therefore, outlines a number of assumptions and starting points with regard to post-modernism and postmodernity to try to head off any such confusion. However, if you find this discussion a little intricate or esoteric, you might want to skip straight to Chapter 4 now, and perhaps return to Chapter 3 later to add further clarification, if necessary (itself, a rather postmodern way of reading the book!).

NOTES

1. Havel, V., "The end of the modern era", *New York Times*, 1 March 1992.

2. The most extensive and definitive review of this field is in Fullan, M. with Stiegelbauer, S., *The New Meaning of Educational Change*, New York, Teachers College Press; Toronto, OISE Press; and London, Cassell, 1991. See also Berman, P. and McLaughlin, M., *Federal Programs Supporting Educational Change*, Vol. VII, *Factors Affecting Implementation and Continuation*, Santa Monica, CA, Rand Corporation, 1977; Huberman, M. and Miles, M., *Innovation Up Close*, New York, Plenum, 1984; and Louis, K. S. and Miles, M., *Improving the Urban High School: What Works and Why*, New York, Teachers College Press, 1990.

3. Merton, R. K., *Social Theory and Social Structure* (rev. edn), New York, The Free Press, 1957.

4. Modernity, modernism and modernization are similar words but with quite distinctive meanings. *Modernity* describes a particular social condition with social, political, cultural and economic components. *Modernism* is an intellectual, aesthetic and cultural form, or the movement through which that form is expressed or brought about. *Modernization* is an economic and political process of development and change.

5. The term "high modernity" is particularly favored by Anthony Giddens. See, for instance, Giddens, A., *The Consequences of Modernity*, Cambridge, Polity Press, 1990, and Giddens, A., *Modernity and Self Identity*, Cambridge, Polity Press, 1991.

6. Turner, B. S., "Periodization and politics in the postmodern", in Turner, B. S. (ed.), *Theories of Modernity and Postmodernity*, London, Sage Publications, 1990, p. 6.

7. See Weber, M., *General Economic History*, New Brunswick, NJ, and London, Transaction Books, 1981. Also Weber, M., *Economy and Society: An Outline of Interpretive Sociology*, New York, Bedminster Press, 1968.

8. Toffler, A., *Powershift*, New York, Bantam Books, 1990, pp. 9-11.

9. Economies of scale were at the center of Fordist patterns of production, named after the production line technologies and patterns of mass production and consumption favored by Henry Ford. See Harvey, D., *The Condition of Postmodernity*, Oxford, Basil Blackwell, 1989.

10. For Habermas's discussion of modernity, see Habermas, J., *The Philosophical Discourse of Modernity*, Cambridge, Polity Press, 1987, p. 9.

11. Harvey, D., *The Condition of Postmodernity*, op. cit., note 9, p. 12.

12. Harvey, *op. cit.*, p. 13.

13. Turner, *op. cit.*, note 6, pp. 6-7.

14. The classic and most cited source of this argument is Braverman, H., *Labor and Monopoly Capital: The Degradation of Work in the Twentieth Century*, New York, Monthly Review Press, 1974.

15. There is now a fairly extensive literature which deals with the nature and effects of de-skilling within the labor process of teachers' work. Some of this is dealt with in Chapter 6 in a discussion of the intensification of teachers' work. Other key sources on deskilling and teachers' work include Smyth, J., "International perspectives on teacher collegiality: A labor process discussion based on the concept of teachers' work", *British Journal of Sociology of Education*, 12(3), 1991, 323–46; Apple, M. and Teitelbaum, K., "Are teachers losing control of their skills and curriculum?", *Journal of Curriculum Studies*, 18(2), 177–84; Apple, M. and Jungck, S., "You don't have to be a teacher to teach this unit: Teaching, technology and control in the classroom", in Hargreaves, A. and Fullan, M., *Understanding Teacher Development*, New York, Teachers College Press and London, Cassell, 1992; Lawn, M., "Skill in schoolwork: Work relations in the primary school" in Ozga, J. (ed.), *Schoolwork: Approaches to the Labour Process of Teaching*, Milton Keynes, Open University Press, 1988; Densmore, K., "Professionalism, proletarianization and teachers' work", in Popkewitz, T. (ed.), *Critical Studies in Teacher Education*, Lewes, Falmer Press, 1987.

16. The late 1970s and early 1980s saw a proliferation of theorizing on the role of the state in contemporary capitalist societies. Sample readings can be found in McLennan, G., Held, D. and Hall, S., *State and Society in Contemporary Britain*, Oxford, Polity Press, 1984. Three of the many classic references on the subject at the time were Habermas, J., *Legitimation Crisis*, London, Heinemann Books, 1976; Offe, C., *Contradictions of the Welfare State*, London, Hutchinson, 1984; and Poulantzas, N., *Political Power and Social Classes*, London, New Left Books. While these sources, like most at the time, tended to emphasize the political, ideological and economic role of the state, the military aspect of the state's role as a bounded political entity was taken up perhaps most articulately by Giddens, A., *The Nation State and Violence*, Cambridge, Polity Press, 1985.

17. See Giddens, A., *The Consequences of Modernity*, op. cit., note 5.

18. The most authoritative and extensive theoretical discussion of the relationship between education, the modern state, and the politics and economics of capitalism is Dale, R., *The State and Education Policy*, Milton Keynes, Open University Press, 1989.

19. Althusser, L., "Ideology and ideological state apparatuses", in *Lenin, Philosophy and Other Essays*, London, New Left Books, 1971.

20. Goodson, I. F., *The Making of Curriculum*, New York and Philadelphia, Falmer Press, 1988; Hamilton, D., *Towards a Theory of Schooling*, New York and Philadelphia, Falmer Press, 1989.

21. Powell, A., Farrar, E. and Cohen, D., *The Shopping Mall High School: Winners and Losers in the Educational Marketplace*, Boston, Houghton Mifflin, 1985; Hargreaves, D., *The Challenge for the Comprehensive School*, London, Routledge & Kegan Paul, 1982.

22. These educational needs in restructured schools have been listed in the form repeated here by Lieberman, A., Darling-Hammond, L. and Zuckerman, D., *Early Lessons in Restructuring Schools*, New York, National Center for Restructuring Education, Schools, and Teaching (NCREST), 1991.

23. Leinberger, P. and Tucker, B., *The New Individualists: The Generation after the Organization Man*, New York, HarperCollins, 1991.

24. Leinberger and Tucker, *op. cit.*, note 23, p. 142.

25 Whyte, W. H., Jr., *The Organization Man*, New York, Simon & Schuster, 1956, p. 161.

26. Whyte, *op. cit.*, note 25, p. 167.

27. This was most striking in Goffman, E., *The Presentation of Self in Everyday Life*, Harmondsworth, Penguin, 1959.

28. Berne, E., *Games People Play*, Harmondsworth, Penguin, 1967.

29. Mead, G. H., *Mind, Self and Society*, Chicago, University of Chicago Press, 1934.

30. Laing, R. D., *Self and Others*, Harmondsworth, Penguin, 1969.

31. Nias, J., *Primary Teachers Talking*, London, Routledge, 1989. Nias's original arguments can be found in two earlier papers, "Teaching and the Self", *Cambridge Journal of Education*, 17, 1987 and "The definition and maintenance of self in primary teaching", *British Journal of Sociology of Education*, 5, 1984. See also Woods, P., *Sociology and the School*, London, Routledge, 1983.

32. Westbury, I., "Conventional classrooms, 'open' classrooms and the technology of teaching", *Journal of Curriculum Studies*, 5(2), 1973; Woods, P., "Teaching for survival", in Woods, P. and Hammersley, M., *School Experience*, London, Croom Helm, 1977, pp. 271–93. My own work on coping strategies is developed in three interconnected papers. They are: Hargreaves, A., "The significance of classroom coping strategies", in Barton, L. and Meighan, R., *Sociological Interpretations of Schooling and Classrooms: A Reappraisal*, Driffield, Nafferton Books, 1978; Hargreaves, A., "Strategies, decisions and control", in Eggleston, J., *Teacher Decision-Making in the Classroom*, London, Routledge & Kegan Paul, 1979; and Hargreaves, A., "Progressivism and pupil autonomy", *Sociological Review*, 25(3), 1977.

33. One of the clearest accounts of this struggle between the situation and the self in teaching is Woods, P., "Strategies, commitment and identity: Making and breaking the teacher role", in Barton, L. and Walker, S., *Schools, Teachers and Teaching*, Lewes, Falmer Press, 1981.

34. Examples are identified and explained in Nias, J., *Primary Teachers Talking, op. cit.*, note 31.

35. The classic description of the adaptations which inner-city teachers can come to make here is to be found in Becker, H., "The career of the Chicago public school-teacher", *American Journal of Sociology*, 57, March 1952.

36. One of the most graphic portrayals of this phenomenon is to be found in Riseborough, G., "Teacher careers and comprehensive schooling: An empirical study", *Sociology*, 15(3), 1980. More general patterns are described in Huberman, M., *The Lives of Teachers*, New York, Teachers College Press and London, Cassell, 1993.

37. See Harvey, D., *The Condition of Postmodernity, op. cit.*, note 9.

38. O'Connor, J., *The Fiscal Crisis of the State*, New York, St Martin's Press, 1973.

39. For an account expanding this line of explanation, see Dale, R., *The State and Education Policy, op. cit.*, note 18.

40 Habermas, J., *Legitimation Crisis*, London, Heinemann, 1976.

41. Taylor, C., *The Malaise of Modernity*, Concord, Ontario, House of Anasi Press, 1991. Also Habermas, J., *Towards a Rational Society*, London, Heinemann, 1972.

42. Shedd, J. B. and Bacharach, S. B., *Tangled Hierarchies: Teachers as Professionals and the Management of Schools*, San Francisco, Jossey-Bass, 1991, p. 6.

43. In their study of whole-school curriculum development in several English primary schools, for example, Nias and her colleagues confess that the sample which resulted from their request to study positive examples in this field contained the qualities of middle classness and ethnic homogeneity mentioned here. See Nias, J., Southworth, G. and Campbell, P., *Whole School Curriculum Development in the Primary School*, London and Washington, DC, Falmer Press, 1992.

44. Tendencies towards somewhat paternalistic (or maternalistic) styles of leadership even in highly collaborative primary schools are noted in an earlier study by Nias and her colleagues. See Nias, J., Southworth, G. and Yeomans, R., *Staff Relationships in the Primary School*, London, Cassell, 1989.

Chapter 3

Postmodernity or Postmodernism?
The Discourse of Change

INTRODUCTION

Teachers work within a changing world. To describe that world as a postmodern one is to make particular claims about it — about its social, political, cultural and economic characteristics. The next chapter analyzes some of the key characteristics of postmodernity and their implications for education and teaching. Here, I want to clear up some potential misunderstandings about the term *postmodernity* itself.

While writing about postmodern society has become very fashionable, it does not express any unanimity of opinion. Discussions of postmodernism and postmodernity have expressed different viewpoints, different cultural perspectives, different understandings of basic terms, even. There are different overlapping discourses of texts and terms through which postmodernity and postmodernism respectively are expressed and understood. I want to engage with these discourses and the assumptions they contain so as to clarify and delineate my own basic standpoints in relation to postmodernity. My purpose is to try to thread a clear conceptual path through what can otherwise seem a rather complex and confusing field. This, I hope, will establish a clearer basis in the next chapter for analyzing the concrete conditions of postmodernity with all their implications for teachers and their work.

POSTMODERNITY AND POSTMODERNISM

1. First, my prime concern in this book is with *postmodernity*, not postmodernism. *Postmodernism* is an aesthetic, cultural and intellectual phenomenon. It encompasses a particular set of styles, practices and cultural forms in art, literature, music, architecture, philosophy and broader intellectual discourse — pastiche, collage, deconstruction, absence of linearity, mixture of periods and styles and the like. *Postmodernity*, by contrast, is a social condition. It comprises particular patterns of social, economic, political and cultural relations. From this standpoint, postmodernism is part of the broader phenomenon of postmodernity. It is a component and a consequence of the postmodern social condition. In many ways, postmodernism is an *effect* of postmodernity.

Several writers appear to confuse or conflate the concepts of postmodernity and postmodernism. Maxcy, for instance, uses the terms interchangeably in his discussion of educational criticism.[1] Aronowitz and Giroux, meanwhile, select the single term "postmodernism" to describe "an intellectual position, a form of cultural criticism, as well as . . . an emerging set of social, cultural and economic conditions that have come to characterize the age of global capitalism and industrialism."[2] Using postmodernism in this way, to refer to *both* an intellectual position *and* a set of societal conditions, establishes a seemingly necessary or essential tie between the two. This is misleading. One does not, of course, have to accept or adopt a postmodern intellectual position in order to acknowledge or understand the nature of the postmodern social condition. In this respect, my purpose in this book is to *understand* the condition of postmodernity and its implications for teachers, and not to *advocate* postmodern programs, postmodern pedagogies or postmodern principalship, for instance. This leads to my second point.

2. In this book, postmodernity and postmodernism are topics to be analyzed and explained. They are not also exclusive intellectual resources for analyzing those topics. The distinction I am making here is similar to that drawn by theorists who differentiate between a *sociology of postmodernism* and a *postmodern sociology*.[3] A *sociology of postmodernism* seeks to locate postmodern culture in a particular social, economic and political context and makes clear claims about the social reality of that context.[4] A *postmodern sociology* by contrast might, in Turner's words, "seek to deconstruct such foundational assumptions and . . . would regard the social as problematic."[5]

Adopting a postmodern theoretical position involves denying the existence of foundational knowledge on the grounds that no knowable social reality exists beyond the signs of language, image and discourse. There can, therefore, be no agreed way in which we can understand things we call social systems, or even other human selves, for they too have no inner essence beyond language, image and discourse. Truth, reality and reason itself are therefore unavailable to human knowledge and understanding. All that is available, analytically, to the postmodern theorist is the practice of deconstructing existing versions of social reality, and of giving voice to other versions which are normally neglected or suppressed. In some kinds of postmodern theory known as critical pragmatism, those versions of reality to which voice is given are selected not according to any search for truth or more complete knowledge (since truth and certain knowledge cannot be determined) but on the pragmatic grounds of what social and political interests will best be served by articulating those voices.[6] Thus, the critical pragmatic perspective and the interpretations it generates are guided not by intellectual principles entailing a search for truth or understanding, but by political and ethical principles entailing the realization of such things as justice, fairness and equity.

This theoretical position strikes me as being deeply problematic. There are, of course, methodological advantages in adopting aspects of a postmodern stance *for a while* during one's research, as an intellectual strategy. Looking at things another way, turning them on their heads, considering perspectives that have not yet been voiced can help us take a more critical, open and comprehensive stance towards what we are studying and how we are studying it.[7] But to deny the possibility of any foundational knowledge of social reality is not only practically unhelpful; it is also philosophically inconsistent. For as critics like Habermas and Turner note, in order to overthrow the existence of reason, one has to use the tools of reason.[8] Equally, in order to deny the existence of foundational knowledge, one needs foundational knowledge about its lack of existence. And, in order to assert the end of theoretical or scientific certainties, one needs some certainty about the presence of this ending.

To claim to be without foundation (in terms of one's claims to knowledge) is therefore intellectually somewhat disingenuous. To assert, as critical pragmatists do, an alternative basis for understanding and interpretation founded on the pragmatic fulfillment of particular political and ethical interests is to court ideological dogmatism. By rejecting all claims to truth and establishing the goal of realizing particular political interests in their place, critical pragmatists erect ideologically arbitrary and intellectually privileged interpretations of social reality while also protecting them from criticism, counter-evidence and disconfirmation, on the grounds that verifiable evidence and knowable truth do not exist. In this way, their own theoretical claims are rendered ideologically unassailable — but only insofar as their criticisms of foundationalism continue to hold. As we have seen, however, they do not, for anti-foundationalism is itself without foundation!

My intellectual stance is not, therefore, a postmodern one. While I am interested in such things as the collapse of scientific certainty as a social phenomenon and its implications for education, I do not myself embrace that absence of certainty in the way I analyze it! This book is not a postmodernist book. It is a book *about* the social condition of postmodernity and its implications for the changing world of teachers' work.

3. My account of postmodernity is therefore a rather modernistic one. It seeks to offer a coherent and integrated explanation of what postmodernity *is*, of what its constituent themes and elements are, and of how they connect together. To critics and especially to those who regard themselves as postmodernists, this might seem a perverse and paradoxical position to take. Jameson summarizes the postmodernist critical response in this way:

> If what is historically unique about the postmodern is thus
> acknowledged as sheer heteronomy and the emergence of random
> and unrelated subsystems of all kinds, then, or so the argument
> runs, there has to be something perverse about the effort to
> group it as a unified system in the first place. The effort at
> conceptual unification is, to say the least, strikingly inconsistent
> with the spirit of postmodernism itself.[9]

However, Jameson continues, "a system that constitutively produces differences remains a system".[10] It is not necessary, one might add, to explain madness insanely, chaos chaotically or individualism idiosyncratically. Similarly, in the case of postmodernity, it is quite possible to explain difference and differentiation in an integrated and coherent way.[11] Indeed, not only is it possible to explain difference systematically; it may be extremely desirable to do so. For as Jameson points out, it is often through their very creation of difference, fragmentation, plurality and constant change in the workplace, the mass media and elsewhere that powerful social groups are able to mask their own existence and agency.[12] Differentiation and fragmentation can be very effective in muddying the waters of social perception. The principle of divide and rule can be achieved conceptually as well as politically. As Harvey puts it, "The rhetoric of postmodernism ... avoids confronting the realities of political economy and the circumstances of global power."[13] We will see some evidence of this in the next section.

If my own approach to explaining postmodernity is unapologetically modernistic, I do not also view it as being Olympian and incontestable. As with most attempts at social science generalization, my analysis is a provisional "best shot" at understanding the condition of postmodernity – open to modification or even refutation as other evidence and argument comes along, or even as the subject of analysis (what currently counts as postmodernity) itself undergoes change over time. My explanation of the postmodern condition is therefore offered with some confidence but also with due caution; a combination I consider to be proper in all social analysis. Here, my sentiments are very much with Max Weber in his celebrated essay on Science as a Vocation.

> In science, each of us knows that what he has accomplished will
> be antiquated in ten, twenty, fifty years. That is the fate to
> which science is subjected; it is the very *meaning* of scientific
> work. . . . Every scientific "fulfillment" raises new "questions"; it
> *asks* to be "surpassed" and outdated. Whoever wishes to serve
> science has to resign himself to this fact . . . for it is our common
> fate and, more, our common goal. We cannot work without
> hoping that others will advance further than we have.[14]

4. The nature of the postmodern condition is not given; nor is it fixed. The development of postmodernity is not steered by evolutionary necessity. Its historical fate is not predetermined. Postmodernity is constituted through a set of social, economic, political and cultural tendencies which can vary over historical time and across geographical space. These tendencies are powerful and influential but they are not ineluctable or irresistible. There are two reasons for this.

For one thing, postmodernity, like all social systems, does not exist independently of the actions of people who comprise and construct it, just as these people's actions do not exist independently of the context or systems in which they are embedded. The postmodern social condition, that is, is subject to the general principle of what Giddens calls *the duality of structure*; a principle which acknowledges that social structures are at once the medium *and* the outcome of human interaction.[15] Postmodernity, therefore, frames the possibilities for and probabilities of human interaction, but at the same time continues to exist only through the fulfillment of these interactions. This generic principle of the duality of structure alerts us to how social structures are always both potent (as frameworks for action) and precarious (being vulnerable to change through such action). This simultaneous potency and precariousness applies to postmodernity just as much as it does to any other social condition.

The nature and meaning of postmodernity is also precarious for a second, more specific reason. As a relatively recent phenomenon, postmodernity is still in formation, still unfolding. The tendencies and effects of postmodernity are in certain times and places actively resisted by those who want to retain modern structures, modern paradigms, modern forms of control, and who have much to gain from them. Decentralizers are opposed by centralizers. Advocates of process-based learning which acknowledges the uncertainty of knowledge are overruled by imposers of facts-based mandated curricula. Locally based or school-based teacher development is superseded by system-wide training. Postmodern structures and processes do not therefore occur "naturally". They often have to be asserted in the face of considerable opposition.

Beyond this struggle between the forces of modernity and postmodernity are continuing struggles over the meaning and consequences of postmodernity itself. To take just one issue: what will be the consequences of growing decentralization within systems, coupled with increasing emphasis on self-definition and self-actualization as an active social project among individuals? In theory and in practice, many outcomes are possible. These twin tendencies can create forces in professional development that are empowering and emancipating for teachers — and they are often presented in just those terms. But they can just as easily lead to forms of professional development that are narcissistic and self-indulgent (by placing exclusive and excessive emphasis on the personal aspects of teachers' knowledge and development); to ones which are dissipated and disconnected (devoid of any sense of community, consensus or common purpose among the teaching group); or to ones which are conservative and controlling (because they focus predominantly on the local and the personal, and insulate teachers from access to knowledge of and control over the system conditions which shape and frame their workplaces and what they can achieve there). Empowerment, narcissism, chaos or control are equally likely consequences of the postmodern social condition; and we shall see shortly how these consequences can play themselves out. For now, it is important simply to recognize that the meaning of postmodernity is not something to be conceded. It is something to be constructed and contested.

5. Because postmodernity and postmodernism have many different meanings, they can also be evaluated in very different ways. Postmodernism in

particular has been the subject of extensive and somewhat anarchic celebration.[16] Postmodern lifestyles and their emergent patterns of organization have also been portrayed heroically in some of the corporate and popular futurist literature as heralding the emergence of more dynamic forms of work and production, greater representation of women in leadership, and an overall "triumph of the individual".[17] Those who cast doubt on these demonstrable positive benefits of the new age are swiftly dismissed as mere "doomsayers"![18] At the same time, postmodernism has been viewed as a form of resistance, through its critique of tradition, its deconstruction of dominant ideologies and "master narratives" as Lyotard calls them, and through the way it gives vent to dissident voices of women, minorities and other socially oppressed and marginalized groups.[19] Alternatively, it has been criticized for contributing to a loss of cultural and moral high ground, and encouraging the demise of the working class work ethic, the end of bourgeois values and the general spread of decadence.[20] And neo-Marxists have denounced or dismissed it for restructuring and reproducing the dominant interests of capital, by disguising and dissipating their influences and effects.[21]

For me, the point is not to embrace the postmodern condition uncritically — to promote a postmodern curriculum, or advocate the creation of postmodern school organizations as learning organizations, for example. Nor is it to shrug off postmodernity as a capitalist charade which merely reinscribes traditional patterns of dominance and control within more elaborate and elusive structures. Postmodernity has no single inherent meaning or value. Rather, it offers a new social arena in which moral and political values and commitments in education can be played out. Postmodernity offers new opportunities for these commitments to be realized and also presents new constraints. This book's purpose is to understand and evaluate these in all their complexity.

6. Postmodernity and postmodernism, we have seen, can be viewed as panaceas or pariahs; carnivals or clichés.[22] Beyond these criticisms is a further charge that the very terms "postmodernity" and "postmodernism" are nothing more than rhetorical fads, just another set of *isms*, which do not describe a distinctive set of social conditions at all.[23] They are just trendy new labels for old, familiar bottles. These criticisms can constitute easy sneers for those who know little or have read little about postmodernity and postmodernism and dismissively want to legitimate their own continuing ignorance by imputing irrelevance and irrationality to the field. There are, however, much more studied and well grounded critiques of the concepts of postmodernism and postmodernity than this and these merit more serious attention.

Giddens, for instance, prefers the term *high modernity* to postmodernity, arguing that we are now in a more radical phase of modernity, not something different altogether:

> The disorientation which expresses itself in the feeling that
> systematic knowledge about social organization cannot be

> obtained . . . results primarily from the sense many of us have of being caught up in a universe of events we do not fully understand, and which seems in large part outside of our control. To analyze how this has come to be the case, it is not sufficient merely to invent new terms, like post-modernity and the rest. Instead, we have to look again at the nature of modernity itself. . . . Rather than entering a period of post-modernity, we are moving into one in which the consequences of modernity are becoming more radicalized and universalized than before.[24]

Now, of course, it is possible to exaggerate the differences between modernity and postmodernity. The break is not absolute, clear cut or universal. The struggles and transitions between modernity and postmodernity, I have argued, are active and continuing. And indeed, just as Giddens suggests, some of the components of postmodernity are radicalized or universalized forms of the very things that make up the modern condition. Modernity compresses and collapses time and space; postmodernity does this even more so. Modernity sees the development of monopoly capitalism; postmodernity witnesses its expansion and proliferation across the world. In these respects, what we call postmodernity may very well be an extension and intensification of conditions which preceded it, and not something profoundly new.

However, as the following chapter will show, what many people understand as postmodernity also contains some significant and characteristic differences from its antecedents. Information, for instance, is organized differently, processed more quickly and both accessed and disseminated more pervasively, with immense implications for patterns of communication and control in economic and organizational life. Similarly, the dominance of the image in postmodern society leads to qualitative shifts from phases which preceded it. An instantaneous visual culture with its spectacle and superficiality begins to supersede the moral discourse, studied reflection and rigorous public debate which characterized more oral ones. Such things as these, I will argue, mark profound shifts in the organization and experience of economic, political, organizational and personal life that are more than mere continuations or exaggerations of what went before. What labels we give to these shifts may be as much a matter of semantics or of personal allegiances to particular concepts and traditions as much as anything else. But the shifts that have led to what many call the postmodern condition are substantial and the label "postmodernity" may be as good as any for describing it.

It is time now to look more closely at this postmodern social condition, at the paradoxes and possibilities contained within it, and at the implications for teachers and their work.

NOTES

1. Maxcy, S. J., *Educational Leadership: A Critical Pragmatic Perspective*, Toronto, OISE Press, 1991, pp. 132–5.

2. Aronowitz, S. and Giroux, H. A., *Postmodern Education*, Minneapolis, University of Minnesota Press, 1991, p. 62.

3. See Featherstone, M., "In pursuit of the postmodern: An introduction", *Theory, Culture and Society*, 5(2/3), 1988. Also Smart, B., "Modernity, postmodernity and the present", in Turner, B. S., *Theories of Modernity and Postmodernity*, London, Sage, 1991.

4. Smart, *op. cit.*, note 3, p. 25.

5. Turner, B. S., "Periodization and politics in the postmodern" in Turner, B. S., *Theories of Modernity and Postmodernity*, London, Sage 1991, p. 6.

6. For examples, see Maxcy, *op. cit.*, note 1; Cherryholmes, C., *Power and Criticism*, New York, Teachers College Press, 1988; Rorty, R., *Consequences of Pragmatism*, Minneapolis, University of Minnesota Press, 1982; Bernstein, R. J., *Beyond Objectivism and Relativism*, Philadelphia, University of Pennsylvania Press, 1983.

7. This use of postmodernism as critical method is advocated by Gaskell, J., *Gender Matters from School to Work*, Milton Keynes, Open University Press and Toronto, OISE Press, 1991.

8. Turner, *op. cit.*, note 5; Habermas, J., *The Philosophical Discourse of Modernity*, Cambridge. Polity Press, 1987.

9. Jameson, F., *Postmodernism: Or the Cultural Logic of Late Capitalism*, London and New York, Verso, 1991, p. 342. Aronowitz and Giroux express a similar view when they say:

   > we need to preserve a notion of totality that privileges forms of analysis in which it is possible to make visible those mediations, interrelations and interdependencies that give shape and power to larger political and social systems. We need theories that express and articulate difference, but we also need to understand how the relations in which differences are constituted operate as part of a wider set of social, political and cultural practices.

   See Aronowitz and Giroux, *op. cit.*, note 2, p. 70.

10. Jameson, *op. cit.*, note 9, p. 343.

11. Ibid.

12. Ibid.

13. Harvey, D., *The Condition of Postmodernity*, Cambridge, Polity Press, 1989, p. 117.

14. Weber, M., "Science as a vocation", in Gerth, H. and Mills, C. W. (eds), *From Max Weber*, New York, Free Press, 1946, p. 138.

15. The principle of "duality of structure" is described in many of Anthony Giddens's writings. A particularly succinct account is in Giddens, A., *The Constitution of Society*, Cambridge, Polity Press, 1984.

16. Two by no means identical examples of this position are Lyotard, J., *The Postmodern Condition*, Minneapolis, University of Minnesota Press, 1984 and Baudrillard, J., *Selected Writings*, ed. Porter, M., Stanford, Stanford University Press, 1988.

17. The best-known source here is the best-selling book by Naisbitt, J. and Aberdene, P., *Megatrends 2000: Ten New Directions for the 1990s*, New York, Avon Books, 1990.

18. Naisbitt and Aberdene, *op. cit.*, note 17, pp. 2–3.

19. The reference by Lyotard is to his book, *The Postmodern Condition, op. cit.*, note 16. Aronowitz and Giroux, *op. cit.*, note 2, try to extract such a "progressive" position from postmodernism. A "postmodernism of resistance" is also advocated by Foster, H. (ed.), *The Anti-Aesthetic: Essays on Postmodern Culture*, Port Townsend, WA, Bay Press, 1990.

20. This kind of critique can be seen in embryonic form in Bell, D., *The Cultural Contradictions of Capitalism*, New York, Basic Books, 1976. For a more recent and strident critique, see Bloom, A., *The Closing of The American Mind.*, New York, Simon & Schuster, 1987. One of the most intellectually sophisticated and complex populist critiques of the cultural developments represented by and in postmodernism is Lasch, C., *The True and Only Heaven: Progress and Its Critics*, New York, W. W. Norton, 1991.

21. This is the position of Jameson, *op. cit.*, note 9, p. 62.

22. These possible portrayals of postmodernism are expressed by Lash, S., *Sociology of Postmodernism*, London and New York, Routledge, 1990, p. 2.

23. These charges are more usually to be found in the back rooms of conferences, and in the corners of college common rooms, than in the public forum of print, but they are no less pervasive or pernicious for that. However, the complex mixtures of envy and anxiety that typically accompany the rise of new intellectual discourses can sometimes give rise to less dour and more humorous moments. One such time was at a conference of the International Sociological Association I attended where many of the major speeches had either discussed postmodernism, positioned themselves in relation to postmodernism, or adopted the basic terms of postmodernism as the intellectual currency of debate. Sitting by my hotel swimming pool, I overheard two middle-aged male sociologists complain to one another; "No one seems to be interested in alienation theory any more!" "No, we need some new language, some fashionable new concepts like this postmodernist stuff, to present our field in."

24. Giddens, A., *The Consequences of Modernity*, Cambridge, Polity Press, 1990, pp. 2–3.

Chapter 4

Postmodern Paradoxes
The Context of Change

INTRODUCTION

In *The Coming of Postindustrial Society* Daniel Bell notes that the "sense of . . . living in an interregnum, is nowhere symbolized so sharply as in the widespread use of the word *post*".[1] Whether the transitions we are experiencing are described in terms of postliberalism, postindustrialism or postmodernity, most writers agree that at the heart of the transition is the globalization of economic activity, political relations, information, communications and technology. This does not mean that these trends are entirely clear or consistent. Indeed, their components and consequences are often ironic, paradoxical, perverse. Globalization can lead to ethnocentricism, decentralization to more centralization, flatter organizational structures to concealed hierarchical control. It is these paradoxes and perversities that make postmodernity not only such a fascinating phenomenon, but also one that can be immensely difficult to understand. This chapter examines seven key dimensions of postmodernity where these ironies and paradoxes can be seen. I do not want to claim that these aspects of postmodernity are the only ones and that their discussion exhausts all there is to know on the subject. But they do encompass important elements of the postmodern social condition and are among the ones that are most influential for education and teaching. The seven dimensions are:

- Flexible Economies
- The Paradox of Globalization
- Dead Certainties
- The Moving Mosaic
- The Boundless Self
- Safe Simulation
- Compression of Time and Space

1. FLEXIBLE ECONOMIES

One of the most central defining and determining characteristics of the post-modern, postindustrial order is a new and distinctive pattern of production, consumption and economic life. Various terms have been used to describe this emerging order, such as *flexible accumulation*, *flexible specialization* and the *flexible firm*.[2] While these terms place differential importance on labor markets, patterns of production or the organization of enterprises respectively, the notion of flexibility is central to all of them.

David Harvey picks out *flexible accumulation* as the central, articulating principle of the postmodern economy. For Harvey,

> Flexible accumulation . . . rests on flexibility with respect to
> labor processes, labor markets, products and patterns of
> consumption. It is characterized by the emergence of entirely
> new sectors of production, new ways of providing financial
> services, new markets, and above all, greatly intensified rates of
> commercial, technological, and organizational innovation.[3]

In response to the economic crisis of modernity, with its exhaustion of international markets and long-term debt, flexible accumulation improves profitability by reducing labor costs and increasing *turnover time* in production and consumption. This is achieved in three broad ways: through new work technologies and labor processes, through new relationships between production and consumption, and through new uses of geographical space. Two of them will be discussed here. The third will follow in the next section.

First, postmodern economies are characterized by a whole array of more flexible work technologies and labor processes. Where standardization, job demarcation and mass production characterized modern economies, flexible, postmodern work technologies break down traditional job demarcations and introduce overlaps and rotations in task assignments and job descriptions. They also facilitate rapid and easy adjustments in the size of the workforce through part-time and temporary work, contracting out, and the like. Wage arrangements too are more flexible through the use of devices such as pay-for-performance, discretionary bonuses and merit pay.[4]

A second way in which flexible accumulation is achieved is by articulating and accelerating the interactions between producers and consumers. Unlike old industrial systems of mass production and consumption where standardized technologies fed standardized lifestyles, the new postindustrial economies are characterized by very different connections between production and consumption. For instance, by combining laser technology with instant computation and communication, more and more supermarkets are able to read and relay changing patterns of customer preference and volumes of demand instantaneously to in-store supervisors and external suppliers. As vendors and suppliers are connected more quickly and more closely, the need for stock, inventory and the labor to manage them is drastically reduced.[5] Without the fear of unwanted and unsold goods languishing on supermarket shelves, in warehouse store-rooms or on fashion stores' hangers, consumer fashions and preferences can be differentiated and turned over more quickly. As a result, flexible accumulation is characterized by niche marketing targeted to specialized groups, customized production technologically tailored to individual preferences, and small-batch production that allows rapid responsiveness to shifts in consumer demand. Through marketing and advertising, these patterns are accompanied by strategies to increase and diversify consumer desire and to accelerate the turnover of tastes and fashions.[6]

Flexible accumulation is not solely concerned with producing and consuming goods, however. If anything, knowledge and information are its prime products. With the aid of advances in technology, things like advice, consultancy, tourism, speeches, spectacles and cultural events can be produced and consumed much more quickly than manufactured goods, as can the economic benefits that accrue from them.[7]

The emergence of this knowledge-based economy has brought with it striking changes in the occupational and social structure. Sociologists pointed to the decline of traditional laboring classes and the growth of white collar work in the expanding service sector as long ago as the early 1970s.[8] And the trends have continued. In Canada, for example, while fewer than half of employed people were in the service sector in the 1950s, this had increased to 65 percent by 1979 and 70 percent by 1989.[9]

These new flexible economies with their new definitions and distributions of jobs, call for new qualities and skills from the future workforce and those who educate them. Reich summarizes these needs thus:

> First are the modern problem-solving skills required to put
> things together in unique ways (be they alloys, molecules,
> semi-conductor chips, software codes, movie scripts, pension
> portfolios, or information) . . .
> Next are the skills required to help customers understand
> their needs and how those needs can best be met by customized
> products . . . selling and marketing customized products requires
> having intimate knowledge of a customer's business, where
> competitive advantage may lie, and how it can be achieved. The
> key is to identify new problems and possibilities to which the
> customized product might be applicable. The art of persuasion is
> replaced by the identification of opportunity. Third are the skills
> needed to link problem-solvers and problem-identifiers. People in
> such roles must understand enough about specific technologies
> and markets to see the potential for new products, raise
> whatever money is necessary to launch the project, and assemble
> the right problem-solvers and identifiers to carry it out.[10]

49

Taking up the educational implications of this widely advocated position, Schlechty argues that schools should be in the business of knowledge-work, and their students construed as knowledge workers:

> It is reasonable to expect that, as the American economy
> becomes more information based, and as the mode of labor shifts
> from manual work to knowledge work, concern with the
> continuous growth and learning of citizens and employees will
> increase. Moreover, the conditions of work will require one to
> learn to function well in groups, exercise considerable
> self-discipline, exhibit loyalty while maintaining critical faculties,
> respect the rights of others and in turn expect to be
> respected. . . . This list of characteristics could as well be a list of
> the virtues of a citizen in a democracy.[11]

Schlechty sees a need for new skills and qualities in post-industrial society and for new school structures to generate them. Clearly, educating young people in skills and qualities like adaptability, responsibility, flexibility and capacity to work with others is an important goal for teachers and schools in a postindustrial society. So too is familiarization with the new technologies that will increasingly characterize many work environments. This strongly suggests the need for school environments which can generate the autonomous, individualized and meaningfully collaborative learning essential for the postindustrial workplace. As Schlechty argues, most existing school structures, especially at the secondary level, with their single-lesson, single-classroom, single-teacher formats, are ill suited to these needs.

Flexibility is often portrayed positively as a way of creating work that is more meaningful and holistic for individuals.[12] Because of its economic, organizational and individual benefits, flexibility is frequently presented as a key goal for education and its restructuring. But this is really only one face of flexibility, albeit the most fashionable one. It is the face of the editor, consultant or designer, connected to the world by computer from a cottage in the high peaks of Colorado or on the hillsides of Provence (who also displaces the traditional residents, who can no longer afford to live there!). Or it is the face of the leading edge, high-risk partner or collaborator in a small software company, creating images and information for the future in the heart of Silicon Valley.[13] A rather different face of flexibility, however, is that of the Portuguese maid who cleaned my Vancouver hotel room, protesting "I hate the computer! I hate the computer!" because it allocated and checked all her room assignments after every task, instead of allowing her to exercise her own discretion and control over how and in what order she cleaned her own rooms. Still other faces of "flexibility" are those of the part-time taxi-driver, gas pump attendant or hamburger seller who move in and out of part-time, low-grade, temporary work and perhaps even juggle two or three jobs at once to make ends meet.[14]

"Flexibility" in this sense can create work environments and social structures that are elitist and divisive with autonomy, discretion and more meaningful work being reserved for small technical elites while the remaining workforce is relegated to work that is low-grade, part-time, temporary, unpensioned and assigned in erratic ways.[15] Menzies goes further and cites instances where work which management perceives as "flexible" and enriched is construed very differently by workers. Compared to management, she says:

> The workers are less sanguine, some because they have worked there awhile and can remember when the job was a craft. "Do you think I'd rather be putting in eighty parts and building a board, or putting in six transistors eight hours a day? It's degrading!" Others don't equate job enlargement with job enrichment: "So we can rotate on the slide line. Instead of putting six capacitors in, we can now put six resistors in. Big deal!"[16]

Flexibility and initiative in the most dynamic and creative senses may indeed be needed for future technical and professional elites who will work at the high and medium levels of the new postindustrial economy. But with much traditional manufacturing displaced to regions of cheaper labor outside the West, education for leisure and constructive recreation will also be important, particularly for those part-time, intermittent, low-grade workers who will have less access to opportunities for meaningful work. Equally necessary will be education for citizenship, political participation and social responsibility so that future generations will be ready and willing to engage in discussions and deliberations about constructive and socially valuable uses of technology, along with associated patterns of employment, in the postindustrial world.

Once this broader context of the postindustrial workplace is appreciated, the supposedly generic skills inventories of communication, cooperation, flexibility, initiative and the like, which are produced by writers and policymakers in tune with corporate agendas, begin to seem selective and seductive. Schlechty, for instance, in his vision of *Schools for the Twenty-First Century*, talks of respect, but not of care — either for other persons, or for the environment.[17] Justice and equity are also absent. Productivity is paramount. This doesn't distort, but it does restrict what is seen as appropriate for schools and teachers to do. By contrast, desirable skills and qualities arising from a very different cultural base — that of the Native Indian "Medicine Way" which is used to organize teaching and curriculum in *Children of the Earth* school, an Aboriginal-run school in Manitoba, Canada — include items like truthfulness, guilelessness, courage, compassion, humility and anger at injustice, as important goals for teachers and schools to address.[18]

Flexible economies create important challenges for teaching the knowledge and skills that need to be learned by future generations and for creating more flexible structures and patterns of work organization for teachers through which these things can be achieved. Equally, though, flexible economies pose risks that the purposes of schooling and what its teachers should teach may be narrowed prematurely and perhaps even perniciously to quasi-corporate agendas of a particular kind.

Although flexibility has become an economic and educational buzzword, in practice it can lead equally to enrichment or exploitation, to diversity or divisiveness. It is misleading to celebrate or heroize some of these images of flexibility without also recognizing and responding to the presence of the rest. Educationally, to ignore the needs and demands of flexibility in the postindustrial economy by clinging to ancient subject identities and ossified departmental structures suited to other needs in another time is folly. But to pursue the goal of flexibility with no sense of its various meanings for different sexes, classes and races in the workforce, and with no thought for its consequences for the unemployment, underemployment or undemanding employment to which many workers will be consigned, is to do so selectively and uncritically in ways that benefit some social groups and their interests more than others. In this sense, it is important for teachers and those who work with them to view "flexibility" as an open democratic opportunity requiring commitment and critical engagement, not as a closed corporate obligation demanding unquestioning compliance.

2. THE PARADOX OF GLOBALIZATION

In *The Work of Nations*, Robert Reich observes that:

> We are living through a transformation that will rearrange the politics and economics of the coming century. There will be no *national* products or technologies, no *national* corporations, no *national* industries. There will no longer be national economies, at least as we have come to understand that concept. All that will remain rooted within national borders are the people who comprise a nation. Each nation's primary assets will be its citizens' skills and insights. Each nation's primary political task will be to cope with the centrifugal forces of the global economy which tear at the ties binding citizens together — bestowing ever greater wealth on the most skilled and insightful, while consigning the less skilled to a declining standard of living. As borders become ever more meaningless in economic terms, those citizens best positioned to thrive in the world market are tempted to slip the bonds of national allegiance, and by so doing disengage themselves from their less favored fellows.[19]

In addition to redesigning work technologies and labor processes, and restructuring interactions between producers and consumers, a third way of securing more flexible economies is through new patterns of regulation and control which compress and conquer the boundaries of geographical space. These uses of space in the postindustrial economy are helping to create a second distinctive aspect of postmodern society which I call the *paradox of globalization*.

Postindustrial economies are characterized not by economies of *scale*, but economies of *scope*.[20] The fiscal crisis of the modern state and accompanying doubts about the legitimacy of state intervention have led to its diminished presence in economic affairs as economies have been opened up more to the play of free market forces. These processes of deregulation have been accompanied by new patterns of coordination and control within and between enterprises themselves. With the aid of instantaneous communication and computing, decision-making increasingly cuts across many locations, breaking down the barriers of time and space. Operations and personnel do not now need to be concentrated for efficiency's sake in one place. Units of enterprise are becoming smaller and more maneuverable within the overall corporate structure. Plant location is no longer fixed by tradition and the need for large, loyal labor forces. Company towns are a thing of the past. Geographical *space* is economically flexible. Commitments to the particularities of *place*, meanwhile, persist only as long as is warranted by local markets, favorable land values, and flexible, inexpensive workforces.

These changing patterns of geography and control in postindustrial economies are having immense implications for the preservation and protection of increasingly fragile national and cultural identities. Corporations have begun to spread their interests and expertise across national boundaries, utilizing local markets, labor resources and land opportunities, and maintaining instantaneous connection and coordination across the whole network of operations through modern communications technology. At the same time, computerization along with satellite communication and fiber optic telecommunications have made international trading in information and currency markets ceaseless. With the removal of trade and tariff barriers in the European Community and through the North American Free Trade Agreement, patterns of production and consumption are becoming thoroughly internationalized. National boundaries and local traditions have less and less significance for economic activity and even for the currencies through which it will be transacted. The opening of the Channel Tunnel will merely complete a physical and technological union that is already being achieved economically. On both sides of the Atlantic, economic flexibility has been elevated above national identity.

This globalization of economic life also carries with it environmental consequences of immense scope and risk. Acid rain from the USA kills the lakes and trees of Canada. Logging in the tropical rain forests contributes to the melting of the polar icecaps. And it was the clouds of Chernobyl as much as any qualities of political leadership that first challenged Soviet secrecy and created the silver lining that was glasnost. In the ecology of postmodernity, local catastrophes can have global implications. Air and water show no respect for national borders.[21]

A major paradox of postmodernity is that the anonymity, complexity and uncertainty wrought by globalization herald in an ironic search for meaning and certainty in more locally defined identities. As globalization intensifies, as McDonald's opens in Moscow, sushi bars prosper in New York, and international urban landscapes become ever more alike in the global commodification of community living, we are witnessing the resurgence of ethnic, religious and linguistic identities of a more localized nature. National identities imperilled by economic globalization are frantically being reconstructed. Swedes worry that membership of the European Community will lead to an influx of Mediterranean migrants whose traditional family values will undermine Swedish commitments to gender equality. The British, anxious for closer economic and physical union with mainland Europe, are simultaneously fearful of the loss of their currency, their independent military, their very cultural identity. Latvians, Lithuanians and Estonians secure secession from the former Soviet Union. Yugoslavia falls into disarray. Canada quivers over the future of Quebec. And throughout the Western media, there are xenophobic resurrections and persecutions of inglorious (and by implication, barely dormant) Japanese military pasts. In these respects, the contemporary re-balkanization of Eastern Europe is just a particularly vivid and extreme example of how economic globalization and ideological uncertainty are creating worldwide patterns of retreat to and reconstruction of ethnic, religious and linguistic identities which are more localized, clearly bounded, and sometimes deeply competitive in nature. Nationally, no one seems to know who they are anymore!

The main educational response to this social crisis has been to resurrect old cultural certainties or impose new ones through centralized control of curriculum and assessment requirements. What is at stake here is the protection and reconstruction of national identities, not least through the development of national curricula as described by Goodson, in which elements of national culture and heritage figure strongly.[22]

In the reassertion of traditional academic subjects within the National Curriculum of England and Wales, Goodson sees an attempt to revive and reconstruct a floundering national identity:

> The globalization of economic life, and more particularly of communication, information and technology, all pose enormous challenges to the existing modes of control and operation of nation-states. In this sense, the pursuance of new centralized national curriculum might be seen as the response of the more economically endangered species among nations.[23]

Dealing with the specific case of history, he continues:

> [T]he balance of subjects in the national curriculum suggest [sic] that questions of national identity and control have been

pre-eminent, rather than industrial or commercial requirements. For example, information technology has been largely omitted, whilst history has been embraced as a "foundation subject", even though it is quite clearly a subject in decline within the schools.[24]

This is particularly so, he argues, given the strong emphasis accorded to British history within the history curriculum.

The supposed integrity of British history or Canadian content are the stuff of national cultural reconstruction, where the burden of reinvented traditions is placed, like most other social burdens, on the shoulders of education. Such siege mentalities are leading many educational systems to retreat behind parapets of parochialism in defence of their cultural identities. Many of these attempts to restore traditions and construct senses of heritage inadvertently perpetuate or even reinforce traditional school subjects and their academic content – with profound implications for the continuing balkanization of subject departments at the secondary school level.[25] They make our schools and teachers less flexible, not more so. They also add to teacher overload by creating and consolidating imposed bodies of content which teachers must master.

It is paradoxical that increasing globalization should lead educationally to so much defensive and inward-looking localization; that imposed curricula can be hitched so easily to the wagons of national reconstruction. Reconstructing and reflecting upon local cultures and senses of community, be these native cultures, other ethnic cultures or national cultures, is, of course, important. But teaching young people to be aware of and take some responsibility for the global dimensions of their world matters too. Global education is not just another subject but a perspective which challenges potential ethnocentricism in all subjects.[26] It is therefore difficult to accommodate within the existing subject-based curriculum and the departmental structures which have grown up around it. By contrast, ethnocentric and xenophobic retreats to traditional subject contents tend to consolidate conventional secondary school structures. Much of the future of teachers' work and the structures within which it will be contained, depends on how this paradox will be resolved.

3. DEAD CERTAINTIES

The national and cultural uncertainties created by globalization are not the only uncertainties that make up the postmodern condition. In *Dead Certainties*, a fictionalized history of two deaths almost a century apart, Simon Schama constructs and deconstructs two sets of parallel and interwoven historical narratives in such a way as to question the certainties of historical knowledge, and the linear and singular nature of narrative explanation itself.[27] In the first part of his book, Schama documents what he describes as the many deaths of General James Wolfe. Here he shows how General Wolfe's death at the battle of Quebec in 1759 was first portrayed as that of one common soldier among many on the battlefield. In successive historical accounts and artistic portrayals, Schama argues, Wolfe was drawn ever closer to the center of the battle; a veritable symbol of colonial and imperialist triumph and martyrdom.

In the second part of his book, Schama goes on to document and reconstruct the mysterious death in 1849 of George Parkman, uncle of the renowned historian Francis Parkman, the author of one of the histories of Wolfe's death. By analyzing original judicial records, Schama shows how the evidence which led to the guilty verdict for Parkman's alleged murderer, John Webster, is in retrospect much less convincing and watertight than it once appeared. In an afterword to his book, Schama comments on the significance of his text for historical understanding:

> Both the stories offered here play with the teasing gap
> separating a lived event and its subsequent narration. . . . Both
> dissolve the certainties of events into the multiple possibilities of
> alternative narrations. Thus, General Wolfe dies many deaths,
> and though a verdict is rendered and a confession delivered in
> the case of John Webster, the ultimate truth about how George
> Parkman met his end remains obscure.[28]

Schama's remarkable account deconstructs both the ideological certainty of the greatness and glory of imperial conquest, and the scientific certainties of historical fact and legal evidence. In one text, Schama creates a fascinating allegory of the postmodern intellectual and philosophical condition and the collapse within it of some of our most powerful and deeply cherished forms of knowledge and belief.

In postmodern society, the growth of economic diversity together with the revitalization of local and regional identities is having profound implications for knowledge and belief systems and the expertise that rests upon them. In society as a whole, we are experiencing a shift from a small number of stable singularities of knowledge and belief to a fluctuating, ever changing plurality of belief systems.

Confidence in universalizing, all-encompassing belief systems is in decline. Increasing awareness of the imminent possibilities of environmental catastrophe on a global scale has seriously undermined our faith in technology as a way of reliably predicting and controlling our world in the rational pursuit of progress.[29] Similarly, the globalization of economic life along with the spread of information through satellite television and other means has threatened beliefs in the scientifically predicted inevitability of socialist transformation; a change both symbolized and stimulated by the destruction of the Berlin Wall. Such meta-theories and meta-narratives of human understanding are in disrepute.[30] Even narrative-knowing itself, as something which seeks to understand and articulate the allegedly inherent "narrative unities" that make up people's lives, has been subjected to vigorous criticism on the grounds that people's lives and biographies are characterized as much by inconsistency, contradiction and fragmentation as they are by any purported unity.[31]

The knowledge explosion, meanwhile, has led to a proliferation of expertise; much of it contradictory and competitive, all of it changing. This has begun to reduce people's dependence on particular kinds of expert knowledge but also created a collapse of certainty in received wisdom and established beliefs. Sunshine is good for you, then it is not. Alcohol is assumed to be detrimental to one's health until it is announced that modest consumptions of red wine actually *reduce* cholesterol levels. The reported press release by the Colombian drug cartel that cocaine is high in fiber is a joke that points to the disconcerting pervasiveness and perversity of such scientific uncertainties. Science no longer seems able to show us how to live, at least with any certainty or stability. In postmodern societies, doubt is pervasive, tradition is in retreat, and moral and scientific certainty have lost their credibility.[32]

This shift from cultures of certainty to cultures of uncertainty occurs for a number of reasons.[33]

- Information and sources of understanding are spreading out on an increasingly global scale.

- Communication and technology are compressing space and time, leading to an increasing pace of change in the world we seek to know and in our ways of knowing it. This, in turn, threatens the stability and endurance of our knowledge bases, making them irretrievably fragile and provisional.

- More multicultural migration and international travel are bringing different belief systems into greater contact.

- Rapid communication and a strengthening orientation to knowledge and its continuing development and application are leading to an ever tightening and interactive relationship between social research and development, where the social world changes even as we study it, not least as a result of the very inquiries we make of it.

The collapse of singular political ideologies, the diminishing credibility of traditional knowledge bases, and the declining certainty attached to scientific expertise have far-reaching ramifications for the changing world of education and the place of teachers' work within it.

First, and most obviously, as scientific knowledge becomes more and more provisional, the validity of a curriculum based on given knowledge and incontrovertible fact becomes less and less credible. Processes of inquiry, analysis, information gathering and other aspects of learning-how-to-learn in an engaged and critical way become more important as goals and methods for teachers and schools in the postmodern world. Although these educational principles have deep philosophical roots, and have been the subject of repeated historical advocacy (and resistance), the endemic scientific uncertainties of the post-modern age put them at a particularly high premium.[34]

Second, the decline of the Judaeo-Christian tradition as the prime purpose underpinning schooling and teaching in a context of greater religious, cultural and ethnic diversity raises penetrating questions about the moral purposes of education. One of the greatest educational crises of the postmodern age is the collapse of the common school; a school tied to its community and having a clear sense of the social and moral values it should instill.[35]

Alongside this multicultural challenge to the Judaeo-Christian tradition, the expanding nature of secondary education has raised additional questions about the relevance of the traditional academic curriculum for all students. The cafeteria curriculum of widened course choices was an attempt to accommodate the more diverse needs of a broader secondary school population, but increased diversity brought with it only chronic incoherence in curricular experience and the decline of any sense of community or common purpose in the bureaucratic, fragmented world that secondary schools had become.[36]

For a while, this crisis of educational purpose was met with a characteristically modernistic response which placed scientific and educational faith in a technological apparatus of supposedly known and neutral measures of efficiency and effectiveness. Around the world, educational researchers and those who funded them invested heavily in the development of hard, quantitative research technologies to elicit the generalizable scientific certainties of *school effectiveness*. In many school systems, these attributes of effectiveness — such as high expectations for achievement, a strong focus on instruction, a safe, orderly and supportive school climate, and strong leadership by the principal or headteacher — were zealously applied to the practical world of education as policy goals, or as criteria for monitoring progress and performance.[37] This modernistic faith in the triumph of science and its capacity to determine what makes a school effective has started to dissolve, however. The limitations of effective schools research and practice are becoming increasingly transparent even to their most enthusiastic proponents. Most of these have been succinctly summarized by Reynolds and Parker and include the following.[38]

- Checklists of characteristics do not give a clear, holistic sense of what makes an effective school and how one establishes it. We also need to know what patterns these checklists make and how these patterns hold together in the form of an overall *culture* of the school.

- While we know what effective schools look like, we do not know how to create them. Indeed, attempts to make schools effective, using the effective schools research as a basis for these efforts, have often led to teacher resistance to what they perceive as overload and unwanted, imposed change.

- There is mounting evidence that effective schools do not

necessarily remain stable over time. Even if we knew how to create effective schools, therefore, we still would not know how to sustain them.

- Effective schools embrace rather narrow and conventional definitions of what constitutes effectiveness. Most studies have highlighted academic outcomes and particularly basic skills. Schools which are effective in these conventional and restricted terms might not be at all effective in terms of the demands of the postmodern, postindustrial world. We do not know, for instance, what effective schools which created success in problem-solving, creativity, risk, flexibility, or learning-how-to-learn would look like.

- Our notions of effectiveness are often contextually and culturally specific, limiting what we might imagine schools to be by the settings in which we study and administer them. Thus, strong, heroic and individual leadership is closely correlated with successful outcomes in American and British schools, but not in Dutch ones, where the cultural expectations of leadership are rather different.

While residues of the modernistic legacy of effective schools still remain as surrogate purposes for a number of educators, the faith in generalized and scientifically known principles of school effectiveness has begun to be superseded by commitments to more ongoing, provisional and contextually sensitive processes of school improvement.[39]

The decline of traditional moral and religious certainties, coupled with the collapse of technical and scientific ones, has been responsible within many schools for widespread quests for missions, visions and senses of "wholeness" in the form of whole-school curriculum development and whole-school change. Faith in the product of effectiveness has been transferred to trust in the process of improvement. *Scientific certainty*, the certainty grounded in proven principles of generalized applicability, is being replaced by *situated certainty*; the certainty that teachers and others can collectively glean from their shared practical knowledge of their immediate context and the problems it presents. This school-based search for missions, visions and continuous improvement gives much needed weight to the validity of practitioner knowledge and to the needs and demands of each particular context within which these practitioners work. Yet it also defers and devolves important social, moral and political concerns about the shaping of future generations to a process determined primarily in individual schools and systems.

Solutions which capitulate to collective uncertainty and let schools be moulded by the marketplace of parental choice, reflecting the pressures and particularities of the different localities they serve and the interest groups that dominate them, exacerbate these problems still further.[40] The crisis of educational and social purpose in the postmodern age is, in this sense, a crisis that still awaits resolution. Nor can that crisis be properly resolved by nostalgic retreats to mythical certainties of an ill-remembered past in which real subjects, traditional standards and basic skills were purportedly triumphant.[41] Not only is the solidity of that past a matter of historical doubt, but its appropriateness to the complex, diverse and fast-moving settings of the present is even more questionable.

The third set of implications that cultures of uncertainty raise for teachers and schools concerns teaching strategies. Where teaching methods are involved, the pathways of educational reform are strewn with the discarded certainties of the past. Reading schemes, language laboratories, DISTAR, programmed learning, direct instruction, even open classrooms – reforms such as these would be appropriate exhibits for any museum of educational innovation. Today's solutions often become tomorrow's problems. Future exhibits in our museums of innovation might include whole-language, cooperative learning or manipulative math. Singular models of expertise which rest on supposedly certain research bases are built on epistemological sand.[42]

In recent times, and especially in the United States, efforts at reforming teachers and teaching have often been based on and legitimated by allegedly incontrovertible findings of educational research. Madeline Hunter's renowned model of direct instruction as a basis for effective teaching is one example of this deeply modernistic approach.[43] For a time, this model was widely adopted and mandated in many North American school districts, as a required focus for staff training in methods of supposedly "proven" effectiveness. Indeed, adherence to the model has been used as a basis for teacher evaluation and promotion in many districts.[44]

Yet direct instruction has subsequently been criticized on the grounds that it is not universally applicable but effective only in particular settings – especially those emphasizing basic skills;[45] on the grounds that its widespread adoption in a school prejudices the growth of more risky open-ended teaching strategies;[46] and on the grounds that it fosters dependency and inflexibility among those who use it.[47] When teaching strategies such as direct instruction, cooperative learning or mastery teaching are implemented uncritically on the supposedly solid grounds of educational research, this not only undervalues the practical insight and wisdom of teachers by requiring them to comply with knowledge, expertise and prescriptions that are the property and prerogative of scientific "experts", it also betrays a "stereotypically masculine overconfidence" in the authority of "hard research".[48] Robertson makes this point in a critique of the work of Joyce and Showers, who have sought to implement "models of learning" of supposedly proven effectiveness with the support of peer coaching strategies between skilled and less skilled teachers. Referring to their book in which they cite Ron Edmonds's statement that "We can, whenever and wherever we want, successfully teach all children whose schooling is of interest to us. We already know more than we need to do that",[49] Robertson argues that:

Such certainty and predictability are familiar aspects of a masculine view of reality, as is the dependence on external rather than internal inquiry. . . . The "we" to whom Edmonds is referring is assuredly not classroom teachers; this claim for the power of knowledge and instrumentalism refers only to those whose expertise is validated within hierarchical systems. The authors give no indication that they believe teachers might already know enough to teach more children better, but rather that experts can train teachers in observable and tested behaviors which will produce predicted results.[50]

Reliance on the imposition of singular models of teaching expertise can create inflexibility among teachers and make it hard for them to exercise proper discretionary judgments in their classrooms. It can lead to teacher resistance because of implicit rejections of the worth and value of the rest of a teacher's repertoire, and of the life and the person that has been invested in building it up. It can also lead to an overly narrow focus on particular techniques, which can restrict teachers from establishing and drawing upon a wider repertoire of teaching strategies that they can apply flexibly as the context requires. Multiple and flexible conceptions of teaching excellence, however, are grounded in and arise from collective wisdom in the community of teachers and other educators (including, but not confined to, research). They acknowledge the provisional and context-dependent character of the knowledge base of teaching. They respect and leave space for teachers' discretionary judgments in their own classrooms. And by endorsing the possession and application of broad teaching repertoires, they permit gradual and selective adaptation and integration of new approaches without this necessarily implying wholesale rejection of the old.

Some of the emergent approaches to school-based staff development which offer menus of choice and discretion for teachers instead of mandates of standardized imposition, within a context of commitment to continuous learning and improvement, show signs of acknowledging the value of *situated certainty over scientific certainty* in teacher development.[51] Yet attempts to control teaching and how teachers teach by imposing spurious scientific certainties are among the last bastions of modernity. They justify continuing bureaucratic interventions by educational administrators, and they legitimate the separation and superiority of the academy as a specialized source of scientific wisdom that can direct and decree what teachers must do. The collapse of scientific certainty fundamentally challenges the control of educational bureaucracies as well as the credibility of the academy. No wonder it continues to be resisted with great tenacity.

4. THE MOVING MOSAIC

What kinds of organizations survive or, better still, positively thrive in conditions of extreme complexity and uncertainty? What kinds of organizations cope best in a world where technology and the press for turnover and profitability have compressed space and time to such a degree that the pace of change, decision-making and communication has reached frantic and frenetic proportions? What kinds of organizations can operate competently and creatively in a global context where colleagues, clients, partners and providers are constantly changing – a world where you can never be certain with whom you will be dealing from one day to the next? And what kinds of organizations best accommodate to a world where computers have made information more universally accessible and where knowledge and data can therefore no longer be sequestered or secreted so easily by privileged levels, departments and individuals within the organizational hierarchy?

The collective wisdom of contemporary literature on corporate management and organizational change is that conventional, bureaucratic organizations (and here we would include most secondary schools and their departments) do not fare well in the volatile conditions of postmodernity:[52]

- Specialized functions and the cubbyhole-like structures that arise from them create departmental territories and identities that inhibit identification with and commitment to the organization as a whole and the goals it pursues – especially where responsiveness to emergent conditions and opportunities may require departments and their functions to be redefined and redesigned. Conventional secondary schools which attempt curriculum integration or cross-curricular links constantly run up against such territorial defensiveness among their subject departments[53]

- Structures, roles and responsibilities created for one set of purposes during the organization's development tend to solidify and become unable to adapt to new purposes and opportunities as they arise. New challenges are either ignored, diverted into existing (and often inappropriate) departmental structures, or dealt with by adding yet more departments and responsibilities in a way that only makes the overall organization even more complex and cumbersome. The frequent assignment of AIDS, drug and sex education to teachers of physical education (usually a compulsory subject) rather than teachers of Family Studies or Home Economics (usually optional) is an example of this tendency. Another is the addition of Guidance (in the US) or Pastoral Care (in the UK) to regular "academic" teaching and its ultimate separation from and subordination to such teaching as a parallel system.[54]

- In conventional hierarchies of leadership and supervision, as change accelerates, innovation multiplies and the timeframes expected for decision-making become more compressed, individual leaders and supervisors tend to become overloaded and overwhelmed. In consequence, they may make bad decisions, hasty decisions, or no decisions at all. Anxiety, stress and burnout become their personal pathologies; ineffectiveness, their legacy to the organization. In education, principals and headteachers are frequent casualties of these burdens of overload.[55]

- Patterns of delegation and chains of command that are the rational modernistic response to size and complexity in a relatively stable environment merely fetter the organization during conditions of rapid change. This delays decision-making and responsiveness, and reduces the risk and opportunism that are essential to success in turbulent times when markets are constantly moving, niches are opening and closing, and effective enterpreneurship is at a premium. This can be seen in the tendency of many secondary schools and their teachers to adopt reactive rather than proactive responses to educational change.[56]

The kinds of organizations most likely to prosper in the postindustrial, postmodern world, it is widely argued, are ones characterized by flexibility, adaptability, creativity, opportunism, collaboration, continuous improvement, a positive orientation towards problem-solving and commitment to maximizing their capacity to learn about their environment and themselves. In this respect, inbuilt innovativeness and routine unpredictability are the organizational oxymorons of postmodernity.[57]

These emergent characteristics of postmodern organizations have been described in many ways by theorists of management and change. Rosabeth Moss Kanter and her colleagues provide one of the most succinct descriptions in an account of what they call a "tidal wave", which is becoming "a universal model for organizations, especially large ones":

> This model describes more flexible organizations, adaptable to change, with relatively few levels of formal hierarchy and loose boundaries among functions and units, sensitive and responsive to the environment; concerned with shareholders of all sorts – employees, communities, customers, suppliers and shareholders. These organizations empower people to take action and be entrepreneurial, reward them for contributions and help them gain in skill and "employability". Overall, these are global organizations characterized by internal and external relationships, including joint ventures, alliances, consortia and partnerships.[58]

Kanter and her colleagues go on to say that global economic competition and technological change are

> hastening the evolution of an organizational model that defines the boundaries of organizations as fluid and permeable. It recognizes that influences over organizational acts come from many sources and directions, and through many pathways, rather than "down" a "chain of command". . . . Thus, organizational action in the new model needs to be viewed in terms of *clusters of activity sets* whose membership, composition, ownership and goals are constantly changing, and in which *projects* rather than *positions* are central. In such an image of an organization, the bonds between actors are more meaningful and ongoing than those of single market transactions but less rigid and immutable than those of positions in authority structures.[59]

In this view, the postmodern organization is characterized by networks, alliances, tasks and projects, rather than by relatively stable roles and responsibilities which are assigned by function and department, and regulated through hierarchical supervision.

Such postmodern patterns of organization have far-reaching implications for the people who work within them and who in some respects even help create them. In the modernistic world of *The Organization Man* described by Whyte, to belong to an organization usually meant a clear and predictable career path, clarity and stability of tasks and responsibilities, and gradually accumulating rewards of seniority. Above all else, to be a member of an organization entailed a willing exchange of organizational loyalty for personal stability and seniority.[60]

But when boundaries are permeable, roles are blurred and tasks are constantly changing, what does it mean then to be a member of an organization? In a context lacking in clarity, certainty or stability, what happens to individuals' careers and future investments? If departments close down, responsibilities are reassigned or the whole existence of the organization itself is placed in jeopardy, what happens to loyalty and commitment then; to that basic bond between the individual and the organization?

In a fascinating sequel to Whyte's 1950s study of *The Organization Man*, Leinberger and Tucker offer some answers to these important questions.[61] These writers returned to Whyte's sample and interviewed their children, now in their 30s and 40s. How, they asked, do the working lives of the children compare to those of their parents? How are they experiencing organizational life now? And what does this say about them as individuals and about the organizations they are experiencing?

Compared to the safe, secure and somewhat dull work environments of their parents, the children of the organization men, it seems, work in very different kinds of organizational contexts that are typically smaller, less secure and less stable in character. As individuals of a different generation and different cultural outlook, this new breed of white-collar workers also orient themselves to these organizations, and indeed to work and life more generally, in ways that diverge sharply from their parents.

Demographically and culturally, the children of the organization men are part of a generation who have been reared in the seclusion of suburbia. Protected from the struggles and strictures of the Protestant ethic and the necessities of corporate commitment which first motivated their fathers in postwar America, Whyte's organization children grew up in relatively comfortable conditions where material affluence had been attained, domestic stability secured and "child-centered" parenting philosophies among stay-at-home suburban mothers often prevailed.

The result, say Leinberger and Tucker, was an emerging generation whose work and life goals were articulated not by competitive individualism, material struggle, or the search for stability and security — the things which motivated their fathers and willingly bound them to their employers. Rather, the organization men's children were freed from struggle and necessity to pursue more lofty goals of self-actualization, self-development and self-expression. Yet when they entered the workforce, they encountered organizations that were either indifferent or hostile to their personal goals. Conventional bureaucratic organizations suppressed or subordinated the self to the organization's needs, and were clearly antithetical to any pursuit of self-actualization and self-expression. Worse still, the radical restructurings brought about by economic recession in the 1970s and 1980s, in the form of company closures, strategic break-ups, compulsory redundancies and other bullish tactics of ever-more desperate administrations, ran directly counter to the fashionable rhetorics of individual empowerment, personal growth and corporate collaboration that characterized the new organizational "glitterspeak".[62]

The members of the emergent self-actualizing generation responded to this organizational denial or dismissal of the self in a number of ways. Some retreated from conventional organizational life to become artists, or junior academics, or workers in the marginal economy. A few tried to reform organizations from within, to make them more authentic, collective persons as it were, only to be obstructed in their efforts by the continuing bulwarks of bureaucracy. Several set up organizations themselves, and tried to model and personify the authenticity they valued by heading up small consulting companies or artistic agencies of their own. Most interesting of all, perhaps, were those who exploited organizational structures for their own gain and satisfaction — moving from company to company to work with people they liked, on projects that interested them, with no overall sense of loyalty or commitment to the organization which employed them. As Leinberger and Tucker note, this group was not *anti-organizational*, just *anti-organization* in their approaches to their work.[63] None of the children of the organization men, however, made long-term commitments to organizations in the way their fathers had. Though a few of this group did work for organizations, none were "organization men" (or women) in the conventional sense. For them, the traditional bond between the individual and the organization had been irreparably broken.

Through the working lives of this new and maturing white-collar generation, we can see the emergence of new organizational structures in a new society. Created by economic crisis on the one hand, and demographic and cultural change on the other, these fluid, flexible and dynamic organizations hold their employees' loyalty only as long as is warranted by the fulfillment of the work, the rewards that it brings and the lifestyle that it offers. In these emerging organizations, it is not just the structures but the membership itself that is in constant flux.

Toffler employs the metaphor of *the moving mosaic* to describe these patterns.[64] He outlines the movement of large corporations "from monolithic internal structures to mosaics made of scores, often hundreds of independently accounted units".[56] Toffler asks his readers to picture

> a moving mosaic composed not on a flat, solid wall, but on
> many, shifting see-through panels, one behind the other,
> overlapping, interconnected, the colors and shapes continually
> blending, contrasting, changing. Paralleling the new ways that
> knowledge is organized in data bases, this begins to suggest the
> future form of the enterprise and of the economy itself. Instead
> of a power-concentrating hierarchy, dominated by a few central
> organizations, we move toward a multidimensional mosaic form
> of power.[66]

This model of the moving mosaic is not an unconditionally positive one, as we shall see. But in its most favorable forms, it can contribute very valuably to what Senge calls *organizational learning*, by offering an organizational structure "where people continually expand their capabilities to understand complexity, clarify vision and improve shared mental models" by engaging in different tasks, acquiring different kinds of expertise, experiencing and expressing different forms of leadership, confronting uncomfortable organizational truths, and searching together for shared solutions.[67]

There is evidence that some schools, especially smaller elementary or primary ones, are beginning to take on some of the characteristics of the learning organization as Senge describes it. In Chapter 9, I will describe examples of schools which are committed to continuous improvement, where teachers work together closely as colleagues in planning, decision-making and classroom practice, where all or most teachers are leaders at some point or another, and where, as Barth puts it, the principal or headteacher is the leading learner of all.[68]

But in most schools, and especially in larger secondary schools, Fullan's contention that "the school is not now a learning organization" holds true.[69] Secondary schools in particular are in dire need of some of the benefits that a moving mosaic pattern of organization can bring. Chapter 10 shows vividly how their balkanized, cubbyhole-like structures often lead to departmental defensiveness, resistance to changes which threaten departmental identities and lack of opportunities for teachers to work with or learn from colleagues in departments other than their own. Balkanized staffing structures are deeply inimical to effective organizational learning.

Secondary schools operating more like moving mosaics would have more permeable departmental boundaries; membership of teachers in more than one department; less seniority, permanence and relative reward attached to the leadership position of department head; and more leadership positions across and outside departments. Moreover, these organizational categories, along with leadership of and membership in them, would also be expected to change over time, as circumstances required.

An illustration of a secondary school that exhibits some of the qualities of the moving mosaic is described in Chapter 10. Beyond individual experiments, however, it is likely that attempts to establish more flexible secondary school work structures will continue to be resisted – not just by school system bureaucracies, but by teacher unions too, since the flexible structures of the moving mosaic fundamentally threaten the established career routes and steps to seniority for which teacher unions have fought hard in the later stages of modernity. It is not inconceivable, however, that shifting demographics in the teaching force may in time enhance the acceptance of greater organizational and career flexibility, as a generation of teachers who have grown up accustomed to uncertainty in their personal and professional lives move into positions of greater influence in schools, school systems and, not least, in teacher unions.

As we shall see, teachers' suspicions that organizational "flexibility" and the loosening of their roles and responsibilities may be used against them are not without foundation. Moving targets are notoriously hard to hit and the moving mosaic is no exception. But the appropriate response to such suspicions is not to preserve and protect the status quo of subjects, departments and middle management bureaucracy. To do so only stifles the organization's ability to improve, stunts its teachers' opportunities to learn from colleagues across subject boundaries, and deprives its children of a richer and continually improving education. The overall possibility of and necessity for new organizational scenarios for our secondary schools and their teachers need to be entertained very seriously even if particular versions of these scenarios should be contested.

This brings us to some problematic aspects of the moving mosaic which advocates of the learning organization tend to overlook. While many analysts of postmodern organizations see the emergence of flatter, less hierarchical structures and more collaborative work environments within each unit of the overall enterprise, critics have pointed to important limits which surround such collaboration, and the forms it can take. For instance, collaboration often includes middle-level workers but excludes those below them, creating collaboration for some but subordination for the rest.[70] Management teams can collaborate without their ordinary colleagues, the innovating in-group of teachers without their more skeptical counterparts, teaching staff without support staff, or members of the school without parents in the community.

The parameters of collaboration and site-based decision-making may also be diluted and delimited by the information which management chooses to make available to its employees as a basis for decision-making. Menzies points to a case study of one company where:

> The information provided is often of the company's
> selection — for instance, reams of statistics on sales forecasts
> and defects per million logged in other . . . plants around the
> world, but no forecasts touching on the organization of work and
> the future of jobs in the plant. Workers complained: "They keep
> everybody in the dark." Management's reply: "We tell them as
> much as we think will be beneficial to them and healthy without
> raising hopes or fears."[71]

In this respect, the demands of flexible economies may foster more self-management within individual units of enterprise, but in ways that are paradoxical. Workers (or at least some workers) at site level may be able to exercise greater discretion over how things are produced — but the more controversial aspects of the production process, along with decisions about what is to be produced, tend to remain the prerogative of an inaccessible and unaccountable center which coordinates all the separate units. And should these units prove to be unproductive or uncooperative, they can be closed down and reopened elsewhere, at any time, by exploiting the flexible uses of space in the global economy.[72]

Educationally, the impact of the moving mosaic as the manipulative mosaic can be seen most clearly in the emergence of school-based financing, school-based staff development and the self-managing school, where the principles of postmodern organization have perhaps made their strongest inroads into the system.[73] Predicated on developments in the field of corporate management, school-based management also promises autonomy, empowerment, collaboration, flexibility, responsiveness and release from the grip of meddling bureaucracy. In early experiments, when schools are typically granted the latitude to innovate, self-managing schools can exemplify some of the more positive aspects of these principles rather well. But when developed across entire systems, in a context where self-management or local management is accompanied by the retention of central control over what is produced (through stringent controls over curriculum and assessment), then school-based management is no longer an avenue of empowerment, but a conduit for blame.[74] This is especially true where the curriculum and assessment requirements that are imposed connect poorly with the needs and interests of students who are socially and educationally at risk and may actively contribute to their educational failure. In this respect, school-based management, like corporate self-management, is unlikely to deliver on its promises of teacher empowerment unless the sphere of decision-making is broad, and issues of curriculum, assessment and educational purpose leave ample scope for teacher self-determination.[75]

Renihan and Renihan put it best:

> empowerment is, in its own right, a compelling force in its potential to achieve organizational excellence [but] above all it is imperative that we recognize what empowerment is *not* . . . Empowerment is *not* kidding teachers into thinking preplanned initiatives were their ideas. (That is entrapment.) Empowerment is *not* holding out rewards emanating from positive power. (That is enticement.) Empowerment is *not* insisting that participation is mandated from above. (That is enforcement.) Empowerment is *not* increasing the responsibility and scope of the job in trivial areas. (That is enlargement.) Empowerment is *not* merely concluding that enlarged job expectations just go with the territory. (That is enslavement.) Empowerment is, rather, giving teachers and students a share in important organizational decisions, giving them opportunities to shape organizational goals, purposely providing forums for staff input, acting on staff input, and giving real leadership opportunities in school-specific situations that really matter.[76]

Flexible organizational structures which resemble the metaphor of the moving mosaic are urgently needed in our schools, particularly at the secondary level, to enable schools and teachers to be more responsive to the changing educational needs of students who live in a complex, fast-paced and technologically sophisticated society. But the moving mosaic can easily become the manipulative mosaic, with teachers and schools having responsibility without power as the center retains control over the essentials of curriculum and testing, over the basic products which teachers must turn out. Much of the future of teachers' work and the degrees of empowerment contained within it will be settled by how this emerging context of organizational flexibility is determined and defined.

5. THE BOUNDLESS SELF

Organizational change is helping to create new kinds of selves. Psychological and demographic changes are in turn helping to create new patterns of organization. Postmodernity brings changes not only in *what* we experience, in our organizations and institutions, but also in *how* we experience, in our fundamental senses of self and identity.

If the social crisis of postmodernity is a crisis of moral purpose and cultural identity, the parallel psychological crisis is one of the self and of interpersonal relationships. In the conditions of high modernity, with all their instrumental demands and imperatives, the self tended to be suppressed or denied, trapped by the iron cage of bureaucracy. In postmodern societies, however, the very nature and integrity of the self is placed in doubt.[77] Witness the legal and literary fascination with the existence of multiple personalities as decentered sources of responsibility. In a decentered, postmodern world, the body and the self are no longer contiguous. Even the self no longer has singularity.

In the high-tech world of the instantaneous image, what once stood for the substantial self is increasingly seen as merely a constellation of signs. With the collapse of moral and scientific certainties, of foundational knowledge, the only intelligible reality appears to be that of language, discourse, image, sign and text. But even these have multiple meanings, infinite readings and are open to endless forms of deconstruction. So even the self is now suspect. It has no substance, center or depth. It is "enfolded in language which [it] can neither oversee nor escape".[78] Selves become transient texts, to be read and misread, constructed and deconstructed at will. Human selves become things that people display and other people interpret, not things that have lasting and inner substance of their own. Postmodernity, therefore, sees a "suspicion of the supposed unity and transparency of the disengaged self [and] of the alleged inner sources of the expressive self".[79]

As Giddens suggests, though, the semiotic dissolution of the self – its dissipation into a multitude of signs, displays and constructions – is not the prime psychological characteristic of postmodernity.[80] It is but one effect of a deeper, underlying phenomenon in which the boundaries between the self and the world beyond become progressively blurred.

This blurring of the boundaries of the self has its roots in patterns of childhood socialization and in contemporary forms of social organization. Earlier, I alluded to changing patterns of childhood socialization which emphasized self-actualization, self-expression and self-development. Christopher Lasch sees in these patterns the origins of the narcissistic personality and the genesis of a more pervasive culture of narcissism throughout society as a whole.[81] According to Lasch, narcissism emerges because of the socialization and professionalization of child-rearing techniques which have

> created an ideal of perfect parenthood while destroying parents'
> confidence in their ability to perform the most elementary
> functions of childrearing. The American mother, according to
> Geoffrey Gorer, depends so heavily on experts that she "can
> never have the easy, almost unconscious self assurance of the
> mother of more patterned societies, who is following ways she
> knows unquestioningly to be right".[82]

Lasch continues:

> The narcissistic mother's incessant yet curiously perfunctory
> attentions to her child interfere at every point with the

mechanism of optimal frustration. Because she so often sees the child as an extension of herself, she lavishes attentions on the child that are "awkwardly out of touch" with his needs, providing him with an excess of seemingly solicitous care but with little real warmth. By treating the child as an "exclusive possession", she encourages an exaggerated sense of his own importance; at the same time she makes it difficult for him to acknowledge his disappointment in her shortcomings.[83]

Lasch argues that because of these patterns of parenting (especially when they also include fathers who are separated from their children by demanding work hours and distant commutes), children raised in narcissistic environments often experience "loss of boundaries of the self": an inability to distinguish themselves from their parents because of the limits, differences and discipline which those parents fail to impose.[84]

Narcissism amounts to more than mere self-centeredness, then. Rather, it encompasses a personality where self-esteem turns into forms of self-indulgence and self-importance that know no limit. This brings with it delusions of omni-science and omnipotence, as narcissistic individuals encounter few frustrations or boundaries in their attempts to change and control the world around them. Some of the more morally and politically disturbing expressions of and justifica-tions for this *boundless self*, as I want to call it, are to be found in the excesses of the personal empowerment and human potential movements, to which I shall return shortly.

From the point of view of postmodernity and its implications for the bound-less self, more important than social psychological factors rooted in patterns of childhood socialization is the blurring of psychological boundaries created by changing patterns of social life. In postmodern societies, traditional ties of extended kinship and lifelong marital obligation are weakening. At the same time, the world is increasingly being experienced as rapidly changing and unstable. Moral, religious and ideological belief systems are diverse, pluralistic and in constant flux. Further, the profusion of fleeting media images and sound-bites often makes that world seem ephemeral and superficial. Under these social and organizational conditions, people's selves no longer seem given or settled. Selves have no roots in stable relationships, nor anchors in moral cer-tainties and commitments beyond them.[85]

In the postmodern world, therefore, the fragile self becomes a continuous reflexive project.[86] It has to be constantly and consciously remade and reaf-firmed. Like American freeways or British motorways, it is continuously "under construction". Whole expert systems and volumes of popular literature have been both a source and an outcome of this reflexivity of the self in the form of self-help guides, systems of therapy and support networks. This heightened orientation to the self and its continuing construction can be a source of crea-tivity, empowerment and change (in principle, you can be as you want to be), but also of uncertainty, vulnerability and social withdrawal. Let's look at each of these possibilities.

On the positive side, the end of scientific certainties and the proliferation of contradictory claims to expertise can reduce people's dependence on experts and empower them, individually and together, to make more meaningful choices and exercise greater control over their personal and collective destinies.[87] The growing control that many cancer patients now exercise over their choice of treatments, the extent to which allergies and asthma have been granted increased medical recognition and respectability, and the emerging importance of hospices as places which give dignity to the dying have all arisen from personal and public questioning of medical expertise, and from the quests for self-development and self-determination which such expertise has been seen to deny. The emerging credibility that researchers and staff developers attach to teachers' personal knowledge and practical wisdom creates similar, though slimmer, opportunities for personal and collective empowerment, as teachers do battle with the excessive certainties and inflated claims to expertise of bureaucratic administrations and academic professoriates. Here can be seen some of the real benefits of self-development and personal empowerment when these things are connected to a wider sense of purpose, the personal needs of others, and a shrewd awareness of the micropolitical realities of one's school or system.

This also holds true for the wider search for personal authenticity, which is very much a part of the postmodern condition. At its best, says Charles Taylor, when the search for the authentic self avoids becoming insular and self-enclosed, when it remains rooted in and connected to conceptions of the good, and the welfare of others, important moral benefits can be gained.[88] In particular, the search for authenticity can enhance the development of personal integrity and fidelity when people want to pursue and clarify their social and moral ideals. In teaching, taking just such an interior turn towards self-development and greater authenticity can have extremely positive educational consequences when teachers are able to connect the personal and interpersonal satisfaction they have with their students and their colleagues to social and moral purposes of a broader nature and to the micropolitical realities of the organizations in which they operate.

But self-development can easily degenerate into self-indulgence. As Taylor puts it: "the culture of self-fulfilment has led many people to lose sight of concerns that transcend them. And it seems obvious that it has taken trivialized and self-indulgent forms."[89] In its more worrying forms, the heightened orientation to the self can become a narcissistic one of self-preoccupation or, as Baudrillard puts it, self-referentiality.[90] This orientation is marked by a desperate and deliberate search for biographical meaning and personal narrative unity in an apparently disordered and chaotic social world — an orientation that is reflected in the educational field in increasingly popular research and professional development preoccupations with teachers' narratives, teachers' stories and teachers' lives.[91] The preoccupation with the personal, and the relative neglect of the social and political is a chronic condition of postmodernity.

More than this, the delusions of omnipotence which characterize the boundless self, and the therapies and ideologies of personal growth and human potential which often validate its actions, falsely condense the social into the personal by obliterating the boundaries between them. They overemphasize people's personal responsibility for change. People sense no limits to what they can achieve. Personal change is seen to lead to social change; individual wellness to organizational health. These delusions of omnipotence within the culture of narcissism, with its pious and precious investments in the power of self-development and personal growth, are deeply paradoxical. For with its denial of and inability to interact knowledgeably with contexts which delimit the self, constrain its actions and fragment its connections to others, narcissistic omnipotence and the boundless self create not more personal power but less. As contexts of opportunity and constraint fail to be acknowledged or confronted, they lead to impotence not empowerment.

These tensions and choices between empowerment and narcissism are clearly visible in teachers' work, particularly in the expanding field of teacher development and the increasing importance being attached to the teacher as a person. Leithwood, for instance, points to the value of treating the teacher as a person in his discussion of the principal's role in teacher development.[92] Many other writers also highlight the importance of self-development and self-understanding as keys to professional growth in the teaching force.[93] Personal factors such as personal maturity, stage in the life-cycle, ethnic and gender identity, religious beliefs, ideological commitments and career goals have a clear bearing on teachers' relations with their colleagues, their orientations to change, and the quality of their classroom instruction.

Putting an emphasis on the teacher as a person assists teachers in processes of self-understanding which are grounded in their life and work. It helps others to work with teachers more effectively. And it gives much-needed credibility and dignity to teachers' own personal and practical knowledge of their work in relation to the pronouncements of policy makers and the theoretical claims of the academy.[94] But when moral frameworks are missing, or senses of context are weak, approaching teacher development predominantly or exclusively as a process of self-development has serious limitations.

- First, teacher self-development can become *self-indulgent*. This happens when researchers and professional developers prefer to work with teachers who share their own (broadly child-centered and often humanities-based) values and perspectives and shun other more difficult and demanding ones — like traditional or politically active teachers, or teachers in somewhat more "linear" and less literary subjects whose perspectives may diverge from their own.

- Second, teacher self-development can be *politically naive*. This commonly occurs when teachers are encouraged to reflect on their personal biographies without also connecting them to broader histories of which they are a part; or when they are asked to reflect on their personal images of teaching and learning without also theorizing the conditions which gave rise to those images and the consequences which follow from them. In this respect, when divorced from its surrounding social and political contexts, personal practical knowledge can quickly turn into particular and parochial knowledge.

- Finally, teacher self-development can be misleadingly and narcissistically *grandiose*. This happens when the boundless self of the teacher is invested with unlimited power for personal change, and unrealistic moral obligations for professional improvement that are untempered by any practical and political awareness of the contexts and conditions which currently limit what any one teacher can reasonably achieve; and which teachers and others must confront together if more than trivial gains are to be made. Excessive beliefs in the transformative power of personal knowledge and personal change can lead to pious grandiosity (other teachers too can be as insightful and excellent as me!), or, when personal change is constantly frustrated by organizational constraints, to intolerable guilt. (If only I worked harder, or was a better person, my students could learn more!)

The advent of postmodernity has brought with it an increase in professional collaboration, and some recognition of the need to establish closer ties between teachers' professional performance and their personal and emotional lives which articulate and motivate that performance. At the same time, these postmodern developments suggest a retreat to personal emotions and interpersonal processes among many teachers and teacher developers at the cost of addressing important moral, social and political purposes outside the personal domain. They suggest a focus on the aesthetics of collaboration, self-understanding or partnership, rather than on their politics and their ethics; on what the collaboration, self-understanding or partnership is for; and on how they can be achieved. In this respect, as we shall see in the final chapter, a key challenge of postmodernity is not just to make teacher collaboration work, but to address what it is for and what is beyond it.

6. SAFE SIMULATION

Moral frameworks and a keen awareness of (as well as a willingness to engage with) the micropolitical realities of schooling are essential if the teacher's self is to be a genuinely empowered self; not one that is narcissistic, self-indulgent or piously grandiose about its personal potential to change the world. This need for moral frameworks and micropolitical awareness is even more important in a postmodern world of swirling, fleeting and superficial images, where how things *appear* is often accorded priority over how they actually *are*.

One fascinating feature of postmodern society is its permeation by technologically generated images – television, video, Nintendo, computer simulations, facsmiles, virtual realities and the like. To take the example of Canada: in 1987, Canadians watched an average of 3.4 hours of television a day, a slight increase from the mid-1970s. While teenagers (2.7 hours) and children (3.1 hours) spent less time watching television than adults, they watched more dramas and comedies than did adults and fewer news and public affairs programs. Reflecting the trends toward globalization, it is interesting to note that 98 percent of comedies and 87 percent of dramas came from foreign (mainly US) sources, while 87 percent of news and public affairs programs were Canadian. In 1987, close to 100 percent of Canadian households had a television set and 94 percent had color television. Nearly half of all households had at least two television sets. In addition, 68 percent (up from 47 percent in 1977) of households had cable television, and therefore access to many channels, and 45 percent of households had a videocassette recorder, compared with only 6 percent in 1983.[95]

While the computer is not yet as pervasive a feature of domestic life as is the television set, Canadian data show that by 1989, 82 percent of 15–19-year-olds knew how to use a computer, 63 percent had received formal training in computer use, and 35 percent had a computer at home.[96] Teenagers used computers very often for game playing (92 percent), often for word processing (72 percent) and data entry (61 percent), and less often for programming (49 percent), record-keeping (38 percent) and data analysis (24 percent).[97]

Today's youth are surrounded by and swathed in images. This makes traditional discussions about practical and local relevance as a source for teaching and motivating lower-achieving students somewhat irrelevant – for through a computer bulletin board, for instance, a young person can be more meaningfully connected to someone living hundreds of miles away than they are to their parent, sister or friend sitting right next to them in their own room.[98]

Hi-tech visual images are a pervasive feature of young people's lives. Textbooks, worksheets and overheads are a poor match for these other, more complex, instantaneous and sometimes spectacular forms of experience and learning. In this context, the disengagement of many students from their curriculum and their teaching is not hard to understand. Teachers are having to compete more and more with this world and its surrounding culture of the image. This demands a lot of them in terms of technological awareness and pedagogical change.

At the same time, there are real dangers that the spectacle and superficiality of an instantaneous visual culture may supersede and obliterate the necessary moral discourse and studied reflection of a more oral one. Language, debate and critical verbal analysis are the stuff of a reflective moral culture and it is therefore also important that teachers continue to find ways to protect, promote and validate their contribution. The challenge for teachers in their classrooms is how to engage effectively with the images and technologies of the postmodern world without jettisoning the cultural analysis, moral judgment and studied reflection they threaten to supersede.

Teachers must be both competent users of and innovators with technology, and moral guardians against its most superficial and trivializing effects. But this is not the only way in which teachers and their work are affected by the profusion of visual images that characterize the postmodern world. Like other adults, teachers too are part of a wider world where images are everywhere — where reality tries to live up to its images, becomes suffused with images, and may be indistinguishable from its images. While this profusion of images can give rise to experiences that are exciting, engaging and entertaining, it can also make it difficult to generate serious and sustained moral discourse, public debate, and considered judgment about purposes and values. Aesthetics can be elevated above ethics; how things *look* over how things *are*! Glossy school brochures and color-coded staff development booklets may bear little relation to what actually goes on in these schools or within the staff development practices of school systems. In his book *America*, Jean Baudrillard has encapsulated the potentially trivializing effects of the ubiquitous image in a provocative though also characteristically overstated "cameo" description of what he calls "Reagan's smile":

> And that smile everyone gives you as they pass, that friendly contraction of the jaws triggered by human warmth. It is the eternal smile of communication, the smile through which the child becomes aware of the presence of the others, or struggles desperately with the problem of their presence . . . they certainly do smile at you here [in America] though neither from courtesy, nor from an effort to charm. This smile signifies only the need to smile. It is a bit like the Cheshire Cat's grin: it continues to float on faces long after all emotion has disappeared. . . . The smile of immunity, the smile of advertising: "This country is good. I am good. We are the best!" It is also Reagan's smile — the culmination of the self-satisfaction of the entire American nation — which is on the way to becoming the sole principle of government. . . . Smile and others will smile back. Smile to show how transparent, how candid you are. Smile if you have nothing to say. Most of all, do not hide the fact that you have nothing to say, nor your total indifference to others. Let this emptiness, this profound indifference shine out spontaneously in your smile. . . . Americans may have no identity, but they do have wonderful teeth.

And it works. With this smile, Reagan obtains a much wider consensus than any that could be achieved by a Kennedy with mere reason or political intelligence . . . the whole American population comes together in this toothpaste effect. No idea – not even the nation's moral values in their entirety – could ever have produced such a result. Reagan's credibility is exactly equal to his transparency and the nullity of his smile.[99]

Where people are surrounded by a plethora of images, this can create dramatic spectacles but also moral and political superficiality; aesthetic attractiveness, but also ethical emptiness. In many ways, contemporary images disguise and deflect more unseemly realities. But when technologically generated images are as profuse and pervasive as they are in postmodern society, the relationship between image and reality becomes even more complex than this. Baudrillard captures this complexity in his discussion of "the successive phases of the image" where:

- it is the reflection of a basic reality;
- it masks and perverts a basic reality;
- it masks the *absence* of a basic reality;
- it bears no relation to any reality whatsoever;
- it is its own pure simulacrum.[100]

In this last phase, Baudrillard argues, the image is "no longer in the order of appearance at all but of simulation".[101] Here, technologically complex images which are capable of elaborate design and manipulation have led to increasingly pervasive and popular trends in museums, aquariums and the like, towards creating sophisticated simulations or hyperrealities of Victorian villages, "frontier" gold mines, or entire ecosystems in which dolphins, birds or butterflies appear to be completely at home. Travelling to Disneyworld's Epcot Center and seeing robots which look like humans and which, in many respects, are more perfectly human than humans themselves, one cannot help but marvel at the technological triumph of all this. It is extremely pleasurable to immerse oneself in the self-confirming, simulated world which this contrived imagery has created.

There is more to simulations than this, though. In what they portray, and how they portray it, postmodern simulations also convey moral messages about history, nature and human relationships – messages which are implicit and seductive, rather than explicit and open to debate. This is true, we will see, not just for simulations in entertainment but for certain kinds of "simulated" behavior in organizations and workplaces too, including the workplaces of teachers. But, for illustrative purposes, it is with the world of zoos and museums that I shall begin – for there are powerful analogies and connections here between the simulations of *nature* in postmodern museums and aquariums, and simulations of *culture* in postmodern organizations and workplaces.

What does it mean to simulate something? According to Baudrillard, "To dissimulate is to feign not to have what one has. To simulate is to feign to have what one hasn't."[102] More than this, he says, "simulation threatens the difference between 'true' and 'false', between 'real' and 'imaginary'."[103] Simulations can have powerful effects on our senses and constructions of reality. Umberto Eco illustrates this with his description and analysis of Marine World in San Diego Zoo:

> The symbolic center of Marine World is the Ecology Theater
> where you sit in a comfortable amphitheater (and if you can't sit,
> the polite but implacable hostess will make you, because
> everything must proceed in a smooth and orderly fashion and
> you can't sit where you choose, but if possible next to the latest
> to be seated, so that the line can move properly and everybody
> takes his place without pointless search), you face a natural area
> arranged like a stage. Here, there are three girls with long blond
> hair and a hippie appearance; one plays very sweet folk songs on
> the guitar, the other two show us, in succession, a lion cub, a
> little leopard, and a Bengal tiger only six months old. The
> animals are on leashes, but even if they weren't they wouldn't
> seem dangerous because of their tender age and also because,
> thanks perhaps to a few poppy seeds in their food, they are
> somewhat sleepy. One of the girls explains that the animals,
> traditionally ferocious, are actually quite good when they are in a
> pleasant and friendly environment, and she invites the children
> in the audience to come up on stage and pet them. The emotion
> of petting a Bengal tiger isn't an everyday occurrence and the
> public is spurting ecological goodness from every pore. From the
> pedagogical point of view, the thing has a certain effect on the
> young people, and surely it will teach them not to kill fierce
> animals, assuming that in their later life they happen to
> encounter any. But to achieve this "natural peace" (as an indirect
> allegory of social peace) great efforts had to be made: the
> training of the animals, the construction of an artificial
> environment that seems natural, the preparation of the hostesses
> who educate the public. So the final essence of this apologue on
> the goodness of nature is Universal Taming.[104]

Killer whale and dolphin pools are coming to possess many of the same qualities. In many modernistic "dolphinariums", constructed in the 1970s or thereabouts, a concrete pool painted in garish blue, with clear, sweeping lines and expansive vistas, contains the dolphins, which are made to bounce colored balls, jump through hoops, and somersault over sticks by their youthful, brightly dressed, California surfer-style trainers. Here nature is visibly subjugated, tamed and arguably even improved by the triumph of human technology.

In the postmodern dolphinarium at Chicago's Shedd Aquarium, however, the pool is surrounded on three sides by huge windows so the audience look out onto and feel an inclusive part of what they imagine to be the ocean, even though it is only Lake Michigan, in which a dolphin could never live. The vast oceanarium of which the dolphin pool is a part consists of a sophisticated reconstruction of the Pacific Northwest complete with timber, islands, board-walks, bird calls, and the like. This is more like the Pacific Northwest than the Pacific Northwest itself. Members of the audience perch on rough-hewn steps, seemingly carved out of the very cliffs abutting the pool. The dolphins still do somersaults, slap their tails, and open their jaws on command, but now their quietly spoken, wet-suited and "ecologically correct" trainers assure us that all this behavior is "natural", that they tell the dolphins not *what* to do, only *when* to do it. More than this, they say, having the dolphins open their jaws on command makes it less stressful when they need to have their teeth checked, just as cuddling the dolphins out of the water makes it easier to administer injections when they are sick — all in the interest of their health and natural develop-ment, of course. (Just one day after I first drafted this paragraph, two of the Aquarium's recently captured Beluga whales died after receiving routine injections!)

The dolphins are doing the same tricks as captive dolphins always have — but the simulated imagery gives their behavior a very different meaning. This *simulation* of nature, its order and goodness, is achieved only by *dissimulating* the capture, control and containment of the animals which make the experience possible, and by *dissimulating* the suppression of the spontaneous, dangerous, unpredictable and possibly even unentertaining behavior in which these animals might otherwise indulge if left to their own desires.

This postmodern phenomenon of safe simulation has a significance that extends far beyond the theatrical worlds of zoos, museums and theme parks. Changing approaches to the inservice training and development of teachers have some disconcerting parallels with changing approaches to the training of dolphins! This is most evident in those activities in classrooms and staff-rooms which involve creating cultures of cooperation and collaboration among students, teachers, or both.

One example can be seen in the meteoric rise in North America of what has come to be called cooperative learning. Though there are several leading advo-cates of cooperative learning with different and often highly contested philo-sophies, cooperative learning normally includes a range of specific classroom tasks with names like "Jigsaw" or "Think-Pair-Share", designed to build active, cooperative learning and involvement among students. There is also a somewhat specialized language of principles and procedures (such as five kinds of "positive interdependencies") which teachers are asked to master in order to understand it fully and implement it effectively.[105] Cooperative learning involves students not just working *in* groups, but *as* groups, often in specific roles (for instance, as "encouragers"). Because active group work is uncommon in most classrooms, cooperative learning undoubtedly offers valuable additions to teachers' repertoires of classroom strategies, especially when they are applied with flexibility and discretion. Indeed, I use many such strategies in my own teaching. However, advocates typically make a stronger case for cooperative learning than this.

For writers like Kagan, cooperative learning is not just another string to the teacher's bow, a useful addition to the repertoire. It responds to and compensates for a supposed "socialization void" among many young people, especially culturally and socially disadvantaged ones, in their family and community relationships.[106] Cooperative learning therefore supplies not only improved cognitive learning, but also much-needed social skills. The designated tasks and roles of cooperative learning and the specialized language which surrounds them are therefore seen to address and fill up the social skills void which many children are said to encounter in their homes and on the streets outside their schools.

However, researchers such as Rudduck and Quicke have demonstrated that many students from working class and ethnic minority backgrounds do not lack the social skills of cooperation, nor experience a socialization void at all.[107] Indeed, the cultures of their class and community already supply them with rich, if rather rough and ready, forms of association and assistance of an informal, spontaneous nature. In schools, these things often appear as "cheating" — a form of cooperation that is unwanted and illegitimate in the atmosphere of competitive achievement and hierarchical grading which characterizes school life.

In this way, the insertion of cooperative learning into classroom teaching and learning can be read not as a response to a socialization void in home and community, but in response to a void created by the school itself, with its disciplinary processes, and grading and assessment practices that have already driven more dangerous, spontaneous, desire-laden forms of student collaboration out of the classroom and made them illegitimate. Cooperative learning is then inserted and inscribed as a contrived and controlled set of collaborative structures, practices and behaviors with its own special language: a language that takes lots of expensive training to acquire! It becomes its own self-contained and self-affirming system — a safe simulation of the more spontaneous forms of student collaboration which the school and its teachers have already eradicated.

In Chapter 9, I will document and discuss similar *safe simulations* of collaboration among teachers, which take the form of what I call *contrived collegiality*. This occurs when spontaneous, dangerous and difficult-to-control forms of teacher collaboration are discouraged or usurped by administrators who capture it, contain it and contrive it through compulsory cooperation, required collaborative planning, stage-managed mission statements, labyrinthine procedures of school development planning, and processes of collaboration to implement non-negotiable programs and curricula whose viability and practicality are not open to discussion. The point here is not that contrived collegiality is a manipulative, underhand way of tricking passive teachers into complying with administrative agendas, for we shall see that teachers are very quick to see through such contrivances. Rather, the administratively simulated image of collaboration becomes its own self-sustaining reality, with its own symbolic importance and legitimacy. In this sense, the major problem that the safe simulation of contrived collegiality raises for teachers and their work is not that it is controlling and manipulative but that it is superficial and wasteful of their efforts and energies.

As we move into the postmodern age, a key challenge for schools, administrators and teachers is whether they can live with or even actively encourage full-blown cooperative classrooms, collaborative staffrooms and self-managing schools that are charged with spontaneity, unpredictability, danger and desire; or whether they will opt for safe simulations of these things that are controlled, contrived and ultimately superficial in character.

7. COMPRESSION OF TIME AND SPACE

One of the factors that most propels people towards superficial solutions and the maintenance of surface appearances is shortage of time. This brings me to the seventh and in many ways most pervasive dimension of postmodernity: the compression of time and space.

Since the early days of the Industrial Revolution, with the invention of the mechanical clock and its widespread diffusion among the population, time and the "clock-machine" have become "the Devil's Mill" for workers and their work-places.[108] Through its links to productivity and profitability, time, indeed, is money. Save time and you save money too.

The age of modernity brought accumulating advances in travel and communications which conquered distance and compressed time. Railways, automobiles, telephones and ever-faster air travel all contributed technologically to this intensifying compression of time and space, and to the speed at which business could be contracted as a result. The compression of time and space is nothing new. Things have been getting faster for quite some time.

But postmodernity is characterized by technological leaps which make communication instantaneous, distance irrelevant and time one of the most precious commodities on earth. Fax machines, modems, mobile phones and laptop computers are the technological harbingers of commercial instantaneity: fast food, microwaves and same-day cleaning their life-style accompaniments. Toffler describes some of the developments like this:

> Suddenly in the late 1980s, several things came together: Fax machines could be produced at low cost. Telecommunications technologies vastly improved. AT&T was broken up, helping to cut the cost of long distance services in the United States. Meanwhile, postal services decayed (slowing transaction times at

a moment when the economy was accelerating). In addition, the acceleration effect raised the economic value of each second saved by a fax machine. Together, these converging factors opened a market that then expanded with explosive speed.[109]

In the future, says Toffler:

> The entire wealth-creation cycle will be monitored *as it happens*. Continued feedback will stream in from sensors built into intelligent technology, from optical scanners in stores, and from transmitters in trucks, planes and ships that send signals to satellites so managers can track the changing location of every vehicle at every moment. This information will be combined with the results of continuous polling of people and information from a thousand other sources. The acceleration effect, by making each unit of saved time *more* valuable than the last unit, thus creates a positive feedback loop that accelerates the acceleration. . . .[110] Even now, time itself has become a critical factor of production. As a result, knowledge is used to shrink time intervals.

This compression of time and space brings real benefits. Turnover is increased, travel and communication are swifter, decision-making is quicker, service is more responsive, wait-time is reduced. But the intense compression of time and space which characterizes the postmodern age brings costs as well as benefits to the operation of our organizations, to the quality of our personal and working lives, and to the moral substance of and direction behind what we do. In these more worrying senses, the compression of time and space

- can raise expectations for speed of turnaround and rapid responsiveness to such a level that decision-making is too swift and leads to error, ineffectiveness and superficiality, creating organizations that are chaotic collages rather than moving mosaics;

- can multiply innovation, accelerate the pace of change, and shorten the timelines for implementation so that people experience intolerable guilt and overload and an inability to meet their goals;

- can lead people to concentrate on the aesthetic appearance of change or performance, rather than on the quality and substance of the change or performance itself;

- can exacerbate uncertainty as knowledge is produced, disseminated and overturned at an ever increasing rate;

- can erode opportunities for personal reflection and relaxation, leading to increased stress and loss of contact with one's basic goals and purposes;

- can place such a premium on implementing new techniques and complying with new mandates that more complex, less visible, longer-term and less measurable purposes which involve care for others and relationships with others are diminished in importance, or sacrificed altogether.

The compression of time and space is both cause and consequence of many other aspects of the postmodern condition — accelerated change, organizational flexibility and responsiveness, obsession with appearances, loss of time for the self, and so on. The next three chapters look closely at the place of time in teachers' work, at the nature and effects of its compression upon that work, and at the emotional guilt which teachers experience as they deal with its consequences.

CONCLUSION

If the changes facing teachers seem confusing and disconnected, this is often because what is driving them, the context from which they spring, is unclear. But this is not all. The context itself is also a deeply confusing one. The postmodern condition is complex, paradoxical and contested. Yet it is significant and deeply consequential for education and teaching in areas as diverse as school-based management, collaborative cultures, teacher empowerment, and organizational change. This chapter has explored seven dimensions of postmodernity and their paradoxical character and consequences for teachers and their work. What this analysis has revealed and suggested is that:

- *Occupational flexibility and technological complexity* create needs for diversity but also tendencies towards divisiveness. The need for teachers to develop skills and qualities of flexibility in their students, and to build work structures in which those skills and qualities can be produced, is important. But equally important is the need for discourse and debate to address the uses of technology and the patterns of unemployment and underemployment which many young people will face as adults in the new economic order.

- The paradox of globalization creates *national doubt and insecurity* and carries with it dangers of resurrecting and reconstructing traditional curricula of an ethnocentric and xenophobic nature. Such curricula can reinforce educational inequities among culturally diverse groups, create excesses of content and burdens of overload for teachers to overcome, and reinforce subject-based structures of secondary schooling that inhibit organizational learning.

- *Moral and scientific uncertainty* reduces confidence in the factual certainties of *what* is taught, decreases dependency on scientifically "proven" "best methods" of *how* things are taught, and makes it difficult to secure moral agreement about *why* things are taught. In response, teachers are either becoming more involved in developing their own missions and visions, or are being placed at the moral mercy of the market force of parental choice, or are being directed to extol and expound the virtues of standards, tradition and basic skills by those who nostalgically reconstruct mythical certainties of ill-remembered pasts. The challenge for teachers is to develop *situated* rather than *scientific* certainties in their own schools as collaborative communities. But these should also embrace and be attentive to broader moral frameworks that extend beyond their own particular schools to the domains of policy and public debate.

- *Organizational fluidity* challenges the balkanized structures of secondary school teaching, yet addresses the needs for collaboration and shared occupational learning in contexts that are larger and more complex than small, simple elementary schools. While "moving mosaic" structures of work organization can be flexible and responsive, they can also be manipulative, with the organizational parts being maneuvered by a non-accountable and inaccessible core. This has important implications for school-based management and whether it will become an avenue of empowerment or a conduit for blame.

- *Personal anxiety* and the search for authenticity becomes a continuous psychological quest in a world without secure moral anchors. The focus on staff development as self-development reflects this process. Where teacher self-development is linked to actions which address the contextual realities of teachers' work and which actively seek to change them, this process can be an immensely empowering one. But when the context is ignored, and the powers of self-development and personal change are viewed as boundless, then teacher self-development and its celebration of personal knowledge can become pious, narcissistic and self-indulgent.

- *Technological sophistication and complexity* create a world of instantaneous images and artificial appearances. Safe simulations of reality can be more perfect and plausible than the more untidy and uncontrollable realities themselves. Contrived cooperation in the classroom and contrived collegiality in the staffroom are examples of safe simulations that can denude the collaborative process of its vitality and spontaneity.

- *The compression of time and space* can lead to greater flexibility, improved responsiveness and better communication in our schools, but it can also create intolerable overload, premature burnout, superficiality and loss of purpose and direction. A challenge in reconstructing and redesigning teachers' work is to develop structures and processes which are more flexible and responsive but which also deal effectively and reflectively with the pressures of overload, multiple innovation and accelerated change.

The meanings of postmodernity are still open, and the struggles with the bureaucratic forces of modernity still unresolved. The consequences for teachers and their work, I have shown, are far reaching, but also often fragmented. I have tried in this chapter to show something of their coherence and interconnectedness within the broader social and organizational context. It is time now to look at these struggles and their consequences not in the abstract, from the "top down", but from the "bottom up". It is time, in other words, to move from the broader context of change, to the complexity of teachers' work itself, and to the words through which teachers describe it. That analysis begins with time itself, its social organization within teachers' work, and the ways in which teachers and administrators experience it.

NOTES

1. Bell, D., *The Coming of Postindustrial Society*, New York, Basic Books, 1973, p. 51.

2. On flexible accumulation, see Harvey, D., *The Condition of Postmodernity*, Cambridge, Polity Press, 1989. Flexible specialization is described and defined by Piore, M. and Sabel, M., *The Second Industrial Divide*, New York, Basic Books, 1984. On the flexible firm, see Atkinson, J., "Flexibility: Planning for an uncertain future", *Manpower Policy and Practice*, 1, Summer 1985. These various facets of flexibility are reviewed in MacDonald, M., "Post-Fordism and the flexibility debate", *Studies in Political Economy* 36, Fall 1991, pp. 177–201.

3. Harvey, D., *op. cit.*, note 2, p. 147.

4. See MacDonald, *op. cit.*, note 2.

5. Harvey, *op. cit.*, note 2.

6. Ibid.

7. Ibid.

8. As Bell puts it, "the first and simplest characteristic of a post-industrial society is that the majority of the labor force is no longer engaged in agriculture or manufacturing, but in services, which are defined, residually, as trade, finance, transport, health, recreation, research, education and government" (Bell, D., *The Coming of Postindustrial Society*, *op. cit.*, note 1, p. 15). For British figures on changes in the occupational structure in the 1970s, see Westergaard, J. and Resler, H., *Class in a Capitalist Society*, Harmondsworth, Penguin, 1975.

9. Lindsay, C., "The service sector in the 1980s", *Canadian Social Trends*, Spring 1989, pp. 20–2.

10. Reich, R. B., *The Work of Nations*, New York, Random House, 1992, p. 84.

11. Schlechty, P., *Schools for the Twenty-First Century*, San Francisco, Jossey-Bass, 1990, p. 39.

12. See, for instance, Piore and Sabel, *op. cit.*, note 2.

13. These images are most abundant in more popular, futurist texts such as Naisbitt, J. and Aberdene, P., *Megatrends 2000: Ten New Directions for the 1990s*, New York, Avon Books, 1990, and to a lesser extent Toffler, A., *Powershift*, New York, Bantam Books, 1990.

14. See MacDonald, *op. cit.*, note 2 for a sober assessment of these possibilities.

15. Menzies, H., *Fast Forward and Out of Control: How Technology Controls Our Lives*, Toronto, Macmillan, 1989. In the context of Canada, Menzies puts it like this:

    > Canadian society is becoming a balkanized state composed of two tiers, two nations, two solitudes: the over-employed technocratic elite fully engaged in their society, for whom technology is a tool for creativity and communication, and, on the margins, the under-employed technical support staff, who work within technical systems and are controlled by them. (p. 244)

16. Ibid, p. 134.

17. Schlechty, *op. cit.*, note 11.

18. The Medicine Way Path of Learning as a guide for curriculum planning is produced by and available from Children of the Earth Secondary School, Winnipeg, Manitoba, Canada.

19. Reich, *op. cit.*, note 10, p. 3.

20. Swyngedouw, E., "The socio-spatial implications of innovations in industrial organiza-tion", *Working Paper No. 20*, Johns Hopkins European Center for Reciprocal Planning and Research, Lille. The argument about the innovative uses of space within the postindustrial economy is clearly developed by Harvey, *op. cit.*, note 2.

21. The ecological dimensions of postmodern economies and their impact on political and cultural relations and identities are among the less remarked upon features of postmoder-nity. Anthony Giddens, however, has highlighted their importance particularly effec-tively. See Giddens, A., *The Consequences of Modernity*, Cambridge, Polity Press, 1990.

22. Goodson, I. F., "Nations at risk and national curriculum: Ideology and identity", in *Politics of Education Association Yearbook*, London, Taylor & Francis, 1990, pp. 219–52.

23. Goodson, *op. cit.*, note 22, p. 220.

24. Ibid, p. 221.

25. See Hargreaves, A., *Curriculum and Assessment Reform*, Milton Keynes, Open Univer-sity Press and Toronto, OISE Press, 1989. Also see the arguments later in this book on balkanization in Chapter 10.

26. See Hargreaves, A., Baglin, E., Henderson, P., Leeson, P. and Tossell, T., *Personal and Social Education: Choices and Challenges*. Oxford, Basil Blackwell, 1988.

27. Schama, S., *Dead Certainties (Unwarranted Speculations)*, New York, Alfred A. Knopf, 1991.

28. Schama, *op. cit.*, p. 320.

29. See Harvey, *op. cit.*, note 2 for a development of this argument.

30. The decline of metanarratives as all-encompassing theories of the natural or social world is central to the position of Lyotard, J., *The Postmodern Condition*, Minneapolis, University of Minnesota Press, 1984.

31. See, for instance, Willinsky, J., "Getting personal and practical with personal practical knowledge", *Curriculum Inquiry*, 9(3), Fall 1989, 247–64.

32. On this point, see Giddens, *op. cit.*, note 21. Of additional interest here is the growing popularity of chaos theory in science. See, for example, Gleick, J., *Chaos: Making a New Science*, Harmondsworth, Penguin Books, 1987.

33. Ibid.

34. Among the many advocates of these principles of teaching and learning in the postmodern age are Schlechty, *op. cit.*, note 11 and Sizer, T., *Horace's School: Redesigning the American High School*, Boston, Houghton Mifflin, 1992.

35. This decline of the common school has been analyzed by Holmes, M., "The victory and failure of educational modernism", *Issues in Education*, II(1), 1984, 23–35.

36. For an elaboration of this diagnosis in the United States, see Powell, A., Farrar, E. and Cohen, D., *The Shopping Mall High School: Winners and Losers in the Educational Marketplace*, Boston, Houghton Mifflin, 1985. For an analysis of the British comprehensive school at the end of the modern era, see Hargreaves, D., *The Challenge for the Comprehensive School*, London, Routledge & Kegan Paul, 1982.

37. See Purkey, S. C. and Smith, M. S., "Effective schools: A review', *Elementary School Journal*, 83(4), 1983, 427–52; Lezotte, L. W., "School improvement based on the effective schools research", in Gartner, A. and Lipsky, D. K. (eds), *Beyond Separate Education: Quality Education for All*, Baltimore, MD, Paul H. Brookes, 1989.

38. Reynolds, D. and Parker, A., "School effectiveness and school improvement in the 1990s", in Reynolds, D. and Cuttance, P. (eds), *School Effectiveness: Research, Policy and Practice*, London, Cassell, 1992.

39. For reviews of research on school improvement in comparison with school effectiveness, see Clark, D. L., Lotto, L. S. and Astuto, T. A., "Effective schools and school improvement: A comparative analysis of two lines of enquiry", *Educational Administration Quarterly*, 20(3), 41–68; and Stoll, L., "School effectiveness and school improvement: A meeting of two minds", *International Journal of Educational Research*, forthcoming, 1993.

40. This is the fundamental problem of Holmes' proposed market-based solution to the collapse of the common school he ably identifies in historical terms. See Holmes, *op. cit.*, note 35. Arguably the most influential advocates of markets and choice in education are

Chubb, J. E. and Moe, T. E., *Politics, Markets and America's Schools*, Washington, DC, The Brookings Institution, 1990. I have developed the critique of patterns of educational policy which appeal to the market force of parental choice in Hargreaves, A. and Reynolds, D., "Decomprehensivization", in Hargreaves, A. and Reynolds, D., *Educational Policies: Controversies and Critiques*, London and Washington, DC, Falmer Press, 1989.

41. David Harvey in *The Condition of Postmodernity* (*op. cit.*, note 2, p. 292) argues that

> The greater the ephemerality, the more pressing the need to discover or manufacture some kind of eternal truth that might lie therein. The religious revival that has become much stronger since the late sixties, and the search for authenticity and authority in politics . . . are cases in point. The revival of interest in basic institutions (such as the family and community) and the search for historical roots are all signs of a search for more secure moorings and longer lasting values in a shifting world.

Part of the postmodern condition, he says, is the existence of "an individualistic society of transients [which] sets forth its nostalgia for common values" (p. 288). The reinventions of tradition which result, he continues, most benefit those social elites whose knowledge such reinventions value. Christopher Lasch in *The True and Only Heaven: Progress and Its Critics*, New York, W. W. Norton, 1991, puts it even more simply. Nostalgia, he says, is "the abdication of memory" (p. 82). "Nostalgia does not entail the exercise of memory at all, since the past it idealizes stands outside time, frozen in unchanging perfection" (p. 83).

42. In this respect, the complaints of teachers and others about capricious shifts in educational fads and fashions, about pendulums swinging too far, or babies being thrown out with bathwater are less trite than their cliché-ridden expression suggests. Embodied in them is a deep distrust of excessive administrative or political confidence in singular and certain solutions of educational reform, which overlook and override the practical wisdom of teachers and the peculiarities of the different settings in which they work.

43. See, for example, Hunter, M., "Knowing, teaching and supervising", in Hosford, P. (ed.), *Using What We Know About Teaching*, Alexandria, VA., Association for Supervision and Curriculum Development, 1984, pp. 169–92.

44. For example, see Popkewitz, T. and Lind, K., "Teacher incentives as reforms: Teachers' work and the changing control mechanisms in education", *Teachers College Record*, 90(4), 1989, 575–94.

45. See Hallinger, P. and Murphy, J., "Instructional leadership in the school context", in Greenfield, W. (ed.), *Instructional Leadership: Concepts, Issues and Controversies*, Boston, MA, Allyn & Bacon, 1987, pp. 17–203.

46. See the articles in *Educational Evaluation and Policy Analysis*, 12(3), Fall 1990.

47. Smyth, J. and Garman, N., "Supervision as school reform: A critical perspective", *Journal of Education Policy*, 14(4), 1989, 343–61.

48. Robertson, H., "Teacher development and gender equity", in Hargreaves, A. and Fullan, M. (eds), *Understanding Teacher Development*, London, Cassell and New York, Teachers College Press, 1992, p. 46.

49. Robertson's reference is to Joyce, B. and Showers, B., *Student Achievement through Staff Development*, New York, Longman, 1988. The reference to Edmonds's work cited by

Joyce and Showers is Edmonds, R., "Some schools work and more can", *Social Policy*, 9(5), 1979, 28–32.

50. Robertson, *op. cit.*, note 49, p. 46.

51. The advocacy for menus over mandates in teaching strategies and staff development practice, is developed in Hargreaves, A., "Restructuring restructuring: Postmodernity and the prospects for educational change", *Journal of Education Policy*, forthcoming; and in Fullan, M. and Hargreaves, A., *What's Worth Fighting For?: Working Together for Your School*, Toronto, Ontario Public School Teachers' Federation; Milton Keynes, Open University Press, The Network, North East Lab, US; and Melbourne, Australian Council for Educational Administration, 1991.

52. On organizations in general, see Drucker, P. F. "The coming of the new organization", *Harvard Business Review*, 66(1), January/February, 1988. Also Drucker, P., *The New Realities*, Oxford, Heinemann Professional Publishing, 1989. In education, the burden of bureaucracies has been outlined in the following way by Shedd and Bacharach:

> Bureaucracies . . . are the natural result when administrative superiors are compelled to rely on the discretion of subordinates to apply general principles to unique and unpredictable situations, and when superiors resort to general rules and procedures (rather than specific instructions and direct supervision) to control the performance of their subordinates.

See Shedd, J. B. and Bacharach, S. B., *Tangled Hierarchies: Teachers as Professionals and the Management of Schools*, San Francisco, Jossey-Bass, 1991, p. 5. The implications of changing patterns of organization for the theory and practice of educational administration are outlined in Taylor, W., *The New Political World of Educational Administration*, paper presented to 1991 Australian Council for Educational Administration conference, Sea World NARA Resort, Gold Coast, September 1991.

53. The nature and effects of these *cubbyhole* structures are described and defined in Toffler, A., *Powershift*, New York, Bantam Books, 1990. The gravitational pull of subject departmentalization on efforts to move toward curriculum integration are described in Chapter 10.

54. These patterns are described in Hargreaves, A. and Earl, L., *Rights of Passage*, Toronto, Queen's Printer, 1990, and in Inner London Education Authority, *Improving Secondary Schools*, London, ILEA, 1984.

55. The effects of time–space compression and accelerated change on organizational decision-making in general are described in Leinberger, P. and Tucker, B., *The New Individualists: The Generation after the Organization Man*, New York, HarperCollins, 1991. The more specific effects of overload on educational leadership are described in Fullan, M., *What's Worth Fighting For in the Principalship*, Toronto, Ontario Public School Teachers' Federation, 1988.

56. See Toffler, *op. cit.*, note 53 and Reich, *op. cit.*, note 10. Examples and explanations of proactive and reactive stances to change among a range of secondary schools and their consequences for the teachers concerned are to be found in Hargreaves, A., Davis, J., Fullan, M., Wignall, R., Stager, M. and Macmillan, R., *Secondary School Work Cultures and Educational Change*, final report of a project funded by the OISE Transfer Grant, Toronto, Ontario Institute for Studies in Education, 1992.

57. See, for example, Leinberger and Tucker, *op. cit.*, note 55, and Taylor, W., *op. cit.*, note 52.

58. Kanter, R. M., Stein, B. A. and Jick, T. D., *The Challenge of Organizational Change*, New York, The Free Press, 1992, p. 3.

59. Kanter *et al.*, note 58, pp. 12–13.

60. Whyte, W. H., Jr, *The Organization Man*, New York, Simon & Schuster, 1956.

61. Leinberger and Tucker, *op. cit.*, note 55.

62. I take the term "glitterspeak" here from a document titled *Beyond the Glitterspeak*, which analyzes and outlines strategies for collaborative networks and processes among the different partners in education. See Ontario Teachers' Federation, *Beyond the Glitterspeak*, submission to the Ontario Government cabinet, Toronto, Ontario Teachers' Federation, 1992.

63. Leinberger and Tucker, *op. cit.*, note 55.

64. Toffler, *op. cit.*, note 53.

65. Ibid, p. 215.

66. Ibid, p. 216.

67. Senge, P., *The Fifth Discipline*, New York, Doubleday, 1990.

68. Barth, R.S., *Improving Schools from Within*, San Francisco, Jossey-Bass, 1990.

69. Fullan, M., *Change Forces*, London and Washington, DC, Falmer Press, 1992.

70. Menzies, H., *Fast Forward and Out of Control*, *op. cit.*, note 15.

71. Ibid, p. 151.

72. These spatial aspects of the postmodern economy are described by Harvey, *op. cit.*, note 2.

73. See Caldwell, B. and Spinks, J., *The Self-Managing School*, Lewes, Falmer Press, 1988 and Caldwell, B. and Spinks, J., *Leading the Self-Managing School*, London and Washington, DC, Falmer Press, 1992.

74. I have developed this argument elsewhere particularly with regard to the implications of the local management of schools (LMS) in England and Wales. See Hargreaves, A. and Reynolds, D., *op. cit.*, note 40.

75. I have argued this more extensively in Hargreaves, A., *Curriculum and Assessment Reform*, Milton Keynes, Open University Press and Toronto, OISE Press, 1989.

76. Renihan, F. I. and Renihan, P., "Educational leadership: A renaissance metaphor", *Education Canada*, Spring 1992, p. 11.

77. See Giddens, A., *Modernity and Self-Identity*, Cambridge, Polity Press, 1991; Also Gilbert, R., "Citizenship, education and postmodernity", *British Journal of Sociology of Education*, 13(1), 1992, 51–68.

78. Taylor, C., *Sources of the Self*, Cambridge, MA, Harvard University Press, 1989, pp. 487–8.

79. Ibid, p. 488. These are Taylor's characterizations of the postmodern position, and not the position which he himself holds.

80. See Giddens, A., *Modernity and Self-Identity*, *op. cit.*, note 77.

81. Lasch, C., *The Culture of Narcissism*, New York, W. W. Norton, 1979.

82. *Op. cit.*, p. 120.

83. Ibid, p. 171.

84. Ibid, p. 171.

85. Giddens, *op. cit.*, note 77.

86. See Leinberger and Tucker, *op. cit.*, note 55.

87. The empowerment side of the argument is put most forcefully by Giddens in *The Consequences of Modernity*, *op. cit.*, note 21.

88. Taylor, *op. cit.*, note 78.

89. Taylor, C., *The Malaise of Modernity*, Concord, Ontario, House of Amansi Press, 1991, p. 15.

90. Baudrillard, J. *Simulations*, Columbia University, New York, Semiotext, 1983.

91. This is not an argument against researching lives, stories and narratives in teaching, but it is an argument against studying them in isolation from their social context.

92. Leithwood, K., "The principal's role in teacher development", in Fullan, M. and Hargreaves, A., *Teacher Development and Educational Change*, Philadelphia, Falmer Press, 1991.

93. On teacher development as self-development, see Clark, C. K. M., "Teachers as designers in self-directed professional development", in Hargreaves, A. and Fullan, M., *Understanding Teacher Development*, London, Cassell and New York, Teachers College Press, 1992; Oberg, A. and Underwood, S., "Facilitating teacher self-development: Reflections on experience", in Hargreaves and Fullan, *op. cit.*, Hunt, D., *Beginning with Ourselves*, Toronto, OISE Press, 1987.

94. On the distinctive properties of teachers' personal practical knowledge, see, for example, Connelly, F. M. and Clandinin, D. J., *Teachers as Curriculum Planners: Narratives of Experience*, New York, Teachers College Press, 1988; Clandinin, D. J., *Classroom Practice: Teacher Images in Action*, London and Philadelphia, Falmer Press, 1986; Elbaz, F. L., *Teacher Thinking: A Study of Practical Knowledge*, London, Croom Helm, 1983.

95. Young, A., "Television viewing", *Canadian Social Trends*, Autumn 1989, 14–15.

96. Lowe, G., "Computer literacy", *Canadian Social Trends*, (19), Winter 1990, 13–14.

97. Ibid.

98. This retort to relevance in the conventional sense has been made very effectively by Egan, K., *Teaching as Storytelling*, London, Routledge, 1988.

99. Baudrillard, J., *America*, London and New York, Verso Press, 1988, pp. 33–4.

100. Baudrillard, J., *Simulations*, *op. cit.*, note 90, p. 11.

101. Ibid, p. 12.

102. Ibid, p. 5.

103. Ibid, p. 5.

104. Eco, U., *Travels in Hyperreality*, San Diego, CA, Harcourt Brace Jovanovich, 1990, pp. 50–1.

105. Johnson, D. W. and Johnson, P. T., "Social skills for successful group work", *Educational Leadership*, 47(4), 1989/1990, 29–33.

106. Kagan, S., "Constructive controversy", *Cooperative Learning*, 10(3), 1990, 20–6.

107. Rudduck, J., *Innovation and Change*, Milton Keynes, Open University Press and Toronto, OISE Press, 1990; and Quicke, J., "Personal and social education: A triangulated evaluation of an innovation", *Educational Review*, 38(3), 1986.

108. Thompson, E. P., "Time, work-discipline and industrial capitalism", *Past and Present*, 38, 1967, 56–97.

109. Toffler, *op. cit.*, note 53, p. 229.

110. Ibid, pp. 390–1.

PART TWO

TIME AND WORK

Chapter 5

Time
Quality or Quantity? The Faustian Bargain

INTRODUCTION

Time is the enemy of freedom. Or so it seems to teachers. Time presses down the fulfillment of their wishes. It pushes against the realization of their wants. Time compounds the problem of innovation and confounds the implementation of change. It is central to the formation of teachers' work.

Teachers take their time seriously. They experience it as a major constraint on what they are able and expected to achieve in their schools. "No time", "not enough time", "need more time" — these are verbal gauntlets that teachers repeatedly throw in the path of enthusiastic innovators.

The relationship of time to the teacher runs still deeper than this. Time is a fundamental dimension through which teachers' work is constructed and interpreted by themselves, their colleagues and those who administer and supervise them. Time for the teacher is not just an objective, oppressive constraint but also a subjectively defined horizon of possibility and limitation. Teachers can take time and make time, just as much as they are likely to see time schedules and time commitments as fixed and immutable. Through the prism of time we can therefore begin to see ways in which teachers construct the nature of their work at the same time as they are constrained by it. Time, that is, is a major element in the *structuration* of teachers' work.[1] Time structures the work of teaching and is in turn structured through it. Time is therefore more than a minor organizational contingency, inhibiting or facilitating management's attempts to bring about change. Its definition and imposition form part of the very core of teachers' work and of the policies and perceptions of those who administer it.

This chapter identifies and analyzes different dimensions of time and their implications for teachers' work. These dimensions are not just competing or complementary theoretical perspectives; different ways of looking at time by the theorist. They also constitute different facets of how time itself is constructed and interpreted in the social world at large and within teachers' work in particular.

This analysis of time and teachers' work arises from a study of elementary principals' and teachers' perceptions and uses of preparation or planning time within the school day. Full details of the study are provided in the next chapter. For now, it is necessary to know only that the study took place in 12 elementary schools in two school boards in Ontario, Canada where, as a result of collective bargaining agreements, elementary teachers had acquired a guaranteed minimum amount of scheduled time — usually 120 minutes per week, sometimes more — for purposes of preparation, planning and other support activities. The study focused not just on perceptions and uses of preparation time in particular, but also on the broader aspects of teachers' work outside their scheduled class time. This chapter develops understandings of the relationship of time to teachers' work which emerged from the project as data were being analyzed. References to the study are at this point illustrative in character, selected to highlight particular features of the theoretical framework. More systematic discussion of the data and findings of the study are presented in succeeding chapters.

There are four interrelated dimensions of time I want to pick out for discussion, particularly as they apply to teachers' work. They are technical–rational time, micropolitical time, phenomenological time and sociopolitical time.

1. TECHNICAL–RATIONAL TIME

Within the *technical–rational* dimension of time, time is a finite *resource* or *means* which can be increased, decreased, managed, manipulated, organized or reorganized in order to accommodate selected educational purposes. This dimension of time is dominant within forms of administrative action and interpretation which embody and are organized around modernistic principles of technical rationality. As writers like Habermas and Schön have pointed out, and as I argued in Chapter 2, technical–rational forms of thought and action involve a clear separation between means and ends.[2] Ends and purposes, here, belong to the value-based domains of philosophical, moral or political choice. Once ends have been chosen, the most efficient means of determining them, it is thought, can be identified instrumentally and scientifically, then implemented managerially and administratively. Time, in such a view, is an objective variable, an instrumental, organizational condition that can be managerially manipulated in order to foster the implementation of educational changes whose purpose and desirability have been determined elsewhere. The purpose of educational research and administration, therefore, is to identify and institute allocations and uses of teacher time which facilitate the realization of desired educational objectives.

In an important and insightful paper, Walter Werner defines this view of time as "objective time", "public time" or "fixed time". Such time, he notes, is the very basis of planning:

> It is particularly the point of view of the curriculum developer,
> who may be responsible for initiating change, and of

administrators who conceive implementation along timelines or
think of successive stages or levels of program use.[3]

Within this view, if implementation problems are encountered, objective time
can be administratively adjusted or reallocated accordingly.

The objective, technical–rational dimension of time is important not only in
the more obvious areas of efficient management or productive use of time,[4] to
which I shall return later, but also in enhancing or inhibiting preferred educational changes which affect the character and orientation of teachers' work.
Reviewing work on curriculum development and change, Fullan has concluded
that the provision of small amounts of time can create real benefits.[5] In the
United States, Bird and Little have argued that time is particularly important
for breaking down teacher isolation and developing norms of collegiality:

> The most important resource for improvement is time with
> colleagues; time for teachers to study, analyze and advance their
> practices; time for principals, assistant principals, department
> heads and teacher leaders to support improvement; time for
> faculties to examine, debate and improve their norms of civility,
> instruction and improvement. Considerably more time for these
> activities should be made in the normal school day, either by
> addition or by the elimination of activities that are less
> important.[6]

In Britain, Campbell has concluded that current "teacher working conditions . . . seem stuck on the anachronistic assumption that there is no need to
provide time for curriculum development".[7] Campbell has identified four kinds
of time that were used to carry out and support school-based curriculum development in the ten schools he studied. These were *group time*, for collaborative
planning, conducted after school and perceived as a voluntary, moral commitment; *snatched time* of rushed consultation with other teachers during the
school day; *personal time* out of school for individual reading, planning and
attendance of courses; and *other contact time* (or preparation time) where
teachers are scheduled away from their class. He found that "other contact" or
scheduled preparation time was extremely scarce in British primary schools.

In all these cases, increased amounts of scheduled time available for
teachers outside the classroom are viewed as an exceptionally important condition of staff collegiality and curriculum development. Time here is a scarce
resource worth supplying in greater measure to secure school improvement.
However, while extensions and reallocations of teacher time away from class
may indeed be conditions of increased collaboration and collegiality, they are not
entirely sufficient in this regard. Campbell has noted that on the rare occasions
when preparation time *was* made available in British primary schools, it was
used more for relaxation and individual preparation and marking than for
collaborative planning and review. In Chapter 8, we will see that in one of the

school boards involved in the preparation time study, such time was also used mainly for individual rather than collaborative purposes. Moreover, even in the second board, which was explicitly committed to collaborative planning, not all teachers who were interviewed planned with their colleagues, and many of those who did preferred to plan at times other than during their scheduled preparation periods.

In terms of being a technical means or resource for realizing educational purposes of staff collaboration and curriculum development — for changing the nature and understanding of teachers' work — time therefore has its limitations, however generously it is made available. Additional time does not itself guarantee educational change. In that case, from the innovator's standpoint, there is, or there ought to be, more to teacher time than its technically efficient allocation, planning and scheduling. How that time is used and interpreted is also important. The contribution of dimensions of time other than the technical-rational one to the formation and reformation of teachers' work must therefore be considered.

2. MICROPOLITICAL TIME

Once they are in place in a school, once they have taken on a certain external objectivity, scheduled time distributions between different teachers, grades and subjects are more than informative guides as to who is where and at what time.[8] They are more even than rationally calculated, technically efficient ways of distributing time according to educational need within the limits of available resources such as rooms and staff expertise. Time distributions also reflect dominant configurations of power and status within schools and school systems. They have micropolitical significance.

The micropolitical significance of time scheduling in schools is apparent in several ways. Within the curriculum, for instance, the higher-status subjects, most notably the "academic" subjects, receive more generous time allocations, are granted more favorable scheduling slots and are more likely to be made compulsory than the lower-status, practical subjects.[9] These time distributions, and the staffing needs they generate, both reflect and reinforce the strength and size of departments in the higher-status areas, creating more opportunities for senior appointments and the flexible working conditions which come with these. Time granted to certain curriculum areas therefore rebounds on time available to the teachers working within those areas. This simple fact of vested, material interests accruing to the teacher is one reason why allocations granted to more favored subjects are protected and defended so vehemently.[10]

Within the wider domain of teachers' work, the way in which elementary teachers in particular have virtually all their scheduled time allocated to the classroom reveals that the dominant, overwhelming conception of teachers' work is *classroom* work. Classroom work forms the heart of teaching, as it is usually understood. Relatively speaking, all other activities are peripheral or supplementary by comparison. Time away from this fundamental core commitment to plan, prepare, evaluate and consult is as much an indicator of status and power which permits the teacher concerned to be "away", as it is of any specific educational need.

As one moves up the hierarchy of power and prestige in educational administration, one also moves further away from the classroom, from the conventional, core definition of what a teacher is. Principals and headteachers have more time away from class than assistant principals and deputy headteachers. They, in turn, have more time away than "regular" teachers. Such differences are to be found *within* the regular teaching community, too, reflecting differences of status and power between its constituent parts. In this respect, the fact that secondary school teachers receive more preparation and planning time than elementary teachers, or that intermediate or junior high school teachers have until recently received more of this time than kindergarten or primary teachers, does not so much reflect substantial and substantive differences in planning and preparation needs, as it does historically grounded and sex-related differences between two very different traditions of teaching. One of these is deeply rooted in an elite, male-dominated, schoolmaster tradition devoted to the education of able pupils for university entrance, business and the professions. The other is rooted in a female-saturated elementary tradition devoted to the compulsory education and socialization of the young.[11] Much of the struggle to secure increased time away from class for elementary teachers therefore has to do with fundamental issues of parity and status within the teaching profession, with attempts to redress an historical legacy of inequity between the work of (usually female) elementary and (more often male) secondary school teachers, respectively.

The arguments surrounding increased preparation and planning time for elementary teachers are therefore only partly related to rational cases concerning actual preparation and planning needs. Such arguments are also bound up with competing status claims within the teaching profession, in particular with attempts to extend the definition of elementary teachers' work beyond the classroom. Time for the elementary teacher to be away from class is, in this respect, more than a technical issue of administrative adjustment or improved resourcing. It is an issue awash with micropolitical implications.

3. PHENOMENOLOGICAL TIME

In schedules and timetables, in timeliness and time constraints, time can seem external to the teacher, as if it had an existence all of is own. Yet there is also an important *subjective* dimension to time. Indeed, we shall see later that time is essentially and unavoidably a subjective phenomenon. What counts and comes to be seen as objective time, even in the form of clock time, is in fact nothing more than an agreed, intersubjective convention. Schedules and timetables which we may experience as external, constraining and unalterable are actually the product of subjective definition and decision-making. Structures of time are, in this sense, the outcome of human action, although once in place they also provide a context for such action. This is the fundamental principle of the *structuration* of time. It is a principle that leads us to question the apparent naturalness of existing time allocations and distributions and to investigate their social origins and interpretation.

There is a further aspect to subjective time. This resides not in the very constitution of time itself, but runs alongside and is at variance with the ordered, linear schedules of objective time. We might call this the *phenomenological* dimension of time. It is one where time is subjective, where time is lived, where time has an inner duration which varies from person to person.[12] A person's inner sense of time may be at variance with clock time and may seem to "fly" or "drag" by comparison.[13] People's senses of time may also be at variance with one another. Time often passes differently for us than it does for our fellows.

Subjective variations in our senses of time are grounded in other aspects of our lives: in our projects, interests and activities, and the kinds of demands they make upon us. Our work, our occupations, the roles we have in life, bundle together these projects, activities and interests in particular ways, so that our senses of time vary with the kinds of work we do and with the kinds of roles we take on in life. Shakespeare, whose writing gains much of its comedic and tragic force from his acute sensitivity to phenomenological differences of understanding and interpretation between his characters, has written with great perceptiveness on subjective differences in senses of time and the ways in which they are bound up with our wider life projects. In *As You Like It*, he presents this conversation between Rosalind and Orlando:[14]

> *Ros:* I pray you, what is't o'clock?
>
> *Or:* You should ask me, what time o'day; there's no clock in the forest.
>
> *Ros:* Then there is no true lover in the forest; else sighing every minute and groaning every hour would detect the lazy foot of Time as well as a clock.
>
> *Or:* And why not the swift foot of Time? Had not that been as proper?
>
> *Ros:* By no means, sir. Time travels in divers paces with divers persons. I'll tell you who Time ambles withal, who Time trots withal, who Time gallops withal, and who he stands still withal . . .
>
> *Or:* Who ambles Time withal?
>
> *Ros:* With a priest that lacks Latin, and a rich man that hath not the gout; for the one sleeps easily because he cannot

study, and the other lives merrily because he feels no pain;
the one lacking the burden of lean and wasteful learning,
the other knowing no burden of heavy tedious penury.
These Time ambles withal.

Or: Who doth he gallop withal?

Ros: With a thief to the gallows; for though he go as softly as
foot can fall he thinks himself too soon there.

Or: Who stays it still withal?

Ros: With lawyers in the vacation, for they sleep between term
and term, and then they perceive not how Time moves.

As Shakespeare's lines suggest, subjective time varies with occupation and preoccupation. In this respect, the occupations, preoccupations and related time senses of administrators and innovators on the one hand, and ordinary teachers on the other, are very different.

Werner has usefully outlined some of these differences in time perspective and their importance for the process of curriculum implementation. For Werner, it would seem that administrators and innovators are very much the guardians of "objective" time:

> Program documents and the strategies for their implementation,
> together with the school's organization, assume a notion of time
> that is objective, rationalized and administrative in interest. As
> such, implementation is shaped by objective-time, not only as
> measured by the classroom clock, but also by the structure of
> the new program.[15]

Werner describes how teachers, within the context of their own classroom structures, experience time in a way that conflicts with the time assumptions built into the administrator's innovation schedules. He presents data showing that, in the context of innovation, teachers feel pressure and anxiety because of excessive time demands, along with guilt and frustration because they are implementing the new program less quickly and efficiently than the administrative timelines require. From the teacher's standpoint, new program requirements are imposed with little regard for the teacher's existing pressures and demands, and with little guidance as to how the new requirements can be integrated with existing practices and routines. To the teacher, the time expectations built into the innovation therefore seem excessive and a conflict of time perspective emerges between the teacher and the administrator. Here, the administrator appears insensitive to the teacher's subjective time perspective and the working conditions in which it is grounded. It is at this point that teachers' requests and demands for more time, additional planning time or relaxed innovation timelines are likely to be strongest.

From the standpoint of the classroom, there are, then, almost certainly

Table 5.1 Monochronic and polychronic time-frames [17]

Monochronic time-frames	Polychronic time-frames
One thing at a time	Several things at once
Completion of schedules	Completion of transactions
Low sensitivity to context	High sensitivity to context
Control over completion of schedules	Control over description and evaluation of tasks
Orientation to schedules and procedures	Orientation to people and relationships
"Western" cultures	Amerindian and Latin cultures
Official sphere of business and professions	"Unofficial" sphere of informality and domestic life
Large organizations	Small organizations
Male	Female

major differences of subjective time perspective between administrators and teachers which have important implications for the management of educational change. A useful way of conceptualizing some of these differences is in terms of a distinction drawn by the anthropologist, Edward Hall, between *monochronic* and *polychronic* conceptions of time. [16]

According to Hall, people operating with a *monochronic* time-frame concentrate on doing one thing at a time, in series, as a linear progression through a set of discrete stages. They focus their energies on completing schedules and dispatching the business as well as they can within those schedules (rather like the way some doctors deal with long lists of patients). There is little sensitivity to the particularities of context or the needs of the moment within this time-frame. It is the schedule and its successful completion that have priority. Indeed, those who exercise administrative control within a monochronic time-frame try to exert high control over timelines and schedules to ensure that the work of the organization is successfully completed (but they are, however, less precise about the task itself; about what would count as successful completion). Within such work, the completion of tasks, schedules and procedures predominates over the cultivation of relationships with people. Monochronic time is pervasive throughout most Western cultures (though not Mediterranean ones); it overwhelmingly dominates the worlds of business and the professions; it is characteristic of large, bureaucratic organizations; and, perhaps most interestingly of all, it is most widespread among males. (See Table 5.1).

By comparison, within *polychronic* time people concentrate on doing several things at once, in combination. Their interest is less in meeting schedules than in successfully completing their transactions (for the polychronic doctor, the next patient must wait until the current case has been adequately dealt with, however long that takes). Within polychronic time-frames, there is a heightened sensitivity to context, to the implications and complications of immediate circumstances and surroundings. Those who exercise administrative control from a polychronic perspective allow subordinates high discretion over time schedules, over when tasks are to be completed. However, compared to those operating within a monochronic frame of reference, they are likely to exert much stricter control over the description and evaluation of the task itself. Here, it is important not merely that a job has been completed, but that it has been completed in line with initial intentions and definitions. Relationships predominate in the polychronic time-frame, rather than things. Polychronic time is more people-oriented than task-oriented. It is prominent in Amerindian and Latin or Mediterranean-style cultures; it is common within the spheres of informal relationships and domestic life (an intensive, densely packed sphere of multiple tasks and interpersonal relationships); it is more likely to be found in smaller, more personally led organizations; and it is more usually found among women than it is among men.

Monochronic time-frames and the technical–rational conception of time to which they give rise have the advantage of ensuring that business gets done in large organizations where many separate activities require coordination and integration. However, Hall argues, organizations locked into monochronic time tend to grow rigid and lose sight of their original purpose. They try to bulldoze through changes and impose timelines which are insensitive to the peculiarities of circumstance and context, and to the interpersonal relations which comprise them. They put more emphasis on the *appearance* of performance and change being achieved than on the quality and character of the performance or the change itself. Most important of all, perhaps, they dehumanize the organization in fundamental respects, alienating members from themselves by restricting sensitivity to context. This is particularly true where a dominant, male administrative culture of a monochronic kind comes into contact with a polychronically inclined female membership. Hall puts it like this:

> modern management has accentuated the monochronic side at
> the expense of the less manageable and less predictable
> polychronic side. Virtually everything in our culture works for
> and rewards a monochronic view of the world. But the
> antihuman aspect of M[onochronic] is alienating, especially to
> women. Unfortunately, too many women have "bought" the
> M[onochronic] time world, not realizing that unconscious sexism
> is part of it . . . Women sense there is something alien about the
> way in which modern organizations handle time . . . As soon as
> one enters the door of the office, one becomes immediately locked
> into a monochronic, monolithic structure that is virtually
> impossible to change.[18]

In education, the distinction between monochronic and polychronic time-frames has been applied interestingly to explanations of resistance to schooling among working-class youth. Here, McLaren has shown how, within their street culture, working-class adolescents are oriented to and immersed in rich, poly-chronic time-frames where many things happen at once in a densely packed, complicated and fast-moving set of interpersonal relationships. Such students, McLaren observes, resist the bureaucratically controlled, monochronic world of the classroom, with its depersonalized processing of single tasks in linear, one-at-a-time fashion.[19] Differences in time-frame between teachers and adminis-trators, I want to propose, may be just as significant and illuminating as these time-related differences between teachers and their students.[20]

The world of the school, and of the elementary school in particular, is a world where a predominantly female teaching force comes into contact with a pre-dominantly male administration. As Apple in the United States, Curtis in Canada and Purvis in the United Kingdom have all pointed out, elementary teachers' work is for deep, historical reasons chiefly women's work.[21] The con-trol, administration and supervision of elementary teachers' work is, in this res-pect, overwhelmingly a process whereby supervising men manage the working lives of women. This heavily gendered process in the administration of teachers' work has important implications for the relationship of time to teachers' work and to educational change.

The elementary school teacher's world is profoundly polychronic in charac-ter. This is increasingly so as one moves from the higher to the lower age ranges. It is a complex, densely packed world where the sophisticated skills of the teacher must be directed to dealing with many things at the same time. The simultaneous operation of several learning centers runs on this principle, for instance. As Philip Jackson put it, the elementary school classroom has a paramount feeling of *immediacy* about it.[22] It is a world deeply grounded in intense, sustained and subtly shifting interpersonal relationships among large groups of children, and between these children and their teacher. It is a world less punctuated by the bell and the timetable than the secondary school; a world where projects can be and must be pursued and interests and activities juggled according to the vicissitudes of the moment. The culture of the elementary school classroom – a predominantly female culture – is therefore a culture with high sensitivity to unpredictabilities and particularities of context, to the importance of interpersonal relationships, and to the successful completion of the tasks-in-hand. Characteristically, for the female elementary teacher, the requirements of the immediate context, the activities to be completed in that context, and the people to be catered for in that context take precedence over implementation timelines, or requirements to fill up officially designated pre-paration time with administratively "appropriate" work.

Conflicts and misunderstandings occur when this polychronic culture of female elementary teachers comes into contact with a monochronic culture of male administration which is less sensitive to classroom context. This can occur with inflexible imposition of implementation plans, for instance. Conflicts and misunderstandings can also arise when administrators designate preparation time for particular purposes like collaborative planning and overlook how inappropriate and incongruous those scheduled purposes might be for some teachers, given the particular contexts in which they work. This is the problem of what I call *contrived collegiality*, which I examine in Chapter 9.

As we will see in later chapters, the colleague with whom one is scheduled to collaborate may not be personally amenable or compatible, for instance. The "expert" (for instance, the special education teacher) whom a teacher is time-tabled to meet may have less qualified expertise than the teacher who is meeting him or her. Teachers may find it more convenient and productive to collaborate after school or during the lunch hour rather than in scheduled preparation time — a time they may prefer to use for other purposes like telephoning or photocopying when those facilities are not in heavy demand from other staff. These examples indicate how teachers' needs and demands generated from the particularities of the context may obstruct, undermine or redefine the purposes built into new administrative procedures and the time designations and allocations which accompany them. In this strained juxtaposition of monochronic and polychronic time-frames can be seen much of the reason for the apparent failure of administratively imposed reforms in education.

What are the policy implications of these intersubjective differences in time perspective between teachers and administrators? For Werner, what matters is that administrators become more aware of and sensitive toward the different time perspectives of the teachers their innovations will affect. "Program developers", he states, "can ask themselves what their work assumes about and implies for the teachers' time."[23] More specifically, he argues, "Once a project is underway, there needs to be sensitivity to lived-time and a willingness to continuously modify timelines, as well as an openness to criticism of the reasons for how time is allocated."[24]

Werner's recommendations are important here, insofar as they try to bring the two time-frames (lived and objective) closer together and to increase administrators' awareness and understanding of the complexities of teachers' work. However, I believe they do not go far enough, for two reasons.

First, they allow and do not challenge the implication that "fixed", "objective" or "technical–rational" time has an existential or administrative superiority compared to "lived", "subjective" or "phenomenological" time. They leave open the implication that teachers' subjective time perspectives are important but also imperfect, to be accommodated and incorporated by a more caring but ultimately condescending administration. This begs important questions about the validity, relevance and practicality of time perspectives grounded in one frame of reference (an administrative one) for organizing the details of teachers' work which are grounded in another.

Second, the appeal to heightened administrative sensitivity concerning time issues begs the question of how and why monochronic time-frames have become administratively dominant in the first place. It does not address the significant possibility that issues concerning the control of teachers' work may be located not just in the conflict between a "superordinate", monochronic time perspective which *happens to be* the domain of administration, and a "subordinate" polychronic time perspective which *happens to be* the domain of ordinary teachers, but that such issues may be located in the very principles and constitution of monochronic time perspectives themselves as they are developed and applied through apparatuses of administrative control.

The first matter can be dealt with by reference to the *physics* of time which challenges any spurious objectivity that might be claimed by the advocates and defenders of particular time perspectives. The second poses important questions about the *sociopolitical* nature of time in organizational settings; about the reasons why monochronic time perspectives become administratively dominant in the first place. I shall turn to these next.

The important baseline from which to commence evaluations of the relative merits of different subjective senses of time is Einstein's widely accepted principle that *physical* time is relative. There are no absolute fixed points in space or in time. In this sense, objective time as such has no independent physical existence. It is a human construction and convention around which most of us unquestioningly organize our lives.

In his brilliant and accessible explanation of theories of relativity, Stephen Hawking describes how time is related to the speed of light. For one thing, he explains, time slows down as one approaches the speed of light.[25] For another, time appears to run more slowly when it approaches a massive body like the Earth. Indeed, Hawking describes experiments conducted with clocks mounted at the top and bottom of water towers which resulted in the clocks nearer the Earth running more slowly.[26]

I will return to and expand upon this argument shortly because, as an analogy, it has immense implications for the sociopolitical dimension of time. The simple point I want to establish for the moment is that concerning the physical relativity of time. This is exceptionally important, for, given that physical time is truly relative, defenders of "objective", "monochronic" or "technical–rational" time cannot appeal to the natural laws of the physical world as justification for the worth and superiority of their own particular time perspectives. Claims advanced in favor of or against the monochronic time-frames of administrators must therefore be evaluated on other grounds, including social and political ones.

4. SOCIOPOLITICAL TIME

Monochronic time-frames prevail administratively in education not because they accord more readily with the laws of the natural world, nor because they are necessarily more educationally effective or administratively efficient. They prevail, rather, because they are the prerogative of the powerful. In conflicts between different time perspectives, just as in conflicts between other subjective world views, Berger and Luckmann's principle most usually applies – that those who define reality are those who have the biggest stick.[27] In this respect, the sociopolitical dimension of time, the way in which particular forms of time come to be administratively dominant, is a central element in the administrative control of teachers' work and of the curriculum implementation process. Within the modern realizations of this time dimension, two complementary elements appear to be especially important: *separation* and *colonization*.

Separation

An important part of the sociopolitical dimension of time is the separation of interest, responsibility and associated time perspective between the adminis-trator and the teacher. A return, by analogy, to Hawking's description of the physical properties of time will illustrate what is at issue here:

> Another prediction of general relativity is that time should
> appear to run slower nearer a massive body like the earth. This
> is because there is a relation between the energy of light and its
> frequency (that is, the number of waves of light per second): the
> greater the energy, the higher the frequency. As light travels
> upwards in the earth's gravitational field, it loses energy, and so
> its frequency goes down. (This means that the length of time
> between one wave crest and the next goes up.) To someone high
> up, it would appear that everything down below was taking
> longer to happen.[28]

Although it is always advisable to be cautious when transposing proposi-tions from the physical to the social world, the transfer of this particular time principle leads to some potentially fruitful insights for the field of education. In particular, it suggests the following prediction for the process of implementa-tion and change:

> *That the further one is away from the classroom, from the
> densely packed centre of things, as it were, then the slower that
> time will seem to pass there.*

This principle may well explain the widely documented impatience that administrators have with the pace of change in their schools. From their distant standpoint, they see the classroom not in its densely packed complexity, in its pressing immediacy, as the teacher does. Rather, they see it from the point of view of the single change they are supporting and promoting (and on which their own career reputations may also depend) – a change which will tend to stand out from all the other events and pressures of classroom life. Administrators see the classroom monochronically, not polychronically. And, because of that, the changes they are initiating and supporting there seem to move much too slowly for their liking.[29]

For classroom teachers, meanwhile, the pace of change appears to be far too quick. In their position at the very center of things, where they may have to deal with multiple changes, not just one (a new grade assignment, a new social studies program and a collaborative planning initiative, perhaps), and where they must do all this while still having to cope with the continuing, wide-ranging constraints of classroom life, administrative timelines for change are often seen as too ambitious and unrealistic.[30] For the teacher, the classroom is viewed and experienced polychronically, not monochronically. The tendency, therefore, is to simplify change or to slow it down, so that the complicated, polychronic classroom world can be kept within manageable bounds. This helps explain Werner's finding that teachers often try to accommodate the processes of innovation by working slowly:

> Working slowly in the classroom is the result of trying to simultaneously grasp what a program involves, sorting out doubts about how it may best be used, and trying to do an adequate job under such circumstances.[31]

From this clash between the time perspectives of administrators and teachers emerges a curious and ominous paradox. The quicker and more "unrealistic" the implementation timeline, the more the teacher tries to stretch it out. The more the teacher slows the implementation process down, the more impatient the administrator becomes and the more inclined he or she becomes to quicken the pace or tighten the timelines still further, or to impose yet another innovation, one more attempt to secure change. This adds still further pressures and complexities to the teacher's polychronic world, inducing yet more tendencies to slow down the pace of these additional requirements! And so on! And so on!

The result is what some analysts have called the *intensification* of teachers' work: a bureaucratically driven escalation of pressures, expectations and controls concerning what teachers do and how much they should do within the school day.[32] Much of that somewhat self-defeating process of intensification comes from the discrepant time perspectives and understandings that are embodied in the sharp and widening divisions between administration and teaching, planning and execution, development and implementation. I will look more closely at this process of intensification in the next chapter.

The process of separation gives rise not to minor misunderstandings between administrators and teachers on the question of time and work: not to easily remediable problems of interpretation or gaps in communication between them. Separation, rather, creates deep-rooted and endemic differences in time perspective between two groups whose intuitive feel for, sense of and relationship to the daily demands of classroom life are very different. Therefore, the important policy question posed by this principle of separation between administrators and teachers and its relationship to their different perspectives on time is not one concerning needs for greater communication and understanding between the two groups. The key policy question, rather, concerns how great a distinction and how strong a boundary there should be between administrators and teachers in the first place. Should administrative planning be strictly separated from the execution of those plans in the classroom? Should administrators be responsible for development and teachers only for implementation of what has already been developed? If teachers were given a stronger role in curriculum development and time scheduling at school level, for instance, might this then give rise to more realistic, polychronically sensitive timelines for implementation and improvement?

What is at stake within the sociopolitical time-frame, then, is not minor technical matters of communication and understanding between administrators and teachers, but the fundamental structures of responsibility for curriculum development and the place that working teachers should occupy within those structures. What is at stake, no less, is the empowerment of teachers to take on responsibility for curriculum development, in addition to their current technical obligations regarding implementation.

Colonization

If separation drives the worlds of administration and teaching apart, colonization brings them back together, but in a particular form. Colonization is the process where administrators take up or "colonize" teachers' time with their own purposes. It is a second important aspect of the sociopolitical dimension of time.

The administrative colonization of teachers' work is most noticeable and most significant where the private, informal "back regions" of teachers' working lives are taken over by administrative purposes, converting them into public, formal "front regions". In this way, configurations of time and space that used to mark a domain of private relaxation and relief increasingly mark a domain of public business and supervision.

It was the late Erving Goffman who defined and demarcated "front regions" and "back regions" in social life and described the role they played in occupations which dealt with the public.[33] For Goffman, front regions were places of performance where people were, in a sense, "on stage" in front of their clients, the public or their superiors. When working in "front regions", be it in the dining area as a waiter or waitress, in the showroom as a salesperson or in the classroom as a teacher, people have to be careful to monitor and regulate their conduct: to "keep up appearances". "Backstage" areas, by comparison, provide relaxation, relief and withdrawal from the stresses and demands of these "frontstage" performances. Be they restaurant kitchens, factory washrooms or school staffrooms, back regions allow people opportunity to "let everything hang out", as it were. Goffman put it as follows:

> The backstage language consists of reciprocal first naming,
> cooperative decision-making, profanity, open sexual remarks,
> elaborate griping, smoking, rough informal dress, "sloppy" sitting
> and standing posture, use of dialect or sub-standard speech,

mumbling and shouting, playful aggressivity and "kidding",
inconsiderateness for the other in minor but potentially symbolic
acts, minor physical self-involvements such as humming,
whistling, chewing, nibbling, belching, and flatulence.[34]

Back regions may be tightly bounded in time and space — the staffroom, at
recess, for instance — and may be firmly insulated from contact with or observation by clients in the front region (few staffroom doors are left open!). But this
need not necessarily be so. People may sometimes move into backstage mode
within what is ostensibly a frontstage setting. Teachers who come out of their
classroom doors and pass a few words of exasperation across the corridor before
going back to their "performances", teachers who laugh and joke together about
the parents or the kids while on recess duty — these are examples of backstage
modes being invoked in frontstage settings.

To the casual observer, back-region behavior may seem immature, wasteful or unprofessional. And school administrations which seem to permit and
allow more than minimal time and space for such behavior (through the provision of extra "free periods" or preparation time, for instance) may be seen as
officially condoning wastefulness and unprofessionalism among their teachers.
Such judgments, however, would miss essential points about the important purposes and functions fulfilled by back regions in most social settings, including
teaching.

First, back regions assist and allow for the relief of stress. The tact, control and restraint required "onstage" in the classroom, in official meetings
with one's colleagues or in the presence of one's superiors can be relaxed here.
Humor, by-play, diversion on to non-school topics of conversation, moral
support when difficulties have been encountered with management, students
or parents all help teachers restore and reconstruct themselves for the next
set of "performances".[35]

Second, back regions foster informal relations that build trust, solidarity
and fellow-feeling among teachers. Through that, they provide an interpersonal
platform on which the more formal business and decision-making of school life
can be built without fear of mistrust or misunderstanding.

Third, back regions bounded in time and space (like staffroom "break" time)
give teachers a measure of personally controlled flexibility in managing the
polychronically packed and complex character of their working life. They allow
teachers opportunity to stand back from front-region commitments, or to support and extend them, as appropriate. In the latter case, by using staff lunchtime, say, to photocopy materials, telephone parents, referee sports teams,
mark assignments or meet with colleagues, teachers are conducting "frontregion" activities or working in a "front-region" mode within what is essentially a "back-region" setting. What remains fundamental to this setting, as a
"back-region" one, though, is the teachers' flexibility and control over how such
time and space is to be used — be it in "back-region" mode or "front-region"

mode — according to the necessities of the moment in their polychronic and rapidly changing work environment.

In many ways, teachers' work outside the classroom — in particular, the way that time and space are being used there — is becoming a highly contested region between teachers and administrators in terms of its front- and backstage properties. For preparation time, in particular, a key issue is whether teachers will retain discretion to use it in "back region" or "front region" ways, as they see fit, given the needs and demands of the immediate context. Or will such time be colonized by administration for its own purposes, thereby eroding both the "backstage" characteristics of the region and teachers' discretion in the use of time and space within it? Data from the preparation time study suggest that in a number of schools, non-contact time is increasingly being colonized by administrative purposes, converting private back regions into public front ones, subjecting teachers to increasing administrative surveillance.

Teachers interviewed in the study tended to value discretion and flexibility in how they used preparation time and integrated it with the rest of their work outside the classroom. Stress may sometimes make teachers feel it is better to unwind now and plan later. Easy availability of the telephone or the photocopier (compared to the long queues for these things at lunch) may mean it is often best to meet with colleagues on occasions other than scheduled preparation time — after school, for instance. The flow of the program may mean that planning meetings scheduled in preparation time may need to be used only in some weeks, not all. Flexibility on these counts matters for most teachers.

Principals sometimes see things differently. Some principals reported they regard the conduct of "personal business" like telephoning the garage as an illegitimate use of preparation time, or proudly proclaimed they *never* see their teachers *just* having a coffee during that time (with similar implications of illegitimacy). Some principals require particular teachers to meet as a regular commitment for specified planning periods, and in some cases designate particular rooms for this purpose. Add to this teacher reports of increasing parental presence in elementary school staffrooms (which makes "back-region" behavior more problematic) and the impact of anti-smoking legislation which is driving many teachers away from informal association with their colleagues at lunch and break times into the car-park, shopping plaza or janitor's room, and there is more than a suggestion of a trend towards the administrative colonization of teachers' time and space in many areas.

Now, it should be said that this trend is not universal. It seems stronger where there are administratively driven commitments at the school district level to "planned" change. The trend is also not supported by a number of principals who defend teachers' rights to relax in preparation time if stress generated in the previous lesson requires it, or to use such time for personal business if it is important for teachers to do so (which recognizes that the services they need to contact may not be available later). A number of principals are also protective of teachers' discretion to use preparation time as they see fit, though they may release certain teachers together at the same time to widen the possibilities for consultation, should teachers want to take them up. I shall explore these possibilities and complexities in Chapter 9.

Nevertheless, developments in the administrative colonization and compartmentalization of teachers' time and space are substantial and significant. These developments are driven by concerns for productivity in and control over workers' use of time which have been in existence since the growth of time-related management strategies in early industrial capitalism. Here, time was to be regulated, controlled, compartmentalized and broken down, to ensure it would be used "productively" and not frittered away on unimportant or wasteful activities. Time was to be spent, rather than passed.[36] As Giddens suggests, though, the administrative colonization of time and space has increased and become more sophisticated in recent years with the expansion of forms of surveillance within the modern state.[37] Such surveillance entails not only direct control over, but also increasing disclosure or making visible of what had hitherto been the private plans, thoughts, reflections and intentions of its subjects. With the growth of administrative surveillance, what had previously been private, spontaneous and unpredictable becomes public, controlled and predictable.[38] The colonization and coordination of "back-region" activity in work settings, including teaching, is part of this swing to surveillance, this tendency to fill up and regulate the informal, desire-laden and potentially "unproductive" or even "counterproductive" areas of people's working lives. These patterns of administrative surveillance and bureaucratic control reflect and express the persistence of the modernistic mission within our schools and school systems.

All this should make us watchful and properly skeptical about apparently benevolent, administratively supported moves to increase the amount of scheduled non-contact time available to teachers, however well-intentioned these moves may be. A particular concern is that many teachers (and their unions or federations) may be at risk of becoming trapped in a Faustian bargain, where, for the worldly riches of extra time, they trade something of their professional souls (their control and discretion over how such time is to be organized and used) and their private selves (their access to and emotional indulgence in the spontaneous camaraderie of "back-region" teacher culture). This is not to undermine or minimize the importance of additional non-contact time for teachers. In technical–rational terms, it provides a necessary (if not a sufficient) condition for extending and redefining existing understandings of teachers' work. And micropolitically, it also addresses important status and equity issues across the profession. But the key issue for unions and federations and for teachers more widely may ultimately be not *how much* non-contact time is provided, but how that time is to be used, as well as who is to control that use.

CONCLUSION

Time is relative. Time is subjective. Subjective senses of time, I have argued, tend to differ in important ways between teachers and administrators – although even more so, perhaps, where male administrators are concerned.[39] Administrators, however, have the greater power to make their particular time perspectives stick. Indeed, so firmly can they ingrain their time perspectives and procedures into present administrative structures and routines that administrative time (monochronic, objective, technical–rational time) can come to be regarded as the only reasonable, rational way of organizing time. Administratively driven, technical–rational time, that is, can become hegemonic time[40] – so taken for granted that to challenge it is not to counterpose legitimate alternative time perspectives but to threaten the very foundations of administrative efficiency itself. What we are witnessing in much current educational reform and associated changes in teachers' work is such impositions of modernistic, administrative time perspectives, with all their practical implications, on the working lives of teachers. We are, in effect, witnessing the growing administrative colonization of teachers' time and space, where monochronic, technical–rational time is becoming hegemonic time.

Many Western educational systems are currently seeing an expansion of bureaucratic control and standardization in the development and delivery of their services. With only a few exceptions, and notwithstanding moves towards school-based financing, and school-based staff development in some places, control over curriculum, assessment and the teaching force itself is becoming more centralized and also more detailed. This is creating a widening breach between administration and teaching, between policy and practice, between the broad process of curriculum development and the technical details of program implementation. An irony for teacher development is that teachers are being urged and sometimes required to collaborate *more*, just at the point when there seems less for them to collaborate *about*.[41]

Driven by concerns for productivity, accountability and control, the administrative tendency is to exert tighter control over teachers' work and teachers' time, to regulate and rationalize it; to break it down into small, discrete components with clearly designated objectives assigned to each one. Preparation time, planning time, group time, individual time or, in Britain, "directed time"[42] – all substitutes for what was hitherto understood as "free time", "release time" or "non-contact time" – are symbolic indicators of this shift. This administrative tendency in the definition and control of time is rooted in a monochronic and generically male world of market relations, geared to increasing productivity, the elimination of "waste" and the exertion of control and surveillance.

This monochronic time perspective is divorced from and in conflict with the classroom-based, polychronic perspective of many teachers. The polychronic perspective, with its emphasis on personal relationships more than on things, and its flexible management of simultaneous demands in the densely packed world of the classroom rather than the one-at-a-time fulfillment of linear objectives, poses problems for the implementation of administrative purposes. It creates barriers to implementation, resistance to change.

As the gap widens between administration and teaching, between development and implementation, so too does the difference in administrators' and teachers' time perspectives. Perceptions regarding the pace of change diverge more and more. Administrators compensate by strengthening their control (increasing the gap between administration and teaching) and by multiplying administrative demands (increasing the expectations and compressing the timeliness for change). With these things come reinforced resistance to change and implementation among the teaching force: to the intensification of teachers' work. As they get caught up in the spiral of intensification, bureaucratically driven initiatives to exert tighter control over the development and change process become self-defeating.

The solution to this impasse is not to be found in appeals to more sensitivity and awareness among administrators as they devise and develop new programs and timelines for change. The time-related misunderstandings between administrators and teachers are endemic to the distance there is between their two lifeworlds – a distance which appears to be increasing. It would seem more fruitful to explore solutions which question the strength of the divisions between administration and teaching, between development and implementation, and which question the bureaucratic impulses that support such divisions. In particular, it may be more helpful to give more responsibility and flexibility to teachers in the management and allocation of their time, and to offer them more control over what is to be developed within that time. This is a more postmodern solution. In doing this, we would be recognizing that teacher development is ultimately incompatible with confining teachers to the role of merely *implementing* curriculum guidelines. We would be recognizing that teacher development and curriculum development are closely intertwined.

The ultimate implication is that once we acknowledge what time means for the teacher, there seems a strong case for giving time back to the teacher, both quantitatively and qualitatively, and for giving the teacher educationally substantial things to do with that time. If we do this, then time may no longer be the enemy of teachers' freedom, but its supportive companion.

NOTES

1. On the importance of time as a key element in the principle of structuration, see Giddens, A., *The Constitution of Society*, Cambridge, Polity Press, 1984.

2. Habermas, J., *Towards a Rational Society*, London, 1970, Heinemann; and Schön, D., *The Reflective Practitioner*, New York, Basic Books, 1983.

3. Werner, W., "Program implementation and experienced time", *Alberta Journal of Educational Research*, XXXIV(2),1988, 90–108, quoted from p. 94.

4. Studies in time management exemplify this emphasis. See, for example, Webber, R. A., *Time and Management*, New York, Van Nostrand 1972; and McCary, J. T., *The Management of Time*, Englewood Cliffs, NJ, Prentice-Hall, 1959.

5. Fullan, M., with Stiegelbauer, S., *The New Meaning of Educational Change*, New York, Teachers College Press and Toronto, OISE Press, 1991.

6. Bird, T. and Little, J. W., "How schools organize the teaching occupation", *Elementary School Journal*, 86(4), 493–511, 1986.

7. Campbell, R. J., *Developing the Primary Curriculum*, Eastbourne, Cassell, 1985.

8. See, for example, Brookes, T. E., *Timetable Planning*, London, 1980, Heinemann; and Simper, R., *A Practical Guide to Timetabling*, London, Ward Lock Educational, 1980.

9. See Goodson, I., "Subjects for study: Aspects of a social history of curriculum", *Journal of Curriculum Studies*, 15(4), 391–408, 1983; and Burgess, R., *Experiencing Comprehensive Education*, London, Methuen, 1983.

10. See Ball, S., *Micropolitics of the School*, London, Methuen/Routledge & Kegan Paul, 1987.

11. See Fullan, M. and Connelly, F. M., *Teacher Education in Ontario: Current Practice and Options for the Future*, Toronto, Ontario Ministry of of Education, 1987.

12. See Schutz, A., *Collected Papers*, Vol. I: *The Problem of Social Reality*, The Hague, Martinus Nijhoff, 1973.

13. Ibid.

14. Shakespeare, W., *As You Like It*, Act III, *The Oxford Shakespeare – Complete Works*, New York, Oxford University Press, 1966, p. 230.

15. Werner, W., *op. cit.*, note 3, p. 96

16. Hall, E. T., *The Dance of Life*, New York, Anchor Press/Doubleday, 1984.

17. Derived and adapted from Hall, *op. cit.*, note 16.

18. Ibid, p. 54.

19. McLaren, P., *Schooling as a Ritual Performance*, London, Routledge & Kegan Paul, 1986.

20. On differences in time-frames within the teaching community, see Lubeck, S., *Sandbox Society*, New York, Falmer Press, 1985.

21. Apple, M. W., *Teachers and Texts*, London, Routledge & Kegan Paul, 1986; Curtis, B., *Building the Educational State*, New York, Falmer Press, 1988; Purvis, J., "Women and teaching in the nineteenth century", in Dale, R. *et al.* (eds), *Education and the State*, Vol. 2: *Politics, Patriarchy and Practice*, Lewes, Falmer Press, 1981.

22. Jackson, P. W., *Life in Classrooms*, New York, Holt, Rinehart & Winston, 1968.

23. Werner, *op. cit.* note 3, p. 106.

24. Ibid, p. 107

25. Hawking, S., *A Brief History of Time*, New York, Bantam Books, 1988.

26. Ibid.

27. Berger, L. and Luckmann, S., *The Social Construction of Reality*, Harmondsworth, Penguin, 1967.

28. Hawking, *op. cit.*, note 25.

29. Therefore, the differences in time perspective between teachers and administrators here are not so much generically rooted in the "types" of people respectively. Rather, they arise out of the particular relationship that teachers and administrators respectively have to the context of classroom teaching and teachers' work. In their own offices, the lives of administrators may be just as polychronic as are the lives of teachers in *their* own immediate work environment.

30. This phenomenon is sometimes referred to as *compound innovation*. [Hargreaves, A., *Curriculum and Assessment Reform*, Milton Keynes, Open University Press and Toronto, OISE Press, 1989] or *multiple innovation* [Ball, S., *The Micro-politics of the School*, London, Methuen, 1987].

31. Werner, W., *op. cit.*, note 3.

32. Apple, M., *Education and Power*, London, Routledge & Kegan Paul, 1982; and Apple, M., *Teachers and Texts*, London, Routledge & Kegan Paul, 1986.

33. Goffman, E., *The Presentation of Self in Everyday Life*, Harmondsworth, Penguin, 1959.

34. Ibid.

35. For literature on school staffrooms of this sort, see Woods, P., *The Divided School*, London, Routledge & Kegan Paul, 1979.

36. For the analysis of the economic foundations of contemporary senses of time, read Thompson, E. P., "Time, work-discipline and industrial capitalism", *Past and Present*, 38, 1967, 56–97.

37. Giddens, A. *The Constitution of Society, op cit.*, note 1.

38. See the application of this idea to community education also in Baron, S., "Community and the limits of social democracy: Scenes from the 'politics' ", in Green, A. and Ball, S. (eds), *Progress and Inequality in Comprehensive Education*, London, Routledge & Kegan Paul, 1988; and Hargreaves, A. and Reynolds, D., "Decomprehensivization", in Hargreaves, A. and Reynolds, D. (eds), *Educational Policies: Controversies and Critiques*, New York, Falmer Press, 1989.

39. I am grateful to Saundra Fish for making this point to me.

40. See Hargreaves, A. and Dawe, R., "Paths of professional development: Contrived collegiality, collaborative culture and the case of peer coaching", *Teaching and Teacher Education*, 6(3), 1990, 227–41.

41. As designated, in the latter case, under the teachers' contract of 1987.

42. On male conceptions of time and their rootedness in market relations, see Cottle, T. J., *Perceiving Time*, New York, Wiley, 1976.

Chapter 6

Intensification
Teachers' Work — Better or Worse?

INTRODUCTION

Whatever else might be said about teaching, few would disagree that the nature and demands of the job have changed profoundly over the years. For better or worse, teaching is not what it was. There are the needs of special education students in ordinary classes to be met. Curriculum programs are constantly changing, as innovations multiply and the pressures for reform increase. Assessment strategies are more diverse. There is increasing consultation with parents and more communication with colleagues. Teachers' responsibilities are more extensive. Their roles are more diffuse. What do these changes mean? How do we understand them? For those who perform the work of teaching, is the job getting better, or is it getting worse?

While there is wide agreement about the extent of the change in teachers' work, the meaning and significance of this change is more contested. Two of the broadest contending explanations are those of *professionalization* and *intensification*. Arguments organized around the principle of professionalization have emphasized the struggle for and, in some cases, the realization of greater teacher professionalism through extensions of the teacher's role. Teachers, especially those in elementary or primary schools, are portrayed as having more experience of whole-school curriculum development, involvement in collaborative cultures of mutual support and professional growth, experience of teacher leadership, commitment to continuous improvement, and engagement with processes of extensive, school-wide change.[1] In these accounts, teaching is becoming more complex and more skilled. What Hoyle calls extended teacher professionalism, and Nias and colleagues more cautiously term bounded professionality, is, in this perspective, both an emerging reality and a point of aspiration.[2]

A second line of argument is broadly derived from Marxist theories of the labor process. This argument highlights major trends toward deterioration and deprofessionalization in teachers' work. In these accounts, teachers' work is portrayed as becoming more routinized and deskilled; more like the degraded work of manual workers and less like that of autonomous professionals trusted to exercise the power and expertise of discretionary judgment in the classrooms they understand best.[3] Teachers are depicted as being increasingly controlled by prescribed programs, mandated curricula and step-by-step methods of instruction.[4] More than this, it is claimed, teachers' work has become increasingly *intensified*, with teachers expected to respond to greater pressures and comply with multiple innovations under conditions that are at best stable and at worst deteriorating. Under this view, extended professionalism is a rhetorical ruse, a strategy for getting teachers to collaborate willingly in their own exploitation as more and more effort is extracted from them.

This chapter takes a critical look at the second of these competing perspectives: the intensification thesis. It does so through the voices of teachers themselves; through their own words about their world and their work. This is important, because the evidence for the intensification thesis has so far rested on a rather small number of single- or two-teacher case studies. Empirical support for the thesis, while mounting, can still be regarded as no more than slender. The time is ripe, therefore, to open the intensification thesis to more detailed empirical scrutiny. Drawing on the findings of the preparation time study, this chapter examines the implications of what appears to be a critical case for the intensification of teaching — the scheduling of additional statutory release time for elementary teachers from classroom responsibilities. First, though, it is important to identify the propositions and claimed empirical generalizations that make up the intensification thesis, so that when we listen to teachers' voices, the yardstick for comparison will be clear.

THE INTENSIFICATION THESIS

The concept of intensification is drawn from general theories of the labor process, particularly as outlined by Larson.[5] According to Larson, "intensification . . . represents one of the most tangible ways in which the work privileges of educated workers are eroded".[6] It "represents a break, often sharp, with the leisurely direction that privileged non-manual workers expect" as it "compels the reduction of time within the working day when no surplus is produced".[7] This discussion contains the following claims:

- Intensification leads to reduced time for relaxation during the working day, including "no time at all" for lunch.

- Intensification leads to lack of time to retool one's skills and keep up with one's field.

- Intensification creates chronic and persistent overload (as compared to the temporary overload that is sometimes experienced in meeting deadlines) which reduces areas of personal discretion, inhibits involvement in and control over longer-term planning, and fosters dependency on externally produced materials and expertise.

- Intensification leads to reductions in the *quality* of service, as corners are cut to save on time.

- Intensification leads to enforced diversification of expertise and responsibility to cover personnel shortages, which can in turn create excessive dependency on outside expertise and further reductions in the quality of service.

Discussion of the intensification of *teachers'* work draws extensively and often directly on Larson's broader analysis of the labor process.[8] In the work of Michael Apple, for instance, intensification is particularly evidenced in teachers' work in the growing dependence on an externally produced and imposed apparatus of behavioral objectives, in-class assessments and accountability instruments, and classroom management technologies. This, he says, has led to a proliferation of administrative and assessment tasks, lengthening of the teacher's working day, and elimination of opportunities for more creative and imaginative work – a development which has occasioned complaints among teachers.[9] In his analysis with Susan Jungck of the implementation of computerized instruction, Apple points to one particular effect of intensification on the meaning and quality of teachers' work: reduction of time and opportunity for elementary teachers to show care for and connectedness to their students because of their scheduled preoccupation with administrative and assessment tasks.[10] In addition to the insights they draw from labor process theory, Apple and others point to two aspects of intensification that are specifically grounded in education and teaching.

First, there is the implementation of simplified technological solutions to curriculum change that compensate "teachers for their lack of time by providing them with prepackaged curricula rather than changing the basic conditions under which inadequate preparation time exists".[11] Scarce preparation time, that is, is said to be a chronic and persistent feature of intensification in teachers' work. Solutions to change and improvement focus on simplified translations of externally imposed expertise rather than on the complex evolution of internally developed and shared improvements, along with the time needed for their creation.

Second, among teachers, "the increasing technicization and intensification of the teaching act . . . [is] misrecognized as a symbol of their increased professionalism."[12] Apple reports that the employment of technical criteria and tests makes teachers feel more professional and encourages them to accept the longer hours and intensification of their work that accompanies their introduction.[13] In an analysis of two elementary teachers and the place of intensification in their work, Densmore notes that "out of a sense of professional dedication, teachers often volunteered for additional responsibilities", including after-school and evening activities.[14] One teacher is described as working "quickly and efficiently so that she could include creative supplementary lessons once required lessons were finished. Her own sense of professionalism together with parental pressures for additional effort, propelled her to increase the quantity of lessons taught".[15] The way that such teachers voluntarily consort with the imperatives of intensification, it seems, means that "the ideology of professionalism for teachers legitimates and reinforces . . . intensification".[16]

There are therefore two additional claims about intensification in teaching to add to the earlier list. These are:

- Intensification creates and reinforces scarcities of preparation time.

- Intensification is voluntarily supported by many teachers and misrecognized as professionalism.

Let us now listen to some teachers' voices and compare them to these claims. What do these voices say about teachers' work? And how might they serve as more than mere echoes for preferred theories, leading us instead to question these theories, however uncomfortably, by having authenticity and authority of their own?

PREPARATION TIME: A CRITICAL CASE

In September 1987, elementary teachers in Metropolitan Toronto school boards took strike action in support of their claim for a guaranteed minimum of 180 minutes per week of preparation time. Throughout the province of Ontario, contract negotiations before, during and after this time centered around increased preparation time as a key bargaining issue. In 1988–89, elementary teachers in most Ontario school districts had a guaranteed minimum of 120 minutes or more of preparation time per week.

Such levels of guaranteed time for elementary teachers away from class are unusual in Western schooling systems, yet they have long been advocated as desirable, indeed necessary, conditions for increased collegiality among teachers, for opportunity to commit to and get involved in change and, more recently, for restricting the process of intensification in teachers' work. A study of the uses of increased preparation time, therefore, constitutes a critical case for examining the nature and conditions of teachers' work.

In particular, newly provided preparation time has potentially significant implications for the culture of individualism among teachers and its persistence. One of the most consistently mentioned obstacles to the elimination of individualism and the development of more collaborative working relations among teachers has been shortage of time for teachers to meet, plan, share, help and discuss within the regular school day. A study of the uses and interpretations of teacher preparation time thereby provides a *critical case* of intriguing theoretical possibilities for analyzing the relationships between time, work and culture in teaching. Does scheduled preparation time bring about fundamental change in the teacher culture, inclining teachers more toward developing collaborative relations with their colleagues? Or does it get *absorbed* by the existing culture of teaching, being used to support and extend teachers' present purposes of and preferences for individual, classroom-centered work, such as marking and photocopying? Does it generate closer and more extensive collaborative relationships between teachers and their colleagues? Or are the uses of preparation time defined and absorbed by prevailing patterns of work within the teacher culture of a more individualized, classroom-focused nature?

These questions are at the heart of Chapters 8–10, which analyze the culture of teaching. At the time of the initial research proposal, they had an almost perfect mathematical elegance about them. The social world of education is more complicated and less predictable than the symbolic world of mathematics, however. Not surprisingly, the study's findings were less neat and elegant than its questions. Individualism and collegiality, my colleague Rouleen Wignall and I discovered, were considerably more complex than we and many other writers had imagined. Similarly, in this chapter, we will see that preparation time does not simply halt or restrict the encroaching intensification of teachers' work. Its effects are more complex than that, as is the very process of intensification itself.

The discovery of this complexity was made possible by the study's qualitative and exploratory nature. The key research purpose was to investigate the meanings that teachers and principals attached to preparation time and other non-contact time and the interpretations they put on its use. Here, the project looked not only at specific issues concerning actual, proposed and preferred uses of preparation time, but also at wider patterns of working as a teacher, and the ways that those patterns related to teachers' lives more generally.

The study centered on semi-structured interviews with principals and teachers across a range of school settings. We asked about specific and preferred uses of preparation time. We asked about the usual patterns to the teachers' working day, inside and outside school, weekdays and weekends, term time and vacation time. We asked about professional development and experiences of working with colleagues. Lest references to general patterns should lead to unintended distortion or selective perception on the teachers' part, we also asked quite specific questions about how teachers had used their last three preparation time periods.

All interviews took place in private surroundings, often the principal's office or a resource room, and were taped (with the interviewee's consent) then transcribed, generating almost 1000 pages of typescript for analysis. The transcripts were analyzed by reading and re-reading them to establish close familiarity with the data. We listed emergent themes in the text, then modified and reclassified these as a result of active searches for confirming and disconfirming evidence in the data. This led to important refinements – for instance, in the specification of different forms of collaborative culture among teachers and in drawing distinctions between individualism and individuality. Summary reports of each interview were then written according to the themes, which led to further modification and development of original categories. As a result of this process, data could be searched and analyzed by themes across interviewees or by interviewees across themes (both within and across schools).

The study was conducted with my colleague Rouleen Wignall in 1988–89. It focused on a range of school sites within two school districts (boards) in southern Ontario, Canada. In each board, the principal, a Grade 4 teacher and a Grade 2 teacher were interviewed in each of six schools. Within French immersion schools, where immersion and non-immersion teachers shared responsibility for a class, both teachers were interviewed, so that in two of the schools, four teachers were interviewed, not two.[17] No teacher or principal refused to participate or declined to be taped. The overall data therefore consist of interviews with 12 principals and 28 teachers across two school boards. In the first board, system administrators we contacted regarded preparation time as an uncontentious issue among its teachers, and stated that informal preparation time provision had been in place for a number of years. In this board, where no special initiatives appeared to have been taken regarding the use of non-contact time, we hoped to get an indication of the relationship of preparation time to the individualistic culture of teaching under relatively ordinary circumstances.

In the second board, the sample schools were involved in a three-year initiative to develop cooperative planning among school staff. Judging from the wider literature on teachers' working relations, this group of schools was certainly not typical, but in many respects it constituted a *limiting case* where collaborative relationships between teachers and their colleagues might most be expected, and where the nature and extent of those relationships under circumstances of administrative support and encouragement would be of special interest. It was in these schools that the phenomenon of *contrived collegiality* unexpectedly emerged. Of course, in many other districts, schools would doubtless be grateful if they had some collegiality to contrive in the first place!

Theoretically, the approach taken in reporting, analyzing and conceptualizing the data is broadly humanistic and critical in nature. It looks at how teachers experience their work and also at the context of what it is they experience. Within these widely defined parameters, however, the approach is consciously eclectic. The study is not located within one particular tradition. Instead, I have sought to interrogate the data with different (but not infinite) concepts and theories (e.g. individualism, intensification, postmodernity). Puzzles and surprises in the data also propelled me towards initially unfamiliar concepts and theories (e.g. solitude, persecutory and depressive guilt, monochronic and polychronic time). Where existing concepts or perspectives would not fit, or could not be found, I have constructed new ones (e.g. balkanization, contrived collegiality). Throughout the study, I have tried to sustain a creative dialogue between different theories and the data, in a quest not to validate any presumed perspective, but simply to understand the problems in their social context, as they are experienced by teachers. In similar spirit, my immediate purpose in this chapter is to examine how the data speak to the intensification thesis, and to identify any modifications in our understandings of intensification that we may need to make as a result.

TEACHER TIME AND INTENSIFICATION

The first set of issues arising from the data concerns the changes, pressures and increased expectations that many teachers have experienced in recent years — changes that in a broad quantitative sense would seem to offer some support for the intensification thesis.

One teacher described some of the important ways that teaching had changed for her:

> Teaching is changing so much. There's so much more social work involved in your job now than there ever was before. So many problems, behavioral and social problems, that are sitting in your classroom that have to be dealt with before you can ever attempt to start teaching. I don't think a lot of people realize that . . . it's really a changing job. This is my fifteenth year, and since I first started teaching, you can really see horrendous changes . . . and I don't think a lot of people who've never been in a school and seen a school run know exactly what a person puts up with in a day. Then they say: "What do you need two months off for?"

The effects of special education legislation and the mainstreaming of special education students into regular classes were areas of concern for several teachers, both in terms of the implications for classroom discipline and the demands on the teacher to provide more diversified programs.

> *T*: I know in the beginning, during prep time, there were more teachers who at least had time to take a break, which is sometimes necessary. And now you rarely find a teacher taking a break.
>
> *I*: So how do you explain that?
>
> *T*: I find my workload now is much heavier than it used to be. I just think that although there are times that I know I need to stop, I can't. I have to get things done. So I think that part of it is the changing expectations of teachers. Large class sizes — I have 29 — and when you figure that goes from a Special Ed kid, to enrichment, to ESL, it's a lot of kids that you always seem to be on the tear. I think there's more and more social work going on. If we were to write teachers' descriptions ten years ago, twenty years ago and now, they're vastly different. I think there just isn't the time now for us to sometimes sit down and recuperate.

This teacher went on to describe a number of children and their problems in her class who might previously have been retained in a segregated unit. "You've got all these kids that you never used to have", she said. Nor is it simply a matter of containing them, of maintaining discipline. "We're to meet the individual needs of the kids. Kids don't fail today, really, so we have to keep adjusting the program."

An additional problem for some teachers was what they perceived to be scarce and possibly declining in-class, specialist support and assistance, to help them cope with and prepare programs for the new special needs students. One teacher commented that he had "a very large class", "a low-average class" with two students who were repeating grades, which was "very tough, very demanding" for him. The reason for this concentration of ten to twelve "needy" children in his class, he believed, was that "It's easier for the people in the resource department to schedule time into . . . one class, as opposed to three separate classes." Another teacher pointed out that her paraprofessional, in-class support had been removed because of budget cuts. Therefore she now devotes most of her preparation time to working with individual special needs students to give them the support they need and help them "catch up".

The changing composition of teachers' classes over the years, then, has had implications not only for discipline and stress but for the complexity of programming and preparation too.

> You're always being told that you're constantly responsible for the children. You need to know where they are and what they're doing. You have to be able to program for all the different abilities in your classroom. It's not a simple matter of saying, "Today, we're going to read this story!" It's who can read this story and what am I going to do with the kids who can't? And how do I go about getting these kids to answer in complete sentences while I'm getting this child who's sitting in my Grade 4 and can only read at Grade 1? What am I going to give this person to read, because I have to be there to read with her, but I also have to be there to help these children learn how to do this better than what they're doing.

Accountability to parents and administrators increased the sense of pressure for a number of teachers.

> Especially at this school, we have parents who are very demanding as to what kind of program their children are getting, how it's being delivered, how the paper was marked, how the test was marked that you sent home; all kinds of things like that. So I find that you have to be very accountable to them as well as to

the kids and to the administration too. So therefore it takes a lot of thinking through ahead of time too, as to how you're going to mark a paper or present something.

Accountability has also brought with it more form-filling and paperwork; more accounting for what is being done, has been done, and is intended to be done, for the benefit of parents, administrators and other audiences, as seen in the following statements of teachers.

> Fifteen years ago I didn't have paperwork. Fifteen years ago the paperwork I had, I created for myself . . .

> The paperwork we're getting I'd almost like to give it up. If I didn't enjoy it with the kids so much, I would. . . . What the administration has asked us to do I don't think they have much choice in that either. . . . We have to make plans for everything that we do. . . . We spend so much time sitting and writing out. Maybe that's the way we don't get ourselves into difficulty, I don't know. We have to do a lot of accounting for everything we do. . . .

> It's a lot different than 25 years ago. Paperwork has increased . . . the board's gone out with these pink forms in triplicate, class lists. . . . I must spend 10 minutes each day.

> I'm close to 20 years now and I find from the first year to now, the paperwork has increased.

> They're forever — this year we've all said the same thing — this year seems to have been particularly bad for conferences and workshops. And they want you to attend this and they want you to attend that; there's this new program and that new program. At one point, we had so many things on our plate for the Grade 5s, we finally said "Call a halt! Forget it!. . . ." There was one week, I was out of the school more than I was in it!

> There are people who love meetings. They live for those meetings. I live for a meeting if it's purposeful for me and if it's not, then the meeting is useless and I just cut them right off, which I have done.

These rising demands on and expectations of teachers certainly amount to strong support for the *intensification* thesis, as does the combination of high expectations (e.g. individualized programming) with reduced support (e.g. reductions of in-class assistance).

TEACHER TIME AND PROFESSIONALISM

The high expectations and stringent demands that accompany elementary school teaching did not always clearly emanate from external sources. Working hard was not simply a question of bowing reluctantly to outside pressure. Many of the demands and expectations of teaching seemed to come from within teachers themselves, and frequently teachers appeared to drive themselves with almost merciless enthusiasm and commitment in an attempt to meet the virtually unattainable standards of pedagogical perfection they set themselves. They did not appear to need direction or pressure from above to motivate them in their quest. They drove themselves quite hard enough.

Part of the reason for this phenomenon is to be found in the diffuse definitions and expectations that attach to teaching in Ontario and other similar systems. Comparative studies of the teacher's role by Broadfoot and Osborn have indicated that in France, for instance, the teacher's role is defined tightly and clearly as being specifically concerned with academic learning and performance in school.[18] Teachers there are consequently more certain about their role and more satisfied with their performance. In many other places, like Britain and North America, though, the role is defined and perhaps increasingly being re-defined ever more widely, encompassing social and emotional goals as well as academic ones, concerns for the child's welfare at home as well as performance in school. Goals and expectations defined and understood in such diffuse terms become difficult, indeed impossible to meet with any certainty. Yet dedicated elementary teachers strive hard to meet them. As Flinders puts it:

> More so than other occupations, teaching is an open-ended
> activity. If time and energy allowed, lesson plans could always
> be revised and improved, readings could always be reviewed
> again, more text material could always be covered before the end
> of the term, students could always be given more individual
> attention, and homework could always be graded with greater
> care.[19]

The teachers we interviewed talked a lot about their work in these terms. When describing their use of preparation time, they reeled off activity after activity, giving an urgent, frenetic sense of how densely packed, how compressed that time was. "The time goes really fast," said one. Others remarked that the list of what they do and what they can do "just goes on and on!" "It's endless." "You can always do more." "There are never enough hours in the day." "There's always something I could be doing because I am never finished." In some cases, work became almost an obsession, threatening to overwhelm them. Some stayed late, until after 5:00, so they would not need to take their work and therefore their problems home with them. One had been counseled by his principal to ease back on the work and give more time to his personal life, to his leisure. Many, particularly women with families, spoke wistfully about wishing they could give more time to themselves — "time for me", as they put it.

Many dedicated teachers gave generously of their time and effort to their work, to the students in their charge. The majority took work home in the evenings, taking it out after supper, or once the children had gone to bed. The extraordinary lengths to which their commitment stretched stands out in many individual cases. One teacher regularly stayed until six or seven o'clock, even in winter after the heat had been turned off, when he had to wear his coat and bustle around doing activities that would keep him warm. There was the teacher who spent over $1000 of her own money during the summer on materials and resources for her class. There was the teacher who came to work in his temporary classroom every Sunday and the teacher who came in one Saturday for several hours a month to sort out the staffroom bulletin (display) boards. There was the single-parent teacher with a handicapped child who dashed home at the close of school, two days a week, to take her child for specialist help, and then returned to cook supper, to read to both her children and put them to bed — finally taking out her schoolbooks to start all over again after eight or nine o'clock at night. There was the teacher who had been widowed young, had brought up her children alone, and had commonly worked from 9:00 until 11:00 or midnight after they were asleep — and who was only now, in her middle age, choosing to ease off a little, reduce her commitments some-what as she felt she had "paid her dues" in the past and now deserved the opportunity to develop a life with her new husband. There was the teacher who had shelves and bookcases at home packed with materials and resources that she had made and accumulated over the years. There was the teacher who spent his Sunday mornings compiling tests, quizzes and worksheets on his word processor. There were the teachers who were taking additional quali-fications in computers, or visual arts or teacher librarianship; the teachers who coached sports teams and refereed House Leagues; the teachers who involved themselves with the choir or organized school charities. The list, as one of the teachers said, is endless.

The time and effort these teachers commit to their preparation and teaching comes not so much from grudging compliance with external demands as from dedication to doing a good job and providing effective care within a work context that is diffusely defined and has no clear criteria for successful completion.[20] This internally generated dedication in the context of a diffusely defined occu-pation seems to be grounded in what both Woods and Nias call professional and vocational commitments, commitments that are grounded in the kinds of meanings and purposes that teachers attach to their work.[21] It is churlish, and perhaps also theoretically presumptuous, to dismiss these deeply held commitments and their consequences as merely belonging to a pattern of "professionalism" that misrecognizes and legitimates the intensification of teachers' work.

In these patterns of commitment and care are to be found important modifications to the intensification thesis. The same cautions apply to the data reported here. In certain respects, intensification may be an important feature of the work of the teachers we studied. But this does not mean that all that passes for professionalism is a ruse or a myth. Teachers' commitments and skills cannot be explained away quite that easily.

THE BENEFITS OF PREPARATION TIME

Against these tendencies towards increased workload and pressure, to which intensification has contributed significantly, the advent of preparation time has introduced a measure of compensation and easement.

Some teachers remarked that perhaps the public does not understand what teachers do with their preparation time, or how important it is to them, given the changing nature of the job. When asked if there was anything he would like to add at the end of the interview, one teacher ventured:

> The only thing that I was going to say was that — how much
> better it is for me now than it was. Receiving that prep time
> is really important. I know a lot of people, I think my
> mother-in-law for one of them, sort of wonder what I do during
> that time. . . . I just think she really doesn't have any idea,
> because she's never in [school]. I don't say that meanly
> because . . . she knows that I have a lot of work to do. But I
> think she wouldn't understand, and a lot of people wouldn't
> understand, that it is really nice to have that time when they've
> been in the situation or know somebody who is.

Airing similar concerns about not being fully understood, another teacher commented:

> I just think it is very important for people to understand
> that . . . the job does not start at 8:40 in the morning and end at
> 3:30. . . . We have a lot of parent volunteers and they all say to
> us, "But we had no idea how much you do!"

Teachers reported that increases in preparation time had conferred important benefits on the quality of their work in general and their instruction in particular. First, they pointed out that increased preparation time had been important in reducing stress. Second, it helped restore something to their lives outside teaching, enabling them to give a little more time to their families, their leisure and themselves. Together, these two things helped improve teachers' temperament in the classroom, they argued, improving the quality of interaction they had with their classes. The following quotations give some sense of this commonly noticed relationship between stress, wider life circumstances and classroom temperament:

> It [preparation time] eases the stresses of the job, because all of that planning or duplication would have to be done after school time when you have everybody in the school after the same machines, so you're not waiting your turn for something to become available to you.

> I feel that this year, I'm very much more relaxed. I don't get that same feeling of stress. For instance, having them first thing in the morning, if I've got something I particularly want for that day even, I have time to do it instead of coming in at 7:30, which for me is a real bonus, not being an early-morning person.

> I think it [preparation time] is very vital, because if a teacher is too tired out, too tired and too overworked with homework you are not at your best when you are in contact with the children. Your nerves get a little short. Your children soon pick that up and it's not a good learning atmosphere. I think it's crucial to keep your mental and physical health, and having sufficient time to do the work that you have is a large component.

A third point is that in addition to relieving stress and creating space in other parts of the teacher's life — in addition to making existing work easier, that is — preparation time for many teachers also enables them to do things better. It enables them to be more organized, to be better prepared. For instance:

> I think I'm more organized, and the fact that if there is something that's coming up, I know that I have that time tomorrow to do it in, so that I can do it at that time, rather than staying after school or putting that time in after school, or doing it at lunch time. I can do it during my prep time. It's nice.

> It's most invaluable. Phone calls. For example, you get busy lines and so on. If you're just trying to do it quickly in between classes, it's impossible. And little things like looking over your notes and seeing — looking through my files and seeing what activities I can use to help this group of kids who are having difficulty. Those are invaluable. You just don't have the classroom time to sit down and say "wait" to the kids while you try to find a file for somebody that evening. You just cannot use the time enough.

Preparation time, according to some teachers, also allowed them to do more things, to take on a wider range of activities than they had before. Before preparation time, said one,

> I didn't do as much. I didn't run as many House Leagues. I wasn't involved with as many activities after school because I was just so busy doing all these other things. So I think the

preparation time made me a more efficient person during the day. I can get more done between 8:00 and 4:00 than I could before.

For a number of teachers, the benefits of preparation time were to be found not in time for extra-curricular activities, but in the extra investments they could make in the business of instruction within their own classes. For these teachers, preparation time helped them improve the inventiveness and appropriateness of their pedagogy. They were more able to make games to teach an idea rather "than give a child a piece of paper to write, push a pencil around on". Many teachers also talked about marking, about how preparation time helped them evaluate students' work more effectively.

I don't feel I have to do quite as much rushing at lunch hour to get materials ready and get work marked. I like to mark my work at school so I don't carry big bundles of books home, for one thing. And it's nice to mark it as soon after the kids have done it as possible, so they can see what their mistakes are. If it hangs on for a day or two, it is not as effective.

I feel it's crucial to have the children's work marked as soon as it's done. I get it back to them as soon as possible, because if you leave it two or three days — "What's this?" It's like a week old to children.

Preparation time can be seen as a way of providing teachers with working conditions that are designed to help them catch up with the diversification and changing requirements of the job. Certainly, many teachers spoke vividly about the changes in their work and were unequivocal in their praise of preparation time as a way of helping them cope more effectively with these changes. Preparation time here seems like a clear gain for teachers: a counter to the process of intensification. This is certainly how Ontario teachers' organizations involved in collective bargaining viewed the issue of preparation time when it was in dispute. According to the president of the Ontario Public School Teachers' Federation, "quality education for our children and teachers is what is at issue and, without guarantees of adequate preparation time, that *can't* be obtained".[22] The president of the Federation of Women Teachers of Ontario affirmed this view when she said:

Until we have a serious proposal [on preparation time] that addresses these needs of children, we're at a state of impasse because we as teachers care about the students we teach and we're not about to throw in the towel and give up on the students.[23]

THE PERVERSITIES OF PREPARATION TIME

Preparation time, it seems, can alleviate stress and increase the opportunities for relaxation. It helps reduce chronic work overload and leads to opportunities for the planning and preparation of more creative work. In these respects, preparation time helps counter the effects of intensification. It may even help reverse the spiral. The very existence of preparation time, in fact, constitutes a major challenge to the intensification process. Still, the long-called-for introduction of increased preparation time for elementary teachers does not reverse all the effects of intensification and can to some extent be absorbed by them. The study revealed four ways in which such additional time did not always lead to restrictions of the intensification process.

1. Increased preparation time did not necessarily enhance the processes of association, community and collegiality among teachers. Time itself was not a sufficient condition for collegiality and community. As we shall see in later chapters, unless there was a commitment to collaborative working relationships at the level of school or school district leadership, preparation time became absorbed by the deep-seated culture of individualism and classroom-centeredness that has become historically and institutionally ingrained in the prevailing patterns of teachers' work.

The immediacy of the classroom, its centrality within the teacher's world, and the multiple demands it placed upon the teacher for diversified programming and preparation that would be rationally accountable to others made most teachers predominantly classroom-focused and classroom-centered in their actions, thoughts and preferences. They were practical and classroom-focused not just inside their own classrooms but outside them too, concentrating their energies on what would best and most immediately benefit their own students: preparing materials, ordering resources, marking promptly, and so forth.

Flinders remarks that "isolation is an adaptive strategy because it protects the time and energy required to meet immediate instructional demands".[24] The same can be said of teachers' individualistic uses of preparation time. Indeed, even within one of the boards where there was a system-wide commitment to collaborative planning, a number of teachers referred to preparation time not scheduled for consultation with colleagues as "my time", as time they could use directly for the benefit of their own students. Preparation time was considered too precious and scarce to fritter on activities like relaxation or casual conversation with colleagues. These things were more likely to take place at recess. Hardly any teachers stated that they used preparation time for relaxation. There was simply no time for this. There were too many things to do. As one teacher put it: "If you make the mistake of getting into a conversation with somebody, then [the prep time is] done." Preparation time, therefore, did not automatically assist the process of association between teachers and their colleagues.

2. A second, somewhat perverse consequence of preparation time was that an important minority of the teachers interviewed stated that, while they appreciated the preparation time they now received, they probably did not want the further amounts for which their federations were fighting in order to move closer to the working conditions of secondary school teachers. What was at stake for these teachers was the continuity of the relationship they felt they needed with their classes and the quality of care that relationship would enable them to provide. The ethic of care was a powerful source of motivation and direction for these teachers: not surprisingly, given the importance of care as a key reason among elementary teachers for entering teaching, and given its pervasiveness as a central moral principle among women more generally.[25]

Ironically, while preparation time to a certain extent assisted a process of disintensification in elementary teachers' work, there appeared, for some teachers, to be a point where the law of diminishing returns set in; where further additions to preparation time *reduced* rather than *enhanced* the quality of classroom service provided, because the extra time drew teachers away from their classrooms too much. The data supporting these observations are reported more extensively in Chapter 8, but the words of two teachers capture the prevailing sentiments here:

> I don't think I would like to be away from them too much more, unless it's the same teacher. Even the one teacher that does come in, unless I specifically state what I want, the children don't work as well for her as they do for me.

> I think when they're talking about prep time – I had a letter put in my mailbox the other day and apparently there's some elementary teachers that are in quite a flap, because they are teaching ten minutes longer than the senior school teachers who are teaching [Grades] 7 and 8. And they want this justified. They want that time. And I'm thinking: "What are you here for? Teaching the kids, or trying to find out how much time they don't have to teach them?"

A third teacher summed up the fundamental dilemma and the way she chose to resolve it: "I wonder if I had much time away if I would feel I was losing something with the kids."

These remarks reveal a classroom commitment to quality of care, a professional and vocational commitment that cannot be summarily dismissed as a "misrecognition" of trends towards intensification in the labor process of teaching. On the contrary, these teachers recognize there is a point where it is not so much intensification as disintensification that threatens the quality of service they can provide. For these teachers, concerns about the quality of care superseded ones about the costs of time, even when opportunities to improve the latter were available.

3. A third perversity of preparation time is to be found in the preferred arrangements for preparation time cover. Teachers we interviewed preferred what can be called *segregated* cover arrangements, where a colleague comes in and teaches a self-contained specialty for which he or she holds complete responsibility. *Integrated* cover, where what is taught in preparation time forms part of a wider class program for which responsibility is shared to some degree between the class teacher and the covering teacher, was viewed much less positively. There were several reasons for this.

First, segregated cover saved time. A self-contained program required no prior preparation by the classroom teacher and no consultation with the covering teacher. It was the covering teacher's sole responsibility. In these conditions, there was no need to prepare for preparation time itself.

Second, some teachers had concerns about shared rather than personal accountability. They were worried they might not be able to provide a good or reliable account if they shared responsibility for an "important" subject with a covering colleague. As one teacher put it;

> One of my things that is a pet peeve is that when I talk to a
> parent I want to know that what I'm telling them is something
> I've seen with my own eyes, that I know is a truth and I've seen
> it. If I'm not there, I don't feel that I can comment on that, even
> though I've had feedback from the person [the covering teacher].

Closely related to these concerns about accountability were ones about expertise, which preparation time exposed. One principal put it like this:

> Primary teachers feel OK about handing their kids . . . across to
> somebody who they know can teach particular things better than
> they can. But what they already know they themselves can teach
> well, then it's trickier. We will all be better served if we can
> provide teachers with a sense of comfort and satisfaction that
> what's going on back there [in their classes] is good and valuable.
> We don't feel discomfort sending somebody off to French. It's
> just not there because it's assumed competence. And it's
> assumed incompetence on my part if I send my kids to you.

Therefore, he argued, preparation time is best covered through specialist subjects like music, which are "highly visible, highly valuable".

This was certainly the preferred arrangement for preparation time cover among teachers. They readily acknowledged the specialist expertise of particular colleagues who could teach a specialty better than they could, and they recognized the value of giving students access to this greater competence. Through exchanges of expertise, the clumsy could ensure their students got access to good-quality physical education. Groaning male baritones could secure better-quality teaching in singing and in music more generally. The teacher trying to improve her own visual arts expertise by upgrading her qualifications in the area could meanwhile have this part of the curriculum taught by another specialist during preparation time. Sharing classes where both teachers' expertise in the chosen subject was adequate or strong, however, exposed differences, and raised doubts about whose expertise might be weaker – doubts that teachers preferred to keep suppressed.

These problems of accountability and expertise that were exposed by the administration of preparation time sometimes led to covering teachers who were responsible for sharing "important" subjects like mathematics with the class teacher being assigned routine drills of a safe, self-contained nature. This did little to assist the quality of classroom instruction. More usually, as I noted earlier, teachers searched hard for subjects they disliked or in which they were weak, and which colleagues could cover. Where expertise in the covering subject was strong, this arrangement appeared to work well. The separation of powers between the classroom teacher and the covering teacher was counterbalanced by a collegial respect for complementary subject expertise. But where expertise in the covering subject was weak, the segregated pattern of cover appeared to undermine rather than enhance the quality of instruction. In some cases, this was not perceived as a problem. Of a teacher covering for physical education, for example, it was said that the program guidelines were clear. "It was all set up" and needed no extra preparation. Yet one wonders how far such apparently slavish following of written guidelines would affect the quality of instruction. Interestingly, Apple attributes such patterns of teacher dependency and technical control to processes of intensification in teachers' work. In the context of preparation time, however, such patterns and the shortfalls in quality that result from them, appear to come from seemingly contrary processes of disintensification.

A case of cover in health education serves as a striking example. The classroom teacher was keen for this area of the program to be covered. It was self-contained, and in a French immersion system where she was involved with only half the program anyway (the other half being taught by the French teacher), finding such self-contained areas for cover was not easy.

> I wanted to give the Health, because that's a whole subject in
> itself and it works very well into a short time period. Health
> lessons can be presented and completed in a 40-minute period.

Against the advantages of its being clearly bounded, though, problems arose with selecting this subject as one to be covered. For one thing, there was an apparent overreliance on published guidelines.

> There is a junior Health Course, and most topics such as dental
> health, disease, whatever, are presented in Grades 4, 5 and 6, but
> the objectives change somewhat for each age level, although
> there is a fair bit of overlap. I gave them [the covering teachers]
> sections out of the core and I asked them to be responsible in
> presenting it to the kids.

In a split-grade class, especially where the teacher was strongly dependent on published guidelines, there were also serious difficulties in programming appropriately for each part of the split.

> She tries to cover it with one class. She takes the same core and she will take, depending on the unit and how delicate it is, she might take the objectives from the Grade 6 core or the Grade 5 core and try and blend them a bit. So that's probably the hardest.

In particular, avoiding duplication of the program from one year to the next with split grade students was something achieved more by accident than design.

> The topics are the same [between grades]. It would probably be a different teacher and . . . for example, there's an objective at the top of the page and there are several different ways of attaining that objective. So the chances of them choosing those same activities to meet these same ends are quite low. So they might say to themselves, "Sounds familiar," but they won't be doing the same thing, and they'll be a year older and they'll be looking at it from a different perspective.

This teacher concluded, "It's not the ideal situation"; especially, one might add, where subjects like health education address important social and emotional goals and depend on close, continuous, open and trusting relationships between teachers and their students. Again, the perversity of preparation time is that, in some cases, it can lead not to improvement but to deterioration in the quality of service offered to students, and to deskilling rather than reskilling of the teachers involved.

4. The fourth perversity of preparation time is that while its absence inhibits association among teachers, its presence by no mean guarantees such association. More than this, the kinds of association that are created in the spaces afforded by preparation time may not always be those that enhance teacher development and empowerment. In Chapter 9, I will show that in terms of increased association among teachers, preparation time can help create or reinforce *either* collaborative cultures *or* contrived collegiality in the school community. *Collaborative cultures* comprise relatively spontaneous, informal and pervasive collaborative working relationships among teachers which are both social and task-centered in nature. These entail forms of leadership that support and facilitate these collaborations on an ongoing basis, rather than controlling and constraining them. *Contrived collegiality* is more controlled, regulated and predictable in its outcomes, and is frequently used to implement system initiatives or the principal's preferred programs. We will see in Chapter 9 that in the context of preparation time, the major patterns of teacher association were in fact those more controlled ones of contrived collegiality. More time, less control: this is a central part of the Faustian bargain I described in the previous chapter.

CONCLUSION

What have we learned from this investigation of teacher preparation time and its relationship to the intensification thesis?

First, many of the recent changes that teachers described as occurring in their work are highly compatible with the intensification thesis and offer considerable support for it. Heightened expectations, broader demands, increased accountability, more "social work" responsibilities, multiple innovations and increased amounts of administrative work are all testimony to the problems of chronic work overload documented in the thesis. Pressure, stress, lack of time to relax and lack of time even to talk to colleagues are effects that teachers mentioned, which again are highly consonant with those of the intensification process. Particularly before the advent of preparation time, many aspects of intensification appear to have been at work in the labor process of teaching, even in what was, at the time of the study, a materially favored provincial environment.

There are some qualifications to make to this finding, of course. First, the timescale over which teachers reported changes that were consonant with intensification is a relatively short one of only five or ten years. Evidence over longer timescales is not available in this study, and even when it is inferred from other historical work it is not always convincingly supportive. For instance, many studies of teaching in the nineteenth century indicate that, in quantitative terms, teaching may have been just as hard and demanding as it is now.[26] In qualitative terms, it may also have been less rather than more skilled. Certainly, as Densmore acknowledges, claims and inferences that intensification is part of a long, linear process of degradation in teachers' work are difficult to support through longer-term historical study. The appropriate timescale for intensification and its validity claims therefore remain a matter of open debate.[27]

Second, the evidence of this study is that of reported and retrospective evidence rather than evidence collected longitudinally. Given that such evidence comes from retrospective accounts of individuals, it is also difficult to disentangle *historical* changes in the labor process from *biographical* changes in the life and career cycles of teachers over time, when maturation may bring more responsibilities, or declining physical powers, a sense of reduced capacity to cope.[28]

Third, intensification may not impact on all teachers in the same way. It may be felt particularly keenly by those teachers who are, because of their own commitments or work circumstances (e.g. full-time rather than part-time), rather more work-centered than their colleagues.[29] And it may be felt less keenly by others.

Fourth, this evidence suggests that by no means all instances of broadened commitment and heightened professionalism can be explained in terms of the intensification of the labor process, or as "misrecognition" of that process.[30] Professional commitments to improving the quality of service for clients are often real ones, pursued by teachers themselves in a social context of growing complexity and challenge. These commitments extend far beyond processes structured to extract increased productivity from teachers' work. They are not exclusively reducible to labor process factors.

These four qualifications do not disconfirm the intensification thesis, but they do raise doubts about its scope and singularity as an explanation of changes in teachers' work, suggesting that further inquiry is needed in which other theories and perspectives in addition to those concerned with the nature of the labor process may need to be acknowledged as important for our understanding.

The second broad lesson concerns the potential of preparation time to alleviate many of the problems of intensification, and even to create some elements of disintensification. Preparation time has fulfilled some of its promise. Shortage of time to do and develop things that would enrich their work is a common complaint of teachers and is a key component of the intensification process. Teachers in the preparation time study saw the provision of such time as relieving stress, giving them back a personal life, allowing them to "do more", to contribute more to extra-curricular activities, and to improve the quality of their planning and instruction. If only in the short term (for we have no longer-term evidence), increased preparation time really does appear to help disintensify teaching and to help improve some of the quality of service teachers provide. Its introduction is more than merely cosmetic. In both professional and collective bargaining terms, the benefits it confers appear to be real and worth fighting for.

But preparation time is no panacea. It issues no guarantees. It offers only opportunities. Preparation time can be used for purposes other than its proponents intend, and the organizational contingencies surrounding its implementation can yield a range of unintended consequences that cannot easily be explained within the parameters of labor process theory. Preparation time, that is, has its perversities as well as its potentials. This is the third lesson to be learned from the study.

Beyond a certain point, increases in preparation time reduced rather than improved the quality of service provided to students, as teachers were drawn away from their own classes into other areas of work. Handing over compartmentalized pieces of the program to covering teachers could also create dependency on published guidelines and subject teachers to those very patterns of technical control which proponents of the intensification thesis ironically attribute to the absence of preparation time, not to its presence.

Lastly, when preparation time was used in the context of mandated or *contrived collegiality* and collaborative planning, this created a proliferation of meetings and additional work that intensified teachers' work still further, and subjected them to further administrative control instead of releasing them to develop things themselves.

These perversities point to the unanticipated ironies of complex bureaucratic systems which hold within them only yet more problems for every new solution that is offered. The unintended system consequences of French immersion programming, split-grade responsibilities, local distributions of expertise and the like are important, are not easily predicted and are not reducible to labor process explanations. In addition to the unanticipated consequences of preparation time, we have seen that this promising, if perverse, innovation can also itself serve as a new terrain for traditional struggles for control between administrators and teachers and between bureaucracy and professionalism more generally. In this sense, struggles surrounding preparation time and the Faustian bargains that are at stake within them may not so much solve the problems of intensification as displace the conflicts over intensification and the control of teachers' work to other levels and sites.

Time can seem and has seemed an easy solution to the problems of intensification and change. Perhaps the confidence expressed in the solution of increased teacher's time away from class has, to some extent, been a result of the perceived unlikelihood of its implementation! Sometimes our problems only really begin when our wishes come true. This chapter has shown that intensification is a real and serious problem for teachers and their work. Intensification explains many of the changes we are witnessing in teachers' work as time and space are increasingly compressed in the postmodern world. But intensification and labor process theories more generally do not fully explain what is happening in teachers' work. Our understandings of such work cannot solely be reduced to labor process theory. While time as an antidote to intensification can provide some of the solutions to the problems of teacher development and teachers' work, it can be just as much a source of further problems as well. Reform is often guided by the belief that every problem has a solution. Perhaps the real challenge of reform as a continuous process, though, is acknowledging that every solution has a problem. This is the ultimate perversity of postmodernity. What we can perhaps most hope for is not the achievement of perfect, utopian solutions, but elevation to a better class of problems. In this sense, intensification is an important but not the only source of problems within teachers' work, and preparation time is only partly a solution to it. Sincere commitments of a professional and vocational nature among teachers that amount to more than "ideological misrecognition", the increasingly complex nature of society in the postmodern age and the necessarily widening demands it places on education and educators, the complexities and unanticipated consequences of large bureaucracies, and the displacement of struggles about intensification to new sites even when time has been provided as an antidote to it — these things too must be considered.

The next chapter examines how such wider pressures, demands, expectations and commitments of a more complex kind impact on teachers' work and help structure the ways that teachers experience it emotionally in ways that impact on the quality of what they do.

NOTES

1. Campbell, R. J., *Developing the Primary School Curriculum*, London, Cassell, 1985; Nias, J., Southworth, G. and Campbell, P., *Whole School Curriculum Development*, London, Falmer Press, 1992; Nias, J., Southworth, G. and Yeomans, R., *Staff Relationships in the Primary School*, London, Cassell, 1989; Lieberman, A. and Miller, L., "Teacher development in professional practice and schools", *Teachers College Record*, 92(1), 1990, 105–22; Fullan, M. with Stiegelbauer, S., *The New Meaning of Educational Change*, London, Cassell; New York, Teachers College Press; and Toronto, OISE Press, 1991; Rosenholtz, S., *Teachers' Workplace: The Social Organization of Schools*, New York, Longman, 1989; Lieberman, A., Darling-Hammond, L. and Zuckerman, D., *Early Lessons in Restructuring Schools*, New York, National Center for Restructuring Education, Schools, and Teaching (INCREST), 1991.

2. Hoyle, E., "The study of schools as organizations", in MacHugh, R. and Morgan, C. (ed.), *Management in Education*, Reader 1, London, Ward Lock, 1975; Nias, Southworth and Yeomans, *op. cit.*, note 1.

3. Barth, R. S., *Improving Schools from Within: Teachers, Parents and Principals Can Make a Difference*, San Francisco, Jossey-Bass, 1990.

4. Apple, M., *Teachers and Texts*, New York, Routledge & Kegan Paul, 1989; Apple, M. and Jungck, S., "You don't have to be a teacher to teach this unit: Teaching, technology and control in the classroom", in Hargreaves, A. and Fullan, M. (eds), *Understanding Teacher Development*, London, Cassell and New York, Teachers College Press, 1992; Densmore, K., "Professionalism, proletarianization and teachers' work", in Popkewitz, T. (ed.), *Critical Studies in Teacher Education*, Lewes, Falmer Press, 1987.

5. Larson, S. M., "Proletarianization and educated labor", *Theory and Society*, 9(1), 1980, 131–75.

6. Ibid, p. 165.

7. Ibid, p. 166.

8. Ibid.

9. See, for instance Apple, *op. cit.*, note 4; Apple and Jungck, *op. cit.*, note 4.

10. Apple and Jungck, *op. cit.*, note 4.

11. Ibid, p. 54.

12. Apple, *op. cit.*, note 4, p. 45.

13. Ibid.

14. Densmore, *op cit.*, note 4, pp. 148–9.

15. Ibid.

16. Ibid, p. 149.

17. For those readers unfamiliar with the Canadian educational system, in French immersion schools many or all subjects are taught in French, the chosen language of instruction,

which is not the first language of the students. In many such schools, the program may be divided into two different groups of subjects, one set of which will be taught in English and the other in French.

18. Broadfoot, P. and Osborn, M., "What professional responsibility means to teachers: National contexts and classroom constraints", *British Journal of Sociology of Education*, 9(3), 1988, 265–87.

19. Flinders, D. J., "Teacher isolation and the new reform", *Journal of Curriculum and Supervision*, 14(1), 1988, 17–28.

20. This point will be developed in some detail in the following chapter, through the analysis of teacher guilt.

21. Woods, P., *Sociology and the School*, London, Routledge & Kegan Paul, 1985; Nias, J., *Primary Teachers Talking*, London, Routledge & Kegan Paul, 1989.

22. Quoted in *The Toronto Star*, 24 September 1987.

23. Quoted in *The Toronto Star*, 27 September 1987.

24. Flinders, *op cit.*, note 19, p. 25.

25. This argument is expanded in the next chapter.

26. See, for example, Curtis, B., *Building the Educational State: Canada West*, Philadelphia, Falmer Press, 1989; Tomkins, G., *A Common Countenance: Stability and Change in the Canadian Curriculum*, Scarborough, Ontario, Prentice-Hall, 1986; Prentice, A., "From household to school house: The emergence of the teacher as servant of the state", *Material History Bulletin*, 20, 1984, 19–29.

27. Densmore, *op cit.*, note 4.

28. On such career cycle issues, see Huberman, M., *The Lives of Teachers*, London, Cassell and New York, Teachers College Press, 1993.

29. See Poppleton, P. and Riseborough, G., "Teaching in the mid-1980s: The centrality of work in secondary teachers' lives", *British Educational Research Journal*, 16(2), 1990, 105–24.

30. See also Acker, S., "Teachers' culture in an English primary school: Continuity and change", *British Journal of Sociology of Education*, 11(3), 1990, 270.

Chapter 7

Guilt
Exploring the Emotions of Teaching

INTRODUCTION

One of the central purposes of educational practice and research is the improvement of learning. But behind the mastery of learning stands the mystery of teaching. Understanding teaching, unmasking the mysteries of its practice has presented a persistent and formidable challenge to those who have sought to improve the quality of teaching and learning over the years.

Over time, we have come to understand a lot about how teachers teach, and about the kinds of teaching that can be educationally effective in the classroom. More recently, we have learned much about how teachers think while they teach; how they plan and decide on different courses of action. And we have also come to understand more about what teachers think about their teaching; about how they reflect on their teaching, even as they do it. However, while what teachers do and how teachers think is now more familiar territory to those who study teaching, we know much less about how teachers *feel* while they teach; about the emotions and desires which motivate and moderate their work. Moreover, much of the research and writing that *has* addressed the emotions of teaching has started less from teachers themselves and what they have to say than from preconstituted theoretical agendas and concepts that have then been applied to teachers and teaching. Researchers have tended to have their own theoretical preoccupations with concepts like pride, commitment, uncertainty, creativity and satisfaction, and have asked interview questions or interpreted data in relation to these constructs.[1] There has been rather less focus on how teachers themselves talk about the emotional dimensions of their work.

Routinely, though, as one scans accounts of teachers and their work, it is clear that teachers *do* talk extensively about their emotional responses to their work, but in rather different terms than many theorists do. Where researchers talk about pride, commitment and uncertainty, teachers talk about emotions like anxiety, frustration and guilt.[2] This chapter focuses on just one of these experienced emotions of teaching: that of guilt. Where does teacher guilt come from? What does it mean? What are its consequences for teachers and teaching?

I will address these questions by sampling *three* different kinds of teaching context. I shall refer to and recontextualize some of the findings of the preparation time study; I shall present some insights from a doctoral study of teachers' interpretations of and responses to Employee Assistance Programs (EAPs) by Betty Tucker, a former graduate student of my department at the Ontario Institute for Studies in Education. Lastly, I shall document the case of a secondary school teacher who works in a highly innovative and highly pressured "lighthouse" school that forms part of a wider study of secondary school work cultures, some aspects of which will be reported in Chapter 10.

TEACHING AND GUILT

Guilt is a central emotional preoccupation for teachers. It recurs frequently when they are asked to talk about their work and their relation to it. As one teacher in the preparation time study expressed it: "Teaching is a profession that you go home, you always have stuff that you think about. You think, 'I should be doing this': I feel guilty sitting down half the time."

The feelings of guilt and frustration that teachers commonly experience can be profound and deeply troubling for them. This is not to say that guilt is inherently bad for teachers or consistently damaging in its effects. As many priests will testify, a little guilt can be good for one. Indeed, according to Taylor, "recognition of guilt is a first step towards salvation".[3] The repair work that comes from the need or wish to expiate guilt can be a powerful stimulus to personal change and social reform. Guilt experienced in modest proportions can be a great spur to motivation, innovation and improvement.[4] But in the way that teachers often talk about it, when guilt is bound up with overwhelming feelings of frustration and anxiety, it can become demotivating and disabling in one's work and one's life.

While guilt is a deep personal trouble for many teachers, it should also be remembered, as C. Wright Mills persuasively argued, that within many of our personal troubles reside compelling public issues. The challenge of the sociological imagination, he asserted, is to illuminate the connection between the two.[5] Following Mills's lead, my purpose in this chapter is to understand and interpret some of the emotional dynamics of teacher guilt and to locate them within the social context of teaching; in how the work of teaching is structured and organized.

In teaching, there are both *guilt traps* and *guilt trips*. *Guilt traps* are the social and motivational patterns which delineate and determine teacher guilt; patterns which impel many teachers towards and imprison them within emotional states which can be both personally unrewarding and professionally unproductive. *Guilt trips* are the different strategies that teachers adopt to deal with, deny or repair this guilt. They are ways of coping with or responding to guilt that teachers have developed over the years.[6] Burnout, exit, cynicism and denial are among these major guilt trips of teaching. Teacher behaviors that otherwise seem irrational, uncaring or unproductive can emerge in a very different light once it is understood they are guilt-ridden and guilt-driven. Strategies that teachers adopt to cope with undesirable amounts of guilt can themselves lead to further undesirable consequences in teacher behavior. Guilt, in this sense, is not so much a problem in itself as a generator of further problems beyond it. In the words of Hamlet's mother: "So full of artless jealousy is guilt. It spills itself in fearing to be spilt."[7] Throughout the course of this chapter we will see how these consequences of teacher guilt surface and resurface within teachers' work. My major preoccupation, however, is with the guilt traps of teaching: with the social conditions of teachers' work that generate excesses of guilt in the first place.

TWO KINDS OF GUILT

In his essay "The politics of guilt", Alan Davies argues that "at the centre of the feeling of guilt is self disappointment, a sense of having done badly, fallen short, of having betrayed a personal ideal, standard or commitment."[8] Davies's work highlights two particular forms of such guilt: *persecutory guilt* and *depressive guilt. Persecutory guilt* arises from doing something which is forbidden or from failing to do something which is expected by one or more external authorities.[9] In teaching, persecutory guilt is guilt that comes with accountability demands and bureaucratic controls. Such guilt looks backwards at tasks that have failed to be completed. It also anticipates and scans the future, evaluating potential actions to see if they will comply with the demands and requirements of authorities outside one's classroom.

Persecutory guilt is the kind of guilt that leads many teachers to concentrate on covering the required content, rather than ignoring it or subverting it to develop more interesting materials and approaches of their own. It is the guilt that inhibits innovation in "basic" subjects for fear of prejudicing the test scores by which one will ultimately be held accountable. It is the guilt that encourages overt yet superficial compliance with innovations that are unwanted, or whose validity and practicality are doubted, when open discussion and constructive criticism of the innovation and the problems it raises might provide a more productive foundation for change instead.

Depressive guilt, like all guilt, has much of its origins in early childhood. It appears to spring from early aggressive impulses felt towards an object, especially the mother, who is loved. The emotional experience of the mother understanding and welcoming the child's attempts to repair any such guilt gives rise to learned attempts "to repair and replenish – to give, and not always to take and deplete".[10] In later life, depressive guilt is called out in situations where "individuals feel they have ignored, betrayed or failed to protect the people or values that symbolize their good internal object".[11] In adulthood, this depressive guilt emerges from "having to admit . . . [one has] . . . injured, betrayed or failed to protect a good internal object or its external representation".[12]

Depressive guilt is at its most intense, perhaps, when we realize we may be harming or neglecting those for whom we care, by not meeting their needs or by not giving them sufficient attention. When we have failed to act on our early suspicions that one of our pupils was being abused at home; when we discover from a parent that one of our good, high-achieving pupils is secretly afraid of our loud, reprimanding voice; when we have no time to hear a child's problem, nor patience to listen to their faltering thoughts — this is when we can experience depressive guilt in our work.

Those who work in the caring professions, imbued as they are with the impulse to repair and replenish, are especially prone to depressive guilt. Nurses, for instance, are highly susceptible to feelings of guilt when the demands of the task draw them away from their care for the person.[13] And as we shall see shortly, those teachers whose purposes are strongly shaped by the commitment to care, especially teachers of younger children, are particularly prone to depressive guilt as well.

For some writers, the issue of depressive guilt and how one deals with it is not just a psychological matter, but also a philosophical question of moral choice. Rawls, for instance, describes guilt as a moral emotion which is felt when we recognize we are doing harm to others. For Rawls, such guilt does not only do harm to individuals. It also offends a moral principle of right.[14] In this, more moralistic sense, the distinction between depressive and persecutory guilt is rather like that which R. D. Laing drew between *true* and *false* guilt.

> True guilt is guilt at the obligation one owes to oneself to be
> oneself. False guilt is guilt felt at not being what other people
> feel one ought to be or assume one is.[15]

The contrast between true and false guilt and the definition of guilt in moral terms can place a heavy burden of responsibility on teachers and other carers — as if "true" guilt and its resolution were mainly a matter of personal, principled moral choice; of values and virtue. In the context of teaching, doing or failing to do what is right is more than a matter of personal moral choice, though. It also involves the context of caring and the extent to which that context enables or restricts the exercise of such choice. Teachers may, for instance, be prevented from doing what is right or caring as they wish by insoluble dilemmas or impossible constraints. It is in such dilemmas and constraints, in fact, that many of the sources of teacher guilt, of not being able to do the right things or the good things, are to be found. Teacher guilt and its resolution are, in these respects, as much matters of occupational constraint and expectation as ones of individual responsibility and choice. These patterns of constraint and expectation constitute the *guilt traps* of teaching.

GUILT TRAPS

The guilt traps of teaching, I want to argue, are socially located at the intersection of four specific paths of determination and motivation in teachers' work: the commitment to goals of care and nurturance, the open-ended nature of the job, the pressures of accountability and intensification, and the persona of perfectionism. These four paths of determination create powerful and perplexing combinations of depressive and persecutory guilt in the working lives of many teachers that pose serious problems for their effectiveness and integrity. I will review two of the paths somewhat briefly here as I have already discussed the issues they raise in the previous chapters. But the first and last paths of determination are more complex and difficult, and will be reviewed more extensively.

1. Commitment to Care

The commitment to goals of care and nurturance is a significant source of depressive guilt among teachers. The more important that care is to a teacher, the more emotionally devastating is the experience of failing to provide it. In this respect, the more one cares, the more susceptible to depressive guilt one is likely to be. A key question, then, is just how exclusive and extensive does the commitment to care need to be? Are overwhelming feelings of guilt the unavoidable cost of care? Or do they result from commitments to particular kinds of care that are restrictive or destructive in their effects?

There is no doubt that commitment to care is especially strong among elementary school teachers. It figures largely in their reasons for becoming teachers of younger children.[16] It is also a major source of job satisfaction for them.[17] Elementary teachers frequently feel concern, affection, even love for their pupils. Moreover, Nias's work shows that while the ethic of care, nurturance and connectedness is often seen to be a common and perhaps even characteristic quality of morality and interpersonal relationships among women, the sentiments of care, affection and love for students were pervasive among the men primary teachers she interviewed also.[18] The very metaphors through which elementary teachers characterize their teaching – metaphors which portray them in such terms as "rescuers" or "haven-makers" – also reveal the primacy of the care orientation in elementary teaching.[19] It is principles of warmth, love and self-esteem that underpin the lives and work of many of these closely observed elementary teachers, much more than principles of cognitive learning or instructional effectiveness.

Care seems central to the ethic and organization of elementary teaching, then. Care has many possible meanings, however, and it is important to analyze which of these particular meanings of care are salient for elementary teachers. What form does care take for them? What principles does it embody?

In the main, existing evidence suggests that for teachers as for many members of other "caring professions", care appears to be interpreted as the interpersonal experience of human nurturance, connectedness, warmth and love.

This association of care with interpersonal affiliation and affection is a common one both philosophically and practically, but there are other possible interpretations and realizations of care as well as this.[20] In the field of nursing, for instance, Watson has argued that

> human caring in nursing . . . is not just an emotion, concern,
> attitude, or benevolent desire. Caring is the moral ideal of nursing
> whereby the end is protection, enhancement and preservation of
> human dignity. Human caring involves values, a will and a
> commitment to care, knowledge, caring actions and consequence.[21]

Watson's work reveals that there is more to human caring than interpersonal sharing. Care in this wider sense carries with it social and moral responsibilities as well as interpersonal ones.

Nias's work suggests that a minority of British primary teachers are already able to put care into perspective like this; to value it alongside and in conjunction with other educational commitments.[22] For this minority, "to 'care for' children was to teach well and to accept the need for continuing self improvement". "Most of these teachers", Nias continues, "also saw themselves as interested in educational ideas as well as the practicalities of teaching." For them, she says, "caring was not a soft option".[23]

However, following Nias, it seems that it is indeed only a minority of elementary and primary teachers who can or do make these connections. For many elementary teachers, the purposes of personal care take precedence over all others. More than this, there is evidence that a narrow or exclusive orientation to care as personal care can actually lead to less care rather than more.

Book and his colleagues, for instance, found that entering teacher candidates tend to emphasize the interpersonal aspects of teaching, and minimize the academic ones.[24] These authors warned that when teaching is seen as an extension of the kinds of caring and nurturing relationships that typify parenting, this diminishes teachers' valuing of pedagogy courses and professional attitudes. Similarly, in the context of community health care services for the mentally retarded, Jensen has shown that when care is seen as an extension of nurturing family relationships, community health care professionals can find themselves ironically snared in practices of neglect that run contrary to their commitments to care.[25] Fears of intruding on privacy and concerns to respect patients' wishes led to one patient not eating a hot meal because he had never been instructed how to use the oven, to another patient suffering from poor dental hygiene, to another showering with clothes on and so forth. Because of the preoccupation with personal care, argues Jensen, there was insufficient analysis of problems, little use of professional knowledge, and indecision and neglect due to lack of discussion and consensus about the interventions needing to be made. Similarly, in the elementary school context, a teacher studied intensively by Crow, who had deep commitments to providing care and comfort for her students, was reluctant to breach these principles by showing authoritativeness towards them and developing her managerial skills. Irony was the outcome. Care was not the cure. "Each day was a battle to control the students." The classroom was no longer a "haven", "it was a miserable place to be, a war zone".[26]

When the purposes of care are balanced with those of group management and instructional effectiveness, and when care is construed in social and moral terms as well as interpersonal ones, its contribution to quality in education can be exceptionally valuable. Indeed, a strong care orientation, balanced with other goals such as ones directed to providing focused and intellectually challenging work, has been found to be strongly associated with positive school climates that in turn foster student achievement.[27] But when teachers focus on care too narrowly, too exclusively and too much, its benefits can become outweighed by its costs: costs to instructional efficiency, to collegial consensus and even, as we have seen, to care itself. Teachers, it seems, *can* care too much. They can become committed *by* care as well as *to* it.

It has become fashionable in recent years to attend to the personal knowledge of teachers, the voice it articulates, and the care it expresses.[28] In many respects, this has been a useful emphasis, bringing with it rightful redress for the way that teachers' voices had been ignored and excluded in educational research and policy for many years. But in many cases, those who have helped us hear the teachers' voice have moved beyond humanistic understanding to uncritical celebration and endorsement. Listening to the concerns teachers have for care has corrected a historically skewed preoccupation with technical efficiency and rationality.[29] Care clearly does matter to teachers. But we have seen that commitments to care which are parochial and pervasive in nature can also help form a trap that leads to ineffectiveness, possessiveness and guilt. If we can reconstruct our commitments to care to embrace a broader social and moral perspective and balance these commitments with other educationally important ones, this guilt trap may prove to be an avoidable one. This is not a case of encouraging teachers to care less or to be careless.[30] It is a matter, rather, of caring better and of having more to offer than care itself.

2. The Open-Endedness of Teaching

A second component of the guilt traps of teaching is the open-ended nature of the job. Teaching is a "never ending story".[31] The work is never over; the job is never done.[32] There are always more books to mark, more assignments to prepare — and more care to give to one's pupils.

As we saw earlier, teaching in many Western societies is suffused with notorious uncertainties that can create dissatisfaction and frustration for teachers. Interestingly, as we saw in the previous chapter, in countries like France, where the task of teaching is defined in more circumscribed academic terms, teachers report higher levels of satisfaction with their work.[33] In France, it is clearer when a task has been completed to satisfaction. But elsewhere, teaching is defined very broadly — in social and emotional terms as well as academic ones. The teacher's role is diffuse and not at all clearly defined. In a profession with no agreed knowledge base or accepted technical standards, there are no professionally approved criteria for success. And at the school level, where traditions of teacher isolation persist, as they often still do, there are not even possibilities for collaborative agreement and reduction of uncertainty among smaller communities of teachers.

So while teachers believe it is important to care, they can, in these circumstances, never really care enough. There are no commonly understood criteria for acceptable care or appropriate care. More important still, there is no consensus on the limits to care, on what it is realistically possible to achieve through one's work. Without such commonly understood standards, teachers can experience profound feelings that they are hurting those for whom they care. Especially in early career, they can be impelled to do more in order to care more. Teaching can become an unending process of constant giving. This creates many candidates for burnout.

The bags and briefcases that teachers carry, the piles of work they take home and back in the event that they may catch a few moments to mark some papers or prepare some tests, only to return to school with them mostly unmarked so that they must carry them home yet again next evening, and the next, and the next — like Pilgrim's burden, these are the symbolic burdens of guilt that teachers carry around with them. The bigger the bags, the bigger the guilt! One of the most severe cases I know is of a teacher with so many bags, he had to purchase a bigger bag to put all his other bags in! To leave work behind is to leave care behind, and with it the needs and interests of children. This is hard for teachers to do.

When passionate commitments to care are combined with poor criteria for fulfilling it, guilt and burnout are the outcomes. In response to these difficulties, the literature advocating stronger forms of collegiality and collective senses of certainty among communities of teachers offers a hopeful repertoire of constructive responses. For if shared standards and limits can be established among professional communities of teachers at the level of the school, then it is likely that feelings of excessive guilt can be averted, and the damaging consequences of burnout, cynicism and other responses be avoided. A second possible solution to the guilt glut, therefore, may be the development of stronger forms of collegiality and senses of certainty among smaller professional communities of teachers at the school level.

3. Accountability and Intensification

While care and open-endedness are the major sources of depressive guilt among teachers, accountability and intensification are the prime determinants of persecutory guilt. Studies of teachers' work, including the evidence in the previous chapter, point to major increases in accountability demands over the years.[34] Form filling, meetings, interviews with parents, more extensive reporting systems, more tightly defined curriculum guidelines are all said to have expanded and proliferated. Increasingly, teachers are having to attend more conscientiously to external expectations of growing stringency and they must also do this for a wider range of often competing publics and interest groups.

We have also seen that accountability has been accompanied by intensification of the labor process in teaching, as time and space are more compressed in the postmodern world. While disagreement remains about the extent of this intensification, about the degree to which it has been successfully contested by teachers and their federations, and about the period of time over which it has developed, even the harshest critics find it hard to deny that a good measure of intensification has indeed occurred in teaching over recent times.[35] The time demands of teaching have become more densely packed, multiple innovations have had to be accommodated, the integration of special needs students into ordinary classes has required additional planning, and shared decision-making has also called for extra investments of time. Even the most avant-garde models of educational leadership, in the form of transformational leadership, define their success partly in terms of their capacity to extract extra effort from the teaching force.[36]

Accountability and intensification provide a potent cocktail for inducing feelings of persecutory guilt – pervasive worries and fears that mounting expectations have not been or will not be met. But more than this, the pressing demands of accountability and intensification can fill up the scheduled time demands of teaching to such an extent that little time is left for the informal, interstitial moments to show care and concern: to fulfil the very purpose that many teachers feel to be at the heart of their work. Neufeld, for instance, found that the time demands of performance-based assessment, within the context of a newly developed active learning program, detracted significantly from teachers' opportunities to provide care for their students in terms of hearing their individual problems, or gathering them together to read a story at the end of the day.[37] Similar concerns have been expressed by primary teachers in England and Wales as they strive to cope with the proliferation of curriculum and assessment demands embodied in the new National Curriculum.[38] Indeed, so intense is the sense of loss of ability to provide the fundamental purposes of care among these teachers that Nias, in reviewing their responses, uses the term *bereavement* as an appropriately dramatic indicator of the severity of their emotional reactions. In these senses, accountability and intensification can be major sources of depressive guilt for teachers.

4. The Persona of Perfectionism
The demands of accountability and intensification can be felt particularly harshly where they embody singular views of correct (and, by implication, incorrect) practice.[39] Later, I will document how many of the expectations held of teachers embody singular models of expertise and competence which demarcate good from bad, and fashionable from unfashionable practice. These singular and modernistic models, which are often based on over-confident claims regarding the supposed findings of research about effective practice, make it difficult for

teachers to share expertise, still less to confide their doubts, for different practice may be construed as bad practice. Their very competence as teachers may
be placed in jeopardy. As one participant in a study of teachers' responses to
employee assistance programs (EAPs), undertaken by Betty Tucker, put it:

> Teachers won't seek help through normal channels. They want
> something that is anonymous. There is a fear of not measuring
> up, of having somebody think that they're not doing a good job.
> Teachers are the hardest professionals on themselves. We do not
> want anybody in the classroom watching us teach because we
> might not be doing something right. We might be doing
> something that we shouldn't be doing. We've just been so
> programmed that there are right ways of doing things we don't
> want somebody finding out what's happening in our classroom.
> Even though we are doing a good job, we still hesitate to have
> somebody in to watch us. Our ways may be old fashioned, not up
> to the latest methods. We are very insecure as a profession. . . .
> You know, we think we cannot make a mistake. You must have
> no difficulties whatever, and if you do have difficulties in your
> home life then those never can reflect in the classroom.

It is little wonder that many teachers experience what David Hargreaves
calls fundamental competence anxiety about appearing incompetent to their
colleagues and themselves.[40] Such anxiety, it is commonly recognized, arises, in
part, from there being no certain, technical knowledge base for the profession of
teaching. But it also arises from the arbitrary imposition of expectations for
teaching which contain singular rather than multiple models of competence;
expectations that may mesh poorly with the teacher's personal self or with the
context in which the teacher works.

More than this, competence anxieties can intensify when the public realm
of teaching performance is segregated and divorced from the private realm of
personal feeling; when professional lives and personal lives become strictly
detached from each other. The work of Nias and her colleagues suggests that
strong collaborative cultures of confidence and support both respect and celebrate the interpenetration of personal and professional lives among communities of teachers.[41] In collaborative cultures, teachers reveal much of their
private selves, teachers become friends as well as colleagues, and if bad days or
personal problems are encountered, teachers make allowances and offer practical help to their troubled colleagues.

Many teachers do not work in such collaborative cultures of confidence and
support. In such circumstances, where doubts cannot be aired, and problems
cannot be shared, teachers can become trapped in having to construct and maintain a persona of perfectionism. Personal problems *do* intrude on professional
performance. As one teacher in Tucker's EAP study put it, "It's pretty difficult
to take your other self and hang it on a hook somewhere and then close the door."

Yet to confess or confide personal difficulties is, in many cases, to betray signs of incompetence, inadequacy or unsuitability. A woman teacher with an abusive husband is advised to keep her domestic troubles to herself, "because if they found out, they wouldn't want me teaching at the school, because if my husband was that violent, he might come in and harm the children". Even being seen to approach an EAP for help may be perceived as reflecting on one's professional adequacy and thereby hinder promotion opportunities.

> You don't know how some principals and administrators view it.
> They may see it as a personality flaw, a sign that you can't handle
> responsibility, too much on your plate or something like that.
> You're supposed to be an example to those beneath you. You
> might be overlooked for a promotion if your flaws become known.

In Catholic school districts, where the boundaries between church, state and family are often exceedingly blurred because of the church's assumption of moral authority for the regulation of family life, the fear of personal disclosure and its implications for professional performance can become especially acute. Teachers can become trapped in abusive and unsupportive domestic relationships because separation and divorce might count against them professionally, particularly in terms of promotion. One woman teacher in the EAP study who worked in a Catholic district, for instance, was advised by her principal not to list membership of a Divorced Catholic Group on her résumé, because this might hinder her promotion prospects.

Caught between the pressure of high expectations in the workplace and the lurking possibility of religious and moral disapproval regarding their home life, women teachers in particular can become locked in the remorseless pursuit of personal and professional perfectionism that the "double burden" of work and home places upon them. If they are found personally and professionally wanting, they can simply "try harder". A personnel administrator in the EAP study remarked:

> Sometimes women are in a position that almost everyone in their
> life is drawing in some fashion from them. There is an acceptance
> that you don't complain. You just do your best. You stifle
> yourself. A coping strategy is just to keep on working.
> Sometimes the solution seems to be to work harder at home and
> work harder at [school], but that is not the real solution.

The guilt and perfectionism that come from separating the public and the private domains in teachers' lives are not the exclusive preserve of women, though. As one male teacher in the EAP study commented:

> You are not supposed to have problems. Chauvinism is alive and
> well. Men are still not allowed to be sensitive. Men are still not
> allowed to cry. . . . You are supposed to have your act together.
> You're not supposed to show weakness in any way, shape or

form. The most dangerous one being, "I just can't handle this kid". If you go for help to the principal, then that comes back as a black mark against you, that you can't handle certain situations. The unwritten rule is that if you are going for your permanent [certificate] you stay away from the office, handle your own problems.

The process of perfectionism is central to the determination and delineation of teacher guilt. Paradoxically, such perfectionism is itself an imperfection. In the talk of teachers, just as in the popular self-help literature, this persona is often perceived and treated as a personal, psychological attribute. Yet it is more than simply a product of irrational and treatable personal drivenness. In large part, the emotional dynamics of perfectionism are also structured by the intensifying pressures of the workplace; by singular models of expertise which preclude sharing and the inadequacies it might expose; and by the separation of personal troubles from professional performance for fear of betraying private shortcomings and even sinfulness that might prejudice opportunities and rewards in the workplace.

The socially structured struggle for the perfectionist persona that has no private or public flaws is at best a short-term solution. In the long run, it merely generates more perverse consequences and problems in the form of burnout, cynicism or exit from the profession: the very consequences to which Employee Assistance Programs, Stress Workshops and the like are themselves a response.

A CASE OF GUILT

The case of one teacher, a dedicated teacher, highly valued by her colleagues and her school, whom I interviewed in a study of secondary school work cultures and educational change (which I shall describe in Chapter 10) illuminates how these four different determinants can intersect within one setting to produce powerful guilt traps of teaching. A senior teacher in the school, this woman had worked in the school all year since it had opened as a newly built, high profile, innovative, "lighthouse" school, intending to make creative and radical changes in the ways secondary schools are structured and deliver their curriculum. In the middle of the interview, as she talked generally about her work, she came around to the subject of guilt. She talked first about the unending, open-ended, non-completable nature of the work:

> People will say "how are you doing?" And my response is "I'm exhausted but I'm exhilarated", because there is so much work to be done that it will never get done and I think that that was something we all had to realize that many of us are perfectionists, that the perfect is not here yet. It will take several years to develop and that's important for people to

understand and to realize and once there's that understanding
you can stop beating yourself about what you're not doing.

She continued:

It can be an all-consuming job. And that's the danger of it. The
more that you do, the more you're asked to do. And the more
you do well, even more you're asked to do. And this is what
happens, and then you feel guilty by saying "No". But you have
to learn to say, "No — I can't do anymore. I just can't do it".
And then you run a risk of people saying "Oh well, she's at the
end of it. She can't do anymore. She's stressed out!" What they
don't realize is that "No, you're not stressed out". You're being
real in what you can expect of yourself.

The push to perfectionism was especially strong among her colleagues in the
school, for almost all of them had been specially selected as highly motivated
teachers committed to the mission the school would be pursuing. As one of her
colleagues remarked, "all the teachers in this school are excellent". She herself
reflected:

We all were terrific teachers and we had been told all kinds of
times by people, not only here but in the board, that the best of
the best have been chosen for this school. You know, "you people
are sort of the rising suns".

When people encountered difficulties, as could reasonably be expected in changes
of the scope and pace that the school was undertaking, "they didn't want to let
on that they weren't doing a great job or doing the perfect job". The interviewee
explained it like this:

When you are told that you are the best of the best, then you
have to be the best of the best. You can't be a human being. You
know, you're guilty otherwise, aren't you, if you say, "No, I'm not
perfect, I'm just a human being, I can't do all of this stuff. I'm
not happy with what I'm doing. It's not working. I don't see it as
working. . . ."

This push for perfectionism was compounded by what she saw as "unrealistic expectations placed upon us that people really will try to work toward and
feel guilty if they don't get there". This, she explained, was "why a lot of people
have been as sick as they have been this year", trying to respond to extraordinary expectations for success from the Ministry, the district, the principal and
fellow teachers themselves in a school that has rarely been out of the spotlight.

This teacher cared about "the kids". They were "the most important thing
here". She began to realize that working harder was giving them less rather than
more. "I think if you set standards for yourself that are unattainable, then you

just get frustrated by it and you tend to get things done too quickly, and they're not well done," she said.

So she learned to set expectations that were still high but also realistic and achievable. Her family, by no means a "burden" in her case, proved a positive and constructive resource for her.

> I realized I was human; that there were things that were very important to me in my own life as well as life here. So that you can't do a good job if you're not a happy person, so you have to maintain some sort of level of sanity, whether it's through not taking your briefcase home one night a week and not feeling guilty about it. . . . You just can't do it . . .

Her husband, also a teacher, provided a source of mutual support, allowing professional and personal concerns to be appropriately balanced – at least within the domestic sphere.

> We are beginning to realize that it is important that if you have a family, to spend some time with them, and not feel guilty about it, because I think we are made to feel guilty about it.

This teacher drew her strength from her family and found constructive ways of coping with and setting boundaries around her guilt. Not all her colleagues were this fortunate in their private support systems, nor so steadfast in their setting of priorities. We saw earlier that cultures of collaboration can provide valuable alternative forms of support for teachers, helping them to maintain high but realistic expectations about their work. New schools are often envied by other teachers and administrators because of their freedom to start with a "clean sheet" and "hand picked" staff. Yet one of their greatest difficulties is having to develop new structures and changes with no established culture or framework of relationships in which the changes can be understood and problems regarding them discussed. As the teacher interviewed put it:

> And then when we started teaching here, we were trying to cope with building curriculum, dealing with the evaluation and all of that kind of stuff. And we were completely unknown as far as the kids were concerned, so we might as well have been 35 supply teachers with no reputation. We didn't know each other very well either, as a staff. We'd had parties and stuff but you really don't know people until you've worked with them over a period of time. So that was another problem.

She went on:

> That was certainly the bottom of the frustration for me, trying to keep up with the day-by-day stuff, deal with everything that was going on in the school at the same time, and the kids, get to know the kids, and the staff.

There was no culture through which to develop the new structures. The absence of early trust, support and understanding made it hard to discuss problems and difficulties in an open and constructive way; to admit and cope together with the guilt. Among this constellation of "stars" there was apparently no place for "black holes". The perfectionist persona had to be sustained.

> There was one staff meeting where there was an impassioned speech by one of the women on staff, how she felt so inadequate, and that's not unfortunately what people want to hear. What they really want to believe is that everything is rosy and working. "This is perfect." Well it's not perfect. So you stop and reflect and you re-design . . . but you have to be willing to say "No! It's not working!" It's not a failure. There's lots of good things. But it's not all perfect.

This one teacher's account, in the rather guilt-inducing environment of a new and innovative school attempting brave and bold changes of imagination and scope, reveals how guilt traps of teaching are determined and defined through interlocking patterns of constraint and expectation:

- through her commitment to care for "the kids", "the most important thing here";
- through the nature of the job that "will never get done";
- through the "unrealistic expectations" placed on teachers working in a new, innovative, high-profile school, where they have to cope with the multiple demands of complex change;
- through the push to perfectionism in a school made up of the "best of the best" who "didn't want to let on that . . . they weren't doing the perfect job", especially in a school where the staff themselves still needed time to create cultures of trust, support and collaboration where problems could be explored openly without fear of loss of reputation.

CONCLUSION

For many teachers, guilt is a key feature of their emotional lives. To some extent, such guilt, with its associated impulse for repair and replenishment, can help create and sustain positive sources of caring and concern within the professional community of teaching. But teacher behavior that is excessively guilt-ridden and guilt-driven can become unproductive and unprofessional. In psychological terms, guilt can be dealt with constructively, by setting priorities and limits and defending them against the incursions of others. But in many cases, teachers' behavior can degenerate into exit, burnout, cynicism and other negative responses as they attempt to cope with the intolerable burdens of guilt that are imposed from without and that evolve from within.

There are, I have argued, certain guilt traps in teaching that create such excesses of guilt with all their negative consequences. Narrow, exclusive and excessive commitments to care; open-ended definitions of teaching held only loosely among a community of relatively isolated professionals; the growing time demands of accountability and intensification; and the pervasiveness of the perfectionist persona – this is the quadruple alliance of determinants which conspire to create the guilt traps in which so many teacher anxieties and frustrations are locked.

The remedies commonly proposed for problems of teacher burnout, cynicism and other negative behaviors often strike at the symptoms, not the causes, of such behaviors. They deal with the guilt trips rather than the guilt traps of teaching. This analysis of the guilt traps of teaching suggests three rather different remedies of an interconnected nature. In order of decreasing obviousness, these are:

1. Easing the accountability and intensification demands of teaching. Removing some of the sources of persecutory (and also depressive) guilt by relaxing the constraints of accountability. Holding back the bureaucracy, decreasing the emphasis on test scores and other paper forms of accountability, and increasing preparation time in the school day to cope with the growing expectations for schooling – those are just some of the measures that can be and in some places already have been adopted in this respect.

2. Reducing the dependence on personal care and nurturance as the prime motive of elementary teaching in particular by extending the definition of care to embrace a moral and social dimension as well as a personal one, and by balancing the purposes of care with other educational purposes of equivalent importance. This should be a priority in both initial and inservice teacher education.

3. Relieving the uncertainty and open-endedness in teaching by creating communities of colleagues at the school level who work collaboratively to set their own professional standards and limits, while still remaining committed to continuous improvement. Such communities can also bring together the professional and the personal lives of teachers in a way that supports growth and allows problems to be discussed without fear of disapproval or punishment.

Teacher guilt is socially generated, emotionally located and practically consequential. These consequences are often negative for teachers and their schools.

Such guilt can be eased by reducing the constraints and demands on teachers. It can be alleviated and its consequences neutralized by reconstructing and widening the moral and social purposes of teaching beyond those interpersonally parochial preoccupations with care and nurturance that currently pervade the informal culture of elementary teaching. And it can be eased by creating professional communities of situated (not "scientific") certainty and support. Clearly, teacher guilt is not simply a private trouble. It is a public issue, and an important issue that we should address with seriousness. One way to do so is by reconstructing the culture of teaching, the working relationships which provide teachers with or prevent them from acquiring direction, support and professional learning and which can involve them actively in setting challenging goals while also establishing realistic limits in what they do. These cultures of teaching are the concern of the next three chapters.

NOTES

1. On *pride* in teaching, see Waller, W., *The Sociology of Teaching*, New York, John Wiley, 1932; and Lortie, D., *Schoolteacher*, Chicago, University of Chicago Press, 1975. On *commitment*, see Woods, P., *Sociology and the School*, London, Routledge & Kegan Paul, 1983; and Nias, J., *Primary Teachers Talking*, London, Routledge & Kegan Paul, 1989. On *uncertainty*, see Jackson, P., *The Practice of Teaching*, New York, Teachers College Press, 1988; and Rosenholtz, S., *Teachers' Workplace*, New York, Longmans, 1989. On *creativity*, see Woods, P., *Teacher Skills and Strategies*, London and New York, Falmer Press, 1990. On *satisfaction*, see Nias, J., "Teacher satisfaction and dissatisfaction: Herzberg's 'two-factor' hypothesis revisited", *British Journal of Sociology of Education* 2(3), 1981, 235–46.

2. As recorded, for example, in Nias, J., *Primary Teachers Talking*, London, Routledge & Kegan Paul, 1989.

3. Taylor, G., *Pride, Shame and Guilt: Emotions of Self-Assessment*, New York, Clarendon Press, 1985, p.101.

4. Carroll, J., *Guilt*, London, Routledge & Kegan Paul, 1985.

5. Mills, C. W., *The Sociological Imagination*, Harmondsworth, Penguin, 1963.

6. In this sense, my use of the term "guilt trips" differs somewhat from the conventional one. In common usage, guilt trips are emotional burdens that one places on others when they are seen to be responsible for one's own misfortune or misery. Here, however, guilt trips are understood as the paths which people follow as a consequence of *their own* guilt experiences.

7. From *Hamlet*, Act II, Scene I, in Shakespeare, W. *Complete Works*, London, Oxford University Press, 1966, p.19.

8. Davies, A. F., *The Human Element: Three Essays in Political Psychology*, Harmondsworth, Penguin, 1989.

9. See also Taylor, *op. cit.*, note 3.

10. Davies, *op. cit.*, note 8, p. 59.

11. Ibid.

12. Ibid, p. 65.

13. Menzies, H., *Fast Forward and Out of Control: How Technology Is Changing Our Lives,* Toronto, Macmillan, 1989.

14. Rawls, J., *A Theory of Justice,* Cambridge, MA, Harvard University Press, 1971.

15. Laing, R. D., *Self and Others,* Harmondsworth, Penguin, 1969, p. 107.

16. Book, C., and Freeman, D. J., "Differences in entry characteristics of elementary and secondary teacher candidates", *Journal of Teacher Education,* 37(2), 1986, 47–51.

17. Lortie, D., *Schoolteacher, op. cit.,* note 1; Nias, J., *op. cit.,* note 2.

18. Nias, *op. cit.,* note 2. The gendered qualities of care and nurturance as principles of moral judgment and human relationship are discussed in Gilligan, C., *In a Different Voice: Psychological Theory and Women's Development,* Cambridge, MA, Harvard University Press, 1982.

19. Crow, N., *Personal Perspectives on Classroom Management,* Paper presented at the American Educational Research Association Annual Conference, Chicago, 3–7 April 1991.

20. See, for example, Noddings, N., *Caring: A Feminine Approach to Ethics and Moral Education,* Berkeley, CA, University of California Press, 1984.

21. Watson, J., *Nursing: Human Science and Human Care: A Theory of Nursing,* New York, National League for Nursing, 1988, p. 29.

22. Nias, *op. cit.,* note 2, p. 41.

23. Ibid.

24. Book and Freeman, *op. cit.,* note 16.

25. Jensen, K., "Beyond virtue and command: a study of care", Paper presented at the American Educational Research Association Annual Conference, Chicago, 3–7 April, 1991.

26. Crow, *op. cit.,* note 19, p. 11.

27. Mortimore., P., Sammons, P., Stoll, L., Lewis, D. and Ecole, R., *School Matters,* Berkeley, CA, University of California Press, 1988.

28. See, for example, Elbaz, F. L., *Teacher Thinking: A Study of Practical Knowledge,* London, Croom Helm, 1983; Clandinin, D. J., *Classroom Practice: Teacher Images in Action,* London and Philadelphia, Falmer Press, 1986; Connelly, F. M. and Clandinin, D. J., *Teachers as Curriculum Planners: Narratives of Experience,* New York, Teachers College Press, 1988.

29. Neufeld, J. "Curriculum reform and the time of care", *Curriculum Journal,* 2(3), 1991, 285–300.

30. Jensen, *op. cit.,* note 25.

31. Neufeld, *op. cit.*, note 29, p. 296.

32. Flinders, D., "Teacher isolation and the new reform", *Journal of Curriculum and Supervision*, 14(1), 1988.

33. Broadfoot, P. and Osborn, M., "What professional responsibility means to teachers: National contexts and classroom constraints", *British Journal of Sociology of Education*, 9(3), 1988, 30–51.

34. See Hargreaves, A., "Contrived collegiality: The micropolitics of teacher collaboration", in Blase, J. (ed.), *The Politics of Life in Schools*, New York, Sage, 1991; and Apple, M. and Jungck, S., "You don't have to be a teacher to teach this unit: Teaching, technology and control in the classroom", in Hargreaves, A. and Fullan, M. (eds), *Understanding Teacher Development*, London, Cassell and New York, Teachers College Press, 1992.

35. Apple, M., *Teachers and Texts*, New York, Routledge & Kegan Paul, 1986; and Densmore, K., "Professionalism, proletarianization and teachers' work", in Popkewitz, T. (ed.), *Critical Studies in Teacher Education*, Lewes, Falmer Press, 1987.

36. Leithwood, K. and Jantzi, D., "Transformational leadership: How principals can help reform school cultures", Paper presented at the American Educational Research Association Annual Conference, Boston, MA, April 1990.

37. Neufeld, *op. cit.*, note 29.

38. Osborn, M. and Broadfoot, P., "The impact of current changes in English primary schools on teacher professionalism", Paper presented at the American Educational Research Association Annual Conference, Chicago, April 1991.

39. See Chapter 8.

40. Hargreaves, D., "The occupational culture of teaching", in Woods, P. (ed.), *Teacher Strategies*, London, Croom Helm, 1982.

41. Nias, J., Southworth, G. and Yeomans, R., *Staff Relationships in the Primary School*, London, Cassell, 1989.

PART THREE

CULTURE

Chapter 8

Individualism and Individuality
Understanding the Teacher Culture

THE HERESY OF INDIVIDUALISM

In the fields of educational leadership, school effectiveness, school improvement and staff development it is an increasingly accepted wisdom that schools should have a mission or a sense of mission.[1] Missions mitigate the guilt-inducing uncertainties of teaching by forging common beliefs and purposes among the teaching community.[2] Through building common goals along with a shared expectation that they can be met, missions also strengthen teachers' sense of efficacy, their beliefs that they can improve the achievement of all their students, irrespective of background.[3] Missions build motivation and missions bestow meaning. Particularly for those who have participated in their development, missions mean a lot.

Developing a sense of mission builds loyalty, commitment and confidence in a school community. It is a powerful spur to improvement. But if missions develop loyalty among the faithful and confidence among the committed, they also create heresy among those who question, differ and doubt. The narrower and more fervent the mission, the greater and more widespread the heresy. For the missionary, heresies are beyond the walls of wisdom, the boundaries of belief. Heresies are not to be derogated or dismissed. To deem an idea as heretical is to dismiss it without counsel or consideration. The social construction of heresy is, in this sense, a powerful ideological force. It suppresses proper discussion of choices and alternatives by patronizingly disregarding their seriousness or by undermining the personal credibility of those who advance them. Heretics, then, are not merely dissenting or disagreeable. They are personally flawed. Weakness, madness or badness are the hallmarks of the heretic, the qualities that mark him or her out from the rest.

In his extensive and intriguing discussion of heresy as a social phenomenon, Szasz argues that heresy

> has to do with not believing what everyone else believes or what
> one ought to believe; with proclaiming disbelief when the right
> thing to do is to proffer belief or at least remain silent.[4]

Heresy will be present, says Szasz, "so long as there is tension between the individual and the group".[5] Individuals must think for themselves. That is what makes them individuals. Yet the group wants its members to echo its beliefs. This is what Szasz calls the constant structure of heresy.

Heresy is a commonly understood accompaniment to religious beliefs and doctrines. But it can be associated with scientific and technological ideals, or political and cultural belief systems, too. To proclaim that the Virgin Birth is not a literal truth but a literalized metaphor is a heresy in the Christian tradition. To assert that the West has much to learn from the East (and not merely vice versa) or that progress is not always good is heretical within Western democracies. Educational systems and those who work within them or on behalf of them also have their heresies. That schools might best be run without the office of principalship or headship; that schools should be primarily responsible for the development of their own curricula; that many children with special needs are better off *not* being integrated into regular classrooms: these are heresies of contemporary educational thought. Within contemporary educational systems, heresies such as these are unspeakable. To utter them is not merely to disagree, but to be wicked or weak. Heresies lie beyond the bounds of reason.

All these heresies are what might be called *substantive heresies,* or heresies of content. They are heresies which question, which threaten particular parts of the belief system, particular doctrines which the faithful hold dear. But beneath these heresies are even deeper, more profound ones. These I want to call *generic heresies,* or heresies of form. Generic heresies challenge the central purpose of the mission itself, and the principles on which it is founded. In the fields of school improvement, staff development and educational change, a fundamental generic heresy is the heresy of individualism. The qualities and characteristics that fall under the labels of teacher individualism, isolation and privatism are widely perceived as significant threats or barriers to professional development, the implementation of change and the development of shared educational goals.

Terms like individualism and collegiality are, however, quite vague and imprecise, open to a range of meanings and interpretations. Of collegiality, Little, for instance, has remarked that the term is "conceptually amorphous and ideologically sanguine".[6] Much the same can be said of individualism. Such terms are in many respects used and understood less as accurate descriptions of types of practice, policy or aspiration. Rather, they are mostly symbolic; motivating rhetorics in a mythical discourse of change and improvement. Here, collaboration and collegiality have become powerful images of preferred aspiration; isolation and individualism equally powerful images of professional aversion. Individualism, isolation and privatism have therefore become preoccupations of and key targets for the educational reform movement. Their eradication, like the eradication of all heresy, has become a high priority.

This chapter analyzes the phenomenon of individualism as a generic heresy of educational change. It begins by critically reviewing existing research and other literature on teacher individualism, isolation and privatism, and identifies what are claimed to be their constituent features and patterns of causation. Findings from the preparation time study are then counterposed against this existing knowledge base. This qualitative research reveals teacher-based explanations for individualistic preferences in the use of preparation time that provide interesting and surprising points of contrast with the existing literature. Together, the critical review of the literature and the findings of the preparation time study provide grounds for reinterpreting and reconstructing the concept of teacher individualism and its implications for change in ways that are less consistently negative than many other writers and researchers have led us to believe.

CULTURES OF TEACHING

Individualism, isolation and privatism make up one particular form of what has come to be known as the culture of teaching. But there are other kinds of teacher culture that are also important for and influential on the work that teachers do. In general, these various cultures provide a context in which particular strategies of teaching are developed, sustained and preferred over time. In this sense, *cultures of teaching* comprise beliefs, values, habits and assumed ways of doing things among communities of teachers who have had to deal with similar demands and constraints over many years.[7] Culture carries the community's historically generated and collectively shared solutions to its new and inexperienced membership. It forms a framework for occupational learning. In this respect, the teaching strategies of kindergarten teachers, for instance, evolve differently from those used by teachers of adolescents, because the problems they routinely face are different. In the same way, the teaching strategies of family studies teachers evolve differently from those of mathematics teachers, those of inner city teachers evolve differently from those who teach in the suburbs and so on. If we want to understand what the teacher does and why the teacher does it, we must therefore also understand the teaching community, the work culture of which that teacher is a part.

Cultures of teaching help give meaning, support and identity to teachers and their work. Physically, teachers are often alone in their own classrooms, with no other adults for company. Psychologically, they never are. What they do there in terms of classroom styles and strategies is powerfully affected by the outlooks and orientations of the colleagues with whom they work now and have worked in the past. In this respect, teacher cultures, the relationships between teachers and their colleagues, are among the most educationally significant aspects of teachers' lives and work.[8] They provide a vital context for teacher development and for the ways that teachers teach. What goes on inside the teacher's classroom cannot be divorced from the relations that are forged outside it.

There are two important dimensions to cultures of teaching, as indeed to all cultures: content and form. The *content* of teacher cultures consists of the substantive attitudes, values, beliefs, habits, assumptions and ways of doing things that are shared within a particular teacher group, or among the wider teacher community. The content of teacher cultures can be seen in what teachers think, say and do. It is "the way we do things around here". The essentially normative concept of sharing (shared beliefs, shared attitudes), of explicit or implicit consensus, is central to the content-driven view of teacher cultures – a view which underpins and pervades the wider literature on organizational cultures.[9] It is the *content* of teacher cultures we are describing when we discuss academic cultures, pastoral (guidance) cultures, subject cultures and so forth. It is here that cultural diversity among the teaching force is most obvious. There is undoubtedly important work to be done in classifying such cultures, in examining their origins, their interrelationships and the ways in which they change over time. This is not my chief concern in this book, though. My main concern in this chapter and the following two is with *form*.

The *form* of teacher cultures consists of the characteristic *patterns of relationship* and *forms of association* between members of those cultures. The *form* of teacher cultures is to be found in how relations between teachers and their colleagues are articulated. The normative concept of sharing is not essential to this definition, for the *form* of teacher cultures may be individualistic or antagonistic, for instance. Relations between teachers and their colleagues, or the *form* of their culture, as it were, may change over time. Indeed, it is through the forms of teacher culture that the *contents* of those different cultures are realized, reproduced and re-defined. To put it another way, changes in beliefs, values and attitudes in the teaching force may be contingent upon prior or parallel changes in the ways teachers relate to their colleagues, in their characteristic patterns of association.[10] To understand the forms of teacher culture, therefore, is to understand many of the limits to and possibilities of teacher development and educational change.

There are, it seems to me, four broad forms of teacher culture, each of which has very different implications for teachers' work and educational change. They are:

- individualism;
- collaboration;
- contrived collegiality;
- balkanization.

I will explore and compare each of these in the three chapters within this section. In the concluding chapter, I will also try to delineate the outlines of a fifth form more appropriate to the demands and challenges of the postmodern world than any of these four in their entirety. I want to begin with the much discussed and, in my view, much misunderstood culture of individualism.

INDIVIDUALISM AS A PSYCHOLOGICAL DEFICIT

Most teachers still teach alone, behind closed doors, in the insulated and isolated environment of their own classrooms. Most elementary schools still have what Lortie described as an egg-crate-like structure to them: segregated classrooms dividing teachers from one another so they see and understand little of what their colleagues do.[11]

Classroom isolation offers many teachers a welcome measure of privacy, a protection from outside interference which they often value. Yet classroom isolation brings with it problems too. Although it purges the classroom of blame and criticism, it also shuts out possible sources of praise and support. Isolated teachers get little adult feedback on their value, worth and competence.

The continuing and pervasive presence of isolation, individualism and privatism within the culture of teaching is not a matter of serious doubt or disagreement among writers on the subject.[12] While pockets of collaborative and collegial practice among teachers are acknowledged, these are widely understood to be exceptions to the general rule, requiring special conditions for their development and persistence.[13] Despite numerous efforts at improvement and reform, individualism stubbornly prevails within the teacher culture. Why?

Within the research literature, two kinds of explanation are commonly advanced as determinants of individualism. In the first, more traditional interpretation, individualism is associated with diffidence, defensiveness and anxiety; with flaws and failures in teachers that are partly "natural" and partly a result of the uncertainties of their work.

Dan Lortie, the first to discuss teacher individualism in any systematic way, associated it with qualities of uncertainty and anxiety that led teachers to rely on orthodox doctrines and their own past experience as students when forming their own styles and strategies of teaching.[14] "Uncertainty", observed Lortie, "is the lot of those who teach",[15] for the goals of teaching are diffuse and the feedback on success in achieving them is unreliable. The majority of teachers that Lortie interviewed did not just happen to be isolated from one another by the architecture of the school. They also actively preferred isolation, arguing that if they were allocated more time, they would spend it in relation to their own classrooms, not on working with their colleagues.[16]

In a series of essays on the occupational culture of teaching, David Hargreaves reiterated Lortie's judgment that teacher individualism "is not cocky and self-assured, but hesitant and uneasy".[17] Hargreaves's characterization of teacher individualism is peppered with the metaphorical language of deficiency and pathology. "The cult of individualism", he claims, "has *deeply infected* the occupational culture of teachers."[18] Teachers "guard their autonomy *jealously*".[19] They do not like being observed, still less being evaluated because they are *fearful* of the criticism that may accompany evaluation. Defences of isolation and independence of a more dignified and virtuous nature are dismissed as rationalizations. "Autonomy", claims Hargreaves, "is the polite word used to *mask* teachers' evaluative *apprehension* and to serve as the rationale for excluding observers."[20]

In a study of 78 elementary schools in Tennessee, Rosenholtz identified 15 schools which she called *isolated* and 50 she termed *moderately isolated* in character.[21] Fifty-five teachers were then randomly selected from a subsample of these isolated and moderately isolated schools and interviewed. In this, one of the most comprehensive studies of teachers' collegial relations yet undertaken, Rosenholtz makes some useful, insightful and well-grounded observations on teachers' statements about their behavior in isolated settings. She finds that help-giving is infrequent, that (as in Lortie's study) it rarely extends beyond sharing existing materials and ideas, that planning and problem-solving with colleagues scarcely happens at all, and that "isolated" teachers prefer to keep discipline problems to themselves.

This is an informative and well-substantiated analysis. But when outlining some of the psychological associations and implications of these data, Rosenholtz shifts deceptively beyond them. For instance, one of the key themes in the social organization of teaching that Rosenholtz associates with teacher isolation is what, following Lortie, she calls teacher uncertainty.[22] The isolated teachers Rosenholtz interviewed do not actually *say* they feel uncertain. Rosenholtz, rather, invokes the construct of *uncertainty* to describe the social organization of the teachers' group, of the teaching culture as a whole in isolated settings.[23] Here, she uses "uncertainty" to describe lack of clear agreement, common definition or collective confidence in shared teaching technologies. In this, there is no problem of interpretation. It is perfectly proper to develop and use concepts in this way to articulate, at one remove, the relationships between the more directly visible elements of a social structure or organizational culture.

However, Rosenholtz shifts almost imperceptibly from this use of uncertainty as a property of *social organization* to its use as a *psychological quality* of teachers themselves where teachers are claimed to *feel* certain or uncertain.[24] In this way, a perfectly legitimate use of uncertainty to describe the loose articulation of goals and purposes in the *social organization* of "isolated" settings becomes subtly transformed into a defective *psychological quality* with strong insinuations of individual deficit and personal disorganization. In places, these subtle imputations of psychological shortcoming expand into wider swathes of sweeping invective and hyperbole, as for instance in the following passage:

> Like the oyster that neutralizes an irritating grain of sand by
> coating it with layers of pearl, isolated teachers seem to coat
> their irritating self-doubts and inadequacies with comforting
> layers of self-deception.[25]

The warrant for Rosenholtz privileging her own interpretation of teacher meaning as mere self-deception, over the teachers' own, is not to be found directly in the data. Nor are the psychological attributes of hesitancy and uneasiness to be found directly in Lortie's data either. In an extensive study of the relationship between teachers' senses of efficacy and their working conditions, Ashton and Webb also use a little interpretive license to describe the way that "on the psychological level, insularity functions to protect the professional image of individual teachers by placing a buffer between them and the *criticism they fear* they might receive if others saw them at work" (my emphasis).[26] Here, Ashton and Webb's allegations of "feared criticisms" are not directly observed but functionally imputed. Lastly, David Hargreaves's characterization of teacher individualism rests on no first-hand data at all but on his application to the English context of findings drawn mainly from American research, particularly Lortie's.[27] In all these cases, relatively sound and well-established findings and interpretations concerning the *workplace conditions* of teacher isolation and individualism shift deceptively into attributions of rather unflattering *psychological characteristics* of individual teachers themselves within those workplaces.[28]

Translating the meaning of individualism, isolation and privatism from a property of workplace cultures and structures to a psychological characteristic of teachers themselves has special significance when it occurs in the context of interventions designed to develop collective working relationships between teachers and their colleagues. For such translations of meaning in the context of change and improvement can lead to teacher resistance being interpreted as a problem of the teacher, not the system. The teacher here can all too easily become the scapegoat of unfulfilled change. Bruce Joyce and his colleagues fall into this trap in their account of a school-wide effort to develop closer collaborative working relations among teachers. Commenting on the substantial presence of anxiety among teachers involved in the project, they assert their belief that "anxiety is a natural syndrome that arises from two sources [including] fear of exposure and incompetence in the more public teaching environment".[29] The roots of anxiety here are located not in workplace conditions; not even in any rational objection to what it is the teachers are being asked to collaborate *about;* but in the teachers themselves, in their own "naturally" vulnerable skills and qualities.

None of this is to say that teachers cannot ever be blamed for their preference to remain in splendid isolation. It is possible that the kinds of personalities attracted to teaching feel more comfortable in the company of children than in the company of adults. Such heresies too must be entertained. It is also possible that it *is* primarily diffidence and defensiveness, fear of observation and evaluation that drive most teachers into the imagined security of their classrooms. All these things are possible. But they are not proven. Their presence in the data of the studies reviewed here is not strong. They do not inhere in the data but have mainly been grafted on afterwards. In short, it seems that the privileged interpretation of teacher individualism as embodying a cluster of implied psychological deficits has little or no warrant. There are other candidate explanations that merit equally serious consideration.

INDIVIDUALISM AS A WORKPLACE CONDITION

Revised interpretations of teacher individualism adopt a different tack. They view it less as a personal shortcoming than a rational economizing of effort and ordering of priorities in a highly pressed and constraining working environment. At the simple and most obvious level, teacher individualism is seen as arising from the physical facts of isolation, embedded in the traditional architecture of schools and their cellular patterns of organization into separate classrooms. These physical facts of isolation form a second important strand of Lortie's explanation of individualism, for instance.

But the workplace determinants of individualism extend far beyond the facts of physical isolation, as such. Flinders helpfully distinguishes three different perspectives on teacher isolation here: isolation as a *psychological state,* isolation as an *ecological condition* under which teachers work (in the sense of physical isolation), and his own alternative — isolation as an adaptive strategy to conserve scarce occupational resources. For Flinders, "isolation is an adaptive strategy because it protects the time and energy required to meet immediate instructional demands".[30] Isolation here is something that is self-imposed and actively worked for. It fends off the digressions and diversions involved in working with colleagues, to give focus to instruction with and for one's own students. This need for time to support instruction is felt to be particularly urgent given the open-ended, endless nature of teaching and the constraints of large classes, assessment demands and the like. Isolation in this view, then, is a sensible adaptive strategy to the work environment of teaching. Flinders argues that the rooting of isolation in workplace conditions such as these explains why attempts to eliminate teacher isolation by removing physical barriers (taking down walls), or by developing psychological skills and qualities suited to collaborative work, are not usually successful. They are directed at the wrong causes.

McTaggart outlines a further set of working conditions which explain the persistence of what he calls privatism, even in the circumstances of a specially supported aesthetic education initiative ostensibly devised to promote collaboration among teachers.[31] The disincentives to collaborate in this project, McTaggart observes, were rooted in a system dominated by principles of bureaucratic rationality which stifled teacher initiative and gave teachers little to collaborate about. Systems of accountability and evaluation at the district level placed "basics" at the centre of teachers' priorities, thrusting aesthetics to the periphery. Curricula and textbooks were standardized at district level too. Once changes were made, they then became binding. Teacher participation in curriculum development therefore became circumscribed, controlled, coopted. Reflecting on Joyce's and Fullan's injunctions to "crack the walls of privatism" in teaching,[32] McTaggart concludes from his study that:

It was not the walls of privatism that needed cracking in this school district, but the social milieu and conditions of work which so effectively undermined the confidence and devalued the knowledge, wisdom and credibility of its best teachers.[33]

In these revised interpretations of individualism, the culture of teaching is rooted more realistically in the continuing work context of the job. Individualism is a consequence of complex organizational conditions and constraints, and it is these that need to be attended to if individualism is to be removed. But interestingly, the assumption that individualism and isolation are ultimately harmful and in need of elimination still remains beyond question. It is not at all a matter of doubt.

Clearly, while there are important differences between the traditional and revised interpretations of individualism, there are also some unexpected similarities. In both interpretations, individualism is primarily a shortcoming, not a strength; a problem, not a possibility; something to be removed rather than something to be respected. The heresy of individualism remains largely intact.

REDEFINING THE DETERMINANTS OF INDIVIDUALISM

Individualism, I have argued, has come to be associated with bad and weak practice, teacher deficiencies, and things that need to be changed. Yet in practice, individualism has other meanings and connotations which are not nearly so negative in character. Flinders, for instance, in his analysis of the closely related concept of teacher isolation, notes that "what one . . . group of teachers regards as isolation, others may see in terms of individual autonomy and professional support".[34] Even Lortie, from whom much of the critical writing about teacher individualism springs, pointed to positive as well as negative aspects of the phenomenon. In particular, he drew attention to what he called the *psychic rewards* of elementary school teaching: to the joys and satisfactions that intensive, sustained and caring relationships with children brought to the classroom teacher. Not even for Lortie was individualism all bad. With the long philosophical and political traditions underpinning the concept of individualism, things could scarcely be otherwise. Indeed, reviewing the concept of individualism within social and political philosophy, Steven Lukes has identified no fewer than 11 meanings of the term, including ones associated with human dignity, autonomy, privacy, self-development, possessive individualism, economic individualism, religious individualism and ethical individualism.[35]

Clearly, when we speak of individualism, therefore, we are speaking not of a singular thing but of a complex social and cultural phenomenon with many meanings — not all of them necessarily negative. If we are to develop a sophisticated rather than a stereotyped understanding of how teachers work with their colleagues, and of the benefits and drawbacks of these different ways of working, then it is important to unpack this concept of teacher individualism more carefully and reconstruct it in professionally helpful ways. It is time we approached individualism in a spirit of understanding, not one of persecution.

Three broad determinants of individualism were identified in the preparation time study which have close but not exact parallels with Flinders' typology of teacher isolation.[36] These are *constrained* individualism, *strategic* individualism and *elective* individualism. I will review the first two and arguably more familiar determinants of individualism in brief then concentrate the analysis in more detail on the third.

Constrained individualism (Flinders' ecological condition) occurs where teachers teach, plan and generally work alone because of administrative or other situational constraints which present significant barriers or discouragements to their doing otherwise. In the preparation study, these constraints included non-involving styles of administration; egg-crate structures of school architecture; scarcity and low quality of available space for adults to work together; shortages of supply teachers; overcrowding with its attendant proliferation of segregated temporary classrooms; and difficulties of scheduling teachers to plan together due to timetabling complexities in large schools, the unavailability of released partners in small ones and the complications brought about by split-grade classes in all of them.

Strategic individualism (Flinders' adaptive strategy) refers to the ways in which teachers actively construct and create individualistic patterns of working as a response to the daily contingencies of their work environment. The dedication of teachers to their work, the diffuse goals of the job, and the mounting external pressures and expectations for accountability and for modified programming in relation to the growing number of special education students in ordinary classes all tended to make teachers classroom-centered as they pursued the impossibly high standards and endless work schedules that they set for themselves and that others set for them. Individualism here was a calculated concentration of effort. It was strategic. In this context, preparation time was a scarce resource that could not be wasted in relaxation but needed to be spent on the many little things that made up the endless list of teachers' jobs. The same strategic principle contributed to teachers' preferences for preparation time cover — these being exercised in favor of segregated self-contained specialisms like music and art which would require no further planning with the covering teacher.

Elective individualism refers to the principled choice to work alone, all or some of the time, and sometimes even in circumstances where there are opportunities and encouragement to work collaboratively with colleagues. Elective individualism describes a preferred way of being, a preferred way of working rather than merely a constrained or strategic response to occupational demands and contingencies. It is a form of individualism which is experienced less as a response to forces of circumstance, or less a strategic calculation of efficient investment of time and energy, than as a preferred form of professional action for all or part of one's work. Of course, in practice, voluntary choice and institutional constraint are not so easily segregated as this. Choices themselves are often the result of history, of biography, and of professional socialization. But whatever its ultimate origins, at any one moment, elective individualism describes patterns of working that are preferred on pedagogical and personal grounds more than on grounds of obligation, lack of opportunity, or efficient expenditure of effort.

In our preparation time study, elective individualism comprised three closely interrelated themes. These are *personal care*, *individuality* and *solitude*.

INDIVIDUALISM AND PERSONAL CARE

The greatest satisfactions of elementary school teaching are found, as a rule, not in pay, prestige or promotion but in what Lortie called the *psychic rewards* of teaching:[37] the joys and satisfactions of caring for and working with young people. The teachers in the study talked a lot about the pleasures of being "with the kids". In one or two cases, they preferred to take their recesses and lunches in the classroom with the children rather than in the staffroom with adults. They spoke of the immense pleasure of hearing a child read her first word or sentence. One teacher commented that when children cheered on being given a new project, "that was its own reward". Several were eager to say, at the end of the interview, that while they had been critical of certain ways in which preparation time was allocated or used, they did not want me to think they disliked teaching. Teaching gave them immense satisfaction, they said. For some, it was "a wonderful job". "I think I'm paid too much sometimes." Even when bureaucratic pressures and constraints seemed overbearing, it was the children and being with the children that kept some of these teachers going. A number questioned the value of meetings, required cooperative planning and other administrative initiatives insofar as these took them away from the children.

These psychic rewards of teaching are central to sustaining teachers' senses of self; their senses of value and worth in their work. In many ways, the primacy of these rewards points to the centrality among elementary teachers of what Gilligan calls an *ethic of care*.[38] In this ethic, actions are motivated by concerns for care and nurturance of others and connectedness to others. It is an ethic that is extremely common in women, but not exclusive to them, says Gilligan. Women, of course, make up the vast proportion of elementary school teachers. It is, in many respects, their commitment to the ethic of care that brings many of them to elementary teaching in the first place.

In many respects, administrative justifications to collaborate with colleagues often appear to be presented less in terms of an ethic of care than in terms of a contrary *ethic of responsibility*[39] Professional obligations are emphasized. Improvements to planning and instruction are stressed. In the face

173

of such demands, what looks like a retreat to insecure individualism may actually be a conservation of care.

Classroom care is often surrounded by other sentiments and orientations, though, which make its presence less obvious, its impact more complex. In particular, care is commonly bound up with other orientations toward ownership and control. Ownership entails more than care, nurturance and connectedness in the relationships that teachers develop with their classes. It suggests that teachers have prime, perhaps even sole responsibility for their classes; that students somehow belong to their teachers, like possessions. As one principal observed, "teachers are a very possessive lot". When temporary classrooms isolated teachers from their colleagues, for instance, this tended to make the teachers within them overly possessive and protective about "their own" children.

> Part of it being in portables [temporary classrooms] is, you never
> have team teaching. Even the fact that − this is what I find, is
> the isolation. If I have to go to the washroom, I can't even leave
> my portable − where, in the school, you can knock on the
> teacher's door and say "Keep an eye on my class". But you get
> very mothering. I think even more so out there, because they're
> your family and you have this little house. I don't find people, I
> don't look at them as being intruders, but there just doesn't seem
> to be the flow. Nobody comes. Nobody goes. So you become your
> own little body of people.

On the one hand, ownership can involve taking on onerous responsibility. On the other, it can acquire characteristics of possessiveness, carrying with it a reluctance to share what one has with others. Among the teachers we interviewed, this was most overtly an issue where there were threats to ownership; where decisions about one's children might have to be shared with someone else. This happened in several cases where teachers had been required to meet and program with the special education resource teacher (SERT) for those children in the class who had been identified as needing modified programs. As teachers talked about this consultation, they revealed the existence of conflicts in the early stages of their relationships. Who was responsible for these children? Who had the authority to make decisions? Power struggles appeared to have occurred over the ownership of "special education" students in a number of regular classes, although in most cases, by the time of the interview, these seemed to be settling down. After describing initial difficulties with his SERT, one teacher summed matters up by saying:

> If classroom teachers have the greater responsibility, 85–90
> percent expectation that the programs will be modified, to meet
> the needs of unique or individual learners, then the expectation
> must also be there to have available to them resource personnel,

someone with expertise, someone that can share ideas, so that
the time is well spent.

Notwithstanding the value of consultation and complementary expertise, for this teacher it was absolutely clear where the ownership rested: with the classroom teacher.

If the divisions between care and ownership are unclear, so too are those between care and control. Sometimes, it seems, we can act as if we are being kind to be cruel. Control in social settings comprises the ability to regulate, determine and direct the course of one's life or other lives, and to avoid or resist intrusions and impositions by others which interfere with that ability. Control over one's own destiny and over the destinies of others has both positive and negative implications. The bounded classroom where the teacher has almost exclusive contact with and responsibility for the development of impressionable young minds is rife with control implications. Indeed, there are elements of the control impulse that attract many teachers to that setting. The following interview extract illustrates some of the issues that are at stake here.

> I.   So what's the biggest difference that you've found, moving
> from Special Education to having a class of your own?
>
> T.   Control! I'm in charge. I'm the one that calls the shots, I'm
> the one that says what goes. As a resource teacher, you're
> with other people. You adapt to whatever style, method
> philosophy the other teacher has. . . . I enjoy being in
> charge. I enjoy being in control.

Care, ownership and control are, in any one teacher's sentiments, often combined together in a complicated and subtle mixture. This had important and unexpected implications for preparation time practice, particularly regarding the judgment of a subsample of teachers about the possible drawbacks of still further additions to their preparation time that were then being proposed by their federation representatives. In the board we studied, which was committed to developing collaborative planning in a group of its schools, teachers' and principals' observations on the value of further additions to preparation time were evenly divided between support for and opposition to additional time. Of the ten teachers who gave clear views on the advantages and disadvantages of extending preparation time further, five were at least ambivalent about and, in many cases, strongly critical of the impact that additional preparation time would have on the coherence of their children's program, the stability of the classroom atmosphere and the quality of instruction. Most of these teachers were genuinely torn in their commitments and their desires. They could do with more time, most of them said. But their worry and concern that overrode this desire was the negative consequences that extra time away from class would have for instruction and for what they called classroom "flow".

A little bit of concern that I have is, it's nice to have prep time, and I do appreciate it, but if you start to take more time away, take me away from the children more, then I do get concerned. Because one teacher has one set of standards that they can do, and then another has another set of standards.

Commenting on the push by federations to secure 200 minutes of preparation time to be more comparable with their secondary school colleagues, one teacher said:

T. Two hundred minutes would be nice, but I wonder what impact it will have on the kids. They already deal with a French teacher, a physical education teacher, an art teacher. Now they're dealing with somebody who comes in . . . and a lot of children can't handle all those different teachers in one day. It really throws a lot of kids off.

I. So are you suggesting that 200 minutes may be a ceiling, or it may be slightly too high?

T. Yes . . . other teachers would shoot me for saying that! To me it's nice to have the prep time. And it really is great, especially now when I'm working with the kids. I find I get a lot accomplished and I can keep a lot of kids up to date that way. But I really feel that when you leave the kids behind, you really don't know that what you want to get across is getting across.

Another teacher remarked:

I guess having taught when there wasn't any, I'm so grateful for having some. I think it's hard − I could say, "Yes, I could use more". But you've got to remember that the more time you're out of the classroom − they get different teachers. And there are three teachers right now in my class. To introduce a lot of kids when they hit Grade 4, they could still have a French teacher, two or three different teachers coming in for preps, their own teacher − is this too much for the kids? Is it too much for the classroom teacher trying to keep track of all these other people?

Two other teachers offered similar comments:

I wouldn't want 200 minutes with the one class . . . , unless one program was going to be taken over by the other teacher, because otherwise the kids would be missing out on something.

As it was increased, I thought, "It's fine". But there's an amount you can increase it to and then you are missing your kids. This is what I said to [the principal] the other day. "It's fine having all

these spares, but when do you ever get the kids?" I said, "That's
what we're here for. To be with the kids too."

In the arguments and concerns surrounding the provision of additional
preparation time, it is possible to see how different but closely interrelated
aspects of individualism concerning care, control and ownership combine to play
themselves out. There were concerns about fragmentation of the program for
students, about fragmentation of their contacts with adults, and about teachers
losing touch with children. Care, ownership and control underpinned many
teachers' attachments to their classes and underpinned their concerns about
classroom relationships and program continuity being interrupted and damaged
by too many visiting teachers. Nor, beyond a certain point, was working
with other teachers viewed as being as valuable as spending time with the
children.

Teachers who were critical of additional preparation time feared the consequences of loss of continuous contact with their classes. The combined concerns
of care, control and ownership were paramount. Yet it is also interesting that
these teachers assumed preparation time would necessarily mean time *away*
from their class. For such teachers, where arrangements regarding the use of
additional preparation time are being discussed, it may be important to develop
patterns of use which appeal to and build on these teachers' commitment to the
ethic of care, instead of threatening it. This could mean, first, that some additional preparation time might be spent *with* existing classes in different ways —
with individual and small groups of students, perhaps (while a covering teacher
takes responsibility for the rest) — deepening and extending the commitment to
the ethic of care rather than weakening it. Second, schools and administrators
may need to consider different principles for developing and different ways of
justifying collaborative work relations among their teachers. At the moment,
these are commonly organized and justified according to an *ethic of responsibility* with appeals to professional obligations, instructional effectiveness and
the like. Yet a number of teachers, it appears, are motivated not by this ethic
at all, but by an *ethic of care*. The challenge to administration may therefore be
to show in their deeds that relations with one's colleagues can also be organized
according to the ethic of care: that care need not be confined to the classroom
but can be extended to the collegial community also.

In this case, teachers have the opportunity and the obligation to *receive* care
as well as to give it — to open themselves up to receiving care from others,
instead of being like moral martyrs and always giving the care themselves. The
best advice here might come from Dolly Parton in her movie, *Straight Talk* —
"Come down off the cross — we need the wood!" Should this kind of reciprocal
collegial caring become a priority, it is also important, of course, that principals
and headteachers develop and demonstrate such a commitment to the ethic of
care in their own case as well — in terms of receiving and asking for care, as well
as giving it.

Care is not necessarily tied to individualism. But partly because of its additional association with ownership and control, the two do go strongly together. Many attempts to eliminate the habits of individualism also unintentionally threaten teachers' commitments to care. Some of the suggestions just outlined may make it possible to separate care from its attachment to individualism and to classroom work alone. With that kind of loosening, it may be possible to change the culture of individualism without challenging the ethic of care that teachers hold so dear.

INDIVIDUALISM AND INDIVIDUALITY

Care is an often unseen and misunderstood component of what usually passes for individualism in our schools. Another commonly overlooked component is individuality. In his impressive treatise on individualism, Steven Lukes notes how, from Balzac onwards, many writers and thinkers more generally have drawn a fundamental opposition between *individualism* and *individuality*.[40] For Lukes, the first implies "anarchy and social atomization". The second implies "personal independence and self-realization". *Individualism* leads to the relaxation of social unity — the traditional concern of sociological writers like Durkheim.[41] But the extinction of *individuality* (perhaps in the name of removing individualism) creates only a spurious unity; surrender to public opinion.[42]

In his analysis of heresy, Thomas Szasz fascinatingly describes how its original meaning, derived from the Greek, was that of *choice*.[43] Quoting the *Encylopaedia Britannica*, Szasz describes heresy in its original sense as an act of choosing which came "to signify a set of philosophical opinions or the school professing to them". The original meaning of heresy is actually one of independence of judgment, then. But over time, after its appropriation by Christianity, its meaning took on negative, pejorative associations of illegitimate dissent. By a similar process, the principled dissent and disagreement of *individuality* is commonly presented in the pejorative language of *individualism*. When what is thought to be individualism is eliminated, individuality may be the sacrifice.

The power to make independent judgments, to exercise personal discretion, initiative and creativity through their work — what Schön described as defining the heart of professional action[44] — is important to many teachers. If requirements for teamwork and collaboration seem as if they might be eliminating opportunities for independence and initiative, then unhappiness and dissatisfaction may result. One teacher highlighted these concerns in some detail:

> *T.* It's being encouraged more and more. They've been through all the schools. They want you working as a team.
>
> *I.* Do you think that's good?
>
> *T.* So long as they allow for the creativity of the individual to modify the program. But if they want everything

York St John University
Check-Out Receipt

Customer name: SHANNON, NATALIE

Title: Changing teachers, changing times:
teachers' work and culture in the postmodern
ID: 38025004617091
Due: 25/5/2007,23:59

Title: Management theories for educational
change
ID: 38025004614502
Due: 25/5/2007,23:59

Total items: 2
30/04/2007 13:07

Tel: 01904 876700

> lock-stepped, identical – no, I think it would be disastrous,
> because you're going to get some people that won't think at
> all, that just sit back and coast on somebody else's brains
> and I don't feel that's good for anybody.

I. Do you feel you're given that space at the moment?

T. With [my teaching partner] I am. I know with some others
here, I wouldn't . . . I'd go crazy.

I. How would that be . . . ?

T. Basically controlled. They would want – first of all it
would be their ideas. And I would have to fit into their
teaching style, and it would have to fit into their time slot.
And I don't think anybody should have to work like that . . .

This teacher, a self-confessed "maverick", like his partner, did not approve of sharing for sharing's sake. Indeed, to him, sharing sometimes seemed a way of closing down his options for teaching, rather than opening them up. He described, for instance, a recent inservice experience he had undergone where:

> We were just hearing philosophy. I wasn't hearing any
> practicality. And I like to see practicality and philosophy go
> together, so I'd like to try some of the ideas out, so if I have
> questions, I can ask them about it; and I'm not getting that . . .
> The philosophy has been that you share a lot of ideas, you get in
> contact with a teacher at [another school], and you talk about
> what they're doing there. And you get their ideas and you give
> them your ideas. To me that's a waste of time. Why can't we just
> sit there with a consultant, or whatever, and if we're having a
> meeting that night, plan a couple of sequential meetings where
> we're going to build up this fund of knowledge. It's not up to the
> person (at another school) to tell me!

In this kind of inservice experience, he went on, the fundamental questions he wanted to ask were not addressed. He was invited to go and "share" with someone else instead. He cited another recent case where "there were a lot of questions, but they were just ramming everything down your throat". This was not only frustrating, but also a threat to his own classroom competence, he felt.

> They'll say, "Well, if you have any questions, just let us know."
> Well, it's fine, but you're starting to go through this thing and
> you're saying to yourself, "What's the purpose for this? This does
> not make sense to me and yet I've got to teach it." When you
> teach it, the kids are looking at you and saying "This doesn't
> make sense" too.

Another teacher described ways in which threats to autonomy had been associated with declining competence and sense of professionalism in her own case. In her previous school, she said, her principal had been committed to "whole language" teaching.

> Exceedingly! Whole-language. Totally. All day. You never had a reading group that sat down with a certain reader and a certain story all at the same time. That was forbidden . . .
> "Whole-language" was the current buzz-word, and this one administrator could not allow any structure.

So vigilant was this principal that "you never knew when he was popping in", and "you must not have kids working quietly at the same task". "It was very difficult", she went on, and in the end she simply resorted to "survival tactics".

> You had to put out the work for them. The kids had to choose. They were all choosing different things, all different subjects, all of the time. . . . And I just found the children's skills were not developing.

In important ways, this teacher felt her professional autonomy, her power and right to exercise discretionary judgment, had been breached. By contrast, she was overflowing in her praise for her new principal, who respected her autonomy and judgment; who recognized that "you do have solid workable ideas that are effective". "It's a tremendous reassurance", she said, "to realize that once more, there is someone out there who will trust you."

Individuality, as the power to exercise independent, discretionary judgment, was therefore closely linked to senses of competence. Indeed, threats to individuality, mandated requirements to carry out the less than fully understood judgments of others, were closely linked to senses of incompetence. Efforts to eliminate *individualism* should perhaps proceed cautiously, therefore, lest they also undermine *individuality* and the teacher's competence and effectiveness that go with it. In too many school systems, the purge of individualism has become unrestrained and the eccentricity, independence, imagination and initiative that we call individuality have become its casualties.

INDIVIDUALISM AND SOLITUDE

In teaching, if isolation is the destiny of the diffident, solitude is the prerogative of the strong. Isolation for many teachers is the permanent state of affairs for their teaching: the base of their occupational culture. Solitude is more usually a temporary phase in the work, a withdrawal to delve into one's personal resources; to reflect, retreat and regroup. Isolation is a prison or a refuge. Solitude is a retreat. One of the dangers in seeking to halt the pursuit of privatism is that often it is all too easy to argue that we are benevolently releasing teachers from their enforced isolation when what we are really doing is restricting them in their chance for solitude.

Teachers sometimes like to be alone, not with their classes, but with themselves. Not all teachers are like this, of course. Many thrive on collegiality; on collaborative planning. This can provide them with some of their most creative moments. Asked if she preferred to work with a grade partner, one teacher said:

> Yes I do. Because it lightens your workload and if you bounce
> ideas off each other and compare, they benefit and you benefit
> and hopefully the children benefit.

Brainstorming and bouncing ideas off each other were among the benefits of collaborative work for many teachers; their spurs to creativity.

In the majority of cases, though, preparation time − or planning time as some people called it − was not at all the best time to plan, to work with colleagues. Preparation time was, rather, a way of coping with the immediate demands of instruction as they affected one's students. In particular, it provided a way to cope with these demands in the context of internally driven and externally imposed expectations which were high in standard yet diffuse in focus. Preparation time was precious. It was "my time", the teacher's own time, to be focused on the short-term, practical requirements of the teacher's own class. Time spent in other ways − on relaxation or conversation, for instance − was in many respects regarded as wasted time; a distraction from the central task of classroom instruction. Indeed, so powerful was the emphasis on short-term, classroom-focused practicality that almost no teachers seemed to use preparation time for long-term planning. Long-term planning was instead done at home, alone, in quiet and privacy, away from the hustle and bustle of the school day.

The home and the car were among the best places for many teachers to think and plan, to create for their classes. This might not be true for all teachers, all of the time, but it affected most in some measure. The art specialist who otherwise thoroughly enjoyed working and planning with his grade partner nonetheless preferred to do his art alone, to create this most precious area of his work for himself. He was more productive and got better ideas that way, he said.

Selfish, precious, prima donnas − these are some of the ways we can describe teachers who may often prefer the solitude of their own thoughts to the company of others when they are engaged in those processes of creation that give teaching its interest and its life. But in a thorough and searching analysis of the subject, Storr encourages us to revise these judgments.[45]

Contrary to conventional psychological opinion, a preference for solitude, Storr points out, can display one of the great and more unremarked qualities of intellectual maturity: the capacity to be alone. Solitude can also be sought by those who are in search of intellectual or biographical coherence, who have the capacity to converse with and record their own developing thoughts and work. This kind of solitude, says Storr, is often sought by great writers who engage with and reformulate their work, or by the aged, who engage with and reconstruct their lives. Solitude for many people also expresses the legitimate principle that, for them, interests and work can be as satisfying as interpersonal relationships. Lastly, and perhaps most importantly, solitude can stimulate creativity and imagination. Storr concedes that exceptional creativity in adults may well result from enforced solitude in childhood, but whatever its origins, Storr continues, once they are in place, creativity and imagination, and the interest and acclaim that they generate, can be their own spurs to further work. The chosen solitude of adulthood, it would seem, can be justified even when the enforced solitude of childhood cannot.

If most teachers in a school prefer solitude, this is probably indicative of a problem with the system, of individualism representing a withdrawal from threatening, unpleasant or unrewarding working relationships. If teachers prefer solitude only some of the time, however, or if solitude is the desired state for only a few teachers, then a school and its administration ought to be able to tolerate its presence. A system that cannot tolerate interesting and enthusiastic eccentrics, that cannot accommodate strong and imaginative teachers who work better alone than together, that calls individualists prima donnas and turns creative virtue into non-conformist vice – such a system is a system devoid of flexibility and wanting in spirit. It is a system prepared to punish excellence in pursuit of the collegial norm.

CONCLUSION

One of the particular strengths of qualitative research is its capacity to identify the unexpected and illuminate the odd. In organizations driven by bureaucratic imperatives toward goal consensus and conformity, the unexpected is not easily noticed and the odd all too easily persecuted or expunged. The social construction of heresy that accompanies the narrowed visions that sometimes characterize organizational bureaucracies occasionally spills over into the research enterprises that work with those bureaucracies. Broadly speaking, much of the research associated with organizational improvement is concerned with reforming the faith, not reconstituting it.

Qualitative research can raise important, if uncomfortable, questions about the deepest assumptions and the most taken-for-granted purposes and perceptions in organizations. It can serve as a court of appeal for organizational heresies; a forum for giving them deeper, more considered attention.

This chapter has drawn on the qualitative research of the preparation time study to undertake just such a reinterpretation of teacher individualism. It does not claim that all foregoing research on teacher individualism and its alleged weaknesses is incorrect; only that much of it is unproven. It does not claim that the aspects of individualism discussed here are more typical of teacher individualism as a whole than ones discussed elsewhere in the literature. But it does identify and reappraise particular aspects of individualism that have a different character, serve different purposes and have different consequences than has been commonly assumed until now. Care, individuality and solitude, I have argued, have not been fully given their due, not sufficiently acknowledged and accommodated by reformers and researchers working to improve the quality of schooling. This chapter points to the foolishness of presuming that all teacher individualism is iniquitous. It encourages us to think the unthinkable and actively consider some of its potential strengths before we rush to purge it from our school systems. Vibrant teacher cultures should be able to avoid the professional limitations of teacher individualism, while embracing the creative potentials of teacher individuality. This raises questions, therefore, not just about the need for cultures of collaboration among our teachers in general, but also about the particular forms which collaboration takes in particular – the subject of the next chapter.

NOTES

1. Mortimore, P., Sammons, P., Stoll, L., Lewis, D. and Ecob, R., *School Matters*, Berkeley, CA, University of California, 1988; and Purkey, S. C. and Smith, M., "Effective schools: A review", *Elementary School Journal*, 83(4), 1983, 427–52.

2. Rosenholtz, S., *Teachers' Workplace*, New York, Longman, 1988.

3. Ashton, P. and Webb, R., *Making the Difference*, New York, Longman, 1986.

4. Szasz, T., *Heresies*, New York, Anchor-Doubleday, 1976, p. 1.

5. Ibid, p. 10.

6. Little, J. W., "The persistence of privacy: Autonomy and initiative in teachers' professional relations", *Teachers College Record*, 91(4), 1990, 509–36.

7. In this sense, occupational cultures in teaching are not unlike the group perspectives described by Becker, H. and his colleagues in *Boys in White*, Chicago, University of Chicago Press, 1961.

8. A point first made by Waller, W., *The Sociology of Teaching*, New York, Russell & Russell, 1932.

9. There is a wide literature on organizational cultures and their relationship to education. Key examples can be found in Deal, T. E. and Kennedy, A., *Corporate Cultures*, Reading, MA, Addison-Wesley, 1982; Ouchi, W. G., "Markets, bureaucracies and clans", *Administrative Science Quarterly*, 25, 1980, 125–41; Schein, E. H., "Coming to a new awareness of organizational culture", *Sloan Management Review*, Winter, 1984, 3–16; Schein, E., *Organizational Culture and Leadership*, New York, Jossey-Bass, 1985; Wilkins, A. E. and Ouchi, W. G., "Effective cultures: Exploring the relationship between culture and organizational performance", *Administrative Science Quarterly*, 28(3), 1983, 468–81.

10. This is not unlike the concepts of classification and framing used by Basil Bernstein in his classic essay, "The classification and framing of educational knowledge", in his *Class, Codes and Control*, Vol. 3, London, Routledge & Kegan Paul, 1977. For Bernstein

classification refers to the relationships between contents, whereas frame regulates "the modality of the socialization into the classification". Frame is not quite the same as form in curriculum – a point made by Goodson, I. in his essay, "Curriculum Form", London, Ontario, University of Western Ontario, 1989, but it does point interestingly to the ways in which relationships between contents are constituted and regulated. Form has a similar relationship to content within teacher cultures.

11. Lortie, D., *Schoolteacher*, Chicago, University of Chicago Press, 1975.

12. Zahorik, J. A., "Teachers' collegial interaction: An exploratory study", *The Elementary School Journal*, 87(4), 1987, 385–96; Zielinski, A. K. and Hoy, W. K., "Isolation and alienation in the elementary schools", *Educational Administration Quarterly*, 19(2), 1983, 27–45.

13. Little, J. W., "Seductive images and organizational realities in professional development", *Teachers College Record*, 86(1), 1984, 84–102; and Nias, J., Southworth, G. and Yeomans, R., *Staff Relationships in the Primary School*, London, Cassell, 1989.

14. Lortie, *op. cit.*, note 11, p. 210.

15. Ibid, p. 133.

16. Ibid, p. 185.

17. Ibid, p. 210. While seeking to distance himself a little from his depiction of teachers' individualism by describing it in Hargreaves, D., *The Challenge for the Comprehensive School*, London, Routledge & Kegan Paul, 1982 as a "caricature", Hargreaves's depiction is nonetheless extensive, otherwise unhedged and in other publications not qualified as being a "caricature" at all (e.g. Hargreaves, D., "The occupational cultures of teachers", in Woods, P. (ed.), *Teacher Strategies*, London, Croom Helm, 1980).

18. Hargreaves, D., "A sociological critique of individualism", *British Journal of Educational Studies*, 28(3), 1980, 187–98.

19. Ibid.

20. Hargreaves, 1982, *op. cit.*, note 17, p. 206.

21. Rosenholtz, *op. cit.*, note 2.

22. Ibid. See also Jackson, P. W., *The Practice of Teaching*, New York, Teachers College Press, 1988.

23. Rosenholtz, *op. cit.*, note 2, p. 4.

24. Ibid, p. 209.

25. Ibid, p. 52.

26. Ashton and Webb, *op. cit.*, note 3, p. 47.

27. Hargreaves, 1982, *op. cit.*, note 17.

28. It is through these shifts in and extensions of conceptual usage within much of the literature on individualism that problems of the workplace become transposed into problems of the teachers. Some of my own characterizations of teacher individualism in earlier writing, it should be said, are not entirely immune from this sort of critique either

(e.g. Hargreaves, A., "Teaching quality: A sociological analysis", *Journal of Curriculum Studies*, 20(3), 1988, 211–31; and Hargreaves, A., "Cultures of teaching", in Hargreaves, A. and Fullan, M. (eds), *Understanding Teacher Development*, London, Cassell and New York, Teachers College Press, 1992.

29. Joyce, B., Murphy, C., Showers, B. and Murphy, J., "Reconstructing the workplace: School renewal as cultural change", Paper presented at the Annual Conference of the American Educational Research Association, San Francisco, April, 1989.

30. Flinders, D. J., "Teachers' isolation and the new reform", *Journal of Curriculum and Supervision*, 4(1), 1988, 17–29.

31. McTaggart, R., "Bureaucratic rationality and the self-educating profession: The problem of teacher privatism", *Journal of Curriculum Studies*, 21(4), 1989, 345–61.

32. Joyce *et al.*, *op. cit.*, note 29; Fullan, M., *The Meaning of Educational Change*, Toronto, OISE Press, 1982.

33. McTaggart, *op. cit.*, note 31, p. 360.

34. Flinders, *op. cit.*, note 30, p. 21.

35. Lukes, S., *Individualism*, Oxford, Blackwell, 1973.

36. Flinders, *op. cit.*, note 30.

37. Lortie, *op. cit.*, note 11.

38. Gilligan, C., *In a Different Voice*, Cambridge, MA, Harvard University Press, 1982.

39. Ibid.

40. Lukes, *op. cit.*, note 35, p. 8.

41. Durkheim, E., *Education and Sociology*, Glencoe, IL, Free Press, 1956.

42. Swart, K. W., "Individualism in the mid-nineteenth century (1826–1860)", *Journal of History of Ideas*, XXIII, 1962.

43. Szasz, *op. cit.*, note 4, p. 1.

44. Schön, D., *The Reflective Practitioner: How Professionals Think in Action*, New York, Basic Books, 1983.

45. Storr, A., *Solitude*, London, Fontana, 1988.

Chapter 9

Collaboration and Contrived Collegiality
Cup of Comfort or Poisoned Chalice?

If one of the most prominent heresies of educational change is the culture of individualism, then collaboration and collegiality are pivotal to the orthodoxies of change. Collaboration and collegiality have been presented as having many virtues. They have, for instance, been advanced as particularly fruitful strategies for fostering *teacher development*. Collaboration and collegiality, it is argued, take teacher development beyond personal, idiosyncratic reflection, or dependence on outside experts, to a point where teachers can learn from each other, sharing and developing their expertise together.[1] Research evidence also suggests that the confidence that comes with collegial sharing and support leads to greater readiness to experiment and take risks, and with it a commitment to continuous improvement among teachers as a recognized part of their professional obligation. In this sense, collaboration and collegiality are seen as forming vital bridges between *school improvement* and teacher development.[2] Certainly, those aspects of collaboration and collegiality that take the form of shared decision-making and staff consultation are among the process factors which are repeatedly identified as correlating with positive school outcomes in studies of *school effectiveness*.[3]

If collaboration and collegiality are seen as promoting professional growth and internally generated school improvement, they are also widely viewed as ways of securing effective implementation of externally introduced change.[4] Their contribution to the implementation of centralized curriculum reform is a key factor here.

Where curriculum reform is school-based, the case for and contribution of collaboration and collegiality are relatively straightforward. The creation of productive and supportive collegial relationships among teachers has long been seen as a prerequisite for effective school-based curriculum development.[5] In many respects, collaboration and collegiality bring teacher development and curriculum development together.[6] Indeed, the failure of many school-based curriculum development initiatives is attributable, at least in part, to the failure to build and sustain the collegial working relationships essential to their success.[7]

Many writers have argued that the effective implementation of more centralized curricular reforms also depends on the development of collegial relationships and joint planning among each school's teaching staff; allowing central guidelines to be interpreted and adapted to the context of each particular school; and building commitment and understanding among the teachers responsible for implementing the newly devised curricula.[8] With trends in many systems towards school-based management or local management of schools, the collective responsibility of teachers to implement centrally defined curriculum mandates places even greater reliance on the development of collaboration and collegiality at school level.

Although not quite a cure-all, the claimed benefits of collaboration and collegiality for organizational health and effectiveness therefore appear to be both numerous and widespread. Shulman brings together some of the key arguments when he says:

> Teacher collegiality and collaboration are not merely important
> for the improvement of morale and teacher satisfaction . . . but
> are absolutely necessary if we wish teaching to be of the highest
> order. . . . Collegiality and collaboration are also needed to ensure
> that teachers benefit from their experiences and continue to grow
> during their careers.[9]

These developments, continues Shulman, have important implications for school leadership. In the wake of the "second wave" of educational reforms in the United States, inspired by the reports of the Holmes Group and the Carnegie Foundation, images of leadership have come to prominence where teachers are involved in and exercise substantial leadership at school level. Shulman summarizes the position thus:

> Schools are asked to become like our best corporations,
> employing modern methods of management to decentralize
> authority, to make important decisions at the point where the
> street-level bureaucrats reside. Leadership is not monopolized by
> administrators, but is shared with teachers.[10]

It is in accordance with these kinds of arguments that we have seen increased advocacy for new styles of leadership that have been described variously as instructional leadership,[11] transformational leadership[12] and shared governance.[13] In all these conceptions, the sharing of decision-making on collegial lines figures very prominently.

Collaboration and collegiality, then, form significant planks of policies to restructure schools from without and to improve them from within. Much of the burden of educational reform has been placed upon their fragile shoulders. School improvement, curriculum reform, teacher development and leadership development are all seen to some extent as dependent on the building of positive collegial relationships for their success. Consequently, while collaboration and collegiality are not themselves usually the subject of national, state or provincial mandates, their successful development is viewed as essential to the effective delivery of reforms that are mandated at national or local levels. Among many reformers and administrators, collaboration and collegiality have become the keys to educational change.

CRITIQUES OF COLLEGIALITY

Collaboration and collegiality may have become important focal points for a growing administrative and intellectual consensus about desirable directions for change and improvement, but they have not been without their critics.

Most critiques of collaboration and collegiality have focused on difficulties of implementation, particularly issues of time during which teachers can work together and issues concerning the unfamiliarity that many teachers have with the collegial role.[14] These criticisms are of a relatively specific, technical, managerial nature.

A second set of critiques of collaboration and collegiality concerns their meaning. Collaboration and collegiality are often discussed as if they are widely understood. In practice, though, what passes for collaboration and collegiality takes many different forms. In terms of specific initiatives alone, collaboration and collegiality can take the form of team teaching, collaborative planning, peer coaching, mentor relationships, professional dialogue and collaborative action research, to name but a few. More informally, they can be expressed through staffroom talk, conversation outside the classroom, help and advice regarding resources and scores of other small but significant actions. Beyond teachers working or talking together in some way, there is little else that these many different activities and initiatives have in common.[15]

Judith Warren Little has helpfully distinguished between different kinds of collegial relations in terms of their implications for teacher independence.[16] Telling stories, "scanning" for ideas and resources, giving and receiving aid and assistance and sharing ideas and materials, she says, do not pose serious threats to teacher independence, since all these forms of collaboration and collegiality take place outside the classroom and leave teachers' conceptions of and control over their own practice broadly intact. Joint work, however, requires closer interdependence between teachers and their colleagues; more mutual adjustments at the level of practice. In the sense that all these things involve teachers working together, they are all versions of collaboration and collegiality. But beyond that simple commonality, these activities are quite different and have quite different implications for teacher autonomy and empowerment.

What matters is not that there are many different kinds of collaboration and collegiality but that the characteristics and virtues of some kinds of collaboration and collegiality are often falsely attributed to other kinds as well, or perhaps to collaboration and collegiality in general. Teacher empowerment, critical reflection or commitment to continuous improvement are claims that are commonly made for collaboration and collegiality in general, but in practice they apply only to particular versions of it.[17]

Because there are so many faces of collaboration and collegiality, their professed attractions as a whole should be treated with caution. There is no such thing as "real" or "true" collaboration or collegiality. There are only different forms of collaboration and collegiality that have different consequences and serve different purposes. Moreover, those forms which are most compatible with the widely declared benefits of teacher empowerment and reflective practice are the forms that seem least common. Little's review of collegial practices found, for instance, that joint work at the level of classroom practice was a comparative rarity.[18] And in the preparation time study on which this chapter is based, even in a group of schools committed to developing collaborative planning among their teachers, this planning was mainly restricted to the specific and relatively short-term task of developing new units of work, and rarely extended to critical, collective and reflective reviews about the ethics, principles and purposes of current practice.[19] This finding is replicated by Little and by Leithwood and Jantzi, who found little evidence of *critical* feedback about teaching among teachers in schools that might otherwise be considered "collaborative".[20] In our headlong rush to manage collaboration and collegiality, it therefore seems important that we first take time to understand its meaning.

These questions about the *meaning* of collaboration and collegiality lead, inexorably, to questions about who guides and controls collaboration and collegiality; about their micropolitics. As Cooper puts it in a biting critique of popular conceptions of collaboration and collegiality:

> Whose culture is it anyway? If teachers are told what to be
> professional about, how, where and with whom to collaborate,
> and what blueprint of professional conduct to follow, then the
> culture that evolves will be foreign to the setting. They will once
> again have "received" a culture.[21]

Discussions about and advocacy of collaboration and collegiality have largely taken place within a particular perspective on human relationships: *the cultural perspective*. In the main, this cultural perspective has been grounded in traditions of sociological functionalism, social anthropology and corporate management. It is a perspective that emphasizes what is shared and held in common in human relationships — values, habits, norms and beliefs: the shared content of teacher cultures.[22] This perspective is pervasive in literature on staff cultures in schools and school systems.[23]

There are two problems with this perspective. First, the existence of shared culture is presumed in any organization being studied, no matter how complex and differentiated. All organizations, it is thought, have cultures. This is not a finding but a presumption. The possibility that some highly complex organizations may have no shared culture of any substance or significance is not acknowledged.

Second, the theoretical and methodological emphasis on what is shared in the organization may exaggerate consensus-based aspects of human relationships, according them an importance in research studies that outweighs their significance in practice. In some organizations, the differences, conflicts, and disagreements are more socially significant for the participants than what they may happen to share. As we shall see in the next chapter, this is often true of secondary schools, with their balkanized relations between departments, for instance.[24] In this sense, what I earlier described as the *form* of teacher culture, the pattern of relationships among its members is as important as the *content* of any shared beliefs within that culture.

A second perspective on human relationships that is less well represented in literature and research on educational administration is the micropolitical perspective. According to Blase, this perspective deals with "the use of power to achieve preferred outcomes in educational settings".[25] In the micropolitical perspective, the differences between groups in an organization are highlighted more than the similarities.[26] The ways that some individuals and groups can realize their values at the expense of others, or have the power and influence to shape other values in the image of their own, is a key concern. In the cultural perspective, leadership is a matter of management and legitimacy. In the micropolitical perspective it is more a question of power and control.[27]

These two perspectives present us with very different outlooks on collaboration and collegiality. In the more dominant *cultural perspective*, collaborative cultures express and emerge from a process of consensus building that is facilitated by a largely benevolent and skilled educational management. In the *micropolitical perspective*, collaboration and collegiality result from the exercise of organizational power by control-conscious administrators. In these cases, collegiality is either an unwanted managerial imposition from the point of view of teachers subjected to it or, more usually, a way of coopting teachers to fulfilling administrative purposes and the implementation of external mandates. From the micropolitical perspective, collaboration and collegiality are often bound up with either direct administrative constraint or the indirect management of consent.

Neither the cultural nor the micropolitical perspective possesses a privileged or more accurate interpretation of organizations and collegial relations within them. Neither one has a monopoly on wisdom. But the dominance of the first perspective in research on school culture has given undue emphasis to more consensus-driven interpretations of and prescriptions regarding staff collegiality. In this chapter, I want to draw particular attention to the less well understood and less frequently acknowledged dimensions of school culture and teacher collegiality: those of a micropolitical nature.

Once the micropolitical perspective is adopted, it has important implications for our understanding of collaboration and collegiality and the questions we ask about it. It casts doubt, for instance, on the widely advocated virtues of team teaching, of collegiality at the classroom level, where there are substantial differences of values and beliefs among the teachers involved. As Huberman has expressed it, sculptors may often want to see each other sculpt, talk about sculpting with fellow artists and go to exhibitions of their work, but would never sculpt with a colleague on the same piece of marble.[28] Because of frequent differences in beliefs and approach, teachers, he says, may be no different from sculptors in this respect.

Second, the micropolitical perspective raises questions about the rights of the individual and the protection of individuality in the face of group pressure. Norms of collegiality are sometimes treated as if they were administrative laws of collegiality. Teachers who prefer to continue working alone for all or part of the time can be unfairly ostracized. As I argued in the previous chapter, some teachers plan better in solitude than they do with their colleagues. The protection of their individuality, and their discretion of judgment, is also a protection of their right to disagree and reflect critically on the value and worth of what it is they are being asked to collaborate about. The micropolitical perspective raises questions about the implications of collaboration and collegiality for individuality and solitude.

Third, the micropolitical perspective inquires into the circumstances where collaboration becomes cooptation: as in collaboration with the enemy. It asks where collaboration becomes a commitment not to developing and realizing purposes of one's own but to implementing purposes devised by others. Hartley, for instance, has criticized the tendency towards shorter, school-based, experiential forms of inservice education for teachers on the grounds that they are cooptative because they cultivate emotional commitment to externally mandated changes at the expense of rational deliberation and critique about their worth and applicability.[29]

Fourth, the micropolitical perspective encourages us to discriminate between the different forms that collaboration and collegiality take; to examine who constitutes those different forms and to ask whose interests they serve in each case. In Chapter 4, for instance, I described how some spontaneous and unpredictable forms of collaboration that are steered by the cultural dynamics of students' own families, communities and peer-groups are often redefined through and reinscribed in more bureaucratically contrived and administratively controlled systems of cooperation, such as active learning and cooperative learning. These reforms maintain a focus on developing and supporting cooperation in the classroom but, in doing so, they pass the locus of control over cooperation from the student to the teacher and the community to the school, draining that cooperation of much of its richness, spontaneity and unpredictability.

The micropolitical perspective sensitizes us to the possible existence of similar processes in the construction of collaboration and collegiality among teachers: the substitution of more evolutionary and spontaneous forms of teacher collaboration by administratively controlled, safely simulated forms of collegiality. It is this kind of administratively constructed or *contrived collegiality* that I want to explore in this chapter. I want to do this by drawing a pivotal distinction between *collaborative culture* and what I call *contrived collegiality* as two prominent but very different forms of collaborative and collegial teacher cultures that can be found in teachers' work: a distinction that turns on the kinds of administrative control and intervention that are exercised in each case.

COLLABORATIVE CULTURES

In *collaborative cultures*, collaborative working relationships between teachers and their colleagues tend to be:

- **Spontaneous.** They emerge primarily from the teachers themselves as a social group. They may be administratively supported and facilitated by helpful scheduling arrangements, by principals and headteachers offering to cover classes, or by example in the behavior of educational leaders. In this sense, the spontaneity of collaborative cultures is not absolute nor are such cultures free from administrative contrivance of a facilitative nature. But ultimately, collaborative working relationships evolve from and are sustained through the teaching community itself.

- **Voluntary.** Collaborative work relations arise not from administrative constraint or compulsion but from their perceived value among teachers that derives from experience, inclination or non-coercive persuasion that working together is both enjoyable and productive.

- **Development-oriented.** In collaborative cultures, teachers work together primarily to develop initiatives of their own, or to work on externally supported or mandated initiatives to which they themselves have a commitment. In collaborative cultures, teachers most often establish the tasks and purposes for working together, rather than meet to implement the purposes of others. Teachers, here, are people who initiate change as much as or more than they react to it. When they have to respond to external mandates, they do so selectively, drawing on their professional confidence and discretionary judgment as a community.[30]

- **Pervasive across time and space.** In collaborative cultures, working together is not often a scheduled activity (like a regular planning session) that can be administratively fixed as taking place at a designated time in a designated place. Scheduled meetings and planning sessions may form part of collaborative cultures but they do not dominate the arrangements for working together. In collaborative cultures, much of the way teachers work together is in almost unnoticed, brief yet frequent informal encounters. This may take the form of such things as passing words and glances, praises and thanks, offers to exchange classes in tough times, suggestions about new ideas, informal discussions about new units of work, sharing of problems or meeting parents together. Collaborative cultures are, in this sense, not clearly or closely regulated. They are constitutive of the very way that the teacher's working life operates in the school.

- **Unpredictable.** Because, in collaborative cultures, teachers have discretion and control over what will be developed, the outcomes of collaboration are often uncertain and not easily predicted. In implementation-oriented systems, where most decisions about purpose and program are centralized at the school district or provincial/state/national level, this can be administratively perplexing. In general, therefore, collaborative cultures are incompatible with school systems where decisions about curriculum and evaluation are highly centralized. The difficulty for administrators seeking to help develop collaborative cultures may therefore be a difficulty not so much of human relations but of political control.

One of the schools in the preparation time study illustrated vividly how collaborative cultures rest on relationships that extend persistently and pervasively across the whole school. The principal of this school, in a small rural, dormitory community, recognized the incipient dangers of balkanization, of teachers becoming divided into separate, isolated groups, even within the context of this smaller elementary school.

Teachers can get kind of isolated. They say, "I'm a primary teacher, a junior teacher, an intermediate teacher!" And the primary teachers are afraid of the older kids, and the intermediate teachers are afraid of the little kids.

He felt that irrespective of grade differences:

You all have a bank of strategies to use with kids, and you should all have the same types of practice, the same types of expectations in the personal things, and so on. You've just got different-aged kids.

He worked hard to get teachers to work together with children from different grades on common projects, but also appreciated this would be threatening for them: a major challenge to their identity and security.

If I were to mention to my Grade 1 teacher, "Would you go up and cover the Grade 8 science class?", well, she'd rather go and drive her car into a tree than confront that. And she'd taught them all in Grade 1!

Working with mixed-aged groups alleviated these threats, though, and helped create a stronger sense of the school as one community. The words of one teacher testify to the success of these and other strategies deployed by the principal in his attempts to create a sense of unity. He reflected, in particular, on a recent experience of being involved in the cooperative planning of a whole-school focus on "Olympics".

> That was very involved. We ran a special sports day outside and we went to the arena . . . and we had a Calgary [site of the winter Olympics] day at school, and we had pancakes. We had it written up in the paper and everything. It was really quite a job. We certainly learned a lot about planning, ourselves, and I think we felt pretty proud, because some schools did nothing or very little, and we were involved with it. Of course, I'm biased, but I think the school atmosphere here benefits from the kind of family atmosphere we have. . . . We do things together. There's a lot of junior/primary/senior togetherness in that respect and I don't see such clearcut rivalries between seniors and juniors, and juniors and primaries. . . . I think it's because of staff unity and the way the principal sees the school as a unit, not as separate little divisions.

The modest and unassuming principal of this school modeled what he most expected of his staff. He praised them, sent them notes to thank them, was always visible around the school to see and hear them, and often bought them corsages or other little gifts to show how much he valued them. When teachers needed his advice, he willingly offered it. When he himself needed help, he unashamedly asked for it. And when teachers wanted to spend their preparation times planning together, he fixed the schedule to facilitate it. He promoted rituals and ceremonies (like an Olympic torch-bearing ceremony) to bring the school and the community together. He encouraged experiments in cross-grade groupings of students and links between their teachers to bring teachers together. And he himself sometimes taught classes to show the importance of bringing the principal and the students together. In response, as the teachers' remarks earlier indicate, teachers broke down the barriers, worked closely together and learned a lot from each other. They didn't just collaborate on things initiated from the outside, but also on projects they developed themselves — as when the teacher taking a course on the use of computers secured some release time from the principal to work with a colleague already knowledgeable about computers, so they could develop some classroom software together.

This is just one example of what a collaborative teacher culture is like in action, and of the kinds of leadership that help promote and support it. This is not to say that collaborative cultures are without their problems or limitations. As I have argued elsewhere, collaborative cultures can be *bounded* or *restricted* in nature with teachers focusing on rather safer activities of sharing resources, materials and ideas, or on planning units of study together in a rather workaday fashion, without reflecting on the value, purpose and consequences of what they do, or without challenging each others' practices, perspectives and assumptions. Collaborative cultures can, in these instances, degenerate into comfortable and complacent cultures. Collegiality can be reduced to congeniality.

But in their most rigorous, robust (and somewhat rarer) forms, collaborative cultures can extend into joint work, mutual observation, and focused reflective inquiry in ways that extend practice critically, searching for better alternatives in the continuous quest for improvement. In these cases, collaborative cultures are not cozy, complacent and politically quiescent. Rather, they can build collective strength and confidence in communities of teachers who are able to interact knowledgeably and assertively with the bearers of innovation and reform; able and willing to select which innovations to adopt, which ones to adapt, and which ones to resist or ignore, as best befits their purposes and circumstances.

CONTRIVED COLLEGIALITY

In conditions of *contrived collegiality*, teachers' collaborative working relationships are not spontaneous, voluntary, development-oriented, fixed in time and space and predictable. The comparative, combined features of contrived collegiality, are as follows:

- **Administratively regulated.** Contrived collegiality does not evolve spontaneously from the initiative of teachers, but is an administrative imposition that requires teachers to meet and work together.

- **Compulsory.** Contrived collegiality therefore makes working together a matter of compulsion as in mandatory peer coaching, team teaching and collaborative planning arrangements. Contrived collegiality affords little discretion to individuality or solitude. Compulsion may be direct, or it may be indirect in terms of associated promises of promotion or veiled threats of withdrawal of support for teachers' other favoured projects, for example.

- **Implementation-oriented.** Under conditions of contrived collegiality, teachers are required or "persuaded" to work together to implement the mandates of others — most directly those of the principal, or headteacher, or indirectly those of the school district or the Ministry. Such mandates may take the form of a national curriculum, accelerated learning programs, or cooperative learning strategies, for example. Here, collegial cooperation is closely bound up with administrative cooptation.

195

- **Fixed in time and space.** Contrived collegiality takes place in particular places at particular times. This is part of its administrative regulation. When, for example, peer coaching sessions, collaborative planning meetings in preparation time, and mentor meetings alone constitute teachers' joint working relationships, they amount to trying to secure cooperation by contrivance.

- **Predictable.** Contrived collegiality is designed to have relatively high predictability in its outcomes. This cannot, of course, be guaranteed and, as we shall see, the outcomes of contrived collegiality are sometimes perverse. But control over its purposes and regulation of its time and placement are designed to increase the predictability of teacher collegiality and its outcomes. Contrived collegiality is in these respects a safe administrative simulation of collaboration. It replaces spontaneous, unpredictable and difficult-to-control forms of teacher-generated collaboration with forms of collaboration that are captured, contained and contrived by administrators instead.

CONTRIVED COLLEGIALITY IN ACTION

I now want to explore some practical, school-based realizations of contrived collegiality that emerged in the preparation time study, particularly in the school board dedicated to developing collaborative planning in a group of its schools. As I have already described, we found some clear and distinctive examples of *collaborative cultures* within these schools, but *contrived collegiality* was also clearly present. What follows is not an evaluation of the collaborative planning initiative overall. Nor is it an attempt to estimate in quantitative terms, the strength of contrived collegiality within that initiative. Rather, it is designed to draw attention, from a micropolitical perspective, to aspects of collegiality emerging from the data that have received little or no emphasis thus far in more general, positively inclined discussions of teacher collaboration.

I will focus on three specific realizations of contrived collegiality that emerged from the study and that illustrate both the properties and the consequences of this pattern of teacher collaboration. These realizations of contrived collegiality are mandated preparation time use, consultation with special education resource teachers, and peer coaching.

1. Mandated Preparation Time Use

In debates surrounding the introduction of preparation time in many Ontario school boards, one of the arguments used in its support was that it would enable teachers to meet and consult with their colleagues during the school day. For most teachers we interviewed, preparation time or "planning time" was not at all the best time to plan, however. Preparation time periods were usually fairly short: 40 minutes or less. Many minutes were often lost looking after classes until the next teacher arrived, taking children to the gym for their physical education class with another teacher and supervising them getting changed before that, walking across to the staffroom or library if the teacher's own classroom was in use, and other activities. Three teachers' comments illustrate their concerns here:

> You could get more accomplished in an hour. I'm very conscious of – well, now, I can only really do this job and that job, and then I have to get back. And even as it is, when I try to pick up the kids after music, I miss them, because I've just been that two minutes later running off that little extra job, and they're gone, they're back into the classroom and I've got to retrace my steps and catch up with them. I would use it [the prep time] differently if I had a larger amount.

> Usually, I find my preps go fast, there's only 35 minutes and when you're dismissing your class and going back into your class and moving all around, suddenly that 35 minutes is now 25 minutes and before you know it, if you have to go to the office to do some photocopying, or to the work area to run off dittos, that 25 minutes is now gone. It takes time to get to these places.

> [One 40 minute prep time] doesn't end up being the full time, because my class has to come in from recess, get their coats off. [The covering teacher] has to get his class to French. So right now I would say it's just a good half hour. Then once the bad weather starts, it will be less than that. The kids have to get their snowsuits off. But it's scheduled as the full 40 minutes.

Not surprisingly, therefore, teachers commonly regarded preparation time as too short for sustained planning, be it collective or individual. Indeed, so scarce and pressed was the time that teachers frequently commented they needed to do their planning *before* prep time, at home perhaps, so they knew exactly how the time was going to be used and what jobs they were going to do at that time. Teachers here preferred to plan at other times: at lunch, before school and after school, for instance. Preparation time, rather, was used more to "clear the decks" of the innumerable small tasks like photocopying and telephoning that could be dispatched less efficiently at other times like lunch, when the rest of the school's teachers would be clamoring for the same resources. This pattern of work in preparation time was highly useful for many teachers and freed up time for them to plan in a more sustained way at other points in the school day.

> Usually [in prep time], I have a hundred things to do, and I only get ten of them done. I mark work, I prepare for the next day, I

197

> do bulletin boards, I write letters to parents, I phone parents: a
> multitude of things.
>
> [With one particular teacher-librarian] we would tend to do our
> preparation with him after school. My team partner and I
> couldn't get sprung [scheduled] together, so we would choose to
> go after school and work with our librarian. That's when we
> really could plan, because the air was clear and we really tossed
> ideas back and forth.

Marking, doing stencils, photocopying, cutting and pasting, and doing bulletin
boards were the usual stuff of preparation time for most teachers.

Larger preparation time periods (doubles) were more suited to extended
planning, either alone or with colleagues. A number of teachers preferred some
of their time to be "chunked" in this way to facilitate planning. But when these
extended preparation time periods were designed specifically for collaborating
with colleagues, teachers were still concerned to have scheduled time to prepare
for their own classes.

For other teachers, however, preparation time was ideal for planning
with colleagues. Responsibilities for coaching and refereeing sports teams, for
instance, gave some teachers little opportunity to meet with colleagues at other
times. For a number of women teachers, in particular a single parent with a child
who often had to be taken to psychiatric appointments immediately after school,
pressing domestic responsibilities made it difficult for them to stay long with
colleagues after school. Much of their planning took place at home, often late
at night. For them, preparation time was a good time to work with colleagues.

Teachers' work and life circumstances vary. The teachers' work is highly
contexted. It is not and cannot be standardized in the way that administrators
sometimes want it to be. Preparation time and its uses therefore have an
inevitably complicated and highly contexted relationship to these variable work
and life circumstances. There is no unambiguous administrative formula for
dealing with this. It would be of little value to calculate how many teachers in
one school would support and benefit from scheduled collaborative planning
time and how many would not and then decide, on some percentage basis,
whether mandating such uses for preparation time would be worthwhile. The
important administrative principle, rather, would appear to be one of administrative flexibility and discretion in delegating decisions about how preparation
time periods are to be used to teachers themselves.

That flexibility is important for at least three reasons: to place preparation
time use in the realistic context of teachers' wider life and work circumstances;
to allow preparation time use to be responsive to the day-to-day, week-to-week
variations in required tasks and priorities; and, not least, to acknowledge the
professionalism of teachers as defined by Schön in terms of their rights and
opportunities to exercise discretionary judgment in the best interests of those
students for whom they care and hold responsibility.

Some interview responses from teachers indicated that while they would normally use preparation periods for the collaborative purposes designated by the principal, a proportion of them would retreat to their own room or other space, to work alone for their own classes, clearing away the plethora of little tasks for which preparation time is so important. Yet in doing so, they would feel guilty, aware that they were going against the wishes of their principal.

In a school where grade partners were scheduled to plan together, one teacher related how, every third week, he and his grade partners would work alone instead.

> T: We plan in blocks of months, so our theme works that way, so that as we get to the third week, we'll say to each other, "Now, we know what we're doing next week; these are some of the things that we have to get caught up because we're behind in this." And we'll say, "Bye", and each go our separate way.
>
> I: And would the view about that be that it was OK to do that, if it were known that that's what you did?
>
> T: I don't think so. I think when they make this as a statement that you're working together as a group, and that's the impression I get, that you're to work together as a group for that 40 minutes.

One principal related how he discovered that teachers whose classes he had personally covered so they could be released to plan together were, on the occasion he checked up on them, not planning together at all, but working, preparing and marking alone.

> I used to take the kids myself and do different things with them. . . . I thought the teachers were getting together, planning . . . and I thought, "Oh well, I'll ask somebody to watch the kids while I go and see what's going on in the planning." I walked down the hall and three teachers were all in different rooms, marking. So I said, "Whoa!! There's something wrong here." But you know, they always have a rationalization: "Well we got to the point where we needed to do this! Trust us! We will get together on our own time to do the planning."

Infuriating as it might seem to administrators, especially when they have given up their own precious time to facilitate collaborative planning, it is important, for the reasons reviewed earlier, to allow discretion and flexibility for teachers in their use of preparation time at any particular moment. It is, of course, helpful to use scheduling in order to release teachers together, as a device, or contrivance to *facilitate* collaboration and collegiality, not to *control* it. Difficult as it may sometimes be for them, it is important for principals or headteachers to continue giving their time to covering for teachers so they can be released, even though teachers may not always use that released time to work together, as expected. I am not suggesting here that administrators abrogate their responsibility for fulfilling the school's purposes and priorities. But it is important, for reasons of sheer practicality and of respect for teachers' professionalism, that teachers are awarded high discretion and flexibility in how those priorities are met. With regard to collaborative planning, principals might do better to set expectations for the *task* (preferably through discussion and development with teachers), rather than expectations for the *time*. What teachers would then be held accountable for would be commitment to and completion of the task, not obedience in their use of the *time*.

2. Consultation with Special Education Resource Teachers

A second manifestation of contrived collegiality can be seen in the arrangements for consultation between special education teachers and classroom teachers. Since the early 1980s in Ontario, there has been a shift in the expected role for special education teachers in ordinary schools. With the integration of more special education students into regular classes, the special education teacher's role has been undergoing a shift from a *restorative role*, where identified children would be withdrawn from classes, "treated" by the special education teacher and then "restored" to regular class work at a later stage, to an *integrative* role, where the special education resource teacher supports the regular teacher in adapting instruction for identified children within normal classroom work.[31] One implication for this development has been a need for closer consultation between special education teachers and regular classroom teachers to monitor and create programs for identified children in regular classes. In schools within the collaboratively inclined board in the study, preparation time was often used or scheduled to facilitate this process of consultation with special education resource teachers (SERTS).

In many cases, these consultations were not just expected or administratively facilitated, but directly mandated to occur in particular places at particular times. These required consultations between classroom teachers and special education resource teachers raised issues that were similar to those entailed in required consultations between grade partners in preparation time. Flexibility in use of time was again deemed important by teachers. Teachers perceived special education support from the resource teacher as necessary, important and valuable, although the intensity of that need and the depth of support required varied with the program, the changing nature of students' difficulties and needs, and other factors. Yet setting aside time each week when the teacher was *required* to meet with resource staff was seen by many as unhelpfully inflexible, as unresponsive to the changing needs of the students, the program, the teacher and the classroom. Many teachers emphasized the importance of meeting with special education staff when there was a need to meet, a purpose for the meeting (which might be and often was outside preparation time just as much as within it). Sometimes, however, they would find that on meeting the resource teacher, there was no business to discuss that week, and once again they would tacitly agree to go their own ways and work alone, without informing the principal.

An example from the study illustrates what is at stake here. In it, a teacher describes how he is scheduled to meet with the SERT once a week but how, once every three weeks, he and the SERT do not stick to that arrangement. The principal, he surmises, would not approve of this.

> T: We sit down and we look at what is being done, what has
> to be caught up in the threads for the following week, and
> we say: "Well, this is where we want to go for the following,
> after that, and that next week we'll come with the ideas for
> that period to start off the next one." She goes her way, we
> go ours, and we do planning together at that time.

> I: So you actually use it for a different purpose than it's been
> assigned for?

> T: That's right.

> I: Does anyone mind?

> T: I think the principal would if he found out, but I mean it's
> the only way we can work it out. Sitting there for half an
> hour looking at each other and smiling is not going to
> accomplish anything.

In a second example, a teacher describes how she and her colleagues managed to persuade a SERT to meet them not in scheduled prep time, but at other times, more flexibly, with the result that prep times ("my three prep times", as she calls them) are preserved for her own priorities of individual classroom centred work.

> T: Last year, she [the SERT] wanted one of our prep times
> each cycle, one in three, to talk about children that she had
> from my room that she was working with; children with
> problems. I wasn't too happy with that. Neither were the
> others. I felt that it was too long a time. She didn't need
> 40 minutes.

> I: Has that actually worked out in practice for you — because
> you've had some experience of doing it? Is it your
> experience that it *is* too long?

> T: I didn't need 40 minutes. Actually this year it has changed.
> She was new to the school, and she wanted more time to
> talk to us. This was for each teacher that she saw. She
> wanted to see us for 40 minutes each cycle. . . . But this
> year, she's cut that down. We've chosen our own time now,

>   when we like to see her. So I usually see her on my lunch
>   hour. And I find that's better, because I can eat my lunch
>   at the same time, and I still have my three prep times.

For some teachers, however, preparation time was actually the most helpful and convenient time to meet with the SERT. One teacher who preferred this arrangement and indeed actively initiated it was a teacher with heavy coaching and sports responsibilities at lunch and after school.

> *T*:　I use [one prep period] to talk to . . . the Special Education
>   person about the progress of the three kids that we're
>   monitoring in my class. We keep updates on that, on what
>   she's doing and what I'm expecting and so on. So that's our
>   little chat time.
>
> *I*:　So you usually use a prep period to do that, do you?
>
> *T*:　Yes, that's *my* prep period [emphasis added]. I chose that
>   myself. Some teachers use after school, or mornings. I
>   chose that period mostly because, well, in the Fall, I was so
>   busy with the school team. Either I was on the road with
>   away games, or practising. It was very hard for me to see
>   her after school.

Judging from their accounts of how they consulted with special education teachers, regular teachers, as a group, seem a rather contrary bunch! Teachers who have scheduled time to meet with their SERTS may prefer to do so at other times. Other teachers may initiate consultation arrangements of their own in prep time. And one teacher regretted that special education teachers were not available for consultation during prep time in her school, so that she had to meet with them in short snatches "on the fly" instead. This apparent perversity does not necessarily reveal inconsistency, or any proclivity to oppose whatever arrangements are available. Rather, these comments point once more to the heavily contexted nature of teachers' work, and the difficulty that standardized administrative procedures for developing collegiality have in accommodating these particular and shifting circumstances of teaching.

Two other factors compounded this relationship between classroom teachers, special education resource staff and the use of preparation time. These were *expertise* and *control*.

Expertise is an important criterion for collaboration among teachers. Sharing as such is not itself usually enough. This general principle also applies to relationships between classroom teachers and special education resource staff in particular. Acknowledgement of complementary expertise on the part of the special education resource staff is important. Where classroom teachers have previous special education expertise, or where, as is increasingly common among Ontario elementary teachers, they possess special education qualifications to as advanced a level as the resource personnel themselves, then meetings with

resource staff can seem unnecessary. To teachers in this position, regular scheduled consultations with the special education resource teacher can sometimes
appear to contribute little to their existing expertise and understanding. Because
of this, teachers and resource staff again sometimes tacitly agreed not to meet
on a regular basis, but only as required. One of the teachers put it this way:

> One of them [the prep times] gives me time with the Special Ed.
> person, although I haven't had a need of that this year. In fact, I
> released her from it until she needed, or we felt a need.

She went on to explain that this was partly because, at present, she had very few
"children with problems" in her class. "But also", she continued,

> I find having had some Special Education training . . . I don't
> have a need for the resources as much. In other words, I am my
> own resource . . . I think I have enough expertise and resources
> within myself.

In relations between classroom teachers and special education resource
staff, concerns about expertise are, however, also often closely bound up with
concerns about ownership and control. From the accounts of teachers interviewed in the study, it seemed that as the special education resource teacher's role
had expanded and become more preventive in nature, there had, in some cases,
been something of a struggle with classroom teachers about who had "ownership"
of the "mainstreamed" students. Several instances were reported of initial "personality" clashes with the special education teacher, or of special education staff
allegedly trying to "dictate" to ordinary staff what actions to take with students.
In one case, resistance to the special education teacher's advice, or inability
to implement it, led to an ultimate agreement for that teacher to work in class
with the children themselves, instead of advising the teacher how to do it. In
other cases, the special education teacher left, to be replaced by one who was
more "congenial". And there were claims that in the remaining cases, while the
relationship had been initially problematic, over time it had been negotiated
successfully, so that the parties came to agree on the distribution of expertise, on
the balance of ownership, and on a desirable future pattern for the relationship.

Complaints about what has been termed *contrived collegiality* may sometimes therefore have been motivated less by concerns about rigidity of scheduling and redundancy of expertise than by desires to maintain control over
students and their programming without interference from "outsiders", whatever their expertise. Under these circumstances, administrative contrivance
may have been necessary just to get a relationship started in which a wider brief
for special education support could begin, whatever the initial difficulties. Sometimes, existing structures can obstruct the emergence of vibrant teacher cultures. All cultures are grounded in structures of some kind and if the structures
are overwhelmingly obstructive, they may need to be modified to allow better
cultures to grow. But even if this need for some measure of initial contrivance

203

is acknowledged, the early implementation problems in developing these new relationships could still almost certainly have been eased by reducing some of the other aspects of contrived collegiality (in terms of rigid scheduling of meeting times, etc.).

What implications might be drawn here? First, more sensitivity to classroom teachers' existing expertise in special education might be encouraged. In fact, this principle of acknowledging existing expertise among one's colleagues might also apply to those who find themselves in a position of teacher leadership more generally. Second, even where the expertise in special education is strong among SERTS and particular teachers with whom they consult, there is still a case for colleagues sharing views on special education students and their programming. But this sharing should not be construed as sharing among the skilled and less skilled, the expert and the novice, but among communities of professional equals committed to continuous improvement.[32] Third, expectations for consultation about special education students should perhaps once more be set for the task rather than the time, creating greater flexibility and discretion regarding how and when teachers meet.

3. Peer Coaching

A third area of practice in which elements of contrived collegiality were revealed is peer coaching. While definitions and interpretations of peer coaching vary, it normally consists of a structured process for teachers to work together, usually in pairs, to improve practice. In one of the best-known and earliest elaborations of peer coaching, four discrete stages make up the peer coaching process: presentation of theory underlying a newly advocated approach; demonstration or modeling of that approach; practice of the approach by the teacher new to it; and feedback on how the teacher used the new practice.[33] In the field of peer coaching, there are differences and disagreements in terms of whether the process should be voluntary or compulsory, whether it should focus on practical experience or cognitive reflection about that experience, and whether it should be directed to implementing instructional strategies of allegedly "known" effectiveness, or to making improvements in areas of the teacher's own choosing.[34] Whatever the ideals of any model, though, the muddy realities of practice are often at some variance from those ideas. What is declared as voluntary in principle, for instance, is often perceived as not at all voluntary in practice.[35]

In the sample of teachers in the study, three had recently participated in a new peer coaching program instituted by the board in order to make new initiatives in instruction in the junior division (Grades 4–6). This consisted of six afternoons spent with school board consultants away from the school, with the intention that follow-up activities would be developed and practised with fellow teachers in school. As one teacher described it:

> The Ministry did a review of junior grades a few years ago and
> they were trying to find out what types of program junior

teachers were doing. They found out that there was not enough activity-oriented things going on in the classroom, so the board has put together a little program to try to get teachers stirred up and doing more activity oriented things. It started last year. They sent one junior [division] teacher from each school last year and I'm the representative this year.

Excellent in its rationale and intent perhaps, this program was perceived very differently at the level of practice than it appeared in its ideal form.

One teacher voiced criticisms about lack of consultation in the choice of coaching partners. Unlike the justification made for arranged marriages, this teacher, it seemed, had not learned to love, like or even work effectively with her selected partner over time. This teacher described the program as a series of workshops, "things you could try", followed by "a little homework assignment, things to try in the classroom, and then we go back and discuss how it worked". She went on to say she was "supposed to be working with the person who did it last year". "Are you?" I asked.

> Actually, no I'm not. There's a bit of a personality problem there, so I don't know. I think maybe the people chosen to go to these workshops should be a little more carefully selected. That's my personal feeling.

This teacher further explained that:

> When I volunteered, I didn't realize that I was expected to work with this other person. I've since found that out. I don't know whether the administration knew about it or not. We've had a change of principal, as you know, so the person chosen to go last year was chosen by a different person.

She reflected on the involuntary nature of the partnership with which she was faced:

> She [the partner] manages a classroom completely differently than I do, you know – a whole different way of teaching. It would be stupid for us to try to work together. . . . As well as the personality, there's the teaching strategies involved.

These practice-based remarks resonate with Huberman's insights of a more theoretical nature that most teachers are likely to be able to work productively together at the level of classroom practice only if they have broadly compatible educational beliefs and similar approaches to their teaching.[36] Where these beliefs and approaches are not broadly shared, contrived collegiality in the form of compulsory teaming or coaching is unlikely to be successful.

This first teacher was uncertain whether her teaming with an incompatible colleague was a managerial ploy or an administrative accident. A second teacher felt that both she and her principal had been fundamentally misled by senior board administrators about the purposes of the program:

> We got a report saying how terrible "junior" is and all these things are wrong with junior and I was asked would I like to be part of a group to follow up on this report. And they sent us the report. We read it all, made references. It didn't have anything to do with the report at all. Not a thing. . . . They didn't even mention the report. . . . And I thought, it was going to be a follow-up on how can we make the juniors better. But it wasn't.

What the initiative was, rather, was a set of sessions "laid on" by the board; of things done *to* teachers rather than developed *with* them. Junior science, junior language — these types of topics were the focal points of the board sessions.

> We were told every week what we were going to do. It isn't what my principal thought it was going to be either. We both were under the impression that it was going to be junior teachers' input into how to make the junior division better.

Far from building on and valuing the participating teachers' insight and expertise, this program seemed to overlook and disregard them.

> I didn't get anything out of it that I didn't already know. . . . If you're new to the junior area, I think probably you would have gotten a lot out of it, a lot of good ideas. But having already been in it for 19 years, I felt that it was the wrong way for me to be going. I felt that I was regressing instead of progressing. I would have liked to have some input as to what's wrong in the junior division and how can we change the junior division.

Not only did this approach seem disrespectful of teachers' professionalism, of their existing expertise and discretionary judgment, but it was also impractical with regard to teachers being supposed to coach their colleagues in the newly learned methods back in their own schools.

> You were supposed to be a coach and implement it back in your own room. But . . . a lot of the stuff that they're talking about, we were already doing in our room. I mean, they tell me a lot of people don't do this. I don't know how they can get away with not doing it. It's been board policy for years to plan cooperatively and teach in groups and this stuff. . . . And they tell me people don't do it. I don't know how they get away with it.

Such gaps between the ideal plans of administrators and the practical realities of schools were even starker in the case of a third teacher. He described the principles of the coaching element of the program very clearly: "They want to have these people go out, be inserviced, come back, try it in the classroom, share it with the other staff members, let them try it in their classroom. . . ." The practice, however, was rather different.

> *I:*   Have you been out in connection with this yourself?
>
> *T:*   No, I haven't.
>
> *I:*   Do you know when it starts?
>
> *T:*   It should have started a month and a half ago, but for some reason, I guess with so much going on, I just wasn't aware that I was the one in charge, and that I should have been going to these things!

Perhaps these teachers were unusual. They were only three teachers, after all. But they were not specially selected in the research design. And they did comprise all the teachers in the sample who had been involved in the inservice program. It is tempting to say their experiences were unfortunate or to see their circumstances as special or accidental. Another way of looking at these data, though, is to acknowledge that all circumstances in teaching are special. Incompatible team partners, changing principals and unclear communication about new roles are the stuff of teaching, not isolated interruptions to it.

In these data, this "messiness" seems like a problem. And it mainly seems like a shortcoming of the teachers and the schools in each case. But in many respects, the problem is perhaps more one of centralized, standardized, mandated programs and solutions being imposed insensitively on the specific, variable and rapidly changing settings of teaching. What these responses indicate is not so much the imperfections of practice in general but the way in which contrived collegiality is deeply insensitive to context, to the specifics of the teacher's classroom situation and to the discretionary judgments that teachers need in order to have the flexibility to exercise there, if they are to be successful. District policies and initiatives can be standardized. Classrooms and schools cannot. A more voluntary, development-oriented model of teacher collaboration could build more effectively on the discretionary judgments that teachers exercise in the varying contexts of their work. Mandated, implementation-oriented forms of contrived collegiality of the kind reviewed here are almost certainly too inflexible for that.

CONCLUSIONS AND IMPLICATIONS

The preparation time study began with an elegantly formulated research question which asked whether newly provided preparation time would bring about the development of collaboration and collegiality among teachers, or whether the use of such time would be absorbed into the existing culture of individualism. Yet the qualitative data generated findings more complex and perhaps more interesting than the possibilities posed by either of those alternatives. Collegiality emerged in one board, but not in the other. But even in the board where collegiality was present, more important than its occurrence was its meaning.

One of the realizations of teacher collaboration was what I have called *contrived collegiality*. This reconstituted the cooperative principles of human association among teachers in administratively regulated and predictable forms. In contrived collegiality, collaboration among teachers was compulsory, not voluntary; bounded and fixed in time and space; implementation- rather than development-oriented; and meant to be predictable rather than unpredictable in its outcomes.

The realizations and implications of contrived collegiality emerged in three areas of teacher collaboration: mandated collaboration and joint planning in preparation time; required consultation with special education resource teachers at scheduled times; and participation in a peer coaching program. In micro-political and more broadly sociopolitical terms, contrived collegiality is not merely an example of personal insensitivity, among particular administrators. Rather, it is constitutive of sociopolitical and administrative systems that are less than fully serious about their rhetorical commitment to teacher empowerment. They are systems prepared to delegate to teachers and indeed hold them accountable for the collective, shared responsibility for implementation, while allocating to themselves increasingly centralized responsibility for the development and imposition of purposes through curriculum and assessment mandates. They are systems of state regulation and control in which the business of conception and planning remains broadly separated from that of technical execution.[37] In many respects, and in many instances, humanistic rhetorics of collegiality and empowerment disguise that fundamental division.

Two of the major consequences of contrived collegiality, it was found, are inflexibility and inefficiency – in terms of teachers not meeting when they should, of meeting when there is no business to discuss, and of being involved in peer coaching schemes which they have misunderstood or not been able to work through with suitable partners. In this respect, the sad thing about the safe simulation of teacher collaboration that I have called contrived collegiality is not that it deceives teachers, but that it delays, distracts and demeans them. The inflexibility of mandated collegiality makes it difficult for programs to be adjusted to the purposes and practicalities of particular school and classroom settings. It overrides teachers' professionalism and the discretionary judgment which comprises it. And it diverts teachers' efforts and energies into simulated compliance with administrative demands that are inflexible and inappropriate for the settings in which they work.

Understood in micropolitical and sociopolitical terms, contrived collegiality and its consequences are more than problems of individual insensitivity. More sensitivity and flexibility among school principals and headteachers in the management of collegiality can certainly help alleviate some of its unwanted effects, of course. But the issue underlying contrived collegiality is ultimately one that must be addressed by school systems and educational systems at the highest level. It is an issue of willingness to give to schools and their teachers substantial responsibility for development as well as implementation, for curriculum as well as instruction. It is an issue of commitment to unwriting the details of district, state or nationally driven curriculum guidelines, to give communities of teachers the necessary flexibility to work with each other in developing programs of their own. Ultimately, it is an issue of serious and wide-ranging rather than merely cosmetic empowerment of our teachers and our schools. What remains to be seen, amidst all the rhetoric of restructuring and reform, is whether principals, school system administrators and politicians are prepared to bite that particular bullet.

NOTES

1. Lieberman, A. and Miller, J., *Teachers, Their World and Their Work: Implications for School Improvement*, Alexandria, VA, ASCD, 1984.

2. Rosenholtz, S., *Teachers' Workplace*, New York, Longman; and Bird, T. and Little, J. W., "How schools organize the teaching occupation", *The Elementary School Journal*, 86(4), 1986, 493–512.

3. Mortimore, P., Sammons, P., Stoll, L., Lewis, D. and Ecob, R., *School Matters*, Berkeley, CA, University of California Press, 1988; Purkey, S. C. and Smith, M., "Effective schools: A review", *Elementary School Journal*, 83(4), 1988; Reynolds, D. (ed.), *Studying School Effectiveness*, Lewes, Falmer Press, 1985; Rutter, M., Maughan, B., Mortimore, P., Ouston, J. and Smith, A., *Fifteen Thousand Hours*, London, Open Books, 1979.

4. Huberman, M. and Miles, M., *Innovation Up Close: How School Improvement Works*, New York, Plenum, 1984; Fullan, M. with Stiegelbauer, S., *The New Meaning of Educational Change*, London, Cassell; New York, Teachers College Press; and Toronto, OISE Press, 1991.

5. Campbell, R. J., *Developing the Primary Curriculum*, London, Holt, Rinehart & Winston, 1985; and Skilbeck, M., *School-Based Curriculum Development*, London, Harper & Row, 1984.

6. Stenhouse, L., *Educating Teachers: Changing the Nature of Pedagogical Knowledge*, Lewes, Falmer Press, 1980; and Rudduck, J., *Innovation and Change*, Milton Keynes, Open University Press, 1991.

7. Hargreaves, A. *Curriculum and Assessment Reform*, Toronto, OISE Press, 1989.

8. Campbell, J., "The Education Reform Act 1988: Some implications for curriculum decision-making", in Purdy, M. (ed.), *Approaches to Curriculum Management*, Milton Keynes, Open University Press, 1989.

9. Shulman, L., "Teaching alone, learning together: Needed agendas for the new reforms". A paper prepared for the conference on Restructuring Schooling for Quality Education, Trinity University, San Antonio, TX, 1989.

10. Ibid, pp. 6-7.

11. Hallinger, P. and Murphy, J., "Instructional leadership in the school context", in Greenfield, W. (ed.), *Instructional Leadership: Concepts, Issues and Controversies*, Boston, MA, Allyn & Bacon, 179-203.

12. Leithwood, K. and Jantzi, D., "Transformational leadership: How principals can help reform school cultures". A paper presented at the Annual Meeting of the American Educational Research Association, Boston, MA, April 1990.

13. Glickman, A., "Open accountability for the 1990s: Between the pillars", *Educational Leadership*, 47(7), 1990, 38-42.

14. Little, J. W., "Seductive images and organizational realities in professional development", *Teachers College Record*, 86(1), 1984, 84-102; Bird and Little, *op. cit.*, note 2; Campbell, *op. cit.*, note 5; Gitlin, A., "Common school structures and teacher behaviour", in Beyer, L. E. and Apple, M. (eds), *The Curriculum: Problems, Politics and Possibilities*, Albany, State University of New York Press; Bullough, R., Jr, "Accommodation and tension: Teachers, teachers' role, and the culture of teaching", in Beyer, L. E. and Apple, M. (eds), *The Curriculum: Problems, Politics and Possibilities*, Albany, State University of New York Press.

15. Campbell, P. and Southworth, G., "Rethinking collegiality: Teachers' views". A paper presented at the Annual Meeting of the American Educational Research Association, Boston, MA, April 1990.

16. Little, J. W., "The persistence of privacy: Autonomy and initiative in teachers' professional relations", *Teachers College Record*, 91(4), 1990, 509-36.

17. In her widely cited study of elementary teachers' work relations and their implications for student achievement, for instance, Rosenholtz, *op. cit.*, note 2, makes bold claims for the benefits of teacher collaboration as a whole which are actually founded on a teacher interview instrument that embodies quite specific and rather narrow interpretations of it. Of seven items dealing with collaboration, six refer to giving and receiving advice and help; one to sharing teaching ideas and materials. None deals with critical reflection, shared decision-making, collaborative planning or structured collective reviews and reforms of teaching through such strategies as peer coaching. In fact, Rosenholtz's criteria of collaboration are very much like the kinds of limited sharing and swapping of stories that Lortie, D., *Schoolteacher*, Chicago, University of Chicago Press, 1975, identified as being quite compatible with a basic commitment to individualism and autonomy in the classroom among teachers.

18. Little, *op. cit.*, note 16.

19. Hargreaves, A., "Cultures of teaching: A focus for change", in Hargreaves, A. and Fullan, M. (eds) *Understanding Teacher Development*, London, Cassell and New York, Teachers College Press, 1992, 218-40; Acker, S., "Teachers' culture in an English primary school: Continuity and change", *British Journal of Sociology of Education*, 4(3), 1990, 257-74.

20. Little, *op. cit.*, note 14; Leithwood and Jantzi, *op. cit.*, note 12.

21. Cooper, M., "Whose culture is it anyway?", in Lieberman, A. (ed.), *Building a Professional Culture in Schools*, New York, Teachers College Press, p. 47.

22. Deal, T. E. and Kennedy, A., *Corporate Cultures*, Reading, MA, Addison-Wesley, 1982; Schein, E. H., *Organizational Culture and Leadership: A Dynamic View*, San Francisco, Jossey-Bass, 1985; and Erickson, F., "Conceptions of school culture", *Educational Administration Quarterly*, 23(4), 1987, 11–24.

23. Rosenholtz, *op. cit.*, note 2; Musella, D. and Davis, J., "Assessing organizational culture: Implications for leaders of organizational change", in Leithwood, K. and Musella, D. (eds) *Understanding School System Administration*, New York and Philadelphia, Falmer Press, 1992; and Leithwood and Jantzi, *op. cit.*, note 12.

24. Hargreaves, *op. cit.*, note 19.

25. Blase, J., "The teachers' political orientation *vis-à-vis* the principal: The micropolitics of the school", *Politics of Education Association Yearbook*, 1988, 113–26.

26. Hoyle, E., *The Politics of School Management*, Sevenoaks, Hodder & Stoughton, 1986.

27. Ball, S., *The Micropolitics of the School*, London, Methuen, 1987.

28. Huberman, M., "The social context of instruction in schools". Paper presented at the Annual Meeting of the American Educational Research Association, Boston, MA, April, 1990.

29. Hartley, D., "Instructional isomorphism and the management of consent in education", *Journal of Educational Policy*, 1(2), 1986, 229–37. See also Hargreaves, A. and Reynolds, D., *Educational Policies: Controversies and Critiques*, Lewes, Falmer Press, 1989.

30. Riecken, T., "School improvement and the culture of the school." An unpublished Ph.D. thesis at the University of British Columbia, Vancouver, 1989.

31. Wilson, A., *A Consumer's Guide to Bill 82: Special Education in Ontario*, Toronto, Ontario Institute for Studies in Education, 1983.

32. Rosenholtz, *op. cit.*, note 2.

33. Joyce, B. and Showers, B., *Student Achievement through Staff Development*, New York, Longman, 1988.

34. Ibid. Critiques of peer coaching that adopt a narrow technical approach include Garmston, R. J., "How administrators support peer coaching", *Educational Leadership*, 44(1), 1987, 18–26; and Hargreaves, A. and Dawe, R., "Paths of professional development: Contrived collegiality, collaborative culture and the case of peer coaching", *Teaching and Teacher Education*, 6(3), 1990, 227–41.

35. For example, see Smyth, J., *Educating Teachers: Changing the Nature of Pedagogical Knowledge*, Lewes, Falmer Press, 1987.

36. Huberman, *op. cit.*, note 28.

37. Apple, M., *Education and Power*, London, Methuen, 1982.

Chapter 10

The Balkanization of Teaching
Collaboration That Divides

(with Bob Macmillan)

INTRODUCTION

While I have been writing this book, the most remarkable and dramatic changes have been sweeping across Eastern Europe. State tanks have rolled into Moscow and then, in the face of extraordinary resistance from the people and the President of the Russian republic, swiftly rolled out again. The monolith that was once Soviet power has become a mosaic of independent republics. Meanwhile, Yugoslavia, the nation that to Western eyes had long been the jewel of the Eastern bloc, has been driven apart by ethnic, linguistic and territorial schisms and conflicts of a kind not seen for decades. With Serbians, Croatians and others locking horns in ethnic and political rivalry, the very identity and integrity of Yugoslavian nationhood has fallen into disarray.

On the other side of the world, in a small valley in southern British Columbia, Canada, there is a modest stretch of sand and scrub. In the middle of it, a little town has grown up, most of it in the last three decades. Many of its residents have moved there from other parts of Canada and the world beyond, particularly Europe. One of them is a hairdresser. When I was on vacation there, it was she who cut my hair. She is Slovenian. When she learned I had an old friend in Yugoslavia, she took me through an extended historical and political analysis of the country's problems. She described the intense suspicion and enmity between different ethnic groups, especially Serbians and Croatians, that had its roots not only in ethnicity but also in fundamental differences of religion, language and culture; and of past but not forgotten political conflicts where these differences were so deep-seated and multi-faceted, they were virtually irreconcilable. Only tight control and the imposition of central command, it seemed, could keep these differences suppressed and let order prevail.

Against this portrait of despair, my Slovenian hairdresser then set another picture. There were three hotels in her town, she said; two right next to each other, and a third just down the street. The owners of these hotels had become good friends. They drank together. They socialized together. Nothing unusual in that, perhaps, except one owner was Serbian, one was Croatian and one was Slovenian.

Traditional enemies in one country; loyal friends in another. Differences

212

that seemed irreconcilable and immutable, and rivalries that had become entrenched by culture and history in one context, were not so fixed at all in another. Removed from the cultural boundaries and traditions that kept them separated from and suspicious of one another, members of these ethnic groups, it seemed, could learn to live together in other, more constructive ways. In the Canadian desert, far from the cultural assumptions and distinctions of their own native land, they could even become friends.

In telling this story, I have no wish to trivialize the appalling social and political problems which have been afflicting parts of Eastern Europe. But the story does convey important messages about the nature and consequences of different kinds of culture and collaboration. It shows that collaboration can connect, but that it can just as easily divide. This chapter addresses the kinds of collaboration that divide – that separate teachers into insulated and often competing sub-groups within a school.

This kind of teacher culture is one I term *balkanized*. The balkanized form of teachers' culture, like all other forms, is defined by particular patterns of inter-relationships among teachers. In balkanized cultures, these patterns mainly consist of teachers working neither in isolation, nor with most of their colleagues as a whole school, but in smaller sub-groups within the school community, such as secondary school subject departments, special needs units, or junior and primary divisions within the elementary school.[1]

Simply working and associating with colleagues in small groups does not amount to balkanization, though. Balkanization, I will show, can and does have negative consequences for student learning and teacher learning. By contrast, there are many ways of working with smaller groups of colleagues such as in teaching teams, school improvement teams or curriculum planning groups that can be extremely positive for teachers and students. What is at issue here is not the general advantages and disadvantages of teachers working and associating together with smaller groups of their colleagues, but the particular patterns these forms of sub-group association can and do often take, along with their effects. Balkanization amounts to more than people associating in smaller sub-groups. In their characteristic form, balkanized cultures among teachers and other groups have four additional qualities.

1. **Low permeability.** In balkanized cultures, sub-groups are strongly insulated from each other. Multiple group membership is not common. Balkanized teachers belong predominantly and perhaps exclusively to one group more than any other. Teachers' professional learning occurs mainly within their own sub-group (such as the subject department), and the nature of that professional learning – what teachers come to know, think and believe – varies considerably between those sub-groups. What teachers *know* and *believe* in one department or division, for example, can become quite different from what teachers *know*

and *believe* in another.[2] Balkanization therefore consists of sub-groups whose existence and membership are clearly delineated in *space* with clear boundaries between them.

2. **High permanence.** Once established, the sub-groups which make up balkanization, along with membership of them, also tend to have strong permanence over *time*. In balkanized teacher cultures, few teachers move between groups from one year to the next. Sub-group categories and teachers' membership in them remain relatively stable. Teachers come to see themselves as not just teachers in general, but elementary teachers, chemistry teachers, or special education teachers specifically.[3]

3. **Personal identification.** Within balkanized cultures, people become especially attached to the sub-communities within which most of their working lives are contained and defined. In education, much of this comes through teachers' own school socialization, university education and teacher preparation, where secondary teachers especially learn to identify with their favored subjects, and to see the world from the standpoint of those subjects. The structure of teacher preparation, with its segregation into different stages or panels of specialization, also leads to teachers identifying themselves early as elementary teachers, secondary teachers, or junior-high teachers respectively.

   Socialization into subjects or other sub-groups constructs teachers' identities in particular ways. Active membership of these sub-groups within the school setting adds to these identities a set of assumptions, widely shared in the sub-community, about the nature of learning (is it linear or non-linear; product or process centered?), about workable teaching strategies (frontal teaching, cooperative learning, individualization, etc.) and about student grouping (is tracking/streaming necessary or desirable, etc.?). Induction into a subject or other sub-culture is induction into a particular tradition with its own common understandings about teaching, learning, grouping and assessment.[4] Where cross-membership of sub-groups is rare, induction into one tradition means exclusion and distancing from other, different ones. Communication between staff and consistency of expectations among them are the casualties. In this respect, singular identification with particular sub-groups undermines the capacity for empathy and collaboration with others.

4. **Political complexion.** Finally, balkanized cultures have a political complexion to them. Teacher sub-cultures are not merely sources of identity and meaning. They are repositories of self-interest as

well. Promotion, status and resources are frequently distributed between and realized through membership of teacher sub-cultures. These goods are not distributed evenly, nor are they contested by different sub-cultures on equal terms. Teachers of older students tend to receive more status and rewards than teachers of younger ones; teachers of some subjects more than teachers of others. In balkanized cultures, there are winners and losers. There is grievance and there is greed. Whether they are manifest or muted, the dynamics of power and self-interest within such cultures are major determinants of how teachers behave as a community.[5]

These political behaviors have important educational consequences. Imbalances of power and status between tightly bounded groups make it difficult for teachers to reach common agreement in areas that threaten their career opportunities, resources or conditions of work. When major innovations are introduced, they also divide teachers into supporters who will prosper from the innovation, and opponents who will suffer by it.[6]

These patterns of balkanization are not inevitable, and I will examine some alternatives to them toward the end of the chapter. Before that, I want to describe and analyze two very different cases of balkanization in two secondary schools, to explore what balkanization looks like in practice and to examine the different forms it can take and consequences it can create. These cases are drawn from a study in Ontario, Canada, of eight secondary schools of varying types, and how their teachers are responding to a provincially imposed mandate to destream Grade 9 by the Fall of 1993.[7]

The study is based on interviews conducted in 1991–92 with the principals in each school and with teachers in selected subjects who had taught Grade 9 within the previous two years. The selected subjects were English, French, mathematics, history/geography (whichever was offered in Grade 9), technical or technological studies and family studies. Guidance counselors and special education teachers were also interviewed. Interviews were guided by a semi-structured schedule focusing on teachers' working relations with their colleagues; teachers' perspectives and practices concerning pedagogy, their subject and their career; and teachers' perspectives and practices concerning destreaming and other forms of student grouping. All interviews were tape-recorded and subsequently transcribed.

The first case is of a rather conventional, secondary school — subject-based and academically oriented — which, at the time of the study, was not at all enthusiastic about the destreaming initiative. The second case is a high-profile, innovative secondary school, newly built, and with staff specially appointed to implement destreaming, to establish *cohorts* of students who would stay together for most of their Grade 9 program, and to achieve a number of other changes in student assessment and guidance. There are important contrasts between these two cases of seemingly traditional and innovative schools but we will see that these differences are not at all ones of a secondary school that is balkanized and one that is not. Indeed, it will become clear that for all its innovativeness, our second case of a restructured secondary school has not abolished balkanization at all, but reconstructed and reinscribed it in new forms.

The chapter closes with an analysis of the wider context and consequences of balkanization in secondary schools. Notwithstanding all the challenges of the postmodern age, I will argue, secondary schools and their teachers remain deeply embroiled and enmeshed in the organizational patterns and priorities of modernity. There are ways out of this. And I shall describe one school which offers some clues as to the solutions that might be available. But the grip of modernity remains strong and most secondary teachers show few signs of wanting to release or be released by it.

ROXBOROUGH HIGH: TRADITIONAL BALKANIZATION

Roxborough High School opened in 1957 as the second secondary school in an expanding city in Ontario. Once having had a student population of over 2000 in the late 1970s, at the time of the study it had settled, through school board allocation policies, to a little over 1300. A document prepared by the school for the purposes of the study states that

> the community from which Roxborough draws its students is
> solidly middle class. Most parents hold down managerial or
> professional occupations and have high expectations for their
> children. The student body is overwhelmingly white although
> recently, a growing number of visible minorities have enrolled at
> the school.

The school documents its withdrawal or dropout rate at under 2 percent compared to a regional figure of over 8 percent. Accordingly, in a provincial system which differentiates between academic-level, general-level and basic-level courses in Grade 9, enrolment in general level courses is low, with only 10 percent of students in English registered at the general level, for instance. The arguably lower-status courses of physical education, music, art, family studies, keyboarding and technical education are offered at general level (although they take students of a wider ability range), and are therefore regarded by the principal as *already destreamed*. Clearly, the school is proudly and persistently weighted towards a traditional academic emphasis in its intake, program and values. Its inclusion of a program for French immersion students adds to this emphasis.

The principal unabashedly describes the school as a *traditional* one, as do many of his staff. When approaching the school on behalf of the project team, to invite it to join the study, a school board superintendent stated, tongue in cheek, that we were looking for an "antediluvian school" and asked if the school would want to be included on those grounds. Certainly, in staffing terms, the school is a highly stable one. There are 89 other teaching staff apart from the principal and vice-principal, whose median age is 45 years. Teachers' median years of teaching experience is 18, and the median number of years they have taught at Roxborough itself is 14! A further indicator of the school's holding power on its staff is that 27 (one-third) of the staff have taught nowhere else but Roxborough, and six others have taught there for all but one year of their careers.

Some staff were drawn to Roxborough by its academic, social and community reputation and, like the family studies teacher wanting to move to this city, they held out on other opportunities and "sat tight, waiting for something to fall into my lap". Two of the ten teachers we interviewed had first come to Roxborough on short-term teacher exchanges, and then stayed. Whatever their reasons, once there, most teachers liked to stay, sometimes even at the expense of career opportunities elsewhere. The history teacher's response was typical. Although attracted to the thought of working in other settings and getting new experiences, he said:

> Roxborough feels very comfortable, but comfortable pews are
> like that! . . . I would like to believe that I'm not going to finish
> out my career here, that I should be moving on and getting some
> new experiences, too. It's just making that break. The longer I
> stay, the easier it is to stay.

The mathematics teacher reinforced this interpretation when he said, "Once people get there, they like to stay, unless it's a promotion sort of thing."

There were many factors that kept teachers at Roxborough. Students were foremost among these factors, reinforcing Metz's point that the status and worth of teachers is in many respects defined for them by the qualities and characteristics of their students.[8] One teacher said the reason teachers stayed "has a lot to do with the comfort, with the students, with the community that we have here that makes up the school!" The Special Education teacher claimed that Roxborough kids are "a cut above the rest" academically, which he hears "over and over again" from itinerant teachers, mental health professionals and others who come to the school. He reiterated the comments of one visitor who said:

> There is a different feeling at Roxborough. [She referred to a
> couple of things that were happening around.] It was December
> and it was kids singing carols in the hall; teachers joining in a
> band to play Christmas carols and raise money for charity. . . .
> There's a different atmosphere.

In addition to the students and community, the caliber and characteristics of the staff were another reason teachers liked Roxborough and stayed there. Staff relationships were generally highly valued within the school. As the geography teacher put it:

> Most of the staff are easy to talk to. Most of the staff accept
> their role, and not a lot of whining and bitching and
> complaining. . . . If I have a problem with a student, I can go to
> the teacher and talk. . . . Most staff pull their weight and do the
> job. And that's what's nice.

The English teacher referred to "the quality of education and that reflects on the teaching staff, the quality and dedication of the teaching staff. That's one of the big strengths." The teachers at Roxborough, he said, were "supportive, friendly, committed", Staff relationships were a particular strength for the family studies teacher who had come from a school amalgamation that had divided staff and created dissonance, "sour grapes" and a poor staffroom atmosphere. At Roxborough, therefore, she especially valued the "very positive peer relations at this school". Colleagues were "very positive, very helpful". They spent a lot of time after school in classes with kids. There was "a tone of professionalism". "The whole school works together," she said, right through to the secretaries and the janitor.

More than one teacher observed that despite their overall age, 55 percent of the staff were actively involved in extra-curricular commitments with students. As the math teacher observed, this helped create a good school spirit.

It is important to recognize these teachers' positive perceptions of their students, the community and each other. By the proud admission of the principal and many of his staff, the school is traditionally academic in emphasis. We will also see that in its structure, and in the identifications of its teachers, it is strongly subject-based. Powerful patterns of balkanization, I will show, have built up around these subject structures and identities. But the school is by no means an outmoded and uncaring Dickensian sweatshop. Indeed, the sense of community and commitment among its teachers is at least as strong as in many of its more explicitly innovative counterparts.

It is with this clear sense of context that I want to define and describe the patterns of balkanization of a subject-based nature which permeate Roxborough High. The evidence suggests that this balkanization limits the school's capacity to develop the more nurturing side of its mission (which the special education teacher already felt to be strongly present but insufficiently recognized), and to extend this to embrace the needs of students in general-level classes who are not easily accommodated by the school's academic emphasis. Second, the evidence also suggests that balkanization creates and sustains invidious status distinctions between *academic* and *practical* subjects and therefore between the students who take them, in such a way as to threaten program balance and the viability of self-contained solutions to the problem of students in general level classes. Third, and most importantly, the evidence suggests that balkanization creates and confirms a myth of changelessness in the school, and limits awareness of potential for change that already exists by reducing teachers' opportunities to learn from each other.

1. Subject Identification and Academic Emphasis

At Roxborough High, most teachers identify closely with their subjects, have limited experiences of teaching outside of their subjects, and have developed pedagogical identities that are congruent with their subjects being realized in strongly academic ways. With the length of time that many teachers have spent at Roxborough, these subject attachments and identities have tended to become not only stabilized but even a little entrenched. In these respects, Roxborough exemplifies very clearly the qualities of low permeability and high permanence that are two of the defining criteria of balkanization.

Teachers in the school were, in the words of the math teacher, perceived as "very dedicated to teaching their subjects. I think the teachers are very content-oriented: the academic side of things." In general, he said, there was a "very high percentage of excellent academic teachers". He himself knew that "math was always the subject I was going to teach". He excelled in it in Grades 12 and 13, and studied it at university. He was still "quite interested in math. I enjoy doing math and teaching it quite a lot." Math was now "all part of me," he said.

> It's either right or it's wrong, and there's a definite strategy to it. I don't have to be creative. There's a chance to get it right . . . and getting the right answers is a certain satisfaction for me.

Whatever shortcomings he might have, this teacher felt that "The . . . academic side makes up for it. Because the kids feel comfortable in my class. They tend to learn, *if they choose to*. If they're interested in understanding what's going on, they will." However,

> Some kids perhaps just have no interest . . . that's a challenge, to make them interested that they've had . . . math has never been easy or useful in their minds. And so you've got a mindset in some students, about math.

More generally, he felt that:

> Maybe the kids that don't want to learn would do better if they felt more comfortable in a personal sort of way. . . . I think it goes far beyond just hating math or whatever. It's more into they don't like school and I'm just another teacher . . . math not always usually being a favorite subject for those type of kids. My style doesn't say "Gee this is neat!" . . . and I'm not flashy . . . I do bring in concrete examples and that sort of thing, but that goes to my more structured and orderly way of doing things.

The history teacher listed his subject as one of the main things he liked about his job.

> Definitely one is working with the whole subject matter. I bring to this job an intrinsically curious mind about things dealing

> with . . . politics and history, current events, all that. That is just
> something that comes to me naturally. . . . So I bring a natural
> interest to the subject matter.

This teacher is by no means staid in his approach to the subject. He organizes
visits to Washington so his students can analyze politics with students from
other schools. He suspended the program to look at the Gulf War. He "gets
excited about the material" and communicates this excitement to his students.
But his main teaching style is one of class discussion, he confesses to enjoying
being the center of attention, he is not convinced students are learning when
they are working individually, and he admits to being uneasy when he is not in
control. This style appears to suit many of Roxborough's students but, as with
the math teacher, this teacher also experiences difficulty with slower learners,
who are not as keen on the subject as he is.

The school is built upon strong subject identities with a high academic
emphasis and pedagogies which support that. The decision-making process in
which department heads play a central role as filters for decisions buttresses
these subjects still further. At the time of the study, most teachers acknowledged and were genuinely concerned about the fact that students in general-level
classes were not well catered for within the school. But the solution was to
establish a General Level Committee which dealt with the issue as a self-
contained problem. What was more difficult for staff to see, at this point, was
the extent to which the fortunes and frustrations of students in general-level
classes were shaped by identities, priorities and capacities of teachers that had
their anchors in the academic, subject-based domain and in the more purely
intellectual mentalities of teachers and higher-achieving students alike which
constituted that domain.[9]

2. Status Differentiation

Differences of status between subjects compounded these differences of status
between students. Technical education and family studies were both included in
the range of subjects from which we selected teacher interviewees. Both were
designated as general-level programs by the school, in Grade 9, but were open
to advanced level students also. In practice, though, most of their students were
"general level". The technical teacher estimated that most of his classes were
made up of around ten "general level" students and three to five other students
who were "advanced-level type". The family studies teacher observed that
because her subject was an elective, "a certain kind of person takes family
studies", compared to English, where she also does some teaching and where
"you're exposed to the academic". She estimates that in the present Grade 9
course, 12 out of 18 students are general level.

Differences in status of the students and the levels of program they take are
reflected in and reinforced by differences of status between subjects which are
designated at those respective levels. In technical education, issues of status

and politics have come to threaten the subject's very viability. The advent and expansion of business studies in Ontario, and the associated provincial imposition of a Grade 9 requirement for students to take *either* technology *or* business studies, has led to sharp declines in the number of students taking technical education, and therefore in the size and status of technical education departments too.

At Roxborough, technical education began with nine teachers and "a whole slew of shops". Now it has only four teachers. Provincial requirements and declining enrolments were responsible for this, but so too were parents' attitudes, reinforcing the status decline into which technical education was already locked.

> Roxborough is not . . . how can I put this, we do not have a lot
> of students here who want to get a technical education. It's
> because of the locality. The school's situated in . . . their parents
> want them to be doctors and dentists and that type of thing.

The status problems of family studies were articulated slightly differently. Here, the problems arising from the purported practicality of the subject were intertwined with and overlain by strongly gendered associations of cooking and domesticity. In response to a question about the downsides of teaching the subject, the family studies teacher replied:

> I think there's a lot of people at the school who are older and
> refer to it as home economics and still see it as traditional
> sewing and cooking. But really family studies involves a lot more
> than sewing and cooking. I'd like it if they were more cognizant
> of the subject material.

A little later, she continued,

> *T*: There are about ten or twenty people at the school who say
> "home economics" and see it as a strictly female thing. You
> get the gender jobs in the staffroom and stuff: "Well, let's
> get the home economics people to do the dishes or the
> baking! Aren't you guys baking cookies or having pie
> tasting contests?" Because twenty years ago, I guess that's
> what the home ecs did.
>
> *I*: How do you deal with that?
>
> *T*: Oh well, I correct them when they say home economics. I
> guess that term really bothers me, so I'll tell them it's
> family studies. When they say, "Aren't you baking any
> cookies?", I'll say, "Well, no, we've finished our cooking
> component. We only did it for two months." So they'll
> wonder what we're doing for the next six months of the
> year so you have to sort of lay your curriculum on the table
> and tell them it's a lot more than just cooking!

I: Is this women as well as guys? Do women tend to understand what you're about?

T: The women do, yeah.

I: That's interesting.

T: It doesn't happen a lot, but this is the worst thing about family studies. It's a really good area to teach in, but you'll be standing up in front of your classroom or fishing kids out of the hall into the classroom because you're ready to start, and some male teacher goes, "Mike, what are you doing taking family studies!" The message is, you're the wrong gender.

Given these issues of status and gender, as well as the subject's designation as an elective only, it is not surprising that this teacher should conclude that "We have to work hard to promote our subject."

The potential learning benefits for *all* students of programs of family studies and technical education are immense. The subjects claim broad relevance to the domains of leisure, technical training, parenting and life management, and have argued for compulsory status on these grounds. Among subject departments, they are in the forefront of attempts to integrate theory and practical experience in students' learning. And despite their lower status, or perhaps because of it, they are, in pedagogical and organizational terms, two of the most innovative subjects — sometimes out of sheer necessity as reductions in course enrolments lead to different grades as well as different ability levels being taught at the same time.

And yet, notwithstanding their strengths and contribution, these subjects remain unchosen by many students, ostracized by their parents, and misunderstood by colleagues. Because of their modest departmental size, they also possess little influence in the politics and decision-making of the school. In this way, lower-status students are consigned to lower-status subjects and courses, and the cycle of marginalization of students and subjects alike is reinforced.

3. Subject Insulation and the Myth of Changelessness

The influence of balkanization at Roxborough High also perpetuates a *myth of changelessness* among its teachers, masks the individual initiative that many teachers possess to improve their knowledge and skills, and restricts the opportunities for teachers to learn from each other — particularly across subject boundaries. One teacher acknowledged that "we prepare kids for university well" but also felt that "We shouldn't be sitting back saying, 'We're Roxborough, therefore, you're privileged to be here!' There are a lot of schools doing wonderful innovative things and we've got to be prepared to do these things too." "Some people on staff", he concluded, "tend to feel that 'This is Roxborough. The curriculum is important. We prepare kids for university. And anything that takes away from that is *bad*.'" Another teacher, after granting that "there are a lot of very strong teachers", nonetheless added that she would

> like to see maybe more of an open-mind policy, to try new things and to not feel that everything has to stay the same; that we can change things as we go along. I mean Roxborough [laughs!] doesn't!

Another teacher observed that "We've got an aging staff here and not too receptive to trying new things to start with." A fourth teacher was considerably more vociferous. He complained that to some extent, the school "rides on reputation" for being "a good academic leader" which may not hold up as well as 18 or 20 years ago. He continued:

> Because there aren't many people coming in from other areas, we tend to perpetuate some of these myths. I think they are myths, but as with all myths, I think there is a certain amount of truth and a certain amount of creation that goes along with that. . . . To go with what a couple of people have told me who have taught here and pushed on to other things, and, to use the vernacular, this is a rather tightass type of school compared to some of the others that are around. . . . People not open to change as readily as I would like them to be. I find that frustrating sometimes, and to be with people . . . who think that the smallest things are change. In fact, they don't really have a keen appreciation as to what change is. It became a rather insulated type of staff — not unfriendly for the people who are inside it [but] probably a little harder to crack into it. People are good intentioned, but nevertheless, not much change, not much youth. And at times the energy that comes with youth is a little bit lacking.

While deeply perceptive in many respects, there is also an intriguing irony in this teacher's claims about his colleagues. The school's reputation as an academic leader, he feels, is at least to some extent mythical. Yet there is evidence that his own attributions of changelessness to his colleagues may also be somewhat mythical. One colleague, for instance, while recognizing that the school still holds to "traditional values", also emphasizes that "There's an awful lot of innovation going on here; more so than in other schools, in fact." Our interview transcripts contain many examples supporting this claim. This teacher himself, for instance, while a staunch defender of the English language, who strove to "protect it from deterioration", was also enjoying innovating with computers because "You have to create your own challenge. I don't allow myself to stagnate. I think that's what makes it lots of fun." In family studies and technology, as we have seen, change and innovation were often extensive. The technology teacher, for instance, had retrained several times in completely new branches of technology as the department shrank, had constantly updated his expertise in fast-moving areas like electronics, and had learned to teach multiple grade and ability levels in the class at the same time.

Yet the innovations and changes taking place in specific subject departments were often invisible in the school more generally because these departments and their members were so strongly insulated from one another. A story told by the math teacher clearly illustrates the nature and consequences of this problem.

This math teacher had become interested in cooperative learning. He had been doing "a lot of reading and workshops" on the subject, including professional development sessions on cooperative learning in mathematics within his own district, six months previously, and another workshop just a month before this interview, outside his district. Cautious about innovation, this teacher, even after exposure to workshops, readings and videos, had "tried a bit of cooperative learning" just once, with his Grade 10 computer class. What other people might perceive as a rather small investment in change on his part nevertheless involved substantial risk and uncertainty for him. This is why.

After conclusion of our first interview, this teacher talked about his first practical encounter with cooperative learning. The conversation is summarized in fieldnotes:

> I admired his willingness and the willingness of people like him
> to voluntarily undertake and be interested in change. . . . His
> response to this was that it was important to him and he was
> working on it, but that it was hard making innovations like that
> alone in a school. He said that it was hard doing cooperative
> learning in a school where you were the only one. He drew the
> analogy that it was hard being the only teacher in a school who
> allowed kids to wear hats in class when none of the other
> teachers did, and that this would cause problems. The same
> applied to cooperative learning. If all the other teachers allowed
> students to sit with their friends, it was very difficult as a
> teacher yourself to insist that there were other reasons for them
> to sit together, and other combinations for them sitting together.
>
> Even if you explained this to them fully, this still put you
> out of line with the rest of your colleagues in the school, and the
> kids' expectations that followed from that, he said. He pointed
> out that the cooperative learning experience he had tried in his
> class was mainly successful because of the immense planning he
> put into it — hours of planning in terms of the combinations of
> individuals who would be working in the different groups, and
> playing different roles (it took him five hours just to work out
> where the students would sit!). But generally, he pointed out, it

was quite difficult because of the extent to which he was deviant in what he expected and wanted, compared to his colleagues.[10]

This teacher was on the edge in terms of making innovation. Like many teachers who make changes in isolation, he felt vulnerable and exposed; open to comparison and criticism by teachers and students alike. His exhaustive attention to planning and preparing for his cooperative learning lesson might be construed as a product of his personal and subject identity — feeling the need to approach things in a "step-by-step", linear way, in the way that many mathematics teachers appear to do. But it was also a highly realistic adjustment to the challenge of changing alone and to the very real prospects of deviating from wider teaching norms and failing.

Ironically, however, he was not actually alone in his interest in cooperative learning at all. Several other teachers in the school had also indicated in the interviews that they were becoming interested in this area of change. Yet it was only the evening previous to his interview that the math teacher had discovered this.

> Last night, I was at a cooperative learning workshop. It was a school board workshop, but they invited some people from here to go. . . . I didn't realize it, but we've got a group of teachers [in the school] that sort of have an unofficial committee on cooperative learning that they're just starting to work at it. And I didn't even know that!

The support that this teacher needed to make change and risk failure was already there, not just in theory or outside expertise, but among his own colleagues within the school. These colleagues, though, were in other departments. They were not easily accessible to him, and so neither was their practice. As a result, this teacher had soldiered on alone in imagined isolation. Luckily, he had experienced early success and by accident, within the board, had ultimately discovered the sources of needed support among his colleagues. But it could so easily have been otherwise. Early failure could have led to overwhelming discouragement. Criticism could have created retreat and withdrawal. Success at change was being achieved by a combination of personal tenacity and sheer luck; rather fragile components for success! The possibilities for such success were not actively structured into the school's organization, especially in terms of supportive collegial relationships.

The source of this teacher's imagined and real isolation was the school's departmental balkanization. Few teachers were able to comment on the strengths and weaknesses of other departments unless the products and achievements of those departments were very visible — in art displays, band performances, successes in provincial contests and the like. Mainly, they said, they did not really know what went on in other departments. They could only comment on what went on in their own.

225

Summary

The consequences of balkanization in Roxborough High were twofold. Students in general-level classes and lower-status subjects were rather marginalized in the school's emphases and priorities. This led to imbalances in the program and to students in general-level classes having difficulty achieving in ways the school valued. The problem of the "general level" students and their programs was rooted in what the school emphasized and valued for the rest. Balkanization also created a myth of changelessness among the school's staff. It underestimated and failed to make visible teachers' own individual interests in and capacities to change. And it created serious risks that fledgling attempts at change would be aborted or defeated for want of shared understanding and support. In short, Roxborough High's balkanized character meant that in terms of being interested in change, being able to change and being involved in change, it was considerably better than it collectively imagined. What we can most learn from this case is that if a school's teachers are its own best resources for change, balkanized departmental structures tend to deplete those resources by insulating and isolating them. In balkanized cultures, the organizational whole is less than the sum of its parts!

LINCOLN SECONDARY: BALKANIZATION REINSCRIBED

Lincoln Secondary is in a community on the fringe of a large metropolitan area and sits amid extensive areas of new housing. It is a new secondary school founded as an experiment to interpret and implement some of the guidelines of the provincial government's initiatives for what it calls "The Transition Years (Grades 7–9)". At the center of the experiment is a destreamed cohort system (or mini-school) for the first year of secondary school (Grade 9), designed to ease the transition from the elementary to the secondary level. A new school founded on principles different from the accepted norm might be expected to weaken or transform the balkanized structures found in most other secondary schools. In this second case, balkanization has not been removed, however, but reconstructed and reinscribed within new structures, leading to important gaps between philosophy and action.

Lincoln Secondary School has tried and is still trying with immense effort and imagination to break the balkanization that afflicts most other secondary school structures, in order to create an education that is more fulfilling, rewarding and academically and socially coherent for its students, especially in Grade 9. Teachers at Lincoln are energetic, committed and passionate about their work. They consistently commented on the excellence of their colleagues. Even after hours of complaining in interviews about the difficulties, conflicts and frustrations, when one group of teachers was asked what they would do if the school reverted to a more conventional pattern, all but one said they would hand in their resignations! Their frustrations, difficulties and disagreements are in this sense less rooted in personalities than in the structures and frameworks which surround them.

In this school, however, new patterns of organization ran parallel to and did not challenge traditional subject departmentalization (cohorts versus departments), subject status differences were perpetuated (core subjects versus the exploratories) and micropolitical factions had developed to deal with perceived inequalities developed in relation to the innovation ("Ins" versus "Not-ins"). The question I want to examine here is: what are the implications of this new organizational structure for traditional patterns of balkanization and their consequences that are found in other high schools?

1. Cohorts versus Departments

Lincoln Secondary has undertaken many innovations in its Grade 9 program, but the central one, organizationally, is the cohort system. The cohorts were established to create homogeneous groupings of students who would take most of their program together, with their teachers functioning as a group and coordinating their efforts. The teachers said they had hoped to function as Grade 9 teachers first and as subject specialists second. In line with this principle, each cohort had a cohort leader who coordinated discussions about students and program. The principal described the functioning of the staff within these cohorts in the following manner.

> The teachers in each cohort meet on a regular basis to discuss
> items related to their cohort. Sometimes they have a day off as a
> group to consider student evaluation, and sometimes they meet
> at noon hours, after school, or whenever they can to develop
> program, etc. Cohort meetings are where many of the ideas and
> decisions come in terms of the Grade 9 program.

Following the philosophy behind the cohort system, teachers recalled their optimism when the staff had agreed to develop several cross-curricular themes as a basis for instruction in all subject areas in all of the cohorts. However, teachers' initial optimism was quickly undermined by the strength of older subject loyalties and traditional departmental structures. In the first semester of the school's existence, the attempt to use a thematic approach was modified department by department, with no coordination through the cohorts. Three factors appear to have contributed to this lack of coordination. First, the themes were left for the departments and not the cohorts to implement. Second, the position of Cohort Leader was ill-defined. Third, the principal circumvented the individual cohorts and allowed some departments to opt out of agreed themes.

When the modifications were discovered, departments which had been continuing with the themes were disappointed and resentful. As one teacher said:

> When decisions affecting the content of the curriculum (for
> example, the six themes as agreed upon by all subject areas),

when those were modified as the year progressed, all subject
areas of the school were not notified.

Evidently, whatever was decided during cohort meetings could still be
overidden by departments. In effect, any initial loyalty teachers may have
felt toward a cohort became subordinated to deeper department loyalties. This
was demonstrated most clearly when curriculum content came into conflict
with the student-centered philosophy of the school. When faced with the difficulties of a student-centered curriculum, teachers tended to revert to subject
loyalties.

> Some departments are more tied to curriculum. My point, my
> perception is, being a pilot project we've been released from that
> to try something. But, again, it's difficult because you've done
> things for 20 years one way, or for a lot of years one way, and
> now you have to change.

Difficulties for teachers arose when they had to reconcile the aims of individualized instruction implicit in the design of the cohort system with basic
subject competencies.

> Science? math? You know, both departments have done
> tremendous things in this school but they feel most tied to
> curriculum. In math, the comment that goes over and over is:
> "They got to have algebra. Kids coming out of Grade 10, they
> have to have algebra." And that's a very strong indication. In
> science it's all very . . . they're very tied to curriculum too.

Ironically, one of the reasons given for the persistence of traditional subject
structures and identities was the challenge of showing demonstrable success
within the destreaming initiative itself. As one teacher stated,

> Destreaming itself has created barriers between . . . well no, you
> could say for a better part that it has opened gates between
> departments. But I could see that there are barriers that may
> have not been there before where subjects really need to feel,
> departments, I don't know how to express this, but there's an
> anxiousness, an anxiety that we all have to be treating our
> subject well, and applying it well to the idea and philosophy and
> so on of destreaming.

Departmental structures persisted in various ways at Lincoln High. As we
have seen, departments were permitted to overrule cohorts on decisions about
themes. Teachers were also allowed to regroup physically along departmental
lines. As the principal put it:

> We had the opportunity to build three specific rooms in the
> school that are workrooms, separate from the staffroom. We also

have prep rooms in some of the areas such as science and social science. We did not designate specific rooms to specific subjects, but just allowed teachers to work in any area they desired. We're allowing the teachers to choose where they might like to work and will take a look at how this develops after the first two years. Eventually we'll have more teachers and this will create problems at that time. At the present time, we are letting the places where teachers work be their choice.

When we returned eight months later for the second phase of the study, the patterns of interaction were more clearly defined still. The strength of the departments became even more consolidated. As the school expands, we would predict just such a shift in the balance of power and influence from cohorts to departments. Opening as it did with Grade 9 and 10 students only, with other grades (and staff) to be added year by year, and given that the cohort system operates in Grade 9 only, the school's position is shifting from one of small departments operating alongside a Grade 9 cohort system that makes up half of the school, to an eventual pattern of large departments operating alongside Grade 9 cohorts that are the organizational exception to all other grades.

2. Core Subjects versus the Exploratories

The subjects at the school have been divided into two groups: core and exploratory. This division is based on the amount of time assigned in the timetable and the importance placed on a particular subject by the majority of staff and the principal. Core subjects, which are taken continuously throughout the year's program, are English, mathematics, second-language instruction, science, social science and physical education. Exploratory subjects (visual arts, dramatic arts, music, family studies and technology) which are semestered[11] are assigned only 11 teaching periods each; an arrangement initially thought to be sufficient to introduce students to and allow them to explore a subject as a basis for informed program choices in Grade 10 and beyond.

Whatever its initial intentions, the teachers of the exploratory subjects nonetheless felt they had been marginalized by teachers in the core areas. As one exploratory teacher said:

> We're on the fringe . . . because we would say something and a
> core teacher who had had that person for every other day for
> how many weeks, knew that. And we would say something, our
> perception, if we could remember who it was, and it was taken
> with a grain of salt. In fact I stopped going to them.

Exploratory teachers recounted numerous incidences of marginalization. Each incident was used to demonstrate that the content of the exploratory subjects was considered not sufficiently rigorous by core teachers who clearly voiced their opinions to their exploratory colleagues.

> Oh, there were a couple of comments that I just found so
> insulting. I said I would never come back to another cohort
> meeting and I didn't. There was a comment that I'd made about
> a student; they were putting this student way off to the right of
> the scale, towards independence and he's Mr Wonderful, and he's
> like this and this; and I said: "In my art class, he's at the totally
> opposite end of the scale." And they said: "Oh well, that's just
> art"; and when someone made that comment I thought: "Oh, I've
> never had to deal with that before. This is interesting." And I
> got a little bit angry about it. There was an apology made but
> still that was the way that we were perceived, at least art was
> perceived, and I'm sure the rest of the exploratories were too.
> "You guys don't really count because you're not part of the core."

Some teachers felt that marginalization did not only encompass discussions about students but extended to the distribution of resources and privileges as well. Speaking of his efforts to gain extra resources, one core teacher said that the principal "told us, OK, tell me what your needs are and which was related to the budget, and I received everything I asked for". This was quite different from the experience of one of the exploratory teachers who asked the principal to clarify the rationale behind differential allocation of resources.

> And I feel that I've been affected directly by some of the
> decisions that have been made. When I did approach the
> principal about them I don't think I was really dealt fairly. He
> listened to me and he nodded – he's a very good listener –
> but then his responses were very cut and dried and his decisions
> had been made and that was all there was to it. And there was
> no real answer, no good reason for the decisions he made. And
> that bothered me a lot because I said: "I want to know why you
> made this decision", and he said: "Well, I really don't know right
> now. I have to get back to you", and he never did.

The marginalization of the exploratory subjects was not without benefits. It encouraged teachers to work together in order to maximize their efforts given the brief time allotted to each of them in the schedule. Some collaboration and integration had certainly occurred between the teachers of two of the subjects, and demonstrated the feasibility and benefits of careful cross-curricular planning. The teachers of the exploratory subjects stated that they now intended to pursue such integration with the core subject teachers. Overall, however, the differences and divisions between high- and low-status subjects that pervade most other secondary schools persisted at Lincoln. Indeed, their inscription within new structures that designated and divided what is core (and central) from what is exploratory (and therefore marginal) exaggerated these differences even further.

3. "Ins" versus the "Not-ins"

A third pattern of balkanization at Lincoln was a less formally structured one. Teachers themselves described it in terms of a distinction between "Ins" and "Not Ins".

All new schools face problems of creation and establishment, problems for which existing theories of educational change based on schools moving from one state to another are not particularly helpful. When what is being created is deeply innovative, these problems are magnified. Teachers must create and define novel structures, while simultaneously establishing a culture of working relationships through which the new structures can be developed. This is extra-ordinarily difficult. One teacher put it like this:

> In a certain sense, with a new school, you're working with new people so you're trying to develop relationships by even getting to know people. Like those relationships are already sort of established, but here, everyone is sort of trying to decide who everybody is, where everybody stands, what we're all about. But in addition to that, I think there's the relationships of working together with people who (a) weren't traditionally working together at other schools, and (b) trying to do that cross-curricular thing. And those relationships are the ones I think that are a little tough and are slow in coming.

There was an ambivalence about how these relationships were perceived. Generally the "staff is really good at supporting each other, and really good at not being afraid to try new things":

> To me, the sense of community in this school outshines anything that I've ever experienced. We've been here for a year, and that may not be everyone's experience, but it certainly is mine. I feel that I know everybody far better at Lincoln, everybody on the staff, than I did at the school that I've been at for a number of years. There's less of a sense of isolation here.

Alongside this sense of informal mutual support, though, there was also conflict and dissonance, especially where power and decision-making were concerned. During the first year of operation, factions developed through departmental coalitions to gain access to and control over the decision-making process. In their study of schools engaged in restructuring, Lieberman and her colleagues conclude that conflict is a necessary part of change.[12] This is not surprising because change is a micropolitical process in which competing purposes and interests are at stake. This conflict is normal, not pathological, Lieberman and colleagues note, but it does need to be addressed and resolved constructively rather than avoided if the change process is to succeed. At Lincoln, however, the mechanisms for addressing and resolving such micropolitical conflicts appeared to be weak or absent.

> I think the mechanism to air these complaints, to get teachers
> feeling that they have a voice in what's been happening or some
> sort of control, power, in what will happen — I'm not sure they're
> feeling that. I think that's what the frustration is.

Another teacher observed that this failure to address conflicts openly led to factions becoming reinforced and entrenched.

> [One of the teachers] made a really good statement at this
> session and he [the principal] was there. She said that when
> things were going wrong, people were not . . . the mechanism for
> trying to solve these problems was not there and that people
> were kind of coalescing in little groups and bitching about it.

One notable problem area was the difference between the staff's and the principal's perceptions about how decisions were made. As one teacher put it, "He's not dictatorial because he wants people's input, but only to a certain extent. Draw the line."

One area where a divergence of opinion occurred is the issue of vision and school philosophy. Whereas the principal was given the opportunity to develop a strong sense of the philosophy and the vision he felt was required for a school such as Lincoln, teachers were not given the same amount of time before having to proceed with the practicalities of opening the school. While belief in the principal's philosophy was a criterion used for hiring, many teachers made it quite clear that their translation of the philosophy into a vision and the principal's translation were in conflict. While the principal had had some discussion with others concerning his vision for Lincoln, the staff did not have the sense of participating in the development of Lincoln's publicly articulated vision. As Fullan notes, when educational visions are grounded in the leader's personal and prior vision, they can become not visions that illuminate, but visions that blind.[13]

Although it may be easier from the principal's standpoint to make decisions while consulting or seeming to consult with people about particular issues, this may cause staff to feel a lack of significant involvement in the school. At Lincoln, some of our interviewees certainly expressed feelings of disengagement and exclusion from the decision-making process. One younger teacher, for instance, related how she had been given the responsibility of staff representative on student council and, with it, the task of creating a motto for the school — only to find that several successive mottos which she and the students generated were overturned by the principal! With an air of resignation, she confided that as a younger, more junior teacher, she probably couldn't have much influence in her school and perhaps just needed to wait and get older before other people valued her opinion. When asked what impact such exclusion from decision-making has had on staff, several teachers stated that there appears to be a polarization of staff members. At one end are those who appear to have access to the decision-making process and the principal, and at the other, those who do not.

This was strikingly revealed in a focus group of four staff members during our second phase of the study. Two teachers talked about the efforts that had been made to acquaint an incoming group of staff with the school and its existing staff. A younger colleague retorted that not only had she not been consulted about the induction of new colleagues, she had not even known the program existed.

Part of the reason for this polarization may have been a product of the principal's initial mandate for and his personal investment in establishing the school. He was selected and given the task of building the school and hiring the staff based on aspects of the destreaming and Transition Years initiatives of the Ministry of Education; and in many respects, the school was established as a showcase of innovation within the board. The principal, perceived as a strong leader by board staff and by trustees, selected people with whom he had worked in previous situations or who had demonstrated an interest in the philosophy behind the school. When comparing transcripts of people who had worked with the principal before with those of people who had not, it is the former group who are considered to be a part of what staff called the "Ins". This led some teachers to interpret the decision-making process as being concentrated in the principal's office.

Several teachers specifically mentioned the existence of two groups – the "Ins" and the "Not Ins" – and identified themselves in terms of one or the other. Those who were uncertain could discover which group they were in, as many teachers joked on a staff retreat, by seeing whether they had been given rooms with fireplaces or not! The "Ins" had influence. This was felt to be because their informal leader was particularly close to the principal. One teacher frequently referred to him as "the hip pocket guy"! Several staff also stated that they felt decisions about issues affecting the whole staff were already made with the input of the "In" group prior to general discussion. As one person stated:

> It's my impression that there is a core group of people who make decisions for the school. And it's also my impression that not all views are considered, that in some cases things are very directive and predecided.

The perceived power structure within the school has affected how committees function. While several committees have been struck to deal with many issues in the school, teachers expressed some concern about the authority of these committees.

> I think that people probably want to feel that they are more a part of the decision-making. You know we certainly do a lot of committee work and so forth. I think there is a fear that maybe

we are not going to make some of the changes that staff feel we should make.

Part of the problem may be the perception that "there's no bottom line" and that everything is open for negotiation and can be overturned, even when decisions have been made with a staff majority. In one sense, this process might be seen as exemplifying the much-vaunted change process of integrating bottom-up with top-down decision-making. But this integration was not consistent, nor was it systematic. It was not always clear when decisions were bottom-up or top-down; or would change from one to the other! Teachers seemed to feel that anything could be negotiated and developed methods for operating within this power structure. One teacher described an interesting technique some staff had developed to achieve their desired goals:

> I think . . . what you have to do with [the principal] is to plant the idea and make him think it's his own. And then come back and ask him about it.

"Not-in" groups described other techniques they used to manipulate the structure to their advantage. For example, the exploratory subject specialists developed a common front to defend and promote their common interests. Through this, they had gained an increase in the time allotted to their subjects by deciding collectively what time they needed to make their program work, then going to the principal as a group for discussion, negotiation and approval. The key, they felt, was the solidarity of the group when they made their request, a strategy that was vindicated when the principal accepted their suggestions. In exactly the same way, they also approached the interview team, virtually demanding an audience for discussing their common concerns.

Summary

Notwithstanding all its efforts, Lincoln Secondary School has not eradicated the balkanization of teaching. It has reinscribed it. First, despite the bold attempt to establish cohort groups, the historically, politically and organizationally embedded nature of subject departmentalization continues to exert powerful gravitational forces on any attempts to pull away from that departmentalism — a pattern that has been observed in other cases of school restructuring. As Lincoln expands and the departments grow, the gravitational pull of departmentalism will almost certainly increase.

Second, the uncertainty of the terrain into which the school was moving, the unavoidable swiftness of the implementation process as the school had to create an entirely new vision and structure instead of changing an existing one, and the system's urgent expectations of success that were embedded in the forceful leadership it appointed together created another kind of balkanization. This was between those teachers who had ready influence with the principal and those who did not; between the "Ins" and the "Not Ins".

What we can learn from the case of Lincoln School is that attempts to restructure secondary schools which supplement rather than substitute for existing structures of subject departmentalism are likely to prove deeply problematic and perhaps even self-defeating.[15] We can also learn that attempts to impose singular visions on the large, complex organizations that secondary schools are can divide and blind rather than unite and enlighten.

SEARCHING FOR SOLUTIONS

These two case studies indicate that balkanization remains a dominant feature of contemporary secondary schools, even in those that are striving to become more innovative. Balkanization is characterized by strong and enduring boundaries between different parts of the organization, by personal identification with the domains these boundaries define, and by differences of power between one domain and another. It is an organizational pattern that sustains and is sustained by the prevailing hegemony of subject specialism and its marginalization of more "practical" mentalities; a pattern that restricts professional learning and educational change among communities of teachers; and a pattern that perpetuates and expresses the conflicts and divisions that have come to characterize secondary school life.

In a postmodern world which is fast, compressed, uncertain, diverse and complex, balkanized secondary structures are poorly equipped to harness the human resources necessary to create flexible learning for students, continuous professional growth for staff and responsiveness to changing client needs in the community.

One response to the challenges posed by postmodernity and the needs it creates for educational change has been to try to eliminate or alleviate the stultifying and divisive effects of balkanization by constructing some sense of wholeness in our threatened schools. Whole-school curriculum development, whole-school curriculum change and whole-school commitments to missions and visions of educational purpose are the symbols and realizations of this process.[14] According to Nias, Southworth and Campbell, to be a member of a "whole school" is to aspire to belong to a community, to share the same educational beliefs and aims, to work together as a team, to acknowledge and activate the complementary expertise of colleagues, to relate well to other members of the group, to be aware of and involved in classes beyond one's own, and to value the leadership of the school principal.[15] Although they are difficult to establish, we have seen in earlier chapters that whole-school identities are nonetheless achievable in some elementary schools. Much of the widespread thrust toward teacher collaboration can be interpreted in this light. Even so, research suggests that the whole-school project is only possible or likely under certain conditions: where the school is small, where it is predominantly middle class and not very multicultural in its intake, and where the leadership is in some ways neo-feudal

in character, with a strong, visionary principal caring in a benevolently matri-
archal or patriarchal but nonetheless inclusive way for a *family* of collaborating
teachers.[16]

In larger, more complex schools, especially at the secondary level, whole-
school identity is more difficult, if not impossible, to achieve. Size militates
against it, as do the complex and diverse constituencies that most secondary
schools employ. And the historical and political strength of academic subjects
as sources of personal identity, career aspiration and public accountability
means that most secondary schools continue to operate as micropolitical worlds,
with conflict and competition between their departments being an endemic
feature of their existence. Efforts to surpass these entrenched identities through
principles and practices of curriculum and staff integration appear to depend for
their success on exceptional leadership, on the capacity to appoint energetic
teachers committed to the innovative philosophy, and on the tolerance and support of the school district in allowing the school to operate in experimental ways.
Progress towards establishing whole-school identities of a more innovative kind
at the secondary level, therefore, seems sustainable only as long as teachers
stay, do not burn out, and continue to receive protection from their districts.[17]

In the absence of such exceptional conditions, the evidence of this chapter
and of other studies elsewhere is that most secondary schools persist with or
revert to balkanization by default or design. By default, through the collapse of
innovation and the retreat to traditional subject identities. By design, when
these identities are placed at the heart of newly constructed centralized curricula. The challenge for secondary school teachers of the postmodern age is
how to construct a coherent sense of purpose that neither rests on the fruitless
pursuit of whole-school vision or identity, nor reverts to traditionally balkanized
patterns of departmental conflict or indifference. It is a formidable challenge
indeed.

If balkanization simply meant working and living in smaller groups, then
the antidote to it might be imagined as being either individualism or whole-
community attachment. But the definitions and cases of balkanization described
here point to more complex meanings than this. If balkanization is defined by
strong and lasting boundaries, by personal identification with the territories
they delineate, and by differences of power and status among these territories,
then the antidotes to balkanization have very different properties. What, in this
sense, might a debalkanized world of secondary school teaching imply?

First, educational balkanization springs not only from principles of difference but also from ones of power and divisiveness. Debalkanizing secondary
schools will, in this sense, require active and ongoing struggles to establish some
balance and eradicate or alleviate differences in size, prestige and time allocation
between high- and low-status subjects and the forms of knowledge and achievement they embody. Clearly, this is an issue that extends far beyond the individual school itself to the educational and social community outside it, where
any such struggles to equalize and establish common value between rigor and

relevance, academic and practical mentalities, and high- and low-status knowledge will challenge the interests of the powerful and not be ceded easily — even in the face of postindustrialism and global competitiveness. If equality of commitment is to be realistic and effective, it must be reflected in equality of budgets as well as equality of rhetoric. The development of broad-based technology with associated and continuing budgetary support is an example of the kind of shift it is possible to engineer here. Other similar shifts will also be needed at the level of policy if the hegemony of school subjects and subject status is to be successfully re-defined. These initiatives will need to have more than advisory status.

Second, as we have seen, the departmental specialism of balkanized secondary schools will not be easily or coherently replaced by structures that can support common identity, experience and consensus. Secondary schools are not and cannot be organized simply as if they were "big" elementary schools. The organizational antidote to balkanization might more properly be considered to be what I described in Chapter 4 as the kinetic collage or the moving mosaic. Here, large structures still understandably accommodate different groups and those who work in them do not strive for unattainable goals of common experience and value consensus. What matters, rather, is that both the identity of the sub-groups and membership of them do not become fixed and entrenched. Subject departments may continue to exist but not always in their present form. *Debalkanizing secondary schools does not mean disestablishing school subjects.* However, in debalkanized conditions, subject boundaries will be more blurred, subject status differences more flattened, and other organizational categories will emerge alongside, cross-cut with and attain similar or greater political power to those rooted in subject departments. Subject departments will, for instance, likely persist alongside other units and committees that evolve in response to continuing challenges — the Co-op (or school-work) education team, the school improvement team, the community links team and the like. In the moving mosaic, membership of sub-units changes over time. Department leaderships carry no permanence, or institutional reward greater than you would find for any other leadership role. They are elected, or rotating and temporary. They carry no automatic promise of career advancement. They are neither arteries nor enclaves for school decision-making. The moving mosaic is an organizational structure that is gaining increasing strength outside the educational world as a way of enabling collaborative responsiveness to rapidly shifting pressures and challenges. If it is to be successfully accommodated in the world of secondary schools, then one essential sacrifice will have to be the institutionalized, career position of department leadership.

Elsewhere, with a number of my colleagues I have shown how smaller secondary schools possess some of the qualities of the moving mosaic by necessity, as teachers are constantly required to collaborate and improvise under conditions of continuous staff scarcity. We have also described the case of a secondary school, led by a female principal, which appoints all new teachers

1. *Fragmented individualism*

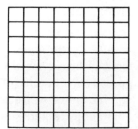

- Isolation
- Ceiling to improvement
- Protection from outside
  interference

3. *Collaborative culture*

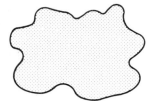

- Sharing, trust, support
- Central to daily work
- "Family" structure may
  involve paternalistic or
  maternalistic leadership
- Joint work
- Continuous improvement

5. *The moving mosaic*

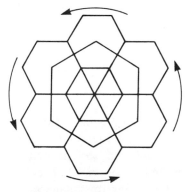

- Blurred boundaries
- Overlapping categories
  and membership
- Flexible, dynamic, responsive
- Also uncertain, vulnerable,
  contested

2. *Balkanization*

- City states
- Inconsistencies
- Loyalties and identities tied
  to particular group
- Whole is less than sum of
  its parts

4. *Contrived collegiality*

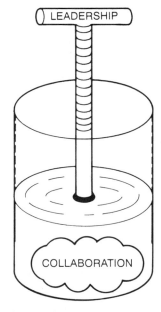

- Strategy for creating
  collegiality
- Also strategy for contriving
  and controlling it
- Administrative procedure
- Safe simulation
- A device that can suppress
  desire

Figure 10.1 Forms of teacher culture.

by interdepartmental committee, assigns workrooms so that each accommodates more than one department, and is administered by five committees — operations, program, public relations, student activities and resources — in which all teachers are involved (each teacher must sit on at least one committee). The result is a complex web of collegial relationships which extend well beyond traditional departmental allegiances and which minimize interdepartmental conflicts as teachers recognize that their strength is increased when they work collectively. Warm human relationships of mutual respect and understanding combined with the toleration and even encouragement of debate, discussion and disagreement create flexibility, risk-taking and continuous improvement among the staff which in turn lead to positive results among the students, and positive attitudes among the staff to changes and innovations which might benefit those students. Moving mosaics are not an abstraction. The beginnings of them can be found in secondary schools that already exist. They may provide the foundation for an emergent fifth form of teacher culture that might be better suited to the challenges of the post-modern world. This fifth form of the teacher culture — the moving mosaic – is portrayed alongside the other forms in Figure 10.1.

Third, in complex postmodern organizations, even though the identity and membership of sub-groups may always be shifting, there will still be ongoing struggles of power, for status and around conflicting interests. If these are not to lead to new status hierarchies, and newly entrenched patterns of balkanization, then these conflicts will need to be clearly and ethically dealt with on an ongoing basis. In this sense, secondary schools, as aspiring postmodern organizations, will need not to repress conflicts, as many now do, but to discuss them and resolve them as a continuous process. Honest, democratic and ethical procedures for decision-making and conflict resolution are, in this sense, an essential component of secondary school teaching in the future.

What is becoming disturbingly clear in our secondary schools is the inability of the present subject system and of modernistic organizational structures to meet the needs of students and indeed the longer-term needs of their staffs in a complex and rapidly changing postmodern society. To meet vital individual and societal needs, education of the future requires a radical reconceptualization of secondary schools, their curricula and their patterns of work organization for teachers as we now know them. This raises the issue of whether and how schools and teaching should be restructured in order to address the challenges of the postmodern world. This is the subject of the final chapter.

NOTES

1. Fullan, M. and Hargreaves, A., *What's Worth Fighting For?: Working Together for Your School*, Toronto, Ontario Public School Teachers' Federation; Milton Keynes, Open University Press; The Network, North East Lab, USA; and Melbourne, Australian Council for Educational Administration, 1991.

2. Goodson, I. and Ball, S. (eds), *Defining the Curriculum*, New York and Philadelphia, Falmer Press, 1985; Ball, S., *Beachside Comprehensive*, Cambridge, Cambridge University Press, 1980.

3. Bernstein, B., "On the classification and framing of educational knowledge", in Young, M. F. P. (ed.), *Knowledge and Control*, New York, Collier-Macmillan, 1971.

4. Goodson, I., "Subjects for study: Aspects of a social history of curriculum", *Journal of Curriculum Studies*, 15(4), 1983.

5. Ball, S., *The Micropolitics of the School: Towards a Theory of School Organization*, London and New York, Methuen, 1987.

6. Riseborough, G., "Teacher careers and comprehensive schooling: An empirical study", *Sociology*, 15(3),1981, 355–81.

7. The complete study is reported in Hargreaves, A., Davis, J., Fullan, M., Wignall, R., Stager, M. and Macmillan, R., *Secondary School Work Cultures and Educational Change*, Final report of a research project funded by the OISE Transfer Grant, Toronto, Ontario Institute for Studies in Education, 1992.

8. Metz, M., "How social class differences shape teachers' work", in McLaughlin, M., Talbert, J. and Bascia, N. (eds), *Contexts of Secondary Schooling*, New York, Teachers College Press, 1990, pp. 40–107.

9. Goodson, I., "On curriculum form: Notes towards a theory of curriculum", *Sociology of Education*, 65(1), 1992, 66–75.

10. The grammar and style of these fieldnotes are not always of the highest standard. But they have been reproduced in the rough form in which they were first composed, rather than "cleaned up" and perhaps therefore distorted for subsequent publication.

11. Semestering, for readers unfamiliar with the system, involves dividing the program into half-yearly cycles, with half of the program range being taught in the first part of the year and the other half in the second part. This is how the exploratories were organized at Lincoln. The remainder of the curriculum (core) operated on a Day 1/Day 2 alternating cycle throughout the year.

12. Lieberman, A., Darling-Hammond, L. and Zuckerman, D., *Early Lessons in Restructuring Schools*, New York, National Center for Restructuring Education, Schools, and Teaching (NCREST), 1991.

13. Fullan, M., "Visions that blind", *Educational Leadership*, 49(5), 1992, 19–22.

14. Nias, J., Southworth, G. and Campbell, P., *Whole School Curriculum Development in the Primary School*, London and Washington, DC, Falmer Press, 1992.

15. Ibid.

16. Nias, J., Southworth, G. and Yeomans, R., *Staff Relationships in the Primary School*, London, Cassell, 1989.

17. Siskin, L., "School restructuring and subject subcultures", Paper presented to the Annual Meeting of the American Educational Research Association, Chicago, April 1990.

Chapter 11

Restructuring
Beyond Collaboration

INTRODUCTION

In 1986, the US Carnegie Forum on "Education and the Economy", in its report
A Nation Prepared, announced the need to "restructure schools".[1] This restructuring, it was thought, would respect and support the professionalism of
teachers to make decisions in their own classrooms that best met local and state
goals, while also holding teachers accountable for how they did that. In the space
of just a few years, restructuring has become common currency in educational
policy vocabulary, right up to the office of the President of the United States
and among Ministers and civil servants in other national and regional policy
contexts too.[2] Yet its meanings are various, conflicting and often ill-defined. As
Tyack observes, where restructuring is concerned, vague is vogue.[3]

Restructuring has many different possible components. According to
Murphy and Evertson, these comprise school-based management, increased
consumer choice, teacher empowerment and teaching for understanding.[4] For
the US National Governors' Association, they include curriculum and instruction redesigned to promote higher-order thinking skills; the decentralization of
authority and decision-making to site level; more diverse and differentiated roles
for teachers; and broadened systems of accountability.[5] At the National Center
for Restructuring Education, Schools, and Teaching (NCREST) in the United
States, Lieberman and her colleagues argue, on the basis of ten cases of restructuring they have been studying, that school restructuring

> aims to create schools that are more centered on learners' needs
> for active, experiental, cooperative and culturally connected
> learning opportunities supportive of individual talents and
> learning styles. Restructurers aim to create these learning
> opportunities within school organizations energized by
> collaborative inquiry, informed by authentic accountability and
> guided by shared decision-making.[6]

For Theodore Sizer and the Coalition for Essential Schools, restructuring is
about nothing more nor less than helping each student to "learn to use one's
mind well".[7] While the specific components of restructuring vary from one

241

writer to another, most seem to agree that what is centrally involved is a fundamental re-definition of rules, roles, responsibilities and relationships for students, teachers and leaders in our schools. Why is restructuring so important? Why is it necessary?

In *The Predictable Failure of Educational Reform*, Seymour Sarason argues that by the criterion of classroom impact, most existing approaches to educational reform have failed.[8] This failure, he says, is predictable. He identifies two factors as responsible for it. First, he notes that the different components of educational reform have neither been conceived nor addressed as a whole, in their interrelationships, as a complex system. If components like curriculum change, professional development, or new teaching strategies are tackled in isolation while others are left unchanged, he says, the success of the reforms will almost certainly be undermined. Sarason supplies numerous historical examples of such failed reforms.

Sarason's argument has two important implications. First, significant change in curriculum, assessment or any other domain is unlikely to be successful unless serious attention is also paid to teacher development and the principles of professional judgment and discretion contained within it. Teacher development and enhanced professionalism must therefore be undertaken in conjunction with developments in curriculum, assessment, leadership and school organization.

Sarason's second and even more challenging contention is that major educational change is unlikely to be successful unless it addresses school power relationships. "Schools . . . remain intractable to desired reform as long as we avoid confronting their existing power relationships," he argues.[9] These include relationships between administrators and teachers, between teachers and parents and between teachers and students. Sarason argues for a fundamental rethink of how schools and classrooms are run. His vision of educational change entails change that is comprehensive in scope, accompanied by significant, not superficial redistributions of existing power relationships among principals, teachers, parents and students.

Restructuring tries to address the emerging learning needs of the post-industrial, postmodern age and the more flexible structures of schooling that are required to meet those needs effectively. It seeks to create alternative learning environments to meet continuing and contemporary student needs. But it is early days in restructuring yet. The patterns are diverse, the outcomes are unclear, the possibilities of moving beyond isolated experiments unknown. Two sets of problems need to be addressed with particular sensitivity.

First, restructuring has already become a fashionable new buzzword which has many different meanings and implications. Some use it to give more power to schools; more of a stake to students as partners in their learning, curriculum, and assessment; more power and involvement for parents; and less dependence among teachers on bureaucratic mandates and requirements. Others, however, use restructuring not to expand students' minds and capabilities in the broadest sense, but to shape and mold them to changing corporate interests by defining the goals and learning outcomes of schooling along with the structures required to provide them, in specifically corporate terms. We saw in Chapter 4 how such definitions of restructuring could become entrapped within the corporate confines of "flexibility".

Restructuring is commonly used to re-define and re-label traditional, outmoded and ineffective patterns of managed change. Some use it to season with slightly more palatable language indigestible and unwanted patterns of top-down reforms that are force-fed to teachers and schools against their will. The most cynical proponents of restructuring of all merely use it as a euphemism or rationale for downsizing school staffing and resources and downgrading the services they can offer. It is as well to remember that in the corporate context of restructuring, where the concept first emerged, restructuring has often been a synonym for the management of recession and retrenchment.

In view of these differing and often conflicting understandings, it is important to be clear about what the key principles and purposes of restructuring are and to ensure, for instance, that restructuring efforts do seriously try to disestablish the traditional structures of schooling; and do re-define relationships between teachers, students, principals and parents in fundamental ways.

Second, the classroom and staffroom realities of restructuring may be very different from the symbolic rhetoric that is often inscribed in administrative visions and documents. The previous chapter, for instance, described a secondary school undergoing fundamental restructuring, which, despite all its best efforts, did not succeed in eradicating subject departmentalization and its influence on teaching and learning, but simply reinscribed it in other ways. Other difficulties are documented in an evaluation by Wehlage and his colleagues of a group of restructuring projects funded by the Casey Foundation in the United States. The Foundation's *Implementation Guide* listed some bold principles for restructuring. These were:

1. Restructuring should result in increased autonomy at the school building level, site-based management, and teacher empowerment that would free educators from centralized bureaucracies and their stifling effects.

2. Teachers needed greater flexibility in scheduling and grouping students in order to create positive environments and innovative curricula that promote achievement for at-risk students.

3. Restructuring was to make schools more responsive to students through various forms of individualization and the elimination of "slow" and "fast" tracks. In addition, schools were encouraged to find incentives that would lead to greater academic success for those now in lower tracks.

4. To support teachers in their efforts with at-risk students, schools needed to offer extensive training or staff development activities.

243

5. Consistent with the overall rationale of New Futures, schools were urged to find ways of collaborating and coordinating with other organizations and agencies, both public and private, in an effort to multiply the potential of existing resources.[10]

Yet despite these ambitious principles combined with strategies for funding support, partnerships, project monitoring and community involvement, the researchers' data suggested that the initiative

has not yet initiated a comprehensive restructuring of schools of the kind needed to address the problems of at-risk students. To be sure, a variety of new programs, policies, and structures were implemented in response to the . . . initiative, and initially some of them looked promising as building blocks towards restructuring. By and large, however, these were supplemental programs that left the basic experiences of students and teachers unchanged, and by the end of the third year of the initiative, the collective impact [of the project] has not led to significant changes in school practice.[11]

Studies such as this serve to remind us about the importance of determining what lies behind the smoke and mirrors of restructuring; about identifying how far the classroom and school reality matches the administrative and policy rhetoric.

RESTRUCTURING AND CULTURES OF COLLABORATION

If restructuring is, in some fundamental sense, about the reconstruction of school power relationships, then we would expect the working lives of teachers to be organized not around principles of hierarchy and isolation, but ones of collaboration and collegiality. Indeed, while there are many meanings of restructuring, the principle of collaboration has become central to almost all of them, be this collaboration among teachers, or between teachers and principals, students, parents and the wider community.

Collaboration has come to comprise a *metaparadigm* of educational and organizational change in the postmodern age. Paradigm shifts — profound alterations in our fundamental understandings of how the social and natural worlds are mutually constituted, what are its central problems, how we can best inquire into them, and how we should act on the basis of this knowledge — are nothing new. Historically, conditions of rapid and radical social change have typically given rise to such paradigm shifts.[12] But the postmodern age, with its qualitative leaps in instantaneous development and dissemination of communications and information, and with the increasing pace of change that results from this, brings into being an acceleration and diversification of paradigm shifts themselves. A fundamental problem of postmodernity, therefore, is one of needing to generate metaparadigms of understanding, analysis, development and change to interpret, analyze, synthesize and respond to the more specific paradigm shifts in technology, organizational life, intellectual thought and the like that are occurring and will occur with increasing speed in years to come within education and outside it.

One of the emergent and most promising metaparadigms of the postmodern age is that of *collaboration* as an articulating and integrating principle of action, planning, culture, development, organization and research. Throughout this book's examination of issues involving leadership, change and the working lives of teachers, the principle of collaboration has repeatedly emerged as a productive response to a world in which problems are unpredictable, solutions are unclear, and demands and expectations are intensifying. In this kind of context, the promise of collaboration is extensive and diverse. Here and elsewhere, it has been proposed as a solution to many areas of challenge and difficulty which educators are having to face. In the context of restructuring and of educational improvement more generally, this collaborative solution embodies many or all of the following principles:

- **Moral support**. Collaboration strengthens resolve, permits vulnerabilities to be shared and aired, and carries people through those failures and frustrations that accompany change in its early stages, and that can otherwise undermine or overturn it.

- **Increased efficiency**. Collaboration eliminates duplication and removes redundancy between teachers and subjects as activities are coordinated and responsibilities are shared in complementary ways.

- **Improved effectiveness**. Collaboration improves the quality of student learning by improving the quality of teachers' teaching. Collaboration encourages risk-taking, greater diversity in teaching strategies, and improved senses of efficacy among teachers as self-confidence is boosted by positive encouragement and feedback. All these things impact upon and benefit student learning.[13]

- **Reduced overload**. Collaboration permits sharing of the burdens and pressures that come from intensified work demands and accelerated change, so that individual teachers and leaders do not have to shoulder them all, in isolation.

- **Synchronized time perspectives**. Collaboration narrows the differences of time perspective between administrators and teachers. Participation in common activities and communication creates shared and realistic expectations about timelines for change and implementation. The same principles also apply to synchronization of time perspectives and expectations between teachers and students when they become partners in the learning process.

- **Situated certainty.** The two worst states of knowledge are ignorance and certainty. Collaboration reduces uncertainty and limits excesses of guilt that otherwise pervade teaching by setting commonly agreed boundaries around what can reasonably be achieved in any setting. Collaboration also creates collective professional confidence that can help teachers resist the tendency to become dependent on false scientific certainties of teaching effectiveness, school effectiveness and the like. Collaboration replaces false *scientific* certainties or debilitating occupational uncertainties with the *situated* certainties of collected professional wisdom among particular communities of teachers.

- **Political assertiveness.** Collaboration, in its strongest forms, enables teachers to interact more confidently and assertively with their surrounding systems and the multiplicity of reasonable and unreasonable innovations and reforms that come from them. Collaboration strengthens the confidence to adopt externally introduced innovations, the wisdom to delay them and the moral fortitude to resist them, where appropriate. In that sense, it also mitigates the effects of intensification and overload mentioned earlier.

- **Increased capacity for reflection.** Collaboration in dialogue and action provides sources of feedback and comparison that prompt teachers to reflect on their own practice. Others become mirrors for one's own practice, leading one to reflect on it and reformulate it more critically.

- **Organizational responsiveness.** Collaboration pools the collected knowledge, expertise and capacities of the teacher workforce to enable it to respond swiftly to changing constraints and opportunities in the surrounding environment, to scan the environment proactively for upcoming changes, and to seek out the opportunities they may offer. By involving members of that environment – parents, business, communities, etc. – in the collaborative process itself, the swiftness and appropriateness of schools' and teachers' responses is enhanced even further.

- **Opportunities to learn.** Collaboration increases teachers' opportunities to learn from each other between classrooms, between departments and between schools. Collaboration is a powerful source of professional learning, of getting better at the job. In collaborative organizations, the whole is greater than the sum of its parts.

- **Continuous improvement.** Collaboration encourages teachers to see change not as a task to be completed, but as an unending process of continuous improvement in the asymptotic pursuit of ever greater excellence on the one hand, and emergent solutions to rapidly changing problems in the other. Because of the way it promotes shared reflection, professional learning and the pooling of collected expertise, collaboration is a central principle of organizational learning.

Notwithstanding its immense and very real promise as a generative principle of educational change and restructuring, however, we have seen that collaboration carries with it great dangers also, in ways that can be wasteful, harmful and unproductive for teachers and their students. Among the more problematic meanings and realizations of collaboration that have emerged in this book are ones where collaboration is:

- **Comfortable and complacent.** Collaboration can be confined to safer, less controversial areas of teachers' work – ones which avoid collaboration in classroom practice, or collaboration through systematic shared reflection, in favor of moral support and sharing of resources and ideas. Such safer forms of collaboration can consolidate rather than challenge existing practice. These kinds of collaboration can be comfortable, cozy and complacent.
- **Conformist.** As my colleague, Michael Fullan, and I have argued elsewhere, collaboration can be conformist. It can lead to groupthink, suppressing individuality and solitude and the creativity of thought which springs from them.[14]
- **Contrived.** Collaboration can be administratively captured, contained and controlled in ways that make it stilted, unproductive and wasteful of teachers' energies and efforts. By making collaboration into an administrative *device*, contrived collegiality can paradoxically suppress the *desires* that teachers have to collaborate and improve among themselves.
- **Co-optative.** Collaboration is sometimes used as an administrative and political ruse to secure teachers' compliance with and commitment to educational reforms decided by others. If these reforms are ethically bankrupt or suspect, such collaboration can become collaboration with the enemy (for which some people in World War II were shot!).

247

If collaboration is central to educational restructuring, its own meanings, like the meanings of restructuring more generally are also neither consistent nor agreed. Collaboration and restructuring can be helpful or harmful, and their meanings and realizations therefore need to be inspected repeatedly to ensure that their educational and social benefits are positive. But more than this, collaboration itself is not synonymous with restructuring, nor is it a sufficient condition for bringing about and working successfully through the project of restructuring. For collaboration, just as for restructuring, what is really important is who controls it, who is involved in it, what are its purposes, and what conditions are necessary for it to be established and maintained.

Exploring and establishing restructuring in education therefore means committing to certain kinds of collaboration, but also to moving beyond them. The agenda for restructuring remains an open one. It comprises many important choices and dilemmas that bear on the issue of collaboration in complex, challenging and not altogether clear-cut ways. These choices and dilemmas involve profound ethical, political and pragmatic decisions about values, purposes and directions.

At the heart of these is a fundamental choice between restructuring as bureaucratic control, where teachers are controlled and regulated to implement the mandates of others, and restructuring as professional empowerment, where teachers are supported, encouraged and provided with newly structured opportunities to make improvements of their own, in partnership with principals, parents and students. Wishes for consensus and desires to maintain the momentum of change often deflect us from addressing these fundamental and difficult dilemmas. Yet failing to grapple with them early, openly and honestly only suppresses them, leading to conflict and confusion that can spread undetected in diffuse and damaging ways. In the remainder of this final chapter, I want to scratch beneath the current consensus of restructuring to expose and explore some central dilemmas of value, purpose and control which I believe we must confront and resolve as we meet the educational challenges of the twenty-first century.

BEYOND COLLABORATION

1. Vision or Voice?

One of the key tensions in restructuring and in collaborative work too is between vision and voice. This tension is not specific to restructuring in education, but has its roots in the restructuring of postmodern society more generally.

Chapter 4 described how the globalization of economic life has created national doubt and insecurity, as seemingly common cultures become fragmented into a multitude of ethnic, linguistic and religious identities. Such trends can be viewed critically as disturbing breakdowns of order and community. At the same time, though, they also represent the emergence in the context of postmodernity of the voices of those who have previously been unheard, neglected, rejected, ignored – the voices of those who have formerly been marginalized and dispossessed. Gilligan's influential book, *In a Different Voice*, draws attention to the undervalued women's perspective on moral development, for instance.[15] As Harvey puts it, "The idea that all groups have a right to speak for themselves, in their own voice accepted as authentic and legitimate, is essential to the pluralistic stance of postmodernism."[16]

In educational change and research, the formerly unheard or undervalued teacher's voice has been accorded increasing respect and authority in recent years. And here, especially in elementary schools, teachers' voices are also usually women's voices. Elbaz notes how much of the emergent work on teachers' knowledge, thinking and empowerment is centrally concerned with the notion of voice. Where the notion of voice is used, she says, the term is always used against the background of a previous silence, and it is a political usage as well as an epistemological one.[17] Goodson argues that teachers' voices are rooted in their lives, their lifestyles and their point in the life-cycle.[18] The teacher's voice, says Goodson, articulates the teacher's life and its purposes. To understand teaching, therefore, either as a researcher, administrator, or colleague, it is not enough merely to witness the behavior, skills and actions of teaching. One must also listen to the voice of the teacher, to the person it expresses and to the purposes it articulates. Failure to understand the teacher's voice is failure to understand the teacher's teaching. For this reason, Goodson suggests, our priority should be not merely to listen to the teacher's voice, but also to sponsor it as a priority within our teacher development work.

Yet the rise of dissident voices threatens traditional centres of power and control. Struggles for regional autonomy and linguistic or ethnic separatism, for instance, challenge long-standing patterns of central domination. Similarly, in education, the bureaucratic impetus to guide processes of change and improvement from the center may lead the teacher's voice that doubts the change or disagrees with it to go unheard, be silenced, or be dismissed as "mere" resistance. In this respect, as the forces of bureaucratic control and teacher-led professional development wrestle with one another, one of the greatest challenges to the emergence of teacher *voice* is the orchestration of educational *vision*.

The development of a common vision, commitment to shared goals or developing clarity in understanding the goals being implemented by others are commonly advocated components of the change and improvement process. They are seen as essential to developing confidence and consistency among a community of teachers. Educational leaders are viewed as vital to the development of motivating visions. According to Achilles, for instance, leaders

> must know what is needed to improve schools. They must know
> how to administer the schools to achieve the desired results. As a
> starting point, principals must envision better schools, articulate
> this vision to others, and orchestrate consensus on the vision.[19]

There is a strong sense here that the vision is primarily the principal's (or head-teacher's) vision, a vision to be articulated to (not developed with) others, a vision around which the orchestration of consensus will follow later.

These criticisms are not intended to dispute the importance of vision, of shared purpose and direction among a school's staff. The crucial question, though, is "whose vision is this?" For some writers, the principal's role in promoting school improvement and helping develop the culture of the school becomes one of manipulating the culture and its teachers to conform to the principal's own vision. Deal and Peterson, for example, urge that once principals have come to understand their school's culture, they should then ask, "If it matches my conception of a 'good school', what can I do to reinforce or strengthen existing patterns?" "If my vision is at odds with the existing mindset, values or ways of acting, what can be done to change or shape the culture?"[20] For Deal and Peterson, who write very much from a corporate perspective, this is part of the solution to the challenge of school leadership. In many respects, though, it can be seen as part of the problem.

"My vision", "my teachers", "my school" are proprietary claims and attitudes that suggest an ownership of the school and of change which is individual rather than collective, imposed rather than earned, and hierarchical rather than democratic. This ownership is also more often male ownership, in which power is exercised over women. With *visions* as singular as this, teachers soon learn to suppress their *voice*. Management becomes manipulation. Collaboration become cooptation. Worst of all, having teachers conform to the principal's vision minimizes the opportunities for principals to learn that parts of their own vision may be flawed; that some teachers' visions may be as valid or more valid than theirs! The ways in which visions can sometimes be repressive rather than enlightening is bitterly portrayed in the characteristically ironic words of songwriter, Leonard Cohen:

> And I thank you
> I thank you for doing your duty
> You keepers of truth
> You guardians of beauty
> Your vision was right
> My vision was wrong
> I'm sorry for smudging the air with my song.[21]

Ultimately, the responsibility for vision-building should be a collective, not an individual, one. Collaboration should mean creating the vision together, not complying with the principal's own. Teachers, support staff, parents and students should also be involved in illuminating the mission and purposes of the school. Leithwood and Jantzi describe a practical example of developing shared school goals for school improvement, where the responsibility for the task was delegated to school improvement teams. This, they note, "prevented the principal's goals from dominating the process", although the authors add ominously in parentheses: "or from being seen to dominate the process".[22]

Exclusive emphasis on vision or voice alone is constructive neither for restructuring in general nor for professional development in particular. A world of voice without vision is a world reduced to chaotic babble where there are no means for arbitrating between voices, reconciling them or drawing them together. This is the dark side of the postmodern world, a world from which community and authority have disappeared. It is a world where the authority of voice has supplanted the voice of authority to an excessive degree. Research studies which go beyond merely understanding teachers' stories to endorsing and celebrating them, and research traditions which give arbitrary credence to teachers' accounts over (neglected) accounts of parents or students, for instance, illustrate some of the difficulties of this postmodern perspective. Voices need to be not only heard, but also engaged, reconciled and argued with. It is important to attend not only to the aesthetics of articulating teacher voices, but also to the ethics of what it is those voices articulate!

We have seen that a world of vision without voice is equally problematic. In this world, where purposes are imposed and consensus is contrived, there is no place for the practical judgment and wisdom of teachers; no place for their voices to get a proper hearing. A major challenge for educational restructuring is to work through and reconcile this tension between vision and voice: to create a choir from a cacophony.

2. Trust in People or Trust in Processes

In the struggle between bureaucratic control and professional empowerment that accompanies the transition to postmodernity, collaborative relationships and the particular forms they take are central. Such relationships, I have argued, can help give vent to the voice of the people, or they can contribute to the reconstitution of central control. Collaborative working relationships are at the core of the restructuring agenda and all its contradictory possibilities.

A pervasive theme that runs throughout the literature of shared leadership and collaborative cultures is the truism of trust. The establishment of trust, it is argued, is essential to the creation of effective and meaningful collaborative work relationships. For Lieberman and colleagues, "trust and rapport . . . are the foundation for building collegiality in a school."[23] Louden, for instance, describes the importance of trust in the establishment of a collaborative relationship between himself as a researcher, and the teacher with whom he worked.

> The trust we developed was quite personal in character. We found that we liked each other, we became friends and the project became more than a piece of work for both of us. I enjoyed working with Johanna and participating in the life of the school, she liked having me around and hoped my study would go well.[24]

The value of such trust in collaborative working relationships is so widely acknowledged and understood that we rarely probe more than superficially into its meaning and nature. One exception is Nias and her colleagues, who note that "to talk of trust as if it explained everything is . . . to make it into a 'black box', an abstract word packed with individual meanings".[25] They argue that trust has two dimensions: predictability and common goals. "For trust to exist," they argue, "people must find one another highly predictable and share substantially the same aims."[26] To paraphrase Nias *et al.*, trust can be understood as a process of personal and predictable mutuality.

This understanding of trust and the social-psychological heritage from which it springs certainly helps illuminate our understanding of the dynamics of interpersonal relationships in the context of small-group collaboration. But it is an understanding that does not illuminate all forms of trust; only trust in particular circumstances. These are ones of interpersonal relationships that remain relatively stable and persistent over time. As Giddens observes, however, there are also other variants of trust. These can be found in contexts where interpersonal relationships are much less stable and persistent over time. Giddens alludes to these contrasts in his core definition of trust:

> Trust may be defined as confidence in the reliability of a person
> or system, regarding a given set of outcomes or events, where
> that confidence expresses a faith in the probity or love of
> another, or in the correctness of abstract principle.[27]

Trust, in other words, can be invested in persons or in processes – in the qualities and conduct of individuals, or in the expertise and performance of abstract systems. It can be an *outcome* of meaningful face-to-face relationships, or a *condition* of their existence.

The movement from small and simple to massified and modernistic societies brought with it transformations in the forms of trust that were dominant in people's lives. These transformations can be seen particularly clearly in the changing relationships between trust and risk. There is a reciprocal relationship between these two things. In simple societies, risk was associated with permanent danger; with threats of wild beasts, marauding raiders, famines and floods. Personal trust in family, friends and community helped people cope with these persistent risks. Risk in simple societies was something to be minimized or avoided. In modern, mass organizations and societies, risk and trust took on different qualities. In modern, mass secondary schools, for instance, there have often been too many adults to know everyone well. Personnel can change frequently, including leaders. Trust in individuals is no longer sufficient. When key individuals leave or leaders move on, exclusive reliance on personal trust can cause massive instability. In part, these sorts of problems in societies of growing industrial complexity explained the rise of and constituted a persuasive case for bureaucratic forms of organization. Advancing change and increasing complexity led to a decline in traditional forms of authority. In modern, mass societies and organizations, another kind of trust was therefore called for: trust in processes and abstract systems.

Tragically and ironically, though, as we saw in Chapter 2 through the work of Max Weber, the iron grip of modern bureaucracy simply perverted the course of system trust.[28] Predictability turned into inflexibility. Relationships and responsiveness became strangled by rules and regulations. Once they had grown and become established, modern bureaucratic organizations often became too inflexible and self-serving to respond to local circumstances and changing needs. The interests of persons were blocked by the inertia of procedure. Trust in impersonal authority and technical expertise therefore declined. Confidence in abstract principles was undermined.

Modern secondary schools, for instance, were and still are criticized for being vast bureaucratic organizations unable to build a sense of community, to secure loyalty and attachment among their students, and to be responsive to the changing social world around them. Similarly, prevailing patterns of educational change and reform have been criticized for their top-down, standardized, bureaucratic application across entire systems in ways that neglect the purposes and personalities of individual teachers and the contexts in which they work.

The transition from modernity to postmodernity marks the emergence of new kinds of process trust along with the reconstruction of more traditional kinds of personal trust. In postmodern societies, the changing form and articulation of corporate activity from the large, mass factory to smaller, dispersed centers of enterprise are giving rise to two important trends in the reconstruction of trust.

First, there is the reconstruction of personal trust. There is extensive and increasing advocacy in the corporate and educational worlds for making the local unit of enterprise more meaningful to those working within it and more empowered to respond to the needs of its local environment. Emphasis is placed on reconstructing intimacy, warmth and personal trust in building rewarding and also productive collaborative work relationships. With these ends in view, many school districts have initiated programs of school-based management. Large and impersonal secondary schools are also looking increasingly generously at the possibilities for creating smaller, self-contained mini-schools or sub-schools within them that are more meaningful and self-determining for students and teachers alike.[29]

This reinvention of personal trust is double-edged, however. Personal trust can build loyalty, commitment and effectiveness in the enhanced capacity that comes from shared decision-making. But it can also reintroduce problems of paternalism and dependency that characterized traditional, premodern forms of authority and organization. Indeed, in Chapter 9 we saw that what appear to be collaborative school cultures seem to prosper most in smaller organizations under conditions of exceptionally strong leadership of a personalized nature.[30] This can transform internal collective confidence into collective complacency,

253

carrying with it reduced capacity and willingness to network and learn from other kinds of expertise from outside that are not grounded in immediate and trusted personal relationships.[31] In conditions such as these, too much reliance can be placed on the principal or headteacher to be responsible for external linkages.

Exclusive reliance on personal trust and the forms of collaboration that are built upon it can lead to paternalism and parochialism, then. Additional trust in expertise and processes helps postmodern organizations develop and solve problems on a continuing basis in an environment where problems and challenges are perpetual and changing. Processes to be trusted here are ones that maximize the organization's collective expertise and improve its problem-solving capacities. These include improved communication, shared decision-making, creation of opportunities for collegial learning, networking with outside environments, commitment to continuous inquiry and so cn. Trust in people remains important, but trust in expertise and processes supersedes it. Trust in processes is open-ended and risky. But it is probably essential to learning and improvement.

This means that in postmodern school systems, risk is something to be embraced rather than avoided. Risk-taking fosters learning, adaptability and improvement. The trust it presumes may need to extend beyond the close interpersonal understandings that make up the collaborative cultures described earlier. These understandings and cultures are important, especially in smaller schools and teams. But larger and more rapidly changing schools require teachers who can invest trust in processes too; who can trust their colleagues provisionally, even before they know them well. This is not to advocate contrived collegiality, which can substitute managerial tricks for organizational trust. But it is to advocate a kind of trust that extends beyond the deep knowledge of interpersonal relationships.

The establishment of trust is central to restructuring education. The challenge of trust is to reconstruct collaborative working relationships among close colleagues that enhance personal meaning without reinforcing paternalism and parochialism. It is also the challenge of building confidence and connectedness among teachers who may not know each other quite so well, by investing mutual trust in complementary expertise – without this also leading to burgeoning bureaucracy.

3. Structure or Culture

A third tension in educational restructuring and the way it is organized is between *structure* and *culture* as a proper focus for change. This is highlighted by Werner in an incisive analysis of restructuring efforts within British Columbia, Canada. Werner refers to the provincial minister's call in 1989 for "a fundamental restructuring of the provincial curriculum with a focus on the development of problem solving and creative thinking".[32] This proposed restructuring included an ungraded primary curriculum; an integrated, common curriculum; and a strengthening of assessment and accountability procedures.

Werner dismisses the proposed restructuring for British Columbia as "a classic curriculum fix", reflecting a pervasive and deep-rooted belief in the power of curriculum reform to secure effective change (especially if supported by some inservice training and supervision). Against this structural orientation to change, Werner suggests an alternative strategy: "to encourage teacher development, strengthen school culture, and build upon those good practices already in place in schools".[33] In effect, Werner supports the strategy of improving schools from within rather than reforming them from without. More significant than centralized control of curriculum development and implementation, he argues, "will be groups of teachers who search out and discuss ways to better understand and organize their programs, and who take action in and within the structure of their own schools".[34]

Werner's concern is that despite rhetorics of empowerment along with an appearance of devolving power to teachers by giving them more responsibility for planning and organizing curriculum integration, the British Columbia ministry "retained control of curriculum by strengthening student testing and program evaluation. In essence, this meant that power relations around the curriculum would change little".[35]

What is being counterposed here by Werner are politically popular *structural* solutions to educational change against less fashionable but more enduring and effective *cultural* ones. The contrast is striking and persuasive. Structural changes of the sort initially proposed for British Columbia underestimate the traditions, assumptions and working relationships that profoundly shape existing practice. Consequently, they also overestimate the power of structural changes to alter such practice, even with the support of inservice training for teachers. The image is of a powerful determining structure acting on a relatively malleable body of practice. The important thing about change here is to get the structures right so they support your educational goals, then have practice conform to them.

The cultural view, by contrast, sees existing practice as heavily determined by deep-rooted beliefs, practices and working relationships among teachers and students that make up the culture of the school and the traditions of the system. In this pattern of deep cultural determination, structural reforms are perceived as small, transient and ineffective; little match for the power of the existing culture. Change, in this view, is brought about by acting on and supporting the culture itself so that teachers are more able to make change as a community in the interests of the students they know best. Promotion of change in this cultural view is achieved by what Werner has elsewhere called policy support strategies — ones which create release time for teachers to work together, assist them in collaborative planning, encourage teachers to try new experiences (like a new practice or grade level), involve teachers in goal-setting, create a culture of collaboration, risk and improvement, and so on.[36] In effect, what Werner is proposing is not school *restructuring* but school *reculturing*.

While there are growing indications that deep cultural changes of this sort are much more likely to be effective in improving classroom practice than quick structural fixes, there are nevertheless limits to reculturing. Reculturing treads a fine line between respecting the beliefs and perspectives of teachers and romanticizing them. In the quest for collaborative professional development and improvement, the inherent generosity and altruism of all teachers cannot be presumed. Teachers' beliefs and practices are grounded not only in expertise and altruism, but also in structures and routines to which they have become attached and in which considerable self-interest may be invested. Such structures, I have shown, have often evolved historically to meet political and moral purposes that are very different from those which many might now consider important. Effective teacher development in the building of collective improvement therefore depends on more than releasing moral virtue. It also depends on controlling vested interests. For example, collegiality in the secondary school work culture may require modifications to the subject-specialist, departmentalized curriculum that currently isolates teachers from many of their colleagues and ties them to the balkanized domains of departmental politics and subject self-interest.[37]

Cultures do not operate in a vacuum. They are formed within and framed by particular structures. These structures are not neutral. They can be helpful or harmful. They can bring teachers together or keep them apart. They can facilitate opportunities for interaction and learning, or present barriers to such possibilities.

In some cases, therefore, it is not possible to establish productive school cultures without prior changes being effected in school structures that increase opportunities for meaningful working relationships and collegial support among teachers. The importance of restructuring may be less in terms of its direct impact on curriculum, assessment, ability grouping and the like, and the demands these place upon teachers, than in terms of how it creates improved opportunities for teachers to work together and support each other on a continuing basis. The challenge of restructuring along the lines of changed power relationships proposed by Sarason, therefore, is not one of choosing between structure and culture as targets of reform. Nor is it one of "managing" school cultures so that teachers cheerfully comply with structural goals and purposes already fixed by the bureaucratic center. Rather, it is a challenge of re-designing school structures away from modernistic models to help teachers work together more effectively as a community in collaborative cultures of shared learning, positive risk and continuous improvement. As an essential precondition for productive interaction, this much at any rate may need to be mandated!

Especially in times of rapid change, modernistic structures of the secondary school kind inhibit innovation, delay organizational responsiveness, restrict professional learning, and tend to protect and perpetuate departmental self-interests against the needs of the organization and its clients as a whole. At the same time, while simpler collaborative structures of the kind found in many smaller schools can create the necessary cultural conditions for collective and continuous improvement, such communities are difficult to establish and maintain in larger organizations, or under conditions of rapid change where leadership and teaching staff turn over quickly. Better secondary schools are not just bigger elementary schools.

The model of the moving mosaic described in Chapters 4 and 10 is among the more promising possibilities for the postmodern age and provides structural grounds for a fifth form of teacher culture. The moving mosaic fosters vigorous, dynamic and shifting forms of collaboration through networks, partnerships and alliances within and beyond the school. These are sometimes consensual, but sometimes conflict-ridden too, for in the moving mosaic, conflict is seen as a necessary part of the change process. The moving mosaic has overlapping structural categories (like department and school improvement teams) and overlapping membership of them, with both the categories and their membership shifting over time as circumstances require. The moving mosaic is not an abstract conception but a working reality, and not just in the corporate world either. The school described in Chapter 10, where teachers are appointed by cross-departmental committee and every teacher sits on one of the five committees that runs the school, represents one emergent form of the moving mosaic. Similarly, Iroquois School in Louisville, Kentucky, one of Sizer's Coalition for Essential Schools, has replaced the traditional position of principal and assistant principals with four coordinators instead. They are responsible for the middle school building, the high school building, the campus, and student services respectively. These coordinators work together as a team, no one of them being dominant. Several other members of the Coalition for Essential Schools are evolving further moving mosaic structures of their own kind.

Beyond schools themselves, there are trends in staff development towards establishing professional networks among teachers where teachers are connected by electronic mail and satellite and can meet in smaller, interconnected sites. These professional development networks are neither course-based in universities or school-districts, nor site-based in individual schools, but can incorporate, extend beyond and interconnect both of these more conventional patterns.[38]

In some districts, teacher unions and federations have also started to move away from the long-standing promotion categories and formulae agreed in established collective bargaining arrangements, to establish new, more flexible categories for promotion and career development that offer greater discretion to individual schools in terms of how particular career paths and categories are defined. For example, Cincinnati Public Schools District's establishment of new career structures and professional review procedures, with the agreement and initiative of the teachers' federation, includes a four-step career ladder of intern, resident, career teacher and lead teacher, promotion through which is based on a process of peer review. The category of "lead teacher" includes many possible designations that may or may not give priority to department heads at the secondary level. Such structures continue to recognize principles of fairness, reward and security in teachers' careers, while unhooking them from particular categories like department headship that have been established in other decades for other purposes. As a result, individual schools have greater organizational flexibility to respond to changing needs and circumstances around them, with the kinds of leadership roles that seem most appropriate.[39]

Similarly, in Australia, more than 80 schools involved in the National Schools Project have agreed to suspend existing collective agreements (or industrial "awards", as they are termed there) on an experimental basis in order to discover new patterns of work organization that are more productive for students and more rewarding for teachers and that might be replicated on a wider basis. This is very different from beginning with baselines of established, yet increasingly outmoded, work patterns, then trying to negotiate them one bit at a time on a piecemeal basis.[40]

Our visions of organizational possibility for schooling and teachers' work are beginning to extend beyond the traditional, egg-crate elementary school, the modernistic cubbyhole-like secondary school, and the smaller collaborative communities that have come to characterize a number of elementary and primary schools. While no single best model of the moving mosaic has yet emerged, and most certainly never will — for the demands of different contexts call for different structural solutions in each case — the basic principles of the moving mosaic represent some of our best hopes, organizationally, for forms of schooling and teaching in the postmodern age that are flexible, responsive, proactive, efficient and effective in their uses of shared expertise and resources in order to meet the continuously shifting needs of students in a rapidly changing world. To build a moving mosaic is to move beyond the principle of collaboration itself to the structures which can best support it in the complex context of postmodernity.

4. Processes and Purposes

As a principle of restructuring, collaboration at the site level can be decentralized to such extent that it becomes chaotic. Leaving the development of missions and visions to the complete discretion of each individual school and its teachers definitely runs this risk. Free-market systems of site-based management and parental choice of school institutionalize the problem even more deeply.

Collaboration can also be controlled and contrived. As in the corporate sphere, despite the existence of participatory decision-making at site-level, overall coordination of the terms and conditions of collaboration can be overly determined at the center.[41] The *process* of collaboration can become bounded by and separated from decisions about its *products*. The *aesthetics* and emotional experience of the collaborative process can eclipse decisions about and rational criticisms of the *ethics* of what is being collaboratively produced. Process can prevail over purpose.

An important challenge for educational restructuring and the principles of collaboration contained within it is to articulate, listen to and bring together different voices in the educational and social community, and also to establish guiding ethical principles around which these voices and their purposes can cohere. Without an ethical discourse about or ethical principles underpinning collaboration and restructuring, contrived collegiality, for instance, can induce teachers' compliance with imposed curricula that are elitist and ethnocentric in nature (such as the English and Welsh National Curriculum with its emphasis on British history and British literature), and thereby prejudice the achievements of those cultural and ethnic minorities who may be estranged from such curricular contents. Similarly, where the form and focus of collaboration is entirely discretionary, teachers in secondary schools may, as McLaughlin and her colleagues have found, collaborate around issues of academics and curriculum development in middle class communities, and around very different preoccupations with young people and their social adjustment in more socially deprived ones.[42] These different emphases may be read as pragmatic responses to the educational and social demands of each particular context, but they can also be seen as ways of perpetuating imbalances and inequities between those contexts.

For these reasons, collaboration and restructuring must be located within an ethical discourse and political parameters that guide the efforts of individual schools, teachers and their communities in the quest to improve as best as they can, within their own settings. Such ethical principles are contestable and should be open to public debate in order to set nationally agreed goals and frameworks (though not specific and detailed contents) which guide the educational systems in which teachers work. From my own value standpoint, the principles of equity, excellence, justice, partnership, care for others and global awareness should be high on that agenda. In an insightful critique of the limits of collaboration, Zeichner has laid out a particularly persuasive case for establishing such ethical principles and frameworks as guides for educational improvement and development. Zeichner points to the "almost total lack of attention to community empowerment in the mainstream educational literature advocating teacher leadership and school restructuring."[43] Having said this, however, Zeichner points to a second danger that even where communities are involved in the collaborative process, "what communities assert for their schools may be in conflict with principles of a democratic society, repressing particular points of view, or discriminating against certain groups of people". The defence of creationism and the imposition of Judaeo-Christian values on multi-faith communities are examples of this. Overall, argues Zeichner:

> Although we need to encourage and support a process of
> democratic deliberation within schools that includes parents and
> students as well as administrators and teachers, we need some
> way of making determinations about the "goodness" of the
> choices that emerge from these deliberations. . . . First, the fact
> that all relevant parties have participated does not mean that

259

everyone has had an influence in the deliberative process. . . .
Second, we need some way of ensuring that the decisions that
emerge from these deliberations do not violate certain moral
standards, such as social justice and equity.[44]

Processes of change in the form of restructuring, reculturing, collaboration
and the like are extremely important things that professionals and policy
makers need to understand and address. But attention to the change process
should never be allowed to detract from or displace the paramount importance
of change purpose and change substance – of what the change is for!

CONCLUSION

Restructuring has no single, agreed definition. Its meaning, rather, is to be
found in the context and purpose of its use. In centralized patterns of curriculum change and assessment demands where restructuring is a camouflage
for top-down reform, it can support reinscriptions of bureaucratic control.
Strong singular visions and imposed inflexible mandates are the stuff of such
control. Equally, though, restructuring can also propel us into a postmodern
world of indeterminacy and ephemerality – into a cacophony of voices of indistinguishable moral validity, without any common vision or purpose; a world in
which the decision-making power invested in school cultures is arbitrarily
shaped by the inertia of historical tradition and ingrained interest rather than
the virtue of collective moral choice.

The challenge of restructuring in education and elsewhere is a challenge of
abandoning or attenuating bureaucratic controls, inflexible mandates, paternalistic forms of trust and quick system fixes in order to hear, articulate and
bring together the disparate voices of teachers and other educational partners
(particularly students and their parents). It is a challenge of opening up broad
avenues of choice which respect teachers' professional discretion and enhance
their decision-making capacity. It is a challenge of building trust in the processes of collaboration, risk and continuous improvement as well as more
traditional kinds of trust in people. And it is a challenge of supporting and
empowering school cultures and those involved in them to develop changes
themselves on a continuing basis.

But in relaxing or relinquishing administrative control, the challenge of
restructuring in postmodern times is also one of not losing a sense of common
purpose and of commitment with it. In trading bureaucratic control for professional empowerment, it is important we do not trade community for chaos as
well.

Similarly, the possibilities for establishing more vibrant and vigorous
teacher cultures are seriously limited by the existing structures in which many
teachers work. If teachers are to interact more flexibly, learn from each other

more extensively, and improve their own expertise continuously, then new structures need to be created pre-emptively which make these learnings and interactions more possible. The future of restructuring is, in this sense, one which embraces the principles of teacher empowerment, without necessarily accepting or endorsing many teachers' existing conceptions of it. Collaboration and empowerment will mean more discretion for teachers in some domains, but, as they work more closely with students and parents as partners in the learning process, considerably less discretion in others.

This book is not a litany of solutions to the complex challenges and problems of restructuring in education but it has sought to sketch out ways of approaching them by understanding the changing work of teachers and the changing world in which it is situated.

People seeking *the* seven steps to educational recovery or *the* nine ways to restructure their schools will not find them in this book. They must go elsewhere for the solace that such false certainties appear to bring. Restructuring is not an end to our problems but a beginning; a chance to set new rules for new purposes and new learnings in a newly constructed world. The possibilities for responding and contributing to the creation of that postmodern world are still immensely open. Almost everything is up for grabs. In tune with the post-industrial paradigm, there is no one best model, no singular certainty. There will be better and worse forms of practice, and practices that suit some contexts more than others. The important task, therefore, should be to identify, assess and portray a range of restructuring models to create menus of choice for educators to apply and adapt in their own settings, rather than mandates of imposition with which they must comply, whatever their circumstances.

What I have tried to make clear throughout this book is that while the prospects for the future remain uncertain, the one sure thing is that we cannot cling to the crumbling edifice of the modernistic and bureaucratic present with its departments, hierarchies and cubbyhole structures of schooling. Nor can we take nostalgic refuge in the reconstruction of mythical educational pasts with their conceptions of traditional standards, conventional subjects and the narrow pursuit of basic skills. Educationally, it makes no sense at all to go back to the future in this way!

Teachers know their work is changing, along with the world in which they perform it. As long as the existing structures and cultures of teaching are left intact, responding to these complex and accelerating changes in isolation will only create more overload, intensification, guilt, uncertainty, cynicism and burnout. Many chapters of this book have documented the words of teachers which clearly testify to these dangers. As schools move into the postmodern age, something is going to have to give. It might be the quality of classroom learning, as teachers and the curriculum are spread increasingly thinly to accommodate more and more demands. It might be the health, lives and stamina of teachers themselves as they crumple under the pressures of multiple mandated change. Or it can be the basic structures and cultures of schooling, reinvented for and realigned with the postmodern purposes and pressures they must now address. These are the stark choices we now face. The rules of the world are changing. It is time for the rules of teaching and teachers' work to change with them.

NOTES

1. Carnegie Forum on Education and the Economy, *A Nation Prepared: Teachers for the 21st Century*, Report of the Carnegie Task Force on Teaching as a Profession, Washington, DC, Carnegie Forum, 1986.

2. Reported in O'Neill, J., "Piecing together the restructuring puzzle", *Educational Leadership*, 47(7), April 1990, 4–10.

3. Tyack, D., "Restructuring in historical perspective: Tinkering toward utopia", *Teachers College Record*, 192(2), Winter 1990, 170–91.

4. Murphy, J. and Evertson, C. (eds), *Restructuring Schools: Capturing the Phenomena*, New York, Teachers College Press, 1991.

5. National Governors' Association, *Results in Education*, 1989, NGA, Washington, DC, 1989.

6. Lieberman, A., Darling-Hammond, L. and Zuckerman, D., *Early Lessons in Restructuring Schools*, New York, National Center for Restructuring Education, Schools, and Teaching (NCREST), 1991.

7. Sizer, T., *Horace's School: Redesigning the American High School*, Boston, Houghton Mifflin, 1992.

8. Sarason, S., *The Predictable Failure of Educational Reform*, San Francisco, Jossey-Bass, 1990.

9. Sarason, *op. cit.*, note 10, p. 5.

10. Wehlage, G., Smith, G. and Lipman, P., "Restructuring urban schools: The new futures experience", *American Educational Research Journal*, 29(1), 51–93; see also Wehlage, G. *et al.*, *Reducing the Risk: Schools as Communities of Support*, Philadelphia, Falmer Press, 1989.

11. Ibid.

12. Kuhn, T., *The Structure of Scientific Revolutions*, Chicago, University of Chicago Press, 1962.

13. See Rosenholtz, S., *Teachers' Workplace*, New York, Longmans, 1989.

14. Fullan, M. and Hargreaves, A., *What's Worth Fighting For? Working Together for Your School*, Toronto, Ontario Public School Teachers' Federation, Milton Keynes, Open University Press; and Melbourne, Australian Council for Educational Administration.

15. Gilligan, C., *In a Different Voice: Psychological Theory and Women's Development*, Cambridge, MA, 1982.

16. Harvey, D., *The Condition of Postmodernity*, Cambridge, Polity Press, 1989, 48.

17. Elbaz, F., "Research on teachers' knowledge", *Journal of Curriculum Studies*, 23(1), 1991, 10.

18. Goodson, I., "Sponsoring the teacher's voice", in Hargreaves, A. and Fullan, M. (eds), *Understanding Teacher Development*, London, Cassell and New York, Teachers College Press, 1991.

19. Achilles, C. M., "A vision of better schools", in Greenfield, W. (ed.), *Instructional Leadership: Concepts, Issues and Controversies*, Boston, Allyn & Bacon, 1987, 18.

20. Deal, T. and Peterson, K., "Symbolic leadership and the school principal: Shaping school cultures in different contexts". Unpublished paper, Vanderbilt University, 1987, 14.

21. Cohen, L., *The Singer Must Die*, lyrics reprinted by permission from Leonard Cohen Stranger Music.

22. Leithwood, K. and Jantzi, D. "Transformational leadership: How principals can help reform school culture", Paper presented at the American Educational Research Association Annual Meeting, Boston, MA, April 1990.

23. Lieberman, A., Saxl, E. R. and Miles, M. B., "Teachers' leadership: Ideology and practice", in Lieberman, A. (ed.), *Building a Professional Culture in Schools*, New York, Teachers College Press, 1988, 148–66.

24. Louden, W., *Understanding Teaching*, London, Cassell and New York, Teachers College Press, 1991.

25. Nias, J., Southworth, G. and Yeomans, R., *Staff Relationships in the Primary Schools*, London, Cassell, 1989, 78.

26. Ibid, p. 81.

27. Giddens, A., *The Consequences of Modernity*, Oxford, Polity Press, 1990, 34, from which much of the following account of trust and risk is drawn.

28. Weber, M., *Economy and Society: An Outline of Interpretive Sociology*, Guenther Roth and Claus Wittoch (eds), New York, Bedminster Press, 1968.

29. For an account of these developments, see Hargreaves, A. and Earl, L., *Rights of Passage*, Toronto, Queen's Printer, 1990.

30. See Nias *et al.*, *op. cit.*, note 25, for example.

31. Acker, S., "It's what we do already but . . . primary teachers and the 1988 Education Act", Paper presented at a conference on Ethography, Education and Policy, St Hilda's College, Oxford, September 1989.

32. Brummet, A. *Policy Directions: A Response to the Sullivan Royal Commission on Education by the Government of British Columbia*, Victoria, BC, British Columbia Ministry of Education, 1989, 10.

33. Werner, W., "Defining curriculum policy through slogans", *Journal of Education Policy*, 6(2), 1991, 225–38. Quotation from p. 228.

34. Ibid.

35. Ibid, p. 234.

36. Werner, W., *Evaluating Program Implementation (School Based)*. Final Project Report, Centre for the Study of Curriculum Instruction, Vancouver, University of British Columbia, 1982.

37. See Hargreaves, A., "Cultures of teaching: A focus for change", in Hargreaves, A. and Fullan, M. (eds), *Understanding Teacher Development*, London, Cassell and New York, Teachers College Press, 1991.

38. Lieberman, A. and McLaughlin, M., "Networks for educational change: Powerful and problematic", *Phi Delta Kappan*, 73(9), May, 1992, 673–77.

39. Buenger, C., *Cincinnati Business Committee Task Force on Public Schools*, Cincinnati, OH, Cincinnati Business Committee, 1991.

40. On the Australian National Schools Project, see Tonkin, D., "The Australian National Schools Project: Some Early Issues", Paper presented to OECD Experts meeting on Rethinking Schooling: Changing Patterns of Work Organization, Perth, Australia, November 1992.

41. Menzies, H., *Fast Forward and Out of Control: How Technology Is Changing Our Lives*, Toronto, Macmillan, 1989.

42. McLaughlin, M., "What matters most in teachers' workplace context?", in McLaughlin, M. and Little, J. W. (eds), *Cultures and Contexts of Teaching*, New York, Teachers College Press, 1992.

43. Zeichner, K. M., "Contradictions and tensions in the professionalization of teaching and the democratization of schools", *Teachers College Record*, 92(3), 1991, 363–79. Quotation cited on p. 368.

44. Ibid, p. 370.

Name Index

Aberdene, P. 86
Achilles, C.M. 249-50, 263
Acker, S. 140, 210, 263
Althusser, L. 36
Apple, M.W. 35, 104, 115, 116, 119, 134, 139, 159, 211
Aronowitz, S. 39, 45
Ashton, P. 169, 183, 184
Astuto, T.A. 87
Atkinson, J. 85

Bacharach, S.B. 33, 37, 89
Baglin, E. 87
Ball, S. 115, 116, 211, 240
Balzac, H. 178
Baron, S. 116
Barth, R.S. 90, 139
Baudrillard, J. 76-8, 91, 92
Becker, H. 37, 183
Bell, D. 46, 47, 85
Berger, L. 107, 116
Berman, P. 34
Berne, E. 30, 36
Bernstein, B. 183-4, 240
Bernstein, R.J. 45
Berry, B. 20
Bird, T. 97, 115, 209
Blase, J. 190, 211
Bloom, A. 46
Book, C. 146, 158
Braverman, H. 35
Broadfoot, P. 126, 140, 159
Brookes, T.E. 115
Brummet, A. 263
Buenger, C. 264
Bullough, R., Jr. 210
Burgess, R. 115

Caldwell, B. 19, 90
Campbell, P. 37, 139, 210, 235, 240
Campbell, R.J. 97, 115, 139, 209, 210

Carroll, J. 157
Cherryholmes, C. 45
Chubb, J.E. 88
Clandinin, D.J. 91, 158
Clark, C.K.M. 91
Clark, D.L. 87
Cohen, D. 36, 87
Cohen, Leonard 250, 263
Connell, R. 13, 21
Connelly, F.M. 91, 115, 158
Cooper, M. 189, 210
Cottle, T.J. 116
Crow, N. 146, 158
Curtis, B. 104, 115, 140

Dale, R. 36, 37
Darling-Hammond, L. 20, 36, 139, 240, 262
Davies, A.F. 143, 158
Davis, J. 89, 211, 240
Dawe, R. 19, 116, 211
Deal, T.E. 183, 211, 250, 263
Dearing, Sir Ron 19
Deleuze, G. 21
Densmore, K. 35, 119, 136, 139, 140, 159
Doyle, W. 20
Drucker, P.F. 89
Durkheim, E. 178, 185

Earl, L. 89, 263
Eco, U. 78, 92
Ecob, R. 183, 209
Ecole, R. 158
Edmonds, R. 60-1, 88-9
Egan, K. 91
Elbaz, F.L. 91, 158, 249, 263
Erickson, F. 211
Evertson, C. 241, 262

Farrar, E. 36, 87
Featherstone, M. 45
Fish, S. 116

Flinders, D.J.   126, 140, 159, 170, 171, 172, 185
Foster, H.   46
Freeman, D.J.   158
Fullan, M.   20, 34, 66, 89, 90, 97, 115, 139, 170, 185, 209, 232, 239, 240, 247, 262

Garman, N.   19, 88
Garmston, R.J.   211
Gaskell, J.   45
Giddens, A.   34, 35, 43-4, 45, 46, 70, 86, 87, 90, 91, 114, 116, 252, 263
Gilbert, R.   90
Gilligan, C.   158, 173, 185, 249, 262
Giroux, H.A.   39, 45
Gitlin, A.   210
Gleick, J.   87
Glickman, A.   210
Goffman, E.   30, 36, 109-10, 116
Goodson, I.F.   27, 36, 54-5, 86, 115, 184, 240, 249, 263
Guattari, F.   21

Habermas, J.   25-6, 32, 35, 37, 40, 45, 96, 114
Hall, E.T.   102-3, 115
Hall, S.   35
Hallinger, P.   88, 210
Halsey, A.H.   5, 19
Hamilton, D.   27, 36
Hammersley, M.   36
Hargreaves, A.   19, 20, 30, 36, 86, 87, 88, 89, 90, 116, 121-2, 159, 185, 209, 210, 211, 239, 240, 247, 262, 263, 264
Hargreaves, D.   6, 19, 36, 87, 159, 167-8, 169, 184
Hartley, D.   211
Harvey, D.   25-6, 35, 37, 41, 45, 48, 85, 86, 87, 88, 90, 249, 263
Havel, Vaclav   23, 34
Hawking, S.   106, 107, 116
Heath, A.   19
Held, D.   35
Henderson, P.   87
Holmes, M.   87
Hopkins, D.   6, 19, 20
Hoy, W.K.   184
Hoyle, E.   117, 139, 211
Huberman, M.   20, 37, 140, 205, 209, 211
Hunt, D.   91
Hunter, M.   60, 88

Jackson, P.W.   104, 115, 157, 184
James, P.D.   21
Jameson, F.   40-1, 45, 46

Jantzi, D.   159, 189, 210, 211, 250-1, 263
Jensen, K.   146, 158
Jick, T.D.   90
Johnson, D.W.   92
Johnson, Lyndon B.   27
Johnson, P.T.   92
Joyce, B.   60, 88-9, 169, 170, 185, 211
Jungk, S.   35, 119, 139, 159

Kagan, S.   80, 92
Kanter, R.M.   63-4, 90
Kennedy, A.   183, 211
Kuhn, T.   262

Laing, R.D.   30, 36, 144, 158
Larson, S.M.   118-19, 139
Lasch, C.   46, 70-1, 88, 91
Lash, S.   20, 46
Lawn, M.   35
Leeson, P.   87
Leinberger, P.   28-9, 36, 64-5, 89, 90, 91
Leithwood, K.   73, 91, 159, 189, 210, 211, 250-1, 263
Lewis, D.   158, 183, 209
Lezotte, L.W.   87
Lieberman, A.   20, 36, 139, 209, 231, 240, 241, 251, 262, 263, 264
Lind, K.   19, 88
Lindsay, C.   86
Lipman, P.   262
Little, J.W.   97, 115, 164, 183, 184, 188, 189, 209, 210
Lortie, D.   157, 158, 167, 168, 169, 170, 171, 173, 184, 185, 210
Lotto, L.S.   87
Louden, W.   251, 263
Louis, K.S.   20, 34
Lowe, G.   91
Lubeck, S.   115
Luckmann, S.   107, 116
Lukes, S.   171, 178, 185
Lyotard, J.   43, 46, 87

McCary, J.T.   115
MacDonald, M.   85, 86
McLaren, P.   104, 115
McLaughlin, M.   20, 34, 259, 264
McLennan, G.   35
Macmillan, R.   89, 240
McTaggart, R.   170-1, 185
Maughan, B.   209
Maxcy, S.J.   39, 45
Mead, G.H.   30, 36
Menzies, H.   51, 68, 86, 90, 158, 264
Merton, R.K.   23, 34

Metz, M. 217, 240
Miles, M.B. 20, 34, 209, 263
Miller, J. 209
Miller, L. 139
Mills, C.W. 142, 157
Moe, T.E. 88
Mortimore, P. 158, 183, 209
Murphy, C. 185
Murphy, J. 88, 185, 210, 241, 262
Musella, D. 211

Naisbitt, J. 86
Neufeld, J. 149, 158, 159
Nias, J. 30, 36, 37, 117, 127, 139, 145, 146,
    149, 150, 157, 158, 159, 184, 235, 240,
    252, 263
Noddings, N. 158

O'Connor, J. 31, 37
O'Neill, J. 262
Oberg, A. 91
Offe, C. 35
Osborn, M. 126, 140, 159
Ouchi, W.G. 183
Ouston, J. 209

Parker, A. 58, 87
Parkman, Francis 56
Parkman, George 56
Parton, Dolly 177
Peterson, K. 250, 263
Piore, M. 85, 86
Ponder, G. 20
Popkewitz, T. 19, 88
Poppleton, P. 140
Poulantzas, N. 35
Powell, A. 36, 87
Prentice, A. 140
Purkey, S.C. 87, 183, 209
Purvis, J. 104, 115

Quicke, J. 80, 92

Rawls, J. 144, 158
Reagan, Ronald 76-7
Reich, R.B. 49, 52, 86, 89
Renihan, F.I. 60, 90
Renihan, P. 69, 90
Resler, H. 85
Reynolds, D. 58, 87, 88, 90, 116, 209,
    211
Ridge, J. 19
Riecken, T. 211
Riseborough, G. 37, 140, 240

Robertson, H. 60-1, 88, 89
Rorty, R. 45
Rosenholtz, S. 21, 139, 157, 168, 183, 184,
    209, 210, 211, 262
Rudduck, J. 80, 92, 209
Rutter, M. 209

Sabel, M. 85
Sammons, P. 158, 183, 209
Sarason, S. 8, 19, 242, 256, 262
Saxl, E.R. 263
Schama, S. 55-6, 87
Schein, E.H. 183, 211
Schlechty, P. 50, 51, 86, 87
Schön, D. 19, 96, 114, 178, 185, 198
Schutz, A. 115
Senge, P. 66, 90
Shakespeare, William 100-1, 115, 157
Shedd, J.B. 33, 37, 89
Showers, B. 60, 88-9, 185, 211
Shulman, L. 187, 209
Simper, R. 115
Siskin, L. 240
Sizer, T. 87, 241, 257, 262
Skilbeck, M. 209
Smart, B. 45
Smith, A. 209
Smith, G. 262
Smith, M. 183, 209
Smith, M.S. 87
Smyth, J. 19, 35, 88, 211
Southworth, G. 37, 139, 159, 184, 210, 235,
    240, 263
Spinks, J.M. 19, 90
Stager, M. 89, 240
Stein, B.A. 90
Stenhouse, L. 209
Stiegelbauer, S. 20, 34, 115, 139, 209
Stoll, L. 87, 158, 183, 209
Storr, A. 181-2, 185
Swart, K.W. 185
Swyngedouw, E. 86
Szasz, T. 163-4, 178, 183, 185

Taylor, C. 32, 37, 72, 90, 91
Taylor, G. 142, 157
Taylor, W. 89
Teitelbaum, K. 35
Thompson, E.P. 92, 116
Toffler, A. 25, 35, 66, 81-2, 86, 89, 90, 92,
    99
Tomkins, G. 140
Tonkin, D. 264
Tossell, T. 87

Tucker, B.   28-9, 36, 64-5, 89, 90, 91, 142, 150
Turner, B.S.   24-5, 26, 35, 39, 40, 45
Tyack, D.   241, 262

Underwood, S.   91

Waller, W.   157, 183
Watson, J.   146, 158
Webb, R.   169, 183, 184
Webber, R.A.   115
Weber, M.   8, 20, 25, 26, 35, 41, 45, 253, 264
Webster, John   56
Wehlage, G.   243-4, 262
Werner, W.   96-7, 101, 105, 108, 115, 116, 254-5, 264
Westbury, I.   30, 36

Westergaard, J.   85
Whyte, W.H., Jr.   28-9, 36, 64, 65, 90
Wideman, R.   10, 20
Wignall, R.   4, 19, 89, 121-2, 240
Wilkins, A.E.   183
Willinsky, J.   87
Wilson, A.   211
Wolfe, James   55-6
Woods, P.   21, 30, 36, 37, 116, 127, 140, 157

Yeomans, R.   37, 139, 159, 184, 240, 263
Young, A.   91

Zahorkik, J.A.   184
Zeichner, K.M.   259-60, 264
Zielinski, A.K.   184
Zuckerman, D.   20, 36, 139, 240, 262

Subject Index

Note: Since this entire book is about teachers, there are no separate references to teachers in the index.

academy 61
accountability 124-5, 133, 134, 136, 148-9, 156, 170
administrative devices 11-12, 81
authenticity 72

"back regions" 109-11, 112
balkanization 18, 28, 67, 86, 193, 212-40
boundaries 64, 109
boundless self 69-74
bureaucracy 26, 28, 29, 32, 61, 68, 112, 113, 137, 170, 208, 248, 251
burnout 144, 148, 155

care 51, 119, 127, 132, 144-7, 148-9, 153, 155-6, 173-8, 183
certainties
  collective 148
  cultures of 57
  dead 55-61
  discarded 60
  false 54-5
  gender and 60
  moral 70, 83
  scientific 58, 59, 61, 70, 83
  situated 59, 61, 83, 246
change 1-92, 255
  accelerating 3, 8, 63, 83
  context 8-10, 23
  mandated 6
  personal 73
  process of 10-12, 23
  purpose 23
  root and branch 6
  substance 5-8
  whole-school 59, 235-6
changelessness, myth of 222-4
cohort groups 227-9

collaboration 17, 33, 79, 113, 120-1, 131, 186-211, 250-61
  aesthetics of 74
  cultural perspective 189-90
  ethics of 74, 259-60
  micropolitical perspective 190-2
  workplace 67, 68
collaborative planning 97-8, 131, 137, 178-9, 181, 198-200
collegiality 97, 120-1, 131, 148, 164, 186-211
  contrived 17, 80-1, 105, 121, 135, 137, 195-209, 238, 247
  critiques of 188-92
colonization, administrative 109-12
commitment 127-8, 132, 136, 138, 144-7
competence anxiety 150
conflict 231, 235, 236, 239
context 104-5, 207
continuous improvement 247
contrived collegiality, see collegiality: contrived
control 175, 203
cooperative learning 60, 79-80, 191, 224-5
cooptation 247, 250
coping strategies 30
cover arrangements 133-5
critical pragmatism 39-40
cubbyhole structures 18, 28, 62, 67
culture 16-18
  balkanized 18, 28, 67, 86, 193, 212-40
  collaborative 17, 33, 121, 135, 150, 156, 192-4, 238, 244-8
  content of 166
  form of 166
  individualistic 17, 65, 120-1, 131, 163-85, 238
  occupational 167

culture (*cont.*)
  organizational 189
  professional 16–17
  teacher 165–240
curriculum development 97, 109, 114, 186,
  192, 255–8
curriculum implementation 104, 108, 114,
  186, 195, 255–8

decision-making 233–4
departmentalization 18, 33, 62, 98, 225–9,
  235, 237, 239
desires, teacher 11–13, 175
deskilling 26, 35, 117–20
development 73, 186, 242
development planning 80
direct instruction 60–1
discipline 124, 146, 168
disintensification 132, 137

economies of scale 25
economies of scope 53
effectiveness 58, 59, 186
elementary education 27, 33, 95–6, 99, 104,
  117–40, 145, 146, 177–83, 193–207, 249
emotions 16, 141
empowerment 42, 63, 68, 69, 71, 72, 73,
  188, 209, 248, 251, 261
expertise
  critiqued 72
  imposed 119
  models of 60, 152
  shared 119, 133–5, 149–50, 202–4
  singular 149–50, 152
  specialist 133–5

Faustian bargains 112, 135, 138
feelings 141
flexibility
  faces of 50, 51
  organizational 62–9, 243
flexible accumulation 48
flexible economies 48–55, 83
flexible firms 48
flexible specialization 48
fluidity, organizational 84
French immersion schooling 137–8, 139–40
"front regions" 109–11

gender 60, 99, 102–4, 113, 126–7, 145,
  150–1, 154, 173, 220–2, 249
global education 55
globalization 5, 22, 28, 52–5, 56, 63, 248–9
  paradox of 52–5, 83

goal diffuseness 126, 147, 164
goal displacement 23
grandiosity 74
guilt 16, 74, 82, 141–59
  depressive 143–4, 149, 156
  persecutory 143, 149, 156
  philosophy of 144
  politics of 143
  psychology of 144
  true and false 144
guilt traps 142, 145–52, 156
guilt trips 142, 156, 157

heresies of thought 163–4, 178
hyperrealities 77

image 44, 70, 71, 75–7
  aesthetics and ethics of 76, 77
  phases of 77
immediacy 104, 107, 131
improvement 59, 186
  continuous 247
individualism 17, 65, 120–1, 131, 163–85,
  238
  constrained 172
  cult of 167
  ecological 170, 173
  elective 172–3
  psychological 170
  strategic 172
  types of 171
  as workplace condition 170–1
individuality 17, 21, 163, 178–80, 191
information 44, 49, 53, 56, 57
instruction 130, 147
intensification 14–16, 108, 114, 117–40,
  148–9, 156
isolation 10, 97, 131, 147, 163–85, 225

Judaeo-Christian tradition 9, 58

knowledge
  economy 49
  explosion 56
  factual 57
  foundational 40, 70
  personal 72, 74
  practical 72, 74
  processes 57, 58
  products 57, 58
  work 50
  workers 50

labor process   26, 35, 48, 117-20, 136-8
leadership   187, 233, 250-1, 253
learning
    organizational   66-7
    professional   223-4, 235, 246-7
lives   128, 150, 156, 249

marketplace of choice   51
mass schooling   27
menus of choice   61, 261
meta-narratives   56
micropolitics   72, 98-9, 190, 231, 236
missions   9, 59, 163, 236
modernism   34
modernity   8-9, 22-37, 81, 253
    crisis of   31-2, 48
    economics of   8, 26, 31, 48
    high   24, 34, 43-4, 69-70
    malaise of   24-30, 32
    organizational aspects   8, 28, 32, 64, 256
    personal aspects   8, 28-9
    politics of   8, 27-8, 31
modernization   26-34
moving mosaic   62-9, 82, 84, 237, 257-8

narcissism   42, 71-5
narratives   55-7, 72
National Curriculum (England and
    Wales)   6, 54-5, 149
national doubt and insecurity   83, 248-9
national identity   52-5
neo-Marxism   43
networks   64, 257
nostalgia   33, 60, 88
nurturance   145-7, 156, 173

open-endedness   147, 152, 155-6, 170
overload   118
ownership   12, 174-5

paradigm shifts   244-5
parents   259
parochialism   33, 55, 254
paternalism   33, 253, 254
peer coaching   204-7
perfectionism   149-52, 153, 155
personal anxiety   84
postindustrialism   3, 47, 85, 261
postliberalism   47
postmodernism   38-46
postmodernity   3-4, 9-20, 23-4, 38-91, 235,
    239, 249, 251, 253, 257-8
    definition of   38

ecology of   53-4, 56, 86
economic aspects   9
modernity and   42
organizational aspects   9
paradoxes   47-91
personal aspects   9
philosophical and ideological aspects   9
political aspects   9
power relationships   242, 256
practicality ethic   12
premodern systems   24, 33
privatism   164, 165, 169, 180
production
    changes in   48, 50
    customized   49
    mass   8, 26, 31, 48
    small-batch   49
professional action   19, 178, 198
professionalism   119, 120, 126-8, 132, 136,
    198, 248, 251
professionalization   14-15, 117
programming   124, 129, 137
psychic rewards   171, 173

rationality   8
rationalization   25
reculturing   255-8
reform   8, 242
resistance   61, 169, 249
responsibility, ethic of   173-4, 177
restructuring   7, 18, 22, 241-64
risk   252-4

school-based management   7, 8, 68, 187
secondary education   8-9, 18, 27-8, 37, 58,
    62-3, 67, 98-9, 215-40, 253, 256
self
    boundaries of   70
    boundless   69-74
    bureaucracy and   65
    context of   73
    delusions of omnipotence   73
    development   72, 73
    indulgence   42, 72
    modern   70
    multiple   70
    narcissistic   73, 74
    referentiality   72
    reflexive   71
    teacher's   29-30
separation, administrative   107-9
simulation, safe   13, 74-81, 196
site-based management   68
solitude   180-3

space 53, 68
special education 123-4, 174-5, 200-4
split grades 135
state, the 27-8, 31, 35, 53, 151
stress 124, 128, 137
structuration 95, 100
structure 254-8
  duality of 42
structures 62, 203-4
  modernistic 256
subject
  boundaries 222-6, 237
  communities 214-15
  "core" 229-30
  "exploratory" 229-30
  identity 214, 219-20
  politics 214-15
  status 98, 215, 220-2, 229-30, 235-7, 239
surveillance 111-12

technical control 26
technical rationality 32, 147
technological complexity 83-4
technology 49-50, 75-6, 84
thinking, teacher 141
time 15-16, 95-140, 192-3, 196
  administrative views of 101, 103-4, 108,
    111-14
  clock 99
  fixed 96-7
  gender and 99, 102-4, 113
  group 97
  hegemonic 113
  innovation and 101, 105, 107-8
  mandated 196-200

micropolitical 98-9
monochronic 102-4, 106-8
objective 96-7, 101
personal 97
phenomenological 99-106
physical 106
polychronic 102-4, 106-7, 108
preparation 95-6, 99, 111, 117-40, 165
public 96-7
snatched 97
sociopolitical 106-12
status and 98-9
structuration of 95, 100
students and 104
subjective 99
synchronized 245-6
technical-rational 96-8
time-space compression 3, 9, 44, 57, 81-3,
  84-5
trust 110, 251-4
truth claims 40
turnover time 48

uncertainty 82
  cultures of 57-61
  ideological 9
  moral 58, 83
  scientific 3, 9, 5?, 83
  teacher 16, 147, 156, 167, 168-9
unions 67, 257

vision 59, 232, 236, 248-51, 260
voice 16, 147, 248-51, 260

whole-school development 59, 235-6